WHO GOVERNS?

WHO GOVERNS?

Democracy and Power in an American City

BY ROBERT A. DAHL

New Haven and London, Yale University Press

Library of Congress catalog card number: 61–16913
ISBN: 0–300–00395–1 (cloth), 0–300–00051–0 (paper)

Published in Great Britain, Europe, and Africa by
Yale University Press, Ltd., London.
Distributed in Canada by McGill-Queen's University
Press, Montreal; in Latin America by Kaiman & Polon,
Inc., New York City; in India by UBS Publishers'
Distributors Pvt., Ltd., Delhi;
in Japan by John Weatherhill, Inc., Tokyo.

Preface

The book that follows is an attempt to throw new light on an ancient question by examining a single American city in New England.

The study began in 1955 on the opposite edge of the United States, where, during a year of reading and reflecting at the Center for Advanced Study in the Behavioral Sciences in Palo Alto, California, I found myself returning incessantly to the central question of this book and, with the patient help of colleagues at the Center, to a quest for solutions to stubborn problems of concept, theory, and method. The actual research began in 1957 and ended in the summer of 1959, after which I resisted the temptation, except for a few cases, to describe more recent events—none of which, I believe, would significantly modify the hypotheses and interpretations set out in the book as it now stands.

The community I chose to study was New Haven, Connecticut, and I chose it for the most part because it lay conveniently at hand. But there are other good reasons for the choice. Though no city can claim to represent cities in general, and though certainly none can claim to display the full range of characteristics found in a national political system, New Haven is in many respects typical of other cities in the United States. (A comparison of New Haven with other American urban areas is found in Appendix A.) And three respects in which it is atypical are advantageous to my purposes. Because only a handful of cities in the United States have an equally long history, New Haven furnishes the advantages of historical perspective. Because, unlike most American cities, it has had a highly competitive two-party system for over a century, it offers analogies with national politics that few other cities could provide. And because, during the last decade, it has undertaken a dramatic effort to rescue itself from creeping decay, in the course of which the political system itself has altered, it provides an opportunity to examine factors making for stability and change.

If the disadvantages and limitations of studying one city are self-evident, the overwhelming and, I hope, compensating advantage is that the enterprise is reduced to manageable proportions. Many problems that are almost unyielding over a larger area can be relatively easily disposed of on this smaller canvas. It is not, perhaps, wholly accidental that the two political theorists who did the most to develop a descriptive political science were Aristotle and Machiavelli, who, though separated by eighteen centuries, both witnessed politics on the smaller, more human scale of the city-state. Nonetheless, I had better make clear at once that explanations presented in this study are tested only against the evidence furnished in the political system of New Haven.

This book is one of three closely related volumes about New Haven to be published by the Yale University Press. The other two have been written by associates who worked with me in gathering and analyzing the data on New Haven. In *Community Power and Political Theory,* Dr. Nelson Polsby examines the "stratification theory" developed in studies of other communities, where a socioeconomic elite seemed to dominate political life. He tests this theory against the data for New Haven, finds it irrelevant, and states the need for a new pluralist theory of community power. In the third volume, *The Politics of Progress,* Dr. Raymond Wolfinger investigates various theories of political leadership in the light of a detailed examination of the activities of political leaders in New Haven, particularly the mayor, in several major decisions.

The volumes by Dr. Polsby and Dr. Wolfinger complement this one in a number of ways, and questions a reader might expect to find dealt with here will sometimes be found instead in the other two.

The data about New Haven used in this book were gained from a variety of sources and by a number of different methods. These are discussed in some detail in Appendix B, but a brief word may be helpful here. Probably the single most useful source of information about New Haven's political life in recent years was a set of lengthy interviews during 1957 and 1958 with nearly fifty persons who had participated actively in one or more important decisions on matters of urban redevelopment, public education, or nominations for local office. In addition, Dr. Wolfinger spent a year in two highly strategic locations in City Hall and provided invaluable background information; some of this was confidential, and though it does not appear in these pages directly, it nonetheless provided me with heightened confidence in the reliability of the evidence contained in the interviews. Three different sample surveys were made under my supervision; one covered several hundred "subleaders," the other two were of registered voters. Moreover, in 1958, graduate students in my seminar at Yale carried out detailed investigations of the events leading up to a proposal for a new charter and its defeat in a referendum; their papers (listed in Appendix B) were a mine of information, both qualitatively and quantitatively.

In order to gain the kind of reliable historical perspective that a method depending solely on interviews could not provide, I have made use of a variety of historical materials, including not only standard historical works but U. S. Census and other documents and records which provided unique and valuable information.

I have written this book with three audiences constantly in mind— my fellow scholars, my fellow citizens of the greater New Haven area, and inquiring readers who, though in neither of these two groups, may hope that by reading a book about the politics of one particular city they may gain a greater understanding of their own communities, American politics, or even democracy itself.

I am painfully aware of the fact that the interests, background information, and, alas, even the specialized vocabularies of these three audiences are not always the same, and no doubt at times I have paid attention to one audience at the expense of the others. In these cases, I hope that the patience and tolerance of the reader will enable him to gain his objectives where I may have failed in mine.

Robert A. Dahl

New Haven, Connecticut
May 1, 1961

Acknowledgments

My heaviest debt is to two persons who began with me on this study as research assistants and ended as close friends and associates, as well as authors of two companion volumes, Nelson Polsby and Raymond Wolfinger.

At a time when I was too busy to provide more than the most general guidance, William Flanigan assumed virtually complete charge of the preparation, execution, and tabulation of the survey conducted in the summer of 1959, and with unfailing geniality, insight, and responsibility helped me in countless ways with the analysis until the very day this book went to press.

For help on the history of New Haven, I have leaned heavily on my friend and colleague, Professor Rollin Osterweis of the Department of History at Yale, whose encyclopedic fund of information about New Haven's past is only partly recorded in his invaluable book on the history of the city.

The research and papers of graduate students in the Department of Political Science at Yale have been of help in a variety of ways; I should like to record my special obligation to Rufus Browning, William Foltz, James Guyot, Richard Merritt, Leroy Rieselbach, Bruce Russett, and James Toscano.

I am indebted for help in laborious tasks of compilation of tables, transcription of interviews, and typing of manuscript to Josh Taylor, Janet Chalmers, Sally Osterweis Kopman, Linda Offenbach Polsby, Carol Oliver, Betsy Abrams, and Ellen Abrams.

A number of colleagues helped me to clarify my ideas and saved me from error by discussions on problems of concept, method, and substance, or by reading parts of the manuscript. I am particularly grateful to Peter Clark, Herbert Kaufman, Norton Long, James March, Douglas Price, Wallace Sayre, Harry Scoble, Bert Swanson, James Tobin, Benjamin Walter, Henry Wells, and James Wilson.

I should like to express my deep appreciation to Marian Neal Ash and Anne Firth Murray of the Yale University Press on behalf not only of myself but also the ultimate beneficiaries of their efforts, my readers. Their sensitive and intelligent contributions on matters of clarity, organization, and style were all the more persuasive because of the disarming graciousness with which they were offered.

A fellowship at the Center for Advanced Study in the Behavioral Sciences gave me time to work out the first outlines of the research and analysis required for this work, and a year as the Ford Research Professor in the Department of Political Science at Yale provided me with both the time and the additional research funds needed to launch and carry out most of the actual research in New Haven. Additional financial assistance, without which the research and writing could not have been completed, was received from the Social Science Research Council, the Ford Foundation, and the American Philosophical Society.

Finally, I acknowledge my deep obligation to all the citizens of New Haven who permitted themselves to be interviewed. Much of the substance and validity of this study was dependent on their cooperation and willingness to share information and opinion. For many reasons, men and women who furnished me with invaluable information must go nameless here, but to all who read these pages and recognize their contributions, and those who do not, I should like to express my thanks.

R. A. D.

Contents

1. The Nature of the Problem

In a political system where nearly every adult may vote but where knowledge, wealth, social position, access to officials, and other resources are unequally distributed, who actually governs?

The question has been asked, I imagine, wherever popular government has developed and intelligent citizens have reached the stage of critical self-consciousness concerning their society. It must have been put many times in Athens even before it was posed by Plato and Aristotle.

The question is peculiarly relevant to the United States and to Americans. In the first place, Americans espouse democratic beliefs with a fervency and a unanimity that have been a regular source of astonishment to foreign observers from Tocqueville and Bryce to Myrdal and Brogan. Not long ago, two American political scientists reported that 96 per cent or more of several hundred registered voters interviewed in two widely separated American cities agreed that: "Democracy is the best form of government" and "Every citizen should have an equal chance to influence government policy," and subscribed to other propositions equally basic to the democratic credo.[1] What, if anything, do these beliefs actually mean in the face of extensive inequalities in the resources different citizens can use to influence one another?

These beliefs in democracy and equality first gained wide acceptance as a part of what Myrdal later called the "American Creed" during a period when the problem of inequality was (if we can disregard for the moment the question of slavery) much less important than it is today. Indeed, the problem uppermost in the minds of the men at the Constitutional Convention in Philadelphia in 1787 could probably have been stated quite the other way around. To men concerned with what was then a unique task of adapting republican institutions to a whole nation, the very *equality* in resources of power that American society and geography tended to generate seemed to endanger political stability and liberty. In a society of equals, what checks would there be against an impetuous, unenlightened, or unscrupulous majority? A half century later, this was also the way an amazing and gifted observer, Alexis de Tocqueville,

1. James W. Prothro and Charles M. Grigg, "Fundamental Principles of Democracy: Bases of Agreement and Disagreement," *Journal of Politics*, 22 (1960), 276–94.

posed the question in probably the most profound analysis of American democracy ever written. For Tocqueville, the United States was the most advanced representative of a new species of society emerging from centuries of development: "In running over the pages of [European] history, we shall scarcely find a single great event of the last seven hundred years that has not promoted equality of condition." So he wrote in the introduction to the first volume of his *Democracy in America*.

> Whither, then, are we tending? [he went on to ask] No one can say, for terms of comparison already fail us. There is greater equality of condition in Christian countries at the present day than there has been at any previous time, in any part of the world, so that the magnitude of what already has been done prevents us from foreseeing what is yet to be accomplished.

In the United States he had looked upon the future, on

> one country in the world where the great social revolution that I am speaking of seems to have nearly reached its natural limits . . . Men are there seen on a greater equality in point of fortune and intellect, or, in other words, more equal in their strength, than in any other country of the world, or in any age of which history has preserved the remembrance.[2]

The America that Tocqueville saw, however, was the America of Andrew Jackson. It was an agrarian democracy, remarkably close to the ideal often articulated by Jefferson.

Commerce, finance, and industry erupted into this agrarian society in a gigantic explosion. By the time the century approached its last decade, and another distinguished foreign observer looked upon the United States, the America of Tocqueville had already passed away. In how many senses of the word, James Bryce asked in 1899, does equality exist in the United States?

> Clearly not as regards material conditions. Sixty years ago there were no great fortunes in America, few large fortunes, no poverty. Now there is some poverty (though only in a few places can it be called pauperism), many large fortunes, and a greater number of gigantic fortunes than in any other country of the world.

He found also an intellectual elite, among whose members the "level of exceptional attainment . . . rises faster than does the general level of the multitude, so that in this regard also it appears that equality has diminished and will diminish further."

2. Alexis de Tocqueville, *Democracy in America* (New York, Vintage Books, 1955), *1*, 5, 6, 14, 55.

It was true that in America there were no formal marks of rank in the European sense. However, this did not

> prevent the existence of grades and distinctions in society which, though they may find no tangible expression, are sometimes as sharply drawn as in Europe . . . The nature of a man's occupation, his education, his manners and breeding, his income, his connections, all come into view in determining whether he is in this narrow sense of the word "a gentleman."

Yet, remarkably, the universal belief in equality that Tocqueville had found sixty years earlier still persisted. "It is in this," Bryce wrote, "that the real sense of equality comes out. In America men hold others to be at bottom exactly like themselves." A man may be enormously rich, or a great orator, or a great soldier or writer, "but it is not a reason for bowing down to him, or addressing him in deferential terms, or treating him as if he was porcelain and yourself only earthenware."[3]

Now it has always been held that if equality of power among citizens is possible at all—a point on which many political philosophers have had grave doubts—then surely considerable equality of social conditions is a necessary prerequisite. But if, even in America, with its universal creed of democracy and equality, there are great inequalities in the conditions of different citizens, must there not also be great inequalities in the capacities of different citizens to influence the decisions of their various governments? And if, because they are unequal in other conditions, citizens of a democracy are unequal in power to control their government, then who in fact does govern? How does a "democratic" system work amid inequality of resources? These are the questions I want to explore by examining one urban American community, New Haven, Connecticut.

I have said "explore" because it is obvious that one cannot do more by concentrating on one community. However, New Haven embodies most of the equalities and inequalities that lend this enterprise its significance. In the course of the book, I shall examine various aspects of these that may be related to differences in the extent to which citizens can and do influence local government. But it will not hurt to start putting a little paint on the canvas now.

One might argue whether the political system of New Haven is "democratic" or "truly democratic," but only because these terms are always debatable. In everyday language, New Haven is a democratic political community. Most of its adult residents are legally entitled to vote. A relatively high proportion do vote. Their votes are, by and large, honestly counted—though absentee votes, a small fraction of the total,

3. James Bryce, *The American Commonwealth* (London, Macmillan, 1889), 2, 602–03, 606–07.

are occasionally manipulated. Elections are free from violence and, for all practical purposes, free from fraud. Two political parties contest elections, offer rival slates of candidates, and thus present the voters with at least some outward show of choice.

Running counter to this legal equality of citizens in the voting booth, however, is an unequal distribution of the resources that can be used for influencing the choices of voters and, between elections, of officials. Take property, for example. In 1957, the fifty largest property owners, in number less than one-sixteenth of one per cent of the taxpayers, held nearly one-third of the total assessed value of all real property in the city. Most of the fifty largest property owners were, of course, corporations: public utilities like the United Illuminating Company, which had the largest assessment ($22 million) and the Southern New England Telephone Company ($12 million); big industries like Olin Mathieson ($21 million) which had bought up the Winchester Repeating Arms Company, the famous old New Haven firearms firm; family-held firms like Sargent and A. C. Gilbert; or department stores like the century-old firm of Malley's. Of the fifty largest property owners, sixteen were manufacturing firms, nine were retail and wholesale businesses, six were privately-owned public utilities, and five were banks. Yale University was one of the biggest property owners, though it ranked only tenth in assessed value ($3.6 million) because much of its property was tax-free. A few individuals stood out boldly on the list, like John Day Jackson, the owner and publisher of New Haven's two newspapers.

Or consider family income. In 1949, the average (median) family income in New Haven was about $2,700 a year. One family out of forty had an income of $10,000 or more; over one family out of five had an income of less than $1,000. In the Thirtieth Ward, which had the highest average family income, one family out of four had an income of $7,000 or more; in the Fifth, the poorest, over half the families had incomes of less than $2,000 a year. (Technically, the First Ward was even poorer than the Fifth for half the families there had incomes of less than $700 a year, but three-quarters of the residents of the First were students at Yale.)

The average adult in New Haven had completed the ninth grade, but in the Tenth Ward half the adults had never gone beyond elementary school. About one out of six adults in the city had gone to college. The extremes were represented by the Thirty-first Ward, where nearly half had attended college, and the Twenty-seventh, where the proportion was only one out of thirty.[4]

4. Assessments are from the city records. The average ratio of assessed value to actual prices on property sold in 1957 was 49.2, according to the New Haven Taxpayers Research Council, "Assessment of Real Estate," *Council Comment*, No.

Thus one is forced back once more to the initial question. Given the existence of inequalities like these, who actually governs in a democracy?

Since the question is not new, one may wonder whether we do not, after all, pretty well know the answer by now. Do we not at least know what answer must be given for the present-day political system of the United States? Unfortunately no. Students of politics have provided a number of conflicting explanations for the way in which democracies can be expected to operate in the midst of inequalities in political resources. Some answers are a good deal more optimistic than others. For example, it is sometimes said that political parties provide competition for public office and thereby guarantee a relatively high degree of popular control. By appealing to the voters, parties organize the un-organized, give power to the powerless, present voters with alternative candidates and programs, and insure that during campaigns they have an opportunity to learn about the merits of these alternatives. Furthermore, after the election is over, the victorious party, which now represents the preferences of a majority of voters, takes over the task of governing. The voter, therefore, does not need to participate actively in government; it is enough for him to participate in elections by the simple act of voting. By his vote he registers a preference for the general direction in which government policy should move; he cannot and does not need to choose particular policies. One answer to the question, "Who governs?" is then that competing political parties govern, but they do so with the consent of voters secured by competitive elections.

However, no sooner had observers begun to discover the extraordinary importance of political parties in the operation of democratic political systems than others promptly reduced the political party to little more than a collection of "interest groups," or sets of individuals with some values, purposes, and demands in common. If the parties were the political molecules, the interest groups were the atoms. And everything could be explained simply by studying the atoms. Neither people nor parties but interest groups, it was said, are the true units of the political system. An individual, it was argued, is politically rather helpless, but a group unites the resources of individuals into an effective force. Thus some theorists would answer our question by replying that interest groups govern; most of the actions of government can be explained, they would say, simply as the result of struggles among groups of individuals with differing interests and varying resources of influence.

The first explanation was developed by English and American writers, the second almost entirely by Americans. A third theory, much more

---

36 (Mar. 9, 1959). Data on incomes and education are from a special tabulation by wards of the data in U.S. Census, Characteristics of the Population, 1950. Income data are estimates by the Census Bureau from a 20% sample.

pessimistic than the other two, was almost exclusively European in origin, though it subsequently achieved a considerable vogue in the United States. This explanation, which has both a "Left" and a "Right" interpretation, asserts that beneath the façade of democratic politics a social and economic elite will usually be found actually running things. Robert and Helen Lynd used this explanation in their famous two books on "Middletown" (Muncie, Indiana), and many studies since then have also adopted it, most notably Floyd Hunter in his analysis of the "power structure" of Atlanta.[5] Because it fits nicely with the very factors that give rise to our question, the view that a social and economic elite controls government is highly persuasive. Concentration of power in the hands of an elite is a necessary consequence, in this view, of the enormous inequalities in the distribution of resources of influence—property, income, social status, knowledge, publicity, focal position, and all the rest.

One difficulty with all of these explanations was that they left very little room for the politician. He was usually regarded merely as an agent—of majority will, the political parties, interest groups, or the elite. He had no independent influence. But an older view that could be traced back to Machiavelli's famous work, *The Prince*, stressed the enormous political potential of the cunning, resourceful, masterful leader. In this view, majorities, parties, interest groups, elites, even political systems are all to some extent pliable; a leader who knows how to use his resources to the maximum is not so much the agent of others as others are his agents. Although a gifted political entrepreneur might not exist in every political system, wherever he appeared he would make himself felt.

Still another view commingled elements of all the rest. This explanation was set out by Tocqueville as a possible course of degeneration in all democratic orders, restated by the Spanish philosopher, Ortega y Gassett, in his highly influential book, *The Revolt of the Masses* (1930), and proposed by a number of European intellectuals, after the destruction of the German Republic by Nazism, as an explanation for the origins of modern dictatorships. Although it is a theory proposed mainly by Europeans about European conditions, it is so plausible an alternative that we cannot afford to ignore it. Essentially, this theory (which has many variants) argues that under certain conditions of development (chiefly industrialization and urbanization) older, stratified, class-based social structures are weakened or destroyed; and in their place arises a

5. Robert S. Lynd and Helen M. Lynd, *Middletown* (New York, Harcourt Brace, 1929) and *Middletown in Transition* (New York, Harcourt Brace, 1937). Floyd Hunter, *Community Power Structure* (Chapel Hill, University of North Carolina Press, 1953) and *Top Leadership, U.S.A.* (Chapel Hill, University of North Carolina Press, 1959).

mass of individuals with no secure place in the social system, rootless, aimless, lacking strong social ties, ready and indeed eager to attach themselves to any political entrepreneur who will cater to their tastes and desires. Led by unscrupulous and exploitative leaders, these rootless masses have the capacity to destroy whatever stands in their way without the ability to replace it with a stable alternative. Consequently the greater their influence on politics, the more helpless they become; the more they destroy, the more they depend upon strong leaders to create some kind of social, economic, and political organization to replace the old. If we ask, "Who governs?" the answer is not the mass nor its leaders but both together; the leaders cater to mass tastes and in return use the strength provided by the loyalty and obedience of the masses to weaken and perhaps even to annihilate all opposition to their rule.

A superficial familiarity with New Haven (or for that matter with almost any modern American city) would permit one to argue persuasively that each of these theories really explains the inner workings of the city's political life. However, a careful consideration of the points at which the theories diverge suggests that the broad question, "Who governs?" might be profitably subdivided into a number of more specific questions. These questions, listed below, have guided the study of New Haven recorded in this book:

Are inequalities in resources of influence "cumulative" or "noncumulative?" That is, are people who are better off in one resource also better off in others? In other words, does the way in which political resources are distributed encourage oligarchy or pluralism?

How are important political decisions actually made?

What kinds of people have the greatest influence on decisions? Are different kinds of decisions all made by the same people? From what strata of the community are the most influential people, the leaders, drawn?

Do leaders tend to cohere in their policies and form a sort of ruling group, or do they tend to divide, conflict, and bargain? Is the pattern of leadership, in short, oligarchical or pluralistic?

What is the relative importance of the most widely distributed political resource—the right to vote? Do leaders respond generally to the interests of the few citizens with the greatest wealth and highest status—or do they respond to the many with the largest number of votes? To what extent do various citizens *use* their political resources? Are there important differences that in turn result in differences in influence?

Are the patterns of influence durable or changing? For example, was democracy stronger in New Haven when Tocqueville contemplated the American scene? And in more recent years, as New Haven has grappled with a gigantic program of urban reconstruction, what has happened to popular control and to patterns of leadership? In general, what are the sources of change and stability in the political system?

Finally, how important is the nearly universal adherence to the "American Creed" of democracy and equality? Is the operation of the political system affected in any way by what ordinary citizens believe or profess to believe about democracy? If so, how?

The answers to these questions which seem best to fit the facts of New Haven will gradually unfold in the chapters that follow. I warn the reader, however, that I shall not attempt to dispose of all these questions in any one place. Each chapter tells only a part of the story; thus I shall not deal directly with the last pair of questions until the final chapter. Since each chapter builds upon those that precede it, the analysis in the final chapters presupposes knowledge of all that has gone before.

EQUALITY AND INEQUALITY IN NEW HAVEN

Book I

FROM OLIGARCHY TO PLURALISM

2. The Patricians

In the course of the past two centuries, New Haven has gradually changed from oligarchy to pluralism. Accompanying and probably causing this change—one might properly call it a revolution—appears to be a profound alteration in the way political resources are distributed among the citizens of New Haven. This silent socioeconomic revolution has not substituted equality for inequality so much as it has involved a shift from cumulative inequalities in political resources—to use an expression introduced a moment ago—to noncumulative or dispersed inequalities. This point will grow clearer as we proceed.

The main evidence for the shift from oligarchy to pluralism is found in changes in the social characteristics of elected officials in New Haven since 1784, the year the city was first incorporated after a century and a half as colony and town.

In the first period (1784–1842), public office was almost the exclusive prerogative of the patrician families. In the second period (1842–1900), the new self-made men of business, the entrepreneurs, took over. Since then, the "ex-plebes" rising out of working-class or lower middle-class families of immigrant origins have predominated. These transformations reflected profound alterations in the community, in the course of which important resources for obtaining influence were fragmented and dispersed. Wealth was separated from social position by the rise of industry, and public office went to the wealthy. Later, popularity was divorced from both wealth and social position by the influx of immigrants, and public office went to the ex-plebes, who lacked wealth and social position but had the advantage of numbers.

It is theoretically possible, of course, that the "real" decision-makers differed from the official decision-makers; if this were so, the real decision-makers might even have come from different social strata than the official decision-makers. However, for reasons I shall discuss later, it is highly unlikely that a set of real decision-makers from different social strata controlled either the patricians or the entrepreneurs. With the ex-plebes, the case is more plausible. We shall return to this question in Chapter 6.

With this reservation in mind, let us now examine the changes that have taken place in the origins, occupations, and styles of life of the leading elected officials, the mayor and the aldermen, over the past century and three-quarters. Ever since 1784, the mayor of New Haven (Table 2.1) has been elected by his fellow citizens. At first, however, once elected, he held office on the pleasure of the General Assembly of the state, which until 1818 was a staunchly Federalist body and hence willing to let Federalist mayors remain in office indefinitely. In 1826 this quaint practice, more congenial to Federalism than the new Democracy, was superseded by annual elections. The members of the Common Council, including the aldermen, were elected annually in a town meeting. Since the 1870s, the mayor and aldermen have been elected for two-year terms.

During the period of patrician government, the typical mayor came from one of the established families of New Haven, went to Yale, was admitted to the bar, retained some connection with Yale, and spent most of his life in public affairs. Yet there were interesting nuances. Roger Sherman, the most distinguished of all New Haven mayors, was one of the few prominent New Haven Federalists who rose to eminence from modest beginnings. Like most New Englanders of the time, he could trace his New World ancestry back to 1634. His father was a farmer near Newton, Massachusetts, and it was there that Roger first learned the shoemaker's trade with which he began his career in New Haven; he then started a store, acquired real estate, and was admitted to the bar. By 1764 his fellow citizens in New Haven thought well enough of him to send him to the colonial legislature, and from that time onward political life was his real career. He was in the senate of both colony and state for two decades; during the same period he was a judge of

TABLE 2.1. *The mayors of New Haven, 1784–1960*

Party	Elected	Mayor	Occupation	
	1784	Roger Sherman	U.S. senator, signed Declaration of Independence	
Dem.-Rep.	1793	Samuel Bishop	judge of probate	
Fed.	1803	Elizur Goodrich	professor of law	
Dem.-Rep.	1822	George Hoadley*	president, Eagle Bank	
Fed.	1826	Simeon Baldwin	judge, congressman	
Dem.-Rep.	1827	William Bristol	judge, state senator	The patricians: law and the professions
Fed.	1828	David Daggett	professor of law, U.S. senator	
Dem.	1830	Ralph Ingersoll	lawyer, congressman, state attorney	
Dem.	1831	Dennis Kimberly	lawyer, major general, U.S senator	
Dem.	1832	Ebenezer Seeley	?	
Whig	1833	Noyes Darling	judge	
Whig	1834	H. C. Flagg	lawyer, editor	
Whig	1839	S. J. Hitchcock	lawyer, law teacher	

TABLE 2.1. *Continued*

Party	Elected	Mayor	Occupation	
Whig	1842	P. S. Galpin	carpet manufacturer and insurance	
Whig	1846	Henry Peck	Durrie and Peck	
Whig	1850	A. N. Skinner	headmaster, classical boarding school	
Whig	1854	Chauncey Jerome	clock manufacturer	
Dem.	1855	A. Blackman	attorney	
Whig	1856	P. S. Galpin	secretary, Mutual Security Insurance Company	
Dem.	1860	H. M. Welch	founder and president, New Haven Rolling Mill, president, First National Bank	
Dem.	1863	Morris Tyler	wholesale boot and shoe dealer	
Rep.	1865	E. C. Scranton	president, Second National Bank	
Dem.	1866	L. W. Sperry	Sperry and Co. (meat-packing)	
Rep.	1869	William Fitch	E. T. Fitch and Co., coach spring manufacturer	The entrepreneurs: business and industry
Dem.	1870	H. G. Lewis	president, New Haven Wheel Co.	
Dem.	1877	W. R. Shelton	president, American Needle and Fish Hook Co.	
Rep.	1879	H. B. Bigelow	Bigelow and Co., machinery manufacturing	
Dem.	1881	J. B. Robertson	vice president, National Life and Trust Co.	
Ind. Dem.	1883	H. G. Lewis	president, New Haven Wheel Co.	
Dem.	1885	G. F. Holcomb	Holcomb Brothers and Co.	
Dem.	1887	S. A. York	judge of probate, lawyer	
Rep.	1889	H. F. Peck	president, Peck Brothers and Co., brass goods manufacturers	
Dem.	1891	J. B. Sargent	president, Sargent and Co., hardware manufacturing	
Rep.	1895	A. C. Hendrick	general inspector, Board of Fire Underwriters	
Rep.	1897	F. B. Farnsworth	president and treasurer, McLagon Foundry Co.	

TABLE 2.1 *Continued*

Party	Elected	Mayor	Occupation	
Dem.	1899	C. T. Driscoll	lawyer	
Rep.	1901	J. P. Studley	judge, Court of Common Pleas	
Dem.	1908	J. B. Martin	lawyer	
Rep.	1910	F. J. Rice°	real estate	
Rep.	1917	S. C. Campner°°	lawyer	
Dem.	1919	D. E. Fitzgerald	lawyer	
Rep.	1925	J. B. Tower	president, Geom. Garage Co., treasurer, J. R. Rembert Co.	The ex-plebes
Rep.	1928	T. A. Tully	assistant secretary, printing business	
Dem.	1931	J. W. Murphy	business agent, Cigar Workers, A.F.L.	
Rep.	1945	W. C. Celentano	secretary-treasurer, Celentano Funeral Home Inc.	
Dem.	1953	R. C. Lee	director, Yale News Bureau	

° Died in office.
°° Succeeded to office on Rice's death in 1916.

the Superior Court; he was a delegate to the Continental Congress; he signed the Declaration of Independence; during his tenure as mayor of New Haven he was sent first to the Constitutional Convention at Philadelphia and then to the United States Senate. In addition to his public life, he was treasurer of Yale College for more than a decade, a sure sign (if any were needed) of his acceptance by the established families of New Haven; in 1768, Yale awarded him an honorary master of arts.[1]

Elizur Goodrich was more typical of the patrician mayors. He could trace his ancestry to Dr. Thomas Goodrich, who had been Bishop of Ely in 1534; his forebears settled in Wethersfield in 1643. His father had graduated from Yale in 1752, was a Congregational minister, a fellow of the Yale Corporation, and at one time a strong candidate for the presidency of the University. Elizur himself went to Yale, was admitted to the New Haven bar, became judge of probate, a position he held for seventeen years, and was judge of the county court for twelve years. He was sent to the United States Congress and in one of John Adams' historic "midnight" appointments (when Adams sought to pack the courts and the federal service against the incoming Jeffersonians) was appointed collector of customs at New Haven. When Jefferson removed him in order to award the office to Samuel Bishop, an aged Republican whose son Abraham was a loyal and active Jeffersonian, some eighty New

1. *Encyclopedia of Connecticut Biography* (New York, American Historical Society, 1917), *1*, 6–7.

Haven merchants purporting to own "more than seven-eighths of the navigation of the port of New Haven" promptly dispatched a letter of protest. Jefferson was not moved. But Goodrich's friends rewarded him by making him a professor of law at Yale, and two years later mayor of New Haven, a position he held for the next nineteen years.[2] The careers of Simeon Baldwin, David Daggett, and Ralph Ingersoll were much the same: Yale families, Yale education, the bar, public life.[3]

The patricians had all the political resources they needed: wealth, social position, education, and a monopoly of public office; everything, in fact, except numbers—and popularity with the rank and file. It is puzzling to know which is the more in need of explanation: their domination over public life or their ultimate downfall.

As for their domination, New Haven, and for that matter the colony and the state of Connecticut, had been ruled for a century and a half by an elite, the "Standing Order," consisting of Congregational ministers, lawyers, and men of business, of whom the ministers had historically furnished most of the leadership. Like Connecticut itself, New Haven was a kind of Congregational theocracy in the trappings of primitive democracy. David Daggett described the operation of the system in 1787, and mourned its decline. "The minister, with two or three principal characters," he said, "was supreme in each town. Hence the body of the clergy, with a few families of distinction, between whom there was ever a most intimate connection, ruled the whole State." [4]

Among the English upper classes, perhaps the leaders of eighteenth-century New England would not have cut much of a figure. By the standards of English society they were at best of middling status, and in religion more akin to the lower middle classes of England. Perry Miller is doubtless right in saying that "what New England took to be the real England was lower-middle class England." [5] But New Englanders were, after all, living in New England; there the patrician families knew no social superiors. By almost any test it seems safe to infer that the elite of New Haven, like the Standing Order in Connecticut, completely dominated the political system. They were of one common stock and one religion, cohesive in their uniformly conservative outlook on all matters, substantially unchallenged in their authority, successful in pushing through their own policies, and in full control of such critical social institutions as the established religion, the educational system (including

2. Ibid., *1*, 88.

3. For brief biographies of Daggett and Baldwin, see ibid., *1*, 73–74 and 74–75. For Ingersoll, see Edward E. Atwater, *History of the City of New Haven* (New York, W. W. Munsell, 1887).

4. Richard J. Purcell, *Connecticut in Transition, 1775–1818* (Washington, American Historical Association, 1918), p. 310.

5. Perry Miller, *Jonathan Edwards* (New York, William Sloan, 1949), p. 109.

not only all the schools but Yale as well), and even business enterprise. Both they and their opponents took their political supremacy as a fact. By 1800 they were so thoroughly accustomed to the habit of ruling that their response to the emerging challenge of Jeffersonian republicanism was a kind of shocked disbelief: a response immediately followed, however, by energetic efforts to stamp out the new political heresy root and branch.

The capacity of the elite to continue its dominant position in New Haven politics through the first half-century of city government was probably a result of several factors. New Haven, though one of the largest towns in Connecticut, was essentially a small town where everyone knew everyone else by appearance, name, position, origins, and social rank. In 1787, the total population of the city was about 3,400. Not more than 800 of these could have been men eighteen years of age or older.[6] Even as late as 1820, the population was barely over 7,000, of whom about 1,600 were males of twenty-one years and older. Voting took place in town meetings where, under a "Stand-Up" Law enacted with great political shrewdness by the representatives of the Standing Order in the General Assembly of the state in 1801, a man had to reveal his choice within full view of the elite. Only a man of unusual courage was likely to display his opposition to the candidates preferred by church, wealth, and, in effect, state. (There was a beautifully contrived system for voting in town meetings on candidates for the upper chamber of the General Assembly. In theory it allowed a voter to cast a paper ballot for any twelve out of twenty nominees; in fact one had to reveal his support of candidates not on the approved list of twelve. So opponents of the Standing Order, lacking the courage of public opposition, took to casting blank ballots for one or more of the twelve nominees of the elite.)[7]

Even the pressures of small-town life and open voting seem insufficient to account for the dominance of the elite, however, for the top group was a remarkably tiny one. In 1811, when the city could not have contained many more than 5,000 people, President Timothy Dwight of Yale, who was surely in a position to know, listed only thirty-two professional men in the whole city: six clergymen, sixteen lawyers, nine physicians, and one surgeon. (Table 2.2) If we add to that number the proprietors of "29 houses concerned in foreign trade" and seven manufacturers, we must come very near to the number of men eligible for membership in the religious, social, and economic elite. A large intermediate social group, a sort of middle class, consisted of dry goods merchants, grocers, owners of lumber yards, and the like, numbering well over a hundred persons;

6. Timothy Dwight, A Statistical Account of the City of New Haven (New Haven, 1811), pp. 57–58. Reprinted from New Haven City Year Book, 1874.

7. Purcell, Connecticut in Transition, pp. 194 ff.

TABLE 2.2. *Distribution of occupations in New Haven, 1811*
(probably incomplete)

The professions	32
Foreign commerce and manufacturing	36
Retail and wholesale firms	122
Artisans	222
Total	412

Source: Dwight, *Statistical Account of New Haven,* pp. 32–33.

probably most of these looked to the elite for leadership. Even so, there were over two hundred artisans in the city, men more predisposed than their social superiors to egalitarian political faiths and to evangelistic dissenting religions like Baptism or Methodism.[8]

However, many of the artisans were doubtless prevented from voting by the state's property qualification for voting, which required a freehold estate equivalent to the value of $7 a year, or a personal estate of $134. It is difficult to know how many potential voters were disfranchised by this requirement, but at the beginning of the period the number seems to have been rather large. In the first city election in 1784, out of 600 adult males only 343 were qualified to vote. A quarter of these failed to take the oath, so that 249 out of the 600 men in the city actually voted in the town meeting to elect the first mayor. (A few days later in a meeting called to elect lesser officials only about 100 men showed up.)[9]

Even so, had grievances run deep enough, the fact that popular elections were the only legitimate means to public office almost certainly would have resulted in more conflict and opposition than the records reveal. The elite seems to have possessed that most indispensable of all characteristics in a dominant group—the sense, shared not only by themselves but by the populace, that their claim to govern was legitimate. If the best families regarded public life as a prerogative, they must also have looked upon it as an honorable career; like the ministry, politics must have carried with it very high prestige. Hence it is reasonable to conclude that until the winds of Jacksonianism blew in from the West, a man of nonpatrician origins must have regarded it as an act of unusual boldness, if not downright arrogance, to stand for public office. Given the perspectives of the time, who after all were more entitled to rule than those who had founded and governed town and colony, city and state for nearly two centuries and who, besides, embodied the highest achievements of a Congregational society? In a community of Calvinists, the idea of an elect was certainly not strange. And who had a better right to be elected than the elect?

8. Dwight, *Statistical Account of New Haven,* pp. 32–33.
9. Atwater, *History of New Haven,* p. 231.

The whole social system, in short, was a hierarchy in which the patricians stood at the apex. In this respect New Haven was closer to Europe across the Atlantic than to the frontier across the Hudson. The outlook that must have prevailed in such a society is difficult to recapture today, but perhaps nothing better symbolized it than two practices. First, until 1765 Yale College, the educational institution for that tiny minority of Congregational ministers and lay leaders who provided the leadership, catalogued her students not alphabetically but according to their social standing; second, it was the custom in Congregational churches to assign seats according to the age, family background, or wealth of the occupant.[10]

Yet the elect did meet with opposition, and once their legitimacy as rulers began to be doubted, they were too few in number to maintain control over public office in a political order where office could be contested in elections. As an examination of the list of mayors (Table 2.1) reveals, the Federalist-Congregationalist-patrician class was occasionally challenged successfully even during this early period. Although opponents to the regime came from various sources, they all seem to have shared a common hostility to the patrician oligarchy. Religion played an important part. For just as dissenters in England were prone to join the opposition to Tories and later Conservatives, so dissenters in New Haven (and in Connecticut generally) resented that Congregationalism was the established church, and that members of other religious bodies were discriminated against in a variety of annoying ways. When Congregationalism became the religion of a minority, the end of patrician rule was in sight. And even by 1787 only about 26 per cent of the New Haven population was actually enrolled in one of the three Congregational churches.[11]

Religious dissent helps to account for the occasional maverick who "betrayed his class" and went over to Jefferson or Jackson. The Republicans of Connecticut first organized themselves in 1800 at the New Haven home of Pierrepont Edwards, a leading lawyer, federal district judge, and member of one of the most aristocratic families in New England.[12] Henry W. Edwards, Pierrepont's son and also a highly successful lawyer, was not only a Jeffersonian but later became one of the leading Jackson men in the state.[13] It is difficult to account for this open hostility to the Standing Order unless one recalls that it was the

10. Purcell, *Connecticut in Transition,* p. 73.
11. Ibid., p. 44.
12. Ibid., p. 232. See also Rollin G. Osterweis, *Three Centuries of New Haven, 1638–1938* (New Haven, Yale University Press, 1953), p. 197.
13. Jarvis M. Morse, *A Neglected Period of Connecticut's History, 1818–1850* (New Haven, Yale University Press, 1933), pp. 70–73 and passim.

Edwards' common ancestor, Jonathan, who set the whole Congregational establishment of New England on its ear after 1734 when he tried to demonstrate, as Perry Miller has put it, "that they had ceased to believe what they professed, and that as a result the society was sick. He did not merely call them hypocrites, he proved that they were." [14] He attacked the mighty, and as often happens it was the mighty who won. It seems not fanciful to suppose that his eleventh and last son, Pierrepont, born only a few months before the Connecticut River barons drove him in defeat from Northampton, felt less than charity and deference toward the class that destroyed his father, even though that class was his own.

The social origins of Ralph Ingersoll were, as I have already indicated, as impeccable as those of Baldwin and Daggett; he was of a family of lawyers, his father having gone to Yale and thence into the law. Young Ingersoll followed his father's path, began his political life as a Federalist, and was a leader of the bar of Connecticut for many years. But the Ingersolls were Episcopalians, and Ralph Ingersoll moved (with his father) into the Toleration party that seized control of the state from the ruling Federalists in 1818; he ended up as a Jacksonian Democrat and a leader of the Democratic party.[15]

The Bishop family was something else again. In their case religion was perhaps less important than class and ideological factors. The origins of Samuel Bishop are somewhat uncertain, but he was not one of the elect. His son Abraham, appointed collector of customs on his father's death, had been sent to Yale and became a wealthy man, but he remained throughout his life a strong Jeffersonian, a bitter opponent of the Federalist-Congregationalist oligarchy, possibly a bit of a scapegrace, and something of an outcast. The elect accused him of atheism and French Jacobinism, but he was a skilled polemicist who gave as good as he got, and charged his enemies with conspiracies against republican institutions and religious freedom.[16] At times bitterness must have covered the small town like a dank fog.

The Bishops reflected still another source of strength available to the opposition. After 1800 the national government was firmly in the hands of the Jeffersonians; in 1818 the Federalist monopoly over the government of the state was finally and forever destroyed. For Republicans these changes in state and national politics meant patronage, political organization, and even a certain legitimacy. New Haven Federalists could fume about Samuel Bishop's appointment, but they could not reverse it. Where before only the Federalist-Congregationalist elite had an effective politi-

---

14. Miller, *Jonathan Edwards*, pp. 108–09.

15. Atwater, *History of New Haven*, p. 247. For Ingersoll's Episcopalian background, see Purcell, *Connecticut in Transition*, p. 335.

16. *Dictionary of American Biography* (New York, Scribner's, 1946), 2, 294–5

cal organization, now their opponents began to develop one. And where
the Federalists were once the party of experience, increasingly they were
the party of the has-beens while the Republicans were men of national
reputation and extensive political experience.

Sooner or later, leaders who knew how to mobilize sheer numbers were
bound to prevail over the old oligarchy. Five factors helped in that
triumph: the secret ballot, the spread of the suffrage, the growth in
population, mobilization of the voters by the political parties, and ideol-

FIGURE 2.1. *Total votes cast in New Haven in elections
for governor, as percentages of males 21 years old
and over, 1813–1850*

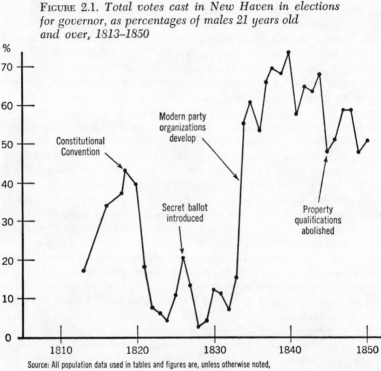

Source: All population data used in tables and figures are, unless otherwise noted,
from the U. S. Census, with linear interpolations between census years.

ogy. Of these, the last two were probably far and away the most
important.

It was not until 1826 that the secret ballot began to be used in town
meetings.[17] Property restrictions prevailed throughout the whole period
of patrician rule although their effect (except to ease the task of Demo-

17. Charles H. Levermore, *The Republic of New Haven, A History of Municipal
Evolution* (Baltimore, Johns Hopkins University, 1886), p. 258.

crats in generating resentments against the oligarchy) seems to have declined, probably because of economic growth and rising property values—and, according to one authority, because "party leaders had often secured the enfranchisement of landless residents by conferring upon them titles to worthless swamp tracts or scrubby acres unfit for cultivation." [18] When property was finally eliminated as a voting re-

FIGURE 2.2. *Population and electorate of New Haven, 1820–1960*

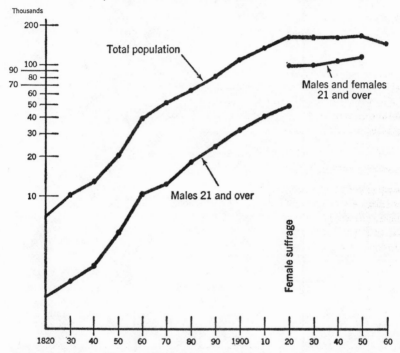

quirement in 1845, the effect on the turnout at elections was negligible not only in New Haven (Figure 2.1) but in the whole state.[19]

Meanwhile, New Haven was rapidly ceasing to be a small village. Between 1820 and 1860 the population grew at the rate of about 4.3 per cent

18. Morse, *A Neglected Period*, p. 323.

19. Total votes cast in presidential elections before and after the elimination of property requirements were (in thousands): 1836, 77.1; 1840, 113.9; 1844, 129.2; 1848, 124.7; 1852, 133.5. See W. Dean Burnham, *Presidential Ballots* (Baltimore, Johns Hopkins Press, 1955), p. 318. As percentages of the total population of the state, assuming a linear increase in population between census years, the presidential votes were: 1836, 25%; 1840, 37%; 1844, 39%; 1848, 35%; and 1852, 35%.

a year. (Figure 2.2) The adult population was getting too big to be managed by the old techniques. Once political organizations were de-

FIGURE 2.3. *Votes cast in New Haven in elections for governor, 1813–1850*

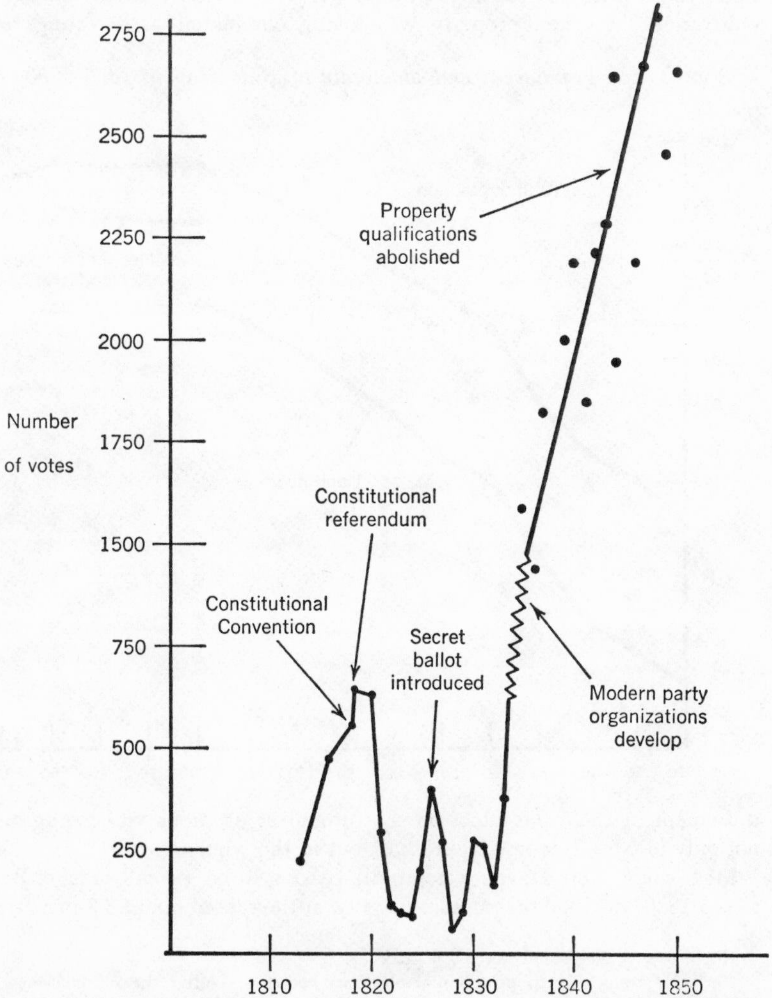

veloped for mobilizing voters at elections, the patricians were bound to be swamped by sheer numbers.

Before the extensive development of political parties more or less in

their modern form, voting turnout was sporadic. (Figure 2.3) Evidently
it depended heavily on the intensity of issues. Thus in contests for state
offices there was a gradual increase in the total turnout as the opposition
began to challenge the Standing Order. In New Haven, the number of
voters rose from 225 in 1813 to 550 for the critical election to the state
constitutional convention in 1818 (a major defeat for the Federalist
oligarchy) and to 648 in the referendum on the constitution itself. After
1820, when the Federalists were clearly a moribund group in the state,
turnout drastically declined. But from 1834 a wholly new phenomenon
appeared. Where voting had oscillated before with the intensity of cam-
paigning and organization, now the development of two nation-wide
political parties, the Democrats and the Whigs, with highly developed
grass-roots organizations at the town and ward level brought the big
swings to an end, and except for small oscillations and long-run changes,
voting participation became relatively stable. A competitive, two-party
system was now at work; and while New Haven voters continued to
support Whig candidates in state and presidential elections pretty generally until the end of the Civil War, clearly the old basis for monopolistic
control over public affairs was now permanently at an end.

The old oligarchs seem to have been crippled by their very ideology,
which justified their own tight rule and left no place for the new competitive party system with its slogans and programs directed toward the
ordinary voter. With the rising threat of Jeffersonian opposition, their
public utterances became one long complaint against novelty, innovation,
and the spread of democratic ideas, and their public actions reflected a
rigidity ill-suited to competitive politics. The rules of the game were,
of course, changing rapidly, and it is not surprising that someone like
David Daggett, who continued to wear the white-topped boots and long
white stockings of the previous age, should find the change uncongenial
and even incomprehensible.

Quite possibly it was this ideological rigidity that finally made the
displacement of the old oligarchs a peaceful one, for when the various
critical tests of strength came, it must have been obvious even to them
that they now commanded such a small following that subversion and
revolt were impossible. They had begun by fighting back, as they did
when Collector of Customs Elizur Goodrich was removed by Jefferson
and Samuel Bishop appointed instead. Beaten on this front, they turned
to darker plans. These eventuated in the ill-famed convention at Hartford in 1814, which with its secrecy, its hint of secession, and the unhappy arrival of its commissioners in Washington just when news of the
American victory at New Orleans and the peace treaty of Ghent had
been received, proved to be the graveyard of Federalism in America.
Thereafter the old Federalists whose memories carried them back to the

days of unchallenged dominion grew feeble and died off one by one, leaving younger conservatives with different memories and traditions, a generation of men who learned politics according to the new rules and who found in the Whig party an instrument better suited to the competitive game of politics. By 1840, the patricians had either withdrawn from politics in order to turn their attention to economic affairs, or they had come to terms with the new order.

And so ended a period when social status, education, wealth, and political influence were united in the same hands. There was never again anything quite like it.

3. The Entrepreneurs

In 1842, Philip Galpin was elected mayor. He was a carpet manufacturer and secretary of a newly organized company specializing in fire and marine insurance. "No New Haven corporation," a local historian wrote of Galpin's "large and successful" insurance company in 1887, "can quote from its directory more well known names." [1]

Galpin ushered in a period during which wealthy entrepreneurs dominated public life almost without interruption for more than half a century. Mayor after mayor was a successful manufacturer, and businessmen virtually crowded all other occupations from the Board of Aldermen and the newly established Board of Finance. (Figure 3.1)

The emergence of the new (but assuredly not idle) rich as occupants of public office reflected an important splitting off of wealth and political influence from social standing and education in New Haven. With the growth of manufacturing a new kind of man rose to the top in the local economic order. Typically he came from the same stock as the patricians; like almost any New Englander he could trace his forebears back to the early colonial period or even to the Mayflower. But he frequently came from humbler origins, quite probably from poverty, turned his hand to hard physical work at an early age, had little opportunity for formal education, got in on the ground floor of some new enterprise, and one day found himself a man of substance. He was, in short, the epitome of the self-made man.

As is often the case, behind these self-made men lay the work of others. In origins, in time, and in life-style, Eli Whitney was a transitional man who stood somewhere between the patricians and the new industrialists. Whitney's father was a Massachusetts farmer who, according to tradition, mortgaged the farm in order to send Eli to Yale. As every American school child knows, Eli went to Georgia to study law and teach on a plantation, and there in 1793 he invented the cotton gin. Less of a businessman than an inventor, he was largely cheated out of the fruits of his invention, and he returned to New Haven where in 1800 he began to manufacture firearms with production methods that made possible a large output of highly standardized interchangeable parts. In this way

1. Atwater, *History of New Haven*, p. 339.

FIGURE 3.1. *Percentage of members of Boards of Aldermen and Finance in various occupations, 1800–1955*

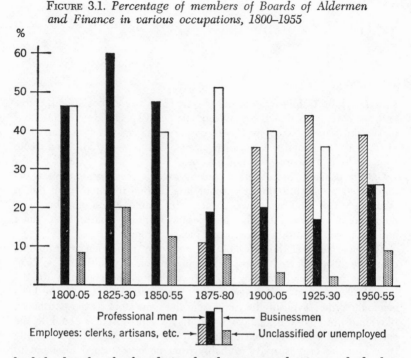

he helped to lay the foundation for the mass production methods that became commonplace during the nineteenth century.[2]

The contest for mayor was frequently a struggle between two leading businessmen. In 1856, after a long interval out of office, Philip Galpin ran again as a Whig and defeated one of the most eminent entrepreneurs in New Haven, James Brewster, who ran on the ticket of the newly formed Republican party. For Brewster, who lost the election by a mere few hundred votes, it must have been nearly the only setback in his entire adult career. Although he was the seventh generation from Elder William Brewster, one of the Mayflower pilgrims, Brewster himself began in social obscurity and hardship. His father, a farmer in Preston, Connecticut, died when James was still a boy in school, and at sixteen the youth was apprenticed in Massachusetts to learn carriage-making. When he was twenty-two he moved to New Haven, began a mechanic's shop, and in the natural course of his trade undertook to make a few of the light new carriages just then replacing the heavy old wagons. Out of these efforts grew one of the largest firms in New Haven. Later Brewster helped to

2. *Dictionary of American Biography*, 20, 157–60.

organize the New Haven and Hartford Railroad, of which he was president for a few years. When he ran for mayor against Galpin at nearly seventy years of age, he was a leading figure in the local business world.[3]

The story of Chauncey Jerome, who was elected mayor between Galpin's first and last terms, is much the same as the others—except for the ending. His father was "a blacksmith and wrought-iron maker in very poor circumstances and Jerome's early life was an extremely hard one." At nine, Jerome went to work making nails in his father's shop in Canaan, Connecticut, and at eleven, when his father died, he sought work on local farms. In due course he became a carpenter; in winter, when work was slack, he made dials for grandfather clocks. When he was thirty, he set up a small clock manufacturing shop of his own in Plymouth, moved to the South, failed there in the depression of 1837, and about twenty years later returned to Windsor, Connecticut to manufacture brass clocks, which were rapidly making obsolete the old-fashioned kind with works of wood. After a fire in Bristol destroyed his main factory and nearly wiped him out in 1845, Jerome concentrated his manufacturing in New Haven, where his use of mass production methods and interchangeable parts in the tradition of Eli Whitney revolutionized the whole clock industry. For a few years his was the biggest clock factory in America, turning out 200,000 clocks a year. But in 1855, only a year after he was elected mayor, the firm failed. Jerome was left a pauper and died in poverty and obscurity.[4]

Jerome's clock company was taken over by James E. English, who, according to a local historian writing in 1887, "more than any other person who has been a citizen of New Haven—unless we except Roger Sherman—is commonly regarded as pre-eminently a self-made man." [5] English was probably New Haven's leading entrepreneur. He had been born into a relatively obscure New Haven family and at twelve began working on a farm. After a few years that included some schooling, he was apprenticed to a contractor to learn the carpenter's trade. He became a journeyman carpenter, then a contractor, ventured into the lumber business, began buying and building vessels, and shipped many of Jerome's clocks to distant markets. When Jerome's clock company failed, owing him large sums, English took it over and under the name of the New Haven Clock Company turned it into a financial success.

---

3. Atwater, *History of New Haven*, pp. 558–59 and Carleton Beals, *Our Yankee Heritage, The Making of Greater New Haven*, 2nd ed. (New Haven, Bradley and Scoville, 1957), pp. 130–39, 147–50, 166, 207, 222.

4. *Dictionary of American Biography*, 3, 27–28, and Beals, *Our Yankee Heritage*, pp. 129 ff.

5. Atwater, *History of New Haven*, p. 577.

He was also one of the founders of the First National Bank and the Connecticut Savings Bank. English, who regarded himself as a Jeffersonian Democrat, was successively honored by his fellow citizens as a selectman, member of the City Council, representative and senator in the state legislature, U.S. representative, governor, and U.S. senator.[6] His partner during one of his early enterprises was Harmanus M. Welch, also a Democrat, who followed Galpin as mayor in 1860; Welch later organized the New Haven Rolling Mill and was for a time president of the First National Bank.

English and Welch serve to remind us that the Democrats were quite as anxious as the Republicans to nominate industrialists. It would be highly misleading to read back into that period recent differences in the leadership of the two national parties, for in social origins, occupations, and achievements (even in outlook) the nominees of both parties were indistinguishable. (Table 3.1) Neither party could be regarded as the

TABLE 3.1. *Occupations of candidates for mayor, 1856–1899*

Occupation	Democratic	Republican
Business		
Manufacturing	8	8
Insurance	1	1
Banking	—	3
Wholesale	1	—
Total	10	12
Law	2	—
Unidentified	4	4
Total	16	16

party of the patricians, and though the Democrats may have had a little more success with the immigrant workers, particularly the Irish, it was assuredly not a working-class party with a working-class program or ideology.

If any evidence were needed as to the Democrats' willingness to endorse industrialists, examine the case of J. B. Sargent. The son of a storekeeper and manufacturer in Leicester, Massachusetts, Sargent had operated a store in Georgia and then a commission firm in New York that soon became one of the country's leading hardware outlets. Among other things, he distributed the products of a hardware firm in New Britain owned by a one-time carpenter named Peck who manufactured hardware and brass goods in New Britain and New Haven. In due course, Sargent secured a tenth of the Peck firm's stock and a few years later

6. Ibid., and Beals, *Our Yankee Heritage*, p. 185.

acquired the entire business. In the middle of the Civil War, Sargent moved his firm to New Haven, bought the Pavilion Hotel from James Brewster, brought down several hundred of his New Britain workers and their families, housed them in the hotel, managed a $9,000 loan from the State Education Fund, contracted for the entire year's output of the Hartford and New Haven brickyards, and rushed eight buildings to completion in record time. The firm made everything, from locks to casket hardware, imported additional workers from Italy, and a century later was still the seventh largest employer in New Haven.[7] J.B. was a Democrat, and as such enjoyed four years in office before being defeated by a Republican. It was appropriately ironic that J.B., who had followed the Peck family into the hardware business and then into New Haven itself, became mayor of New Haven in 1891 hard on the heels of H. F. Peck, a Republican; after losing his job in New Britain when Sargent took over his father's firm, H. F. Peck had come to New Haven, where he ultimately became president of his father's New Haven firm and enjoyed a career in public life as a member of the City Council, Board of Aldermen, Board of Finance, Board of Education, and as mayor. Although they were in opposite parties, the two men never ran for office against each other.

Why this enthusiasm in both parties for the new men of industry? Perhaps the best answer is another question: Who else was a more likely candidate than one of the successful entrepreneurs?

The patricians had been almost totally displaced from the center of public attention; in fact most of the voters probably could not even distinguish between the patricians and the new rich. Moreover the whole emergent style of life in politics and business was against them. In the course of the century politics had taken on some of the flavor of the lower middle classes, with their enthusiasms, emotionalism, and evangelistic religions; frequently the decorum of the preceding period now gave way to buffoonery, dignity was undone by the horselaugh, and the deadly seriousness of the Puritan was replaced by ballyhoo.

Even the new style of economic life seems to have been unsuited to the patricians, none of whom seems to have turned into an important entrepreneur. Tradition drew the patricians toward the professions, commerce, and banking. The three Trowbridge brothers, who could claim descent not merely from one but from two original settlers of the Connecticut Colony, entered their father's countinghouse, which engaged in a prosperous trade with the West Indies, bringing in rum and sugar and exporting farm products and manufactured goods. All three went into banking: T.R. was a director of the Mechanics Bank, Henry became a

7. Beals, *Our Yankee Heritage*, pp. 206–09.

director and vice-president of the New Haven Bank, and E.H. helped organize the Elm City (later the Second National) Bank.[8] The respectability the patricians enjoyed made them useful on boards of directors, but they were not entrepreneurs.

Quite possibly the patricians had a distaste for manufacturing; many of them seemed to think that industry would attract ignorant artisans and thus disrupt the settled order of society. Quite possibly also the entrepreneur had to be a touch too ruthless and aggressive. Perhaps to understand industry and manufacturing, to see and seize the new opportunities, to realize the deficiencies of old methods, and to put together a new business, took a man moving up from hard, concrete experience with poverty, artisans, and machines. There may even have been a kind of failure of imagination, an ingrained habitual incapacity to forget the past and look to the revolutionary future of factories and mass production methods that were already transforming the present. Whatever the reasons, manufacturing and entrepreneurship were evidently not careers for the genteel.

Who else, then, should occupy public office if not the new industrialists? Not the urban workers, who though they more and more outnumbered all the rest were immigrants lacking in status, political know-how, and economic resources. And what is perhaps the most important of all, in a society where each generation of workers was enormously more prosperous than its parents in a seemingly endless expansion of gains, there was no distinctive working-class outlook that could be formed into an ideology and program different from that already expressed in middle-class ideals. As for the middle classes, the matter was probably quite simple: why nominate and elect a grocer as mayor if you can have a manufacturer or bank president?

What is perhaps most interesting of all in retrospect is the fact that the chief elective public offices must still have enjoyed very high prestige. The patricians had perhaps helped to leave that much of a legacy; their prestige had brushed off on politics; the new rich evidently accepted that valuation and by their readiness to stand for the highest public offices must have helped to continue the tradition.

The entrepreneurs had brought about something of a division between two important political resources, wealth and social standing. To be sure, outside the most rarefied circles, where long memories kept old differences alive, social standing followed wealth by a generation or so. Yet entrepreneurs had erected a structure of business in which achievement was to a substantial extent independent of family origins. Henceforth those who had wealth comprised a set of people who overlapped only in part the set with highest social standing. Modern industry—which has often

8. Atwater, *History of New Haven*, p. 577.

been represented as a development that produced a convergence of political resources in the same hands—helped, at least in New Haven, to fragment and disperse political resources to different groups in the community. The process was not, however, a matter of equalizing the distribution of political resources; rather it created what might be called dispersed inequalities.

The monopoly that leading entrepreneurs enjoyed over the chief elective offices of New Haven depended to a considerable extent on a third resource that need not always go with wealth or social standing, namely, popularity. The popularity of the businessman as an elective official in turn required a wide belief on the part of the rank-and-file voter in the peculiar virtues and meritorious attainments of the businessman, a certain measure of respect, and perhaps even some sympathetic identification.

Like the patricians before them, the entrepreneurs suffered from one acute political vulnerability—they necessarily lacked numbers. This weakness was now to be exploited by another band of new men, the ex-plebes, who made up in popularity with their fellow citizens what they frequently lacked in wealth and social standing. As the ex-plebes took over the center of the political stage, the entrepreneurs followed the patricians into the wings.

4. The Ex-plebes

Galpin, the Pecks, Brewster, Jerome, English, Welch, Sargent, and the other entrepreneurs transformed the political, social, and economic life of New Haven: they created a proletariat, and the proletariat—the "ex-plebes"—ultimately displaced them in public office and leadership of the political parties.

COMING OF THE IMMIGRANTS

Throughout the period of patrician rule, the artisan class had been of the same ethnic stock as the patricians themselves. In the 1820s, an Irishman was still a rarity in Connecticut. The number of immigrants entering the port of New Haven between 1820 and 1845 varied each year from six to less than a hundred.[1] But the new industries required workers; the era of the industrial entrepreneur was also the era of immigration. The Irish came first, starting at mid-century, with a small sprinkling of Germans, followed by the Italians and East Europeans in the 1880s. By 1870, 28 per cent of the people in New Haven were foreign-born, a proportion that remained almost exactly the same for the next three decades. By 1900, however, in four of the city's fifteen wards, two persons out of every three were immigrants. By 1910, one-third of New Haven's population was foreign-born and another third had at least one immigrant parent. In every ward in the city except the First Ward, first- and second-generation Americans made up more than half the population; and even in the First, where Yale and a few elegant residential areas still held the middle and upper classes, 46 per cent of the population were either immigrants or second generation. In four wards, nearly nine out of every ten residents were immigrants or had at least one foreign-born parent.

"ETHNICS" AND POLITICS

In New Haven as in many other cities, the "ethnic"—the immigrant, the Catholic, the Jew, the Negro—found that his ethnic identification colored his life, his relations with others, his attitudes toward himself and

1. Morse, *A Neglected Period*, pp. 23, 286.

the world.[2] Ideas of equality and unlimited opportunity, stressed in the American ideology taught in schools and used on ceremonial occasions, often gave rise to expectations among immigrants and Negroes that were frustrated by the actual conditions in which they found themselves. Frequently, too, the ethnic felt a sharp conflict between normal needs for self-respect and the actual treatment he received. Many of his problems arose, of course, not merely because he was of foreign stock but because of all the factors associated with his immigrant origins: his education, speech, dress, demeanor, skills, income, neighborhood, ignorance of American institutions and folkways, and lack of self-confidence. In a nation where some citizens had great power, high prestige, and enormous income, the ethnic was often at the bottom of the pile. And when he looked about him, often the only citizens as badly off in power, prestige, and income were other ethnics; like as not, even some ethnic groups were already higher up the socioeconomic ladder than his own.

Any political leader who could help members of an ethnic group to overcome the handicaps and humiliations associated with their identity, who could increase the power, prestige, and income of an ethnic or religious out-group, automatically had an effective strategy for earning support and loyalty. Politicians themselves, in fact, were often ethnics who knew from personal experience the problems of an out-group. Probably no other political strategy held quite so much promise of capturing the loyalties of citizens for party coalitions. Hence the politics of New Haven became a kind of ethnic politics; it was a politics of assimilation rather than a politics of reform, a politics that simultaneously emphasized the divisive rather than the unifying characteristics of voters and yet played upon the yearnings for assimilation and acceptance.

But neither the strategies of politicians nor the yearnings of the ethnics entailed a root-and-branch attack on socioeconomic inequalities. On the contrary, the object was simply to enlarge the opportunities for ethnics to rise without undue discrimination in a system that contained built-in inequalities in the distribution of resources. Political leaders and their ethnic followings combined to use the political system in order to eliminate the handicaps associated with ethnic identity rather than to reduce disadvantages stemming from the distribution of resources by the existing socioeconomic order itself. The socioeconomic order was not considered illegitimate; discrimination *was*. Local politics—and for that matter state

2. The best examination of this question is in Irvin Child's study of second-generation Italians in New Haven, *Italian or American?* (New Haven, Yale University Press, 1943). For an historical treatment of another ethnic group in New Haven, see Robert Warner, *New Haven Negroes—A Social History* (New Haven, Yale University Press, 1940).

and national politics—was like a rope dangling down the formidable slope of the socioeconomic system. If the ethnic pulled himself up a bit with the help of the rope, he could often gain a toe hold in the system; the higher he climbed, the higher he could reach for another pull upward. He was not greatly interested in leveling the mountain itself.

Yet in spite of this fact, a paradoxical and highly important long-run consequence was to accelerate the transformation of a system of cumulative inequality of political resources into a system of dispersed inequalities.

Since political leaders hoped to expand their own influence with the votes of ethnic groups, they helped the immigrant overcome his initial political powerlessness by engaging him in politics. Whatever else the ethnics lacked, they had numbers. Hence politicians took the initiative; they made it easy for immigrants to become citizens, encouraged ethnics to register, put them on the party rolls, and aided them in meeting the innumerable specific problems resulting from their poverty, strangeness, and lowly position. To obtain and hold the votes, the political leaders rewarded them with city jobs. They also appealed to their desire for ethnic prestige and self-respect by running members of the ethnic group as candidates for elective offices.

Yet ethnic politics, like the politics of the patrician oligarchy and the entrepreneurs, is clearly a transitional phenomenon. The very success of politicians who use the ethnic approach leads to the obsolescence of their strategy. As assimilation progresses, new unities and cleavages supersede the old, and the politician whose only skill is ethnic politics becomes as obsolete as the patrician who responded to nineteenth-century democratic impulses with eighteenth-century techniques of oligarchy. In order to retain their positions, politicians are forced to search for new issues, new strategies, new coalitions.

It will help us to place ethnic politics in perspective if we hypothesize that an ethnic group passes through three stages on the way to political assimilation.

First stage: Members of an ethnic group in this stage are almost exclusively proletarian. They work with their hands, for wages, in shops and factories. In some socioeconomic characteristics, they are highly homogeneous. They are low in status, income, and influence. For leadership, they depend on influential politicians who have come from previously assimilated ethnic groups. Members of the new group serve sometimes as intermediaries between the group and the older leaders, acquiring in the process moderate influence and experience as subleaders. Some of these ethnic subleaders eventually receive nominations for minor offices, such as alderman, where the constituency is drawn predominantly from the subleader's ethnic group. In this stage, the group ordinarily has a high degree of political homogeneity; ethnic similarity is associated with similarity in political attitude, and there is a pronounced tendency toward voting alike. Ethnic ties are partly responsible, but in addition all aspects of life tend to converge and thus to create similar interests and political attitudes. Political homogeneity, then, is a function of socioeconomic homogeneity. Policies that will help an individual to cope with the problems created by his status as a first- or second-generation immigrant are not much different from policies that appeal to him as a wage-earner, a resident of a tenement in a ghetto, a member of a family with a low and uncertain income, a victim of unemployment, a person of little social prestige, or an object of discrimination by middle-class citizens of Anglo-Saxon stock.

Second stage: Socioeconomically, the group has become more heterogeneous. It is no longer predominantly proletarian. An increasing and by now significant proportion of the group have white-collar jobs and other social characteristics of the middling strata. Higher status, income, and self-confidence allow some to gain considerable political influence. They begin to challenge and overthrow the incumbent leaders on whom they hitherto have been dependent; amid charges of betrayal and ingratitude they now move into positions of leadership. Depending on the size of his ethnic group and local attitudes, an ethnic leader may even receive a major party nomination for a leading city-wide office, such as the mayoralty, that cannot be won simply by the votes of his own ethnic group. Although the political homogeneity of the group declines in this stage because of the increasing differentiation of the middling segments from the working-class strata, even the middling segments retain a high sensitivity to their ethnic origins. Consequently, an ethnic candidate who can avoid divisive socioeconomic issues is still able to activate strong sentiments of ethnic solidarity in all strata of his ethnic group; he can command a significantly higher proportion of the votes of his group than can a candidate without the ethnic tie.

Third stage: Socioeconomically, the group is now highly heterogeneous. Large segments are assimilated into the middling and upper strata; they have middle-class jobs, accept middle-class ideas, adopt a middle-class style of life, live in middle-class neighborhoods, and look to others in the middling strata for friends, associates, marriage partners. To these people, ethnic politics is often embarrassing or meaningless. Political attitudes and loyalties have become a function of socioeconomic characteristics. Members of the group display little political homogeneity. Although sentimental and traditional attachments to a particular party may persist, they are easily ruptured. The political effectiveness of a purely ethnic appeal is now negligible among the middling and upper strata. A middle-class or upper-class candidate who happens to be drawn from an ethnic group may use this tie to awaken sentiments of pride; he may win votes, but to do so he must also emphasize socioeconomic issues, even though stressing such issues may split his ethnic group wide open.

In New Haven different ethnic groups have been passing through these stages at different times in the course of the last century. One stage merges so imperceptibly into the next that it would be foolish to attribute much significance to precise dates; but something like the following is perhaps useful as an impressionistic summary of assorted evidence on occupations, residence, and voting patterns.

	First Stage	Second Stage	Third Stage
Germans	1840-1880	1880-1920	1920-
Irish	1840-1890	1890-1930	1930-
"Russians"	1880-1920	1920-1940	1940-
Italians	1880-1930	1930-1950	1950-
Negroes[3]	1784-1950	1950-	

RISE OF THE EX-PLEBES

Long before the last industrialist was elected mayor, the immigrants had secured representation on the Board of Aldermen. As late as 1855 the mayor, the aldermen, the treasurer, the clerk, the collector of taxes, and the members of the Committee on Finance (later called Board of Finance) were all business or professional men of New England stock. But in 1853 the city had been divided into four wards; in 1857 the four wards became six; later they grew to ten, twelve, and by 1900 they numbered fifteen. Once aldermen began to be elected from wards, the immigrants were bound to elect some of their own people.

The first man with a distinctly Irish name appeared on the Board in 1857 as the alderman from the Third Ward; since that time (despite changes in ward boundaries) the Third invariably has elected at least one Irishman[4] as alderman or councilman. In 1900, when 69 per cent of the people in the Third were foreign-born, its two aldermen were a plumber named Corcoran and a painter named McGill. Six of the then twelve wards in the city were evidently electing Irishmen as early as about 1880. The Germans, a smaller group who seem to have moved more

3. In 1791, there were 207 Negroes in New Haven, of whom 78 were slaves; Negroes then comprised 4.5% of the population. In 1830, there were 941 free Negroes and 43 slaves. The proportion of slaves to free Negroes continued to decline until 1848, when slavery was abolished in Connecticut. See Warner, *New Haven Negroes,* p. 300.

4. To avoid cumbersome phrases, I refer throughout this book to Americans of Irish stock as Irishmen, to Americans of Italian stock as Italians, to Americans of English or Scotch-Irish stock long in New England as Yankees, etc. I hope the sensibilities of my readers will not be offended by usages that in other contexts are sometimes meant or felt to be invidious. Here the terms are intended only as convenient, succinct, descriptive, neutral, and widely understood labels.

rapidly out of the working class than the Irish, began appearing on the
Board of Aldermen in 1886; at least four men from well-known German-
Jewish business families served on the Board at various times between
1866 and 1884.

By 1900, the Boards of Aldermen and Finance had been transformed
not only in ethnic but also in occupational composition. The proportion
of businessmen had declined drastically (Figure 4.1) as men with clerical

FIGURE 4.1. *Businessmen on the Boards of Aldermen and Finance
as percentage of total membership during five-year periods,
1825–1955*

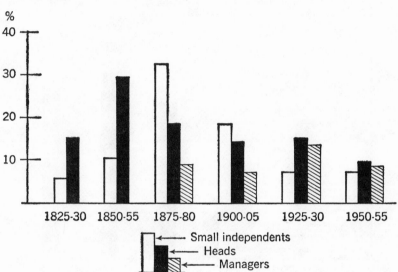

and laboring jobs assumed their places. (Figure 4.2) Of the thirty aldermen in 1900 (two from each ward), the majority were neither patricians
nor leading businessmen. In addition to the plumber and the painter,
there were three saloon keepers, three foremen, three factory employees,
two bill collectors, two druggists, two salesmen, a grocer, a shipping
clerk, a florist, and a linotype operator. One of the two aldermen from
the Fifth Ward was unemployed (the other was one of the three saloon
keepers). The rest included three lawyers, a doctor, an assistant superintendent at Winchester's, and three people who ran their own small
businesses. The president of the Board was the alderman from the
Twelfth Ward, a druggist named Cornelius H. Conway.

In the city elections of 1897, the Democrats had lost when they split
their votes between a Gold Democrat and a Silver Democrat. Two years

later they united around Cornelius R. Driscoll, a lawyer living on Wooster Street in the heart of the old Fifth Ward (the present Tenth Ward), which had been densely populated by the Irish and was then receiving vast numbers of Italian immigrants. Driscoll, an Irishman from County Cork and a Roman Catholic, had helped to found the Knights of Columbus in 1882. He had been sent from the Fifth Ward to the City Council and to the Board of Aldermen. In 1899, with the Democrats behind him, he defeated the Republican incumbent (who was the president and

FIGURE 4.2. *Clerical and working-class occupations on the Boards of Aldermen and Finance as percentage of total membership during five-year periods, 1800–1955*

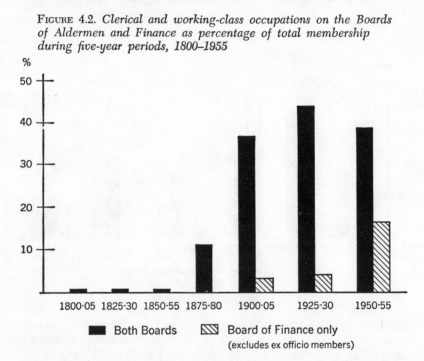

treasurer of a foundry) and thereby became the first immigrant to be elected mayor of New Haven. Since Driscoll's time every victorious Democratic candidate for mayor has been an Irish Catholic.

If the Republicans had not had the foresight to see that in order to survive they would have to break the hold of the Democrats on the recent Americans, doubtless New Haven would soon have become a predominantly one-party community like so many other American cities. But about the time of Driscoll's election, two brothers of German extraction and Jewish faith, Isaac and Louis Ullman, began moving into undisputed control over the New Haven Republican party. In many ways, they were replicas of the Yankee businessmen of the preceding period. Their father, an immigrant coachman, died when they were young; their mother, also an immigrant from Germany, took in washing; the boys themselves began peddling newspapers in their early teens. Later they both went to work for the Strouse-Adler Corset Company, then the largest corset manufacturing concern in the United States and with its 3,000 employees one of the biggest firms in New Haven. Its president, Max Adler, was a leading figure in the business and civic life of New Haven. Isaac Ullman soon became a foreman; Louis was his assistant. Later Isaac married Max Adler's daughter and, with the support of his father-in-law, quickly became president of the firm. Louis married the young widow of Edwin Strouse, a son of the principal owner, and his father-in-law, a pioneer New Haven cigar manufacturer named Lewis Osterweis, bought him a one-third interest in the corset company; Louis, too, became a leading official in the company.

What distinguished the Ullmans from the earlier entrepreneurs, however, was not simply their German-Jewish background but their passion for politics. Indeed, unlike the Yankee businessmen who preceded them in politics, they seem to have preferred political entrepreneurship to business; in fact, when the fortunes of the corset company declined badly after the First World War, critics of their business conduct said that the Ullman brothers had been more interested in winning votes for the Republican party than winning customers for their corsets. However that may be, the Ullmans gained control of the Republican party in the first decade of this century and pretty much ran it for a generation.

They were shrewd enough to know that Republicans could not win against Irish-Catholic Democrats by running wealthy Yankee manufacturers for office and appealing only to Yankee voters. They therefore went into the Italian wards, which had been neglected by the Irish ward leaders in the Democratic party, and helped to pull some of the Italians into the Republican ward organizations. In 1909, the Republicans won the mayoralty election with Frank J. Rice, who was almost the last Yankee to be elected mayor of New Haven. Rice was, however, no great entrepreneur; he had been a trolley conductor, a manager of properties for a real estate firm, and president of the Young Men's Republican Club.[5] On his death in office after his fourth election in 1915, he was succeeded by Samuel Campner, president of the Board of Aldermen. Campner, a Jew, had been born in Russia and brought to New Haven as an infant; he went to Yale College and the Yale Law School and became a prosperous

5. N. G. Osborn, ed., *Men of Mark in Connecticut,* 5 (Hartford, William R. Goodspeed, 1910), 377.

lawyer and distinguished member of the New Haven Jewish community.[6]

The election of 1917 saw Samuel Campner, a Russian Jew, running against David Fitzgerald, an Irish Catholic. Though his parents were Irish immigrants, Fitzgerald himself had been born in New Haven; like Campner he had gone to Yale College and to the Yale Law School, and had become a prosperous lawyer.[7] Both were members of the Racebrook Country Club, a suburban club deliberately organized by a group of Protestants, Catholics, and Jews as an alternative to the New Haven Country Club, which then closed its doors to both Jews and Catholics. In the election Campner carried only five wards out of fifteen, and Fitzgerald won hands down.

From that time on, both parties usually nominated candidates who did not suffer from the handicap of being Yankee. Since Fitzgerald's time, the Democratic party leader has invariably been a Roman Catholic; by the mid-thirties, after the Ullmans had passed from the scene, the acknowledged Republican leader was also an Irish Catholic. In 1939, however, the Republican nominee for mayor was an undertaker of Italian parentage; although this time he lost, he finally won in his second try in 1945. His election marked the growing influence of the Italians, who by that time outnumbered the Irish. In 1959, the Republican town chairman was also of Italian origin; he ran the party in an uneasy coalition with the old Irish-Catholic boss, whose power had waned. The Democratic party was dominated by a triumvirate consisting of the mayor, a Roman Catholic of mixed Irish, English, and Scottish antecedents; the national committeeman, an Irish insurance broker prominent in Catholic lay activities; and the town chairman, a man of Italian ancestry.

Meanwhile equally significant changes were occurring in the occupations of political leaders. Not a single manufacturer or executive of a large corporation has been elected mayor in the twentieth century. Of the eleven mayors in this period, five have been lawyers (though none of these were with the leading law firms of New Haven); the rest include a real estate operator, a garage owner, an official of a printing firm, a business agent for a union, an undertaker, and a director of publicity for Yale.

Nothing less is revealed than a massive invasion of the political system by the ethnics. City jobs, minor offices, major elective and appointive offices—all fell before the irresistible tide of the plebes and ex-plebes of immigrant stock. With respect to city jobs, a survey of 1,600 New Haven families made in 1933 by the Yale Institute of Human Relations furnishes

6. M. H. Mitchell, ed., *History of New Haven County* (Chicago and Boston, Pioneer Historical Publishing Co., 1930), 2, 378–81.

7. Osborn, *Men of Mark*, 5, 511, and Charles W. Burpee, *Burpee's The Story of Connecticut* (New York, American Historical Co. 1939), 4, 848–49.

an interesting snapshot of the state of affairs at that time. (Figure 4.3)
By 1933, the Irish had become by far the most numerous in holding city
jobs; politics was evidently one of the main routes the Irish took to climb
out of the wage-earning class. Although the Irish comprised only 13 per
cent of the families in the sample, they held almost half the jobs in city
government. Not all city positions were, to be sure, white-collar jobs;
but as school teachers, clerks, aldermen, commissioners, and even mayors,
the Irish had gained a place for themselves in the middling strata of New

FIGURE 4.3. *Occupations of family heads in New Haven, 1933*

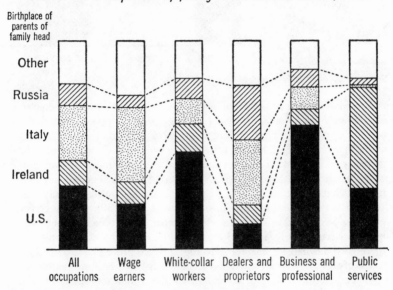

Source: John W. McConnell, The Evolution of Social Classes (Washington, D.C.,
American Council on Public Affairs, 1942) Table I, p. 214.

Haven. By this time they were evidently also receiving a fair share of
white-collar jobs in private industry. They had not yet won their way into
business and the professions, where their connections were still weak,
though some of the business and professional people of American-born
parents, who made up 60 per cent of the total, were no doubt of Irish
extraction. With a foothold in the middle classes gained through politics
and city jobs, in the next two decades the Irish moved rapidly into
business and professional life. Due largely to the Irish, three out of four
family heads in public service in New Haven in 1933 were Catholic,
though Catholics comprised only 56 per cent of the sample.

FIGURE 4.4. *Religious affiliations of family heads in New Haven,
1933*

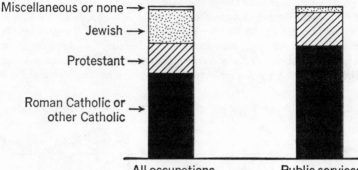

Source: McConnell, Evolution of Social Classes.

Irish domination of government jobs made it more difficult of course for
later immigrants, particularly Italians and East Europeans, to climb the
socioeconomic ladder by pulling themselves up with the help of white-
collar patronage. In addition to this, however, distinctive cultural backgrounds probably promoted a stronger tendency among Jews and Italians
to go into small business. The Irish had brought with them no tradition of
business enterprise or the learned professions. By contrast, immigrants of
Russian origin were mainly Jews whose exodus followed a series of
pogroms beginning in 1881;[8] they were more accustomed to the world of
business, particularly as small shop-owners, and they also brought with
them a traditional respect for learning and the professions. The Italians,
too, were evidently more inclined than the Irish to become peddlers and
shopkeepers. In fact, the Russians and the Italians together made up
almost two-thirds of the shopkeepers in the 1933 family survey. Where the
Irish used politics to surmount obstacles to their advance in the socioeconomic world, Italians and Jews more frequently used gains in the
socioeconomic world to attain elective positions in politics.

Myers has traced the movement of Italians to jobs in the city government from 1890 to 1940.[9] They first began receiving jobs as city employees
between 1900 and 1910, probably as a result of the efforts of the Ullman

8. Osterweis, *Three Centuries of New Haven*, pp. 372 ff.
9. Jerome K. Myers, "Assimilation in the Political Community," *Sociology and
Social Research, 35* (1951), 175–82. See also his "Assimilation to the Ecological
and Social Systems of a Community," *American Sociological Review, 15* (1950),
367–72.

brothers; after 1910 their share of patronage grew rapidly. However, by 1940, a year after William Celentano was defeated in the first bid of an Italian for mayor, they held only about half their "quota" [10] of the lowest jobs in city government—janitors and laborers—and only a third of their "quota" of the top appointive positions. (Table 4.1)

TABLE 4.1. *Italians in city jobs, 1890–1940*

Group	Percentage of Italian "quota" fulfilled in:					
	1890	1900	1910	1920	1930	1940
Appointive boards and commissions	0	0	0	24	13	34
Department heads, city executives	0	0	0	0	0	33
Teachers, professional workers	0	0	3	9	14	22
Clerical workers, firemen, policemen	0	0	2	6	16	21
Janitors, custodians, laborers	0	0	0	15	27	56

Source: Myers, "Assimilation in the Political Community," Tables 2 and 3. Myers made his estimates from names in city directories and manuals. For an explanation of "quota," see footnote 10.

Even though the Italians were to some extent blocked by the Irish and the Yankees from city jobs, the professionals nonetheless found it advantageous to appeal to Italian voters by including Italian candidates for elective office on the party ticket; ever since 1890 Italians have been nominated in considerable numbers. By 1940 leaders of Italian stock were moving into positions of key influence in the Republican party. In the minor elective offices, as Myers shows, the Italians were receiving their fair share by 1940, though they still ran a little behind in the more important elective plums. (Figure 4.5)

In 1945, an Italian Republican candidate for mayor was elected, and the Italians were at last at the top in local politics. After winning the mayoralty election in 1953, the Democrats made vigorous efforts to overcome the historical alienation of Italians from the Irish-dominated Democratic party; among other things the new mayor appointed a man of Italian stock to the politically important post of director of public works. By 1959, the Italians were winning their full share of both major and

10. By "quota," I mean that if the proportion of Italians in city jobs were the same as the proportion of Italians in the population, the "quota" would be fulfilled 100%. Half the quota means that Italians had half as many city jobs as they would if jobs were distributed according to the size of the Italian group in the city population.

FIGURE 4.5. *Italians in elective offices, 1890–1959*

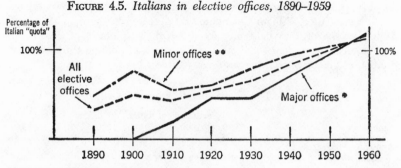

*Mayor, city clerk, treasurer, collector of taxes, sheriff, town clerk, registrar of vital statistics, registrar of voters, aldermen.

**Selectmen, constables, grand jurors, justices of the peace.

Source: For 1890-1940 figures, see Myers, "Assimilation in the Political Community," Table 1 and p. 178. For source of 1959 figures, see Table 4.2.

minor elective offices. In fact, the three largest ethnic groups—Irish Catholics, Italian Catholics, and Jews—were, if anything, all over-represented in elective posts.[11] (Table 4.2)

TABLE 4.2. *Ethnics in elective offices, 1959*

Ethnic group	Registered voters %	Major offices held %	Minor offices held %
Italian	31	34	33
Irish	11	29	11
Jewish	15	19	24
Other	43	17	31
Total	100	99	99
N	525	41	96

Source: Figures for registered voters are from our survey in 1959. Respondent was identified as Italian or Irish only if a parent or grandparent was born there, with father's birthplace determining in case of conflict. "Jewish" represents stated religious preference. Breakdown of major and minor offices follows Myers, "Assimilation in the Political Community." Ethnic affiliation of office holders determined by name or direct information.

ETHNIC POLITICS, 1900–1950

From about 1900 on, political leaders in both parties played the game of ethnic politics. The Democrats were more successful at it, probably

11. Because fourth-generation Americans of Irish or Italian stock would not meet the criteria of Table 4.2, there is undoubtedly some underestimate of those who might identify themselves as Irish or Italian. The Irish in particular are probably significantly underestimated.

because they started first. The Democratic party was overwhelmingly the party of the immigrants by 1900 and remained so until about 1940, when the Republicans began to make new inroads on the loyalties of the ethnics.

In the presidential election of 1904, the proportion of foreign-born residents in a ward was closely related to the percentage of the total two-party vote from that ward that went to the Democratic candidate. (Figure 4.6) In the next two elections, this relationship was weaker, probably because some Italians defected to the Republican party with the encouragement of the Ullmans. The correlation then remained moderately close and steady until 1928, when support from the immigrant wards for Democratic presidential candidates rose to a high level that was sustained until 1940. In that year a decline in the correlation commenced that was only temporarily interrupted by the 1948 election.[12] The story has been

FIGURE 4.6. *Relation between percentage of foreign-born residents in New Haven wards and percentage of two-party vote cast for Democratic candidates for president, 1904–1956*

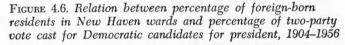

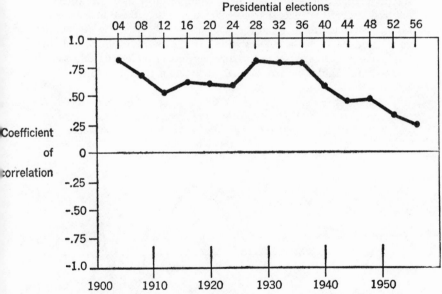

12. An explanation of the statistical basis of Fig. 4.6 and others in this chapter will be found in Appendix B. The significance of the figures rests partly on the assumption that the proportion of foreign-born in a ward is highly correlated with the proportion of persons of recent immigrant background whether or not they were born abroad. A similar assumption is made in identifying Italian, Russian, or Irish wards.

much the same in elections for mayor (Figure 4.7), except that the break-down in the relationship since 1939 is more obvious.

After the split in the mayoralty election of 1897 between Gold Democrats and Silver Democrats, some of the conservative Democrats —business and professional men horrified by William Jennings Bryan, —evidently began to find the Republican party more to their liking. Thus Yankees deserted the Democrats as Irishmen like Cornelius Driscoll moved to the top. By the end of the first decade, a pattern was well-established that held for half a century: in local elections the Irish were mostly in one party, the Yankees in the other. Figure 4.8 shows how the ward with the fewest foreign-born—and presumably the largest number of Yankees—was consistently Republican in every mayoralty election in this century until 1953. By contrast, the ward with the greatest percentage of Irish foreign-born, and probably the heaviest concentration of Irish stock, voted Democratic by a large margin in every election except two throughout the entire six decades.

Obviously the middle-class Yankees were too greatly outnumbered by the proletarian immigrants and their children to retain much voice in a political system that was sharply split on precisely these lines. It was a brilliant strategy, then, when the Ullmans, whose own origins doubtless gave them a much better understanding of the desires of immigrants than the Yankees possessed, set out to lure the Italian proletariat into a coali-tion with the Yankee middle classes. They had a good deal to work with,

FIGURE 4.7. *Relation between percentage of foreign-born residents in New Haven wards and percentage of two-party vote cast for Democratic candidates for mayor, 1903–1959*

including the prestige and wealth of the Yankees, resentments between the Irish and the Italians, and patronage. Although the Ullmans did not succeed in welding the Italians into a solid bloc of Republican votes, their strategy did preserve effective two-party competition in New Haven by providing the Republican party with a base of support among an important immigrant group.

FIGURE 4.8. *Republican vote, as percentage of two-party vote, in ward with highest proportion of Irish residents and ward with lowest proportion of foreign-born residents—mayoralty elections, 1901–1959*

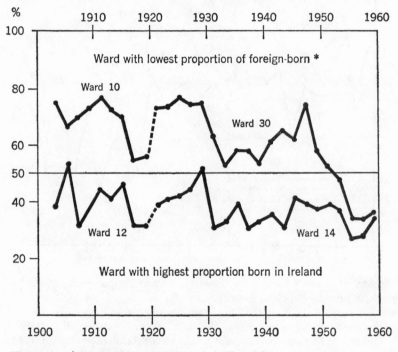

*The Nineteenth Ward, which was 72% Negro in 1950, and the First Ward, heavily populated by Yale students, were excluded.

In the three wards with the greatest number of Italians, the greater the proportion of Italians the smaller the Democratic vote has been in mayoralty elections over the past sixty years. (Figure 4.9) In the Tenth Ward, in 1910, half the population was foreign-born; four out of five of these were Italian; in fact, until the census of 1940, when it was passed by two other wards, the Tenth had the largest proportion of Italian-born

residents. Throughout the century, the Tenth has given more support to
Republican candidates for mayor than the Eleventh, which is the next
most densely Italian-populated. The Eleventh, in turn, has regularly voted
more heavily Republican than the ward with the next highest density of

FIGURE 4.9. *Democratic vote, as percentage of two-party vote,
in three wards with highest proportion of residents born in
Italy—mayoralty elections, 1903–1959*

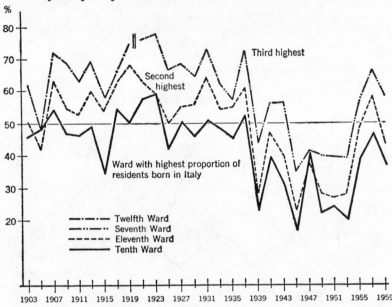

Italian residents.[13] Except for the election of 1948, the same pattern has
held in presidential elections. (Figure 4.10)

Yet despite the fact that the Republicans made inroads in the old
Democratic monopoly among the ethnics, even among the Italians
support for Democratic candidates was high. The densely Italian Tenth
Ward, which gave greater support to the Republicans than any other
immigrant ward, voted more strongly Democratic than the rest of the
city in about two out of three elections for president or mayor up to 1939.
(Figure 4.11) In the same period the next two most densely Italian
wards cast majorities for Democratic mayoralty candidates in every
election except one and generally exceeded the Democratic vote of the
city as a whole by a substantial margin; in every presidential election

13. To avoid confusion I have used present ward numbers.

from 1904 through 1936 these two wards voted more heavily Democratic than the city as a whole by margins never less than 8 per cent and sometimes over 20 per cent.

The fact is that throughout most of this period the Italians of New Haven were in their first stage of political, social, and economic assimilation. They were predominantly workers, near the lower end of the socioeconomic scale. Like other immigrants, they felt the pull of the Democratic party. Normally, the Republican fraction of the Italian voting popu-

FIGURE 4.10. *Democratic vote, as percentage of two-party vote, in three wards with highest proportion of residents born in Italy—presidential elections, 1904–1956*

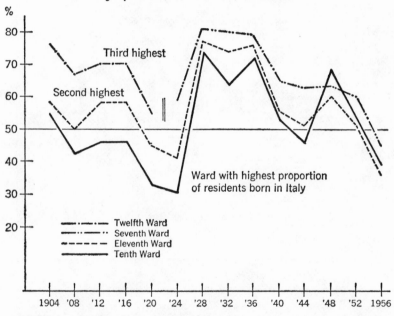

lation should have continued to expand as the middle class grew. But Alfred E. Smith and the Great Depression reversed this trend.

The presidential candidacy of Smith in 1928 gave the Democrats an enormously powerful appeal to all ethnic groups in New Haven, not only because of Smith's Catholicism, which generated sympathy among the Irish and Italians, but also because of his stress on the familiar problems of urban wage earners. The effect of his candidacy on the ethnics of New Haven was electrifying. (Figure 4.6) Smith attracted the Irish, already a dwindling minority in New Haven, but as Figure 4.10 reveals he also won

the Italians. In the three main Italian wards the vote for Smith ran
18–25 per cent higher than in the city as a whole. The Depression,
extensive unemployment among the Italian working classes, and the New
Deal continued the process that Smith had begun. The three most densely
Italian wards supported Roosevelt in 1932 and 1936 as heavily as they
had Smith in 1928.

As jobs became available and war neared, ethnic factors reasserted
themselves locally and nationally among the Italians, who had by this

FIGURE 4.11. *The Tenth Ward: extent to which percentages
of Democratic or Republican votes have exceeded city-wide
percentages in elections for president and mayor, 1903–1959*

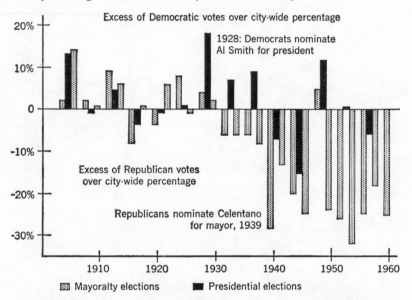

time reached the second stage of assimilation in New Haven. As we have
seen, William Celentano was nominated for mayor by the Republicans in
1939; no person of Italian origin had ever before been nominated for such
a high post. The policies of strict economy pursued by the incumbent
Democratic mayor and the prescriptive right of the Irish to city jobs
weakened any economic or social appeal a Democratic mayor might have
had for Italians. In 1937 the three most densely Italian wards had gone
Democratic. In 1939 there was a net shift in the city of 10 per cent to the
Republicans, but in the three Italian wards, the net shift was about 30
per cent. Celentano lost that election by a small margin, but in the

Tenth and Eleventh Wards he carried more than seven voters out of every ten.

As a burgeoning defense economy soaked up the unemployed and President Roosevelt revealed with increasing frankness his sympathy for the Allies, Italian support for the Democrats also declined at the national level. In 1940, Roosevelt accused Mussolini of delivering a cowardly "stab in the back" to France as she sought vainly to defend herself against the Nazis. War with Italy grew imminent. In the presidential election of 1940, Roosevelt's vote declined sharply in the three Italian wards (as it did in Italian areas elsewhere in the United States); it remained low in 1944. (Figure 4.10) In 1945, Celentano ran again for mayor on the Republican ticket. This time, the disaffection of school teachers and parents added a large bloc of hitherto Democratic voters—many of them Irish—to the Yankee-Italian coalition that had narrowly lost in 1939, and this time Celentano won.[14] In the Italian wards, Celentano's support was even greater than it had been in 1939. (Figure 4.9) Two years later the Democrats managed to split the Italian community by running a dentist of Italian origin for mayor. But they lost so disastrously in the rest of the city that they made no further attempt to repeat the strategy. As a strategy for the Democrats, old-fashioned ethnic politics had obviously become a losing game. After a brief period of success the same thing was destined to happen to the Republicans. By the end of the 1950s, ethnic politics was on the decline in New Haven. And the ex-plebes who knew nothing but the skills of ethnic politics were—like the patricians and the entrepreneurs before them—gradually giving way to new leaders.

What the immigrants and the ex-plebes had accomplished, however, was a further split in political resources. Popularity had been split off from both wealth and social standing. Popularity meant votes; votes meant office; office meant influence. Thus the ex-plebes completed the transition from the old pattern of oligarchy based upon cumulative inequalities to new patterns of leadership based upon dispersed inequalities.

14. This election is described in more detail in Ch. 11.

5. The New Men

In the 1950s, politics in New Haven underwent certain rapid and dramatic transformations. Because the changes are so recent it is probably too much to expect to distinguish correctly between ephemeral alterations that now loom large and durable changes that may now seem minor. However, that politics in New Haven has changed in certain essential respects and that new men are playing new roles—often in coalition with older and more easily recognizable political types—is beyond doubt.

What are the new sources of leadership? How different are the new leaders from the old? What lines of cleavage and cohesion are politicians building on?

CLASS INTERESTS AND ETHNIC POLITICS

To gain perspective on recent events in New Haven, it might help to consider for a moment several possible ways by which individuals or groups benefit from the actions of political leaders.[1] Certain benefits are *divisible* in such a way that they can be allocated to specific individuals; jobs, contracts, and welfare payments are examples of divisible benefits. Other benefits are more nearly *indivisible;* parks, playgrounds, schools, national defense and foreign policies, for example, either cannot be or ordinarily are not allocated by dividing the benefits piecemeal and allocating various pieces to specific individuals. With indivisible benefits, if one person receives benefits many others necessarily must also, though whether or not a particular citizen is affected may depend on the criteria used in allocating the benefits or costs. For the purposes of this chapter, perhaps it is enough to distinguish criteria according to whether they primarily relate to ethnic characteristics, sources and levels of income, or other factors—age, for example, or place of residence. One might, without

1. Here as elsewhere terms such as benefit and reward are intended to refer to subjective, psychological appraisals by the recipients, rather than appraisals by other observers. An action can be said to confer benefits on an individual, in this sense, if he *believes* he has benefited, even though, from the point of view of observers, his belief is false or perhaps ethically wrong. Thus the term is intended to be ethically neutral and independent of "objective" fact other than the perceptions of the recipient. Any reader who feels uncomfortable with this usage may want to read the terms as if they were placed between quotation marks: "benefits," "rewards," etc.

reading too much into the word, refer to differences in sources and levels of income as "class" characteristics. The various possibilities are brought together in Table 5.1. One might say that in ethnic politics politicians seek to win votes by conferring divisible benefits on individuals selected according to ethnic criteria; in class politics, politicians try to win votes by conferring mainly divisible but to some extent indivisible benefits on individuals and groups selected according to the source and size of their incomes.

When an ethnic group is in its first stage, the six categories in Table 5.1 are not sharply distinguished. Politicians who play the game of ethnic

TABLE 5.1. *Criteria for allocating benefits to beneficiaries*

Characteristics of the benefits:	Ethnic	Criteria: Class	Other
Divisible (individual)	(1a)	(2a)	(3a)
Indivisible (shared)	(1b)	(2b)	(3b)

politics confer individual benefits like jobs, nominations, bribes, gratuities, and assistance of all sorts on individuals more or less according to ethnic criteria. But ethnic characteristics serve as a kind of comprehensive symbol for class and other criteria. Moreover, benefits conferred on an individual member of an ethnic group are actually shared to some degree by the rest of the group, for every time one member makes a social or economic breakthrough, others are likely to learn of it, to take pride in his accomplishment, and to find it easier themselves to achieve the same sort of advance. The strategies of politicians are designed to confer specific benefits on particular individuals and thus to win the support of the whole group.

How different is ethnic politics from class politics? A plausible case can be made that if a large part of the electorate is divided along ethnic lines, as it has been in New Haven, the existence of ethnic identifications inhibits the development of class politics based on differences in levels of income, occupations, and other socioeconomic factors. Confronted with his perpetual need to build winning coalitions, the professional politician in New Haven quickly seized upon the most obvious way of categorizing citizens: their ethnic differences. This was by no means the only way, it might be argued, and perhaps not even the most effective way to win elections. Nonetheless, the politician devised his strategies on the assumption that whatever happened in elections could be adequately explained by shifts in ethnic blocs. Because of the uncertainty surrounding voting decisions, these explanations, which then became a part of the local political culture, were too persuasive to be rejected, even when they were incomplete or even wrong. Yet the very fact that the politician exploited ethnic unities and distinctions helped to fortify and maintain—at times perhaps even to create—feelings of ethnic difference among voters of otherwise similar social and economic circumstances. The politicians acted out a self-fulfilling prophecy; by treating ethnic distinctions as fundamental in politics, they *made* them fundamental. Had there been no ethnic distinctions to work with, class or socioeconomic differences would have been more obvious. Politicians probably would have shaped their strategies in order to appeal to socioeconomic groups or classes, and class politics probably would have developed in New Haven, just as it did in more ethnically homogeneous countries like England, Sweden, France, and Germany.

One might argue, in rejoinder, that ethnic politics was not a *substitute* for class politics; it *was* class politics in disguise, for during the first stage of assimilation, the socioeconomic homogeneity of an ethnic group determines its political homogeneity; and as the group moves through the second and third stages, political heterogeneity follows socioeconomic heterogeneity. In other words (it might be said) socioeconomic factors are always paramount; the ethnic tie is always subordinate to socioeconomic factors.

Although there is a large measure of truth in both these views, both probably underestimate the independent force of ethnic feelings. An awareness of ethnic identification is not something created by politicians; it is created by the whole social system. Ethnic similarities are a palpable reality, built into the everyday awareness of the ethnic from early childhood to old age. Nor are they always subordinate to socioeconomic factors; if they were, it would be difficult to account for certain aspects of the political behavior of the New Haven electorate.

The electoral failure of all parties that have shaped their appeals mainly in socioeconomic terms is one such aspect. If socioeconomic factors were invariably paramount, one might reasonably expect that, from about 1880 on, the Socialists, who at one time strongly emphasized the distinctive frustrations encountered by the working man in coping with life in a capitalist system, would have gained an increasing following among the working classes—as Socialist parties did in almost every other major industrial nation. Actually, however, their record in New Haven is one of total inability to win a large following. In nearly a century of effort all the minor parties together have never won more than a quarter of the votes in any election; usually they have won a good deal fewer than that. (Figures 5.1 and 5.2) In recent years, as Socialist candidates have ceased to emphasize class issues and have turned to

questions of economy, efficiency, and public honesty, a Socialist vote
has served largely as an expression of sporadic middle-class discontent
with the candidates of the two major parties. Thus in the mayoralty
election of 1947, when for the only time in the city's history both major
party candidates were of Italian stock, the Socialist candidate suddenly
acquired unexpected popularity (Figure 5.2); his support in working-
class wards was much lower than in the middling and upper residential
areas.

FIGURE 5.1. *Votes cast for third-party candidates for president and*
governor, as percentage of total vote cast in New Haven, 1870–1956

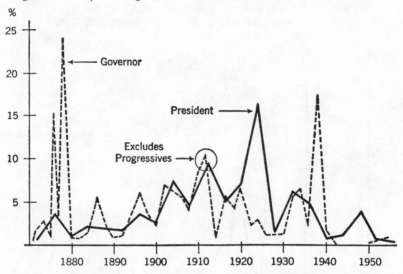

The failures of Socialist and other minor parties in the United States
doubtless cannot be explained by any one factor, but the fragmentation
of urban workers into a variety of ethnic groups undoubtedly created
special obstacles to that rising "solidarity of the working class" for
which Socialists looked in vain. The Socialist parties themselves were
torn by ethnic rivalries. A close student of New Haven's working classes,
who observed them in the middle of the Great Depression, wrote that
even then:

> While it is true that a distinction exists between white-collar work-
> ers and wage earners in their relationships to politics, a much more
> serious type of cleavage is based on nationality groups. . . . The
> dominant political groups that are apparently arising among wage

earners are not groups with a common economic or political philosophy embracing all wage earners, but national groups whose only tie is that of having come to America from the same place. . . . In New Haven nationality groups affiliated with the Socialist Labor Party had been meeting separately for years with much petty friction over the disposition of dues. . . . Nationality and language groups have maintained separate identities within the city central branch of the Socialist Party in New Haven.[2]

Moreover, the hypothesis that socioeconomic differences and similarities outweigh ethnic ties fails to explain the voting behavior of different

FIGURE 5.2. *Votes cast for third-party candidates for mayor, as percentage of total vote cast in New Haven, 1887–1957*

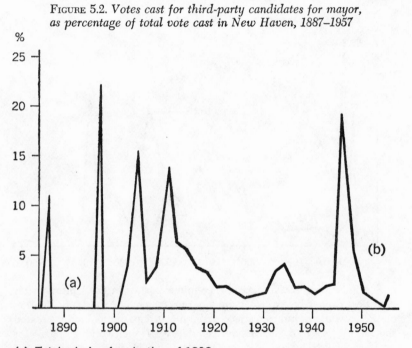

(a) Total missing for election of 1893.
(b) Vote for Malkan, Independent Democrat.

ethnic groups having very similar socioeconomic characteristics. In New Haven, for example, changes in the voting patterns of the Nineteenth Ward, the principal Negro ward in the city, have run directly counter to changes in the Eleventh Ward, which as we have seen is one of the

2. John W. McConnell, *The Evolution of Social Classes* (Washington, D. C., American Council on Public Affairs, 1942), pp. 159 ff.

principal Italian areas. The Nineteenth and the Eleventh are hardly distinguishable in their socioeconomic characteristics. In 1950, both were low-income, working-class wards. (Table 5.2) Yet over the past genera-

TABLE 5.2. *Socioeconomic characteristics of two working-class wards in New Haven, 1950*

	Eleventh Ward	Rank°	Nineteenth Ward	Rank°
Median income	$2,318	26	$2,117	30
White-collar occupations	7.4%	31	7.8%	29
Families with incomes $500 or less	16.9%	27	18.8%	28
Median school years completed, 25 years old or over	8.2	32	8.8	20
Attended college	12.9%	15	5.1%	27

° Out of 33 wards.

tion, the two wards have followed opposite paths. As the Italian ward has become more Republican, the Negro ward has become more Democratic. (Figure 5.3)

FIGURE 5.3. *Percentage voting Republican in two New Haven working-class wards—all elections for president, governor, and mayor, by decades, 1920–1960*

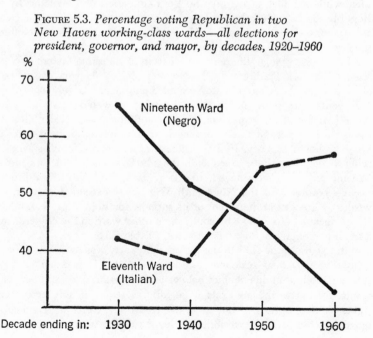

To explain this difference, one does not need to assume that socioeconomic factors are unimportant; the evidence pointing in the other direction is, as we have already seen, too persuasive. But the salience of socioeconomic factors varies just as the salience of ethnic characteristics varies. Neither ethnic nor class factors are constants; on the contrary, both are variables. When an ethnic group is in its first stage, ethnic and socioeconomic factors are *both* likely to be important in the life of the individual and in the way he responds to political appeals. But ordinarily, as we have seen, the two are not in conflict; the life of the ethnic is all of a piece.

So long as *both* sets of factors operate, politicians are likely to shape their appeals to encompass both. In some circumstances, however, the salience of ethnic identifications may decline relative to economic factors; or, conversely, economic factors may grow less salient than ethnic factors. During the Great Depression, problems of jobs, relief, wages, and economic security became paramount among wage earners; during these years, as we have noted, the Italians of New Haven gave strong support to the Democrats. But later, with the decline in unemployment and the development of unemployment compensation, trade unions, and other forms of security, the pressure of economic problems declined. Meanwhile, conflict with Italy and the nomination of Celentano by the Republicans increased the tendency toward ethnic identification. Hence the Italians drifted toward the Republican party, which now offered them greater ethnic rewards than the Democratic.

At the same time, a different combination of the same factors operated among Negroes. Traditionally the Negroes of New Haven, like Negroes elsewhere in the United States, voted Republican, largely because of sentimental ties with the party of Lincoln, as well as patronage and other benefits. The Depression, F.D.R., and the New Deal obliterated these old loyalties. Negroes were harder hit by unemployment than any other group in the city. In 1933 three times as many families were on relief in the Nineteenth Ward as in the city as a whole. Negroes turned, like most of the unemployed, to the party of 'the New Deal. In the decade before 1930 the Nineteenth Ward was exceeded only by the wealthy Fifteenth in the extent of its support for Republican candidates. In the decade before 1960, by contrast, no other ward in the city cast such a small percentage of Republican votes. (Table 5.3)

With Negroes, the shift to the Democratic party was evidently induced primarily by salient economic needs during the Depression. But the shift entailed no undue conflict between ethnic aspirations and economic wants, for northern Democrats were fully as strong in advocating civil rights as Republicans, if not more so. In New Haven, the Democratic mayor elected in 1953 consolidated Negro support with patronage, con-

TABLE 5.3. *Percentage of the two-party vote for Republican candidates in the Nineteenth Ward, 1920–1959*

Decade	Nonwhite %	president %	Elections for governor %	mayor %	All elections %
1920–1929	51	69	67	64	66
1930–1939	66	47	51	55	52
1940–1949	72	34	46	49	45
1950–1959	72	38	31	31	33

Source: Percentages of nonwhites are based on figures from U.S. Census, except for 1950–59, which is based on our 1959 survey of registered voters.

tracts, leading appointments, and support for programs to ease some of the most critical social and economic problems faced by New Haven's Negroes.

Yet if our guiding hypothesis as to the three stages in political assimilation is correct, in the long run ethnic influences must decline and socioeconomic factors must correspondingly increase in importance. As the struggle for respect and acceptance is gradually won and professional and middle-class strata emerge, the old bonds of unity must give way to disunities. Political heterogeneity follows socioeconomic heterogeneity. When this happens, will class politics replace ethnic politics?

THE SHIFT TO COLLECTIVE BENEFITS

Not necessarily. Indeed, judging from New Haven politics in the 1950s one should say, probably not.

By 1950 all ethnic groups in New Haven except the Negroes were rapidly approaching, if they were not already well into, the third stage of political, social, and economic assimilation. Socioeconomic differences within ethnic groups were becoming more noticeable than similarities. For two reasons, however, class politics did not replace ethnic politics. In the first place, in spite of growing assimilation, ethnic factors continued to make themselves felt with astonishing tenacity. The legacy of ethnic politics is sharply revealed in Table 5.4. In the center of the table, the various ethnic groups in our sample of registered voters are ranked according to the percentage that reported working-class occupations in 1959—that is, skilled, unskilled, or manual workers. The proportions range from three out of four among Negroes and six out of ten among Italian Catholics to one out of five among Irish Catholics and one out of six among European Jews. If class position were the dominant influence on party preference, Negroes and Italians would be the most strongly Democratic, and Irish Catholics and Jews would be the most strongly Republican. Yet an inspection of the right side of Table 5.4

TABLE 5.4. *Ethnic groups in New Haven: percentage in working-class occupations and percentage Democratic, 1959*

Number in sample		Skilled, semi-skilled, unskilled manual workers		Democratic	
		%	Rank	%	Rank
47	Negroes	76	1	57	2
157	Italian Catholics	61	2	37	5
53	European Catholics	58	3	48	4
56	European Protestants	35	4	16	6
34	American Protestants°	27	5	9	7
53	Irish Catholics	20	6	64	1
74	European Jews	15	7	52	3

° "American" in this sense means parents and grandparents born in the United States.

Source: The table is based on 474 persons (in an original sample of 525 voters) who could be definitely identified by religion and by place of birth of themselves, parents, or grandparents. The percentages Democratic are those who identified themselves as Democrats in response to the question: "Generally speaking, do you usually think of yourself as a Republican, a Democrat, or what?"

shows a quite different situation. The Negroes, to be sure, are one of the most strongly Democratic groups in the city, but they are exceeded by the Irish and closely followed by the European Jews. The Italian Catholics, on the other hand, are more strongly Republican than all others except European and American Protestants.

In the second place, there was a change in the character of the main political issues. The new issues did not so much emphasize divisible costs and benefits—either to an ethnic group or a class—as shared costs and benefits diffused across many different groups and strata. It is true that the direct effects on incomes from certain policies pursued in the 1950s were felt more strongly by some categories of citizens than others. For example, downtown property owners and construction contractors probably gained more income directly from redevelopment, at least initially, than any other groups of citizens in New Haven. Yet in its appeal redevelopment—far from taking on a class aspect—cut across class or socioeconomic differences more than any local issue has done in decades.

What occurred in the 1950s was a change in the kinds of issues that concerned the political stratum, both nationally and locally. Attention shifted to policies that appeared to allocate shared benefits to citizens less by ethnic or class criteria than by other criteria that were sometimes sharp and sometimes vague but invariably tended to blur ethnic and class lines. It therefore became increasingly difficult to build or hold followings by means of hallowed appeals to ethnic loyalties or effects on income; new electoral coalitions superseded the old. The strategies appropriate to ethnic politics or to class politics were inappropriate to the issues of the 1950s, and the politicians who consciously or unconsciously rejected the older strategies profited most.

In some ways, the following built across the nation by a Republican president, Dwight D. Eisenhower, was remarkably similar to the following developed at the local New Haven level by Richard C. Lee, the Democratic mayor elected in 1953. Both men devel6ped followings that bore only slight resemblance to the party coalitions of their predecessors; in both cases, the followings cut across ethnic and socioeconomic lines to an unprecedented extent; in both cases, their policies emphasized shared benefits to citizens in general rather than to specific categories.

At the national level, problems of war and cold war, defense, foreign policy, subversion, and corruption displaced the issues of the New Deal period. In New Haven, as in many other cities, the presidential election of 1952 shattered the customary patterns of ward voting. The extent of the electoral revolution wrought by Eisenhower is indicated by the remarkably low correlation between the two-party vote in the wards in 1952 and any previous election. In all presidential elections since the present wards were created in 1920, the proportion of the vote each party received in a ward has tended to be rather similar from one election to the next. For example, the correlation of the vote in the various wards for Truman in 1948 with the vote for Smith in 1928 was unbelievably high (0.91). The smallest relationship in any two presidential elections from 1924 to 1948 was between Truman's vote in 1948 and the vote for John W. Davis in 1924; even this correlation, however, was 0.77. By contrast, the correlation between Stevenson's vote in 1952 and Smith's in 1928 was only 0.29; even between Stevenson and Truman, the correlation was only 0.54.

At the local level, a similar change was taking place. Although Lee's election in 1953 rested on the kind of support that had typically served Democrats in the past, once in office he rapidly took advantage of the altered character of the electorate to build up a new following. Neither party could any longer claim to be the party of the ethnics. Perhaps the best symbol of the change is the fact that the Thirtieth Ward, which in 1950 had the highest median income, the highest median school years completed, the largest percentage of college graduates, and the third lowest percentage of foreign-born residents,[3] voted for Lee in 1955, 1957, and 1959 almost as heavily as the Fourteenth, which had the highest percentage of residents born in Ireland. In fact, in these elections the correlation between the various socioeconomic characteristics of the wards and the vote for Lee was, for all practical purposes, zero.

Although Lee did not neglect ethnic issues, particularly with Negroes

3. The ward with the fewest foreign-born was the Nineteenth, which was 72% nonwhite; next was the First, in which Yale is located.

and Italians, or individual benefits to specific socioeconomic groups, his appeal evidently rested in considerable part on his emphasis on the collective benefits to be gained from redevelopment, neighborhood renewal, the attempt to rescue the downtown business area from economic decline, the need for new schools, the possibilities of better parking and more playgrounds, and so on. In 1959, our sample of registered voters was asked, "In your opinion what are the most important problems in New Haven?" Far and away the most commonly mentioned problems were redevelopment, traffic, and parking—the very problems Lee emphasized most heavily. When voters were asked, "Are there things Mayor Lee has done that you particularly like?" far more (46 per cent) mentioned redevelopment than anything else; and only 3 per cent mentioned redevelopment as among things Lee had done that they particularly did *not* like. The change in the nature of issues is indicated by the fact that redevelopment was cited as a problem five times more frequently than unemployment; it was mentioned first ten times more often than unemployment.[4]

Although redevelopment may decline as an important issue during the next decade, the new problems of urban life probably will not. Except among Negroes, the strength of ethnic ties as a factor in local politics surely must recede. Physical and economic deterioration in downtown areas; the flight to the suburbs; the overloading of all public facilities because of rising population, higher incomes, and more automobiles; the clamor for better schools; the intensifying competition for a place in the better colleges; the spread of middle-class tastes, wants, and demands throughout the white-collar and wage-earning strata; the ugliness, limitations, and inconveniences of the metropolitan sprawl; changes in esthetic standards; growing intolerance of civic corruption—all these and still other changes will probably give new importance in the politics and policies of city governments to technicians, planners, professional administrators, and above all to professional politicians with capacities for building durable coalitions out of traditionally noncooperative and even mutually suspicious social strata. The new men in local politics may very well prove to be the bureaucrats and experts—and politicians who know how to use them.

4. In New Haven in 1959 only 8% of our sample mentioned unemployment as a problem. In Gallup polls of a nation-wide cross-section between 1935 and 1939, from 21% to 42% of the respondents mentioned unemployment as "the most vital issue before the American people today." In 1945, 53% said they thought it would be the most important problem facing this country during the next year. Hadley Cantril, ed., *Public Opinion, 1935–1946* (Princeton, Princeton University Press, 1951), pp. 680–81.

6. Shadow and Substance: The Social and Economic Notables

The political leaders who practiced ethnic politics have by no means shuffled off the New Haven stage, but the newer problems of city life are likely to push them gradually into the wings. Meanwhile, what of the present-day patricians and entrepreneurs?

So far most of our evidence for changes in the characteristics of leadership in New Haven over the past century and a half has been drawn from information about *elected public* officials. It is altogether possible, however, that public officials do not represent the *real* decision-makers in a community; they may only be the spokesmen for influential leaders who may not hold public office at all. It seems implausible in the extreme to suppose that covert leaders sat in obscurity behind the patricians, for in view of the social and economic structure of the time it is hard to imagine where the covert leaders might have come from, if not from among the patricians themselves—and evidently the patricians had neither the need nor the wish to rule covertly. Although a case might be made that the entrepreneurs had more liking for the prestige of leading elective offices than they had influence on the governmental decisions of the day, there seems to be no reason to suppose that the leading manufacturers of New Haven were acting as front men for some other covert group in the community. But the suspicion that more recent politicians, who seem to lack some of the most important resources of the patricians and the entrepreneurs, may be political handmaidens of the well-to-do and the elect of New Haven is surely not ill-founded.

Two groups, the Social Notables and the Economic Notables, invite investigation, and in this chapter I shall try to describe the extent and limits of their influence on local governmental decisions.

THE SOCIAL NOTABLES

In the days of the patricians, when birth, wealth, education, and office were joined, it was a simple matter to determine a person's social standing. As these resources have separated from one another in recent years, it has become far from simple.

However, one symbol—perhaps the best—of membership in upper-class

New Haven society today is an invitation to the annual Assemblies held in the New Haven Lawn Club. There are more exclusive criteria, and those who meet tighter criteria might look upon the Assemblies as a trifle undiscriminating. But the Assemblies are the closest approximation modern New Haven has to a list of families of highest social standing.

The Assemblies exist to provide that attenuated version of primitive puberty rites, the social debuts of the daughters of the elect. About 150 families from the greater New Haven area are invited. I shall take two recent years, 1958 and 1959, and arbitrarily select an earlier, 1951, so that members of a somewhat older but still active generation of Social Notables will be included. The continuity over the years is naturally very great; altogether 231 different families were invited to the Assemblies during these three years.

How influential are these Social Notables in public affairs? Do the Notables hold public offices bearing directly on public decisions? Whether or not they hold public offices, are they influential overtly or covertly in the making of government decisions? If they are influential, to what extent is their influence attributable to their social position?

To answer these questions, I have chosen to examine three different "issue-areas" in which important public decisions are made: nominations by the two political parties, urban redevelopment, and public education. Nominations determine which persons will hold public office. The New Haven redevelopment program measured by its cost—present and potential—is the largest in the country. Public education, aside from its intrinsic importance, is the costliest item in the city's budget. It is reasonable to expect, therefore, that the relative influence over public officials wielded by the Social Notables would be revealed by an examination of their participation in these three areas of activity.

What do we find? First, quite unlike the patricians a century and a half ago, very few Social Notables participate overtly in public affairs. Out of nearly 500 elective and party offices in New Haven, in 1957–58 the Notables held only two—both minor positions in the Republican party. Out of 131 higher offices in public education (including members of the Board of Education, superintendent, assistant superintendents, principals, and PTA heads) the Notables held only two. They appeared in larger numbers however, in urban redevelopment. Out of 435 persons who were members of the Redevelopment Agency in executive or policy positions or were on the Citizens Action Commission or any of its numerous committees, some 24 notables appeared. (Table 6.1) Yet even in urban redevelopment an inspection of the names of the Social Notables indicates that with few exceptions their membership was more a result of occupation or economic position than of social standing.

Thus in the two political parties and in public education, the *proportion*

TABLE 6.1. *Number of selected public offices held by Social Notables, 1957–1958*

	Political parties[*] N	Public education N	Urban redevelop-ment N	Duplica-tions[**] N	Total, less duplications N
Social Notables	2	2	24	1	27
Others	495	129	411	38	997
Total	497	131	435	39	1024

[*] Includes major local elective offices and all party offices in the Democratic and Republican parties.
[**] I.e., persons in more than one column.

of higher offices held by Social Notables was infinitesimal. To be sure, it was considerably larger in urban redevelopment, but even there the Social Notables held less than 6 per cent of the offices in 1957 and 1958. It might be argued, of course, that the number of Social Notables in office was *relatively* large, since they were, after all, a very tiny group. If one followed the practices of ancient Athens and filled these offices by random selection, an even smaller proportion of the offices would be held by Social Notables. Indeed, in the case of urban redevelopment, they held about twenty-seven times more positions than one would expect on a purely chance basis. (Table 6.2)

TABLE 6.2. *Percentage of selected offices held by Social Notables, 1957–1958*

	(1) Actual %	(2) Expected [*] %	Ratio (1) ÷ (2)
Political parties	0.4	0.2	2.0
Public education	1.5	0.2	7.5
Urban redevelopment	5.5	0.2	27.5
Percentage in three combined, less duplications	2.7	0.2	13.5

[*] Expected: percentage of Social Notables in total New Haven population 21 years or over.

Looking at the matter in another way, however, the proportion of Social Notables holding office was very small. Even in urban redevelopment, only one out of ten held office in 1957–58; less than one out of a hundred held office in the political parties and in public education. (Table 6.3) Probably not more than two out of ten Social Notables held any public office of any kind—local, state, or national.

TABLE 6.3. *Percentage of Social Notables holding selected public offices, 1957–1958*

	%
Political parties	0.9
Public education	0.9
Urban redevelopment	10.4
Percentage in three combined, less duplications	11.7

One could, no doubt, magnify these tiny proportions into great significance by assuming that the few Social Notables in public life are of extraordinary influence. Alas for such a hypothesis; the evidence to the contrary is devastating. Not only do the Social Notables refrain from participating in public affairs, but when they do participate—overtly or covertly—their influence is evidently not very great.

A rough test of a person's overt or covert influence is the frequency with which he successfully initiates an important policy over the opposition of others, or vetoes policies initiated by others, or initiates a policy where no opposition appears.[1] If we apply this test to the issue-areas of party nominations, public education, and urban redevelopment over the period 1950–59, out of fifty persons who met the test there were only eight Social Notables. What is perhaps most striking of all is that only two of the eight were among the top five men of influence in any of the three sectors, and their influence was strictly confined to public education. (Table 6.4)

The patricians seem therefore to have continued on the course marked out after they were displaced in politics by the entrepreneurs of industry. For the most part, they have eschewed public office. The last Trowbridge to run for office was a Republican candidate for mayor in 1886; he was defeated. A Townshend was elected to the Board of Aldermen from the First Ward in 1904 and subsequently was even elected president of the Board by his fellow aldermen. His wife was an active Republican and was the first woman ever elected to the Connecticut General Assembly. Their son Henry became an alderman and in 1961 the Republican nominee for mayor. A few patricians lingered on in public office by virtue of legal anomalies that permitted them to name their successors on certain boards. Thus five Proprietors of Common and Undivided Grounds were first elected in 1641 for laying out "allotments for inheritance"; today their ancient prerogative still gives them indisputable control over the use of the Central Green. When a proprietor dies, his replacement is elected for life by the surviving proprietors; all are descendants of the

1. A discussion of the definition and measurement of influence will be found in Appendix B.

TABLE 6.4. *Social Notables as leaders, 1950–1959*

	Party nomina- tions N	Urban redevelop- ment N	Public educa- tion N	More than one sector N	Total, less duplications N
TOP LEADERS*					
Social Notables	—	—	2	—	2
Others	9	7	7	2	21
Total					23
MINOR LEADERS**					
Social Notables	1	4	1	—	6
Others	3	15	6	3	21
Total					27
Totals	13	26	16	5	50

* Participants who were successful more than once in initiating or vetoing a policy proposal.
** Participants who were successful only once in initiating or vetoing a policy proposal.

Source: For the method of constructing this table, see Appendix B.

original settlers. (In 1959, the names of the proprietors were Hemingway, Trowbridge, Seymour, Daggett, and Hooker. By way of comparison, another honorific anachronism, the Board of Selectmen, an elected body, consisted of six members named Schlein, Calandrella, Shields, Brown, Kelleher, and Gianelli.)

SOCIAL STANDING AND ECONOMIC LEADERSHIP

Do the Social Notables furnish the economic leaders of New Haven? Let us cast a wide net by including as an Economic Notable in 1957–58 any person in one of the following categories:

The president or chairman of the board of a corporation with property in New Haven assessed in any of the five years 1953–57 at a value placing it among the fifty highest assessments in the city.

Any individual or group of individuals with property in the city assessed in the years 1953–57 at a value of $250,000 or more.

President or chairman of the board of any bank or public utility in the city.

Any individual who was a director of three or more of the following: a firm with an assessed valuation of $250,000 or more, a manufacturing firm with fifty employees or more, a retailing firm with twenty-five employees or more, a bank.

All directors of New Haven banks.

After eliminating duplications, the Economic Notables numbered some 238 persons in 1957–58. By a curious coincidence, this number is almost exactly equal to the number of Social Notables. One might easily leap to the conclusion, therefore, that the two groups were substantially identical. But nothing would be in more serious error, for only twenty-four persons, or about 5 per cent of the total number of names on both lists, were both Social and Economic Notables.

In view of the evolving pattern of economic leadership touched on in Chapter 3, it is not altogether surprising that the two groups have become somewhat distinct. If the entrepreneurs of the last half of the nineteenth century were distinct from the patricians, something like that difference has persisted down to the present day. Nowadays most of the leading executives in the larger corporations have come to top positions in New Haven after careers elsewhere; or if they have grown up in New Haven they have generally started life in circumstances sharply different from those of the socially elect.

James W. Hook, who at the time of his death in 1957 was chairman of the board of the United Illuminating Company and one of the leading business figures in New Haven, was born in Iowa; his successor, then the president of the firm, was born in Texas. The president and later chairman of the board of the Southern New England Telephone Company was a native of New Haven who had started his career as a bookkeeper, supplementing his slender income by leading a jazz band. The chairman of the board of the Armstrong Rubber Company was born in New York, the son of Irish immigrants. Olin-Mathieson executives come to New Haven from a vast national empire of diverse companies. George Alpert, president of the New Haven Railroad, is a Boston lawyer; many of the other top officials in the New Haven offices of the railroad originally came from other parts of the country.

For their part the Social Notables have gone into the professions, particularly law, or play passive roles as corporate directors and owners of real estate. They are particularly prominent among the directors of the leading banks; yet the bank executives themselves, the presidents and vice-presidents, now frequently duplicate the pattern of industry and commerce. Of the twenty-four Social Notables among the Economic Notables, six are bankers, four are lawyers, two are at Yale, and five head their own family firms.

Between the Social and Economic Notables there is a slight discordance, often low but discernible to the carefully attuned ear. One of the Economic Notables put it more bluntly than most:

> Well, we noticed that we weren't readily accepted into the inner circle, you might say, the "sanctorum" of New Haven society, the way these old multi-generation families were. We've only been here for forty years. We're newcomers. We're nouveau riche. We're trying to crash. I mean, the old, long [time] society crowd looks upon us as trying to horn in.[2]

On the other side was the view of one of the twenty-four Social Notables who was an Economic Notable according to our broad criteria but insisted that, "I don't really think I rate being described as an Economic Notable." He expressed his feelings about corporate life:

> I think that there's a growing conviction among all the old families that it's better to be in a profession than [sic] the practices and tempo of business now, which is not according to their taste. . . . It's certainly true with me and I think it's true with a great many people. . . . Business is no more like what it was in '24 than Rome was like what Marco Polo found in China. . . . The tax picture makes for a regal type of living on the part of executives and an outlook on the money standards and the standards of business achievement which is utterly foreign to the Yankee. . . . If you work for General Motors, you're careful what kind of a General Motors car you drive around in, depending on your [place in the] hierarchy. . . . My friend in the Shell Oil Company in Venezuela—there's limousines meeting him everywhere and he flies here and there and everybody gets everything for him and everything's on the expense account. Well, we just haven't grown up with it, that's all—at least most of us haven't.

THE ECONOMIC NOTABLES IN PUBLIC LIFE

The Economic Notables participate more in public affairs than do the Social Notables. In the 1950s, however, their participation was largely confined to only one of the three issue-areas investigated, and this, as might be expected, was urban redevelopment. Forty-eight Economic Notables held offices in urban redevelopment as compared with six in the political parties and none at all in public education. (Table 6.5) One out of every five Economic Notables held some office in urban redevelopment; altogether they held 11 per cent of the offices in that field. (Tables 6.6 and 6.7)

That the Economic Notables should neglect office in the political

2. From an interview. Hereafter, direct quotations from interviews will be given without footnote reference.

parties and in public education might seem surprising and will no doubt astonish anyone who expects to find the hand of an economic ruling elite in every major domain of public activity. But the explanation is not obscure. Most Social Notables and many Economic Notables living in

TABLE 6.5. *Number of selected public offices held by Economic Notables, 1957–1958*

	Political parties N	Public education N	Urban redev. N	Duplica- tions N	Total, less duplications N
Economic Notables	6	—	48	2	52
Others	491	131	387	37	972
Total	497	131	435	39	1024

New Haven send their children to private schools; as a consequence their interest in the public schools is ordinarily rather slight. It is true that expenditures on public schools have a very large bearing on the local tax rate, but—it might be argued—the best place to control taxes is

TABLE 6.6. *Percentage of Economic Notables holding selected public offices, 1957–1958*

	%
Political parties	2.5
Public education	—
Urban redevelopment	20.0
Percentage in three combined, less duplication	21.8

through the mayor and the Board of Finance, about which I shall say something in a moment.

Moreover, to hold office in the parties or in public education one must, with a few exceptions, have a residence in New Haven, and many of

TABLE 6.7. *Percentage of selected offices held by Economic Notables, 1957–1958*

	(1) Actual %	(2) Expected ° %	Ratio (1) ÷ (2)
Political parties	1.2	0.2	6
Public education	—	0.2	—
Urban redevelopment	11.0	0.2	55
Percentage in three combined, less duplication	5.1	0.2	26

° Expected: percentage of Economic Notables in total New Haven population 21 years old or over.

the Economic Notables live in the suburbs. In urban redevelopment, the mayor felt it important to have the support of the Economic Notables, and appointed members to his Citizens Action Commission without regard to where they lived. In 1958, eleven of the twenty-four members of the Citizens Action Commission lived in the suburbs; of the thirteen Economic Notables on the CAC, nine lived in the suburbs. To a lesser degree the manifold special committees operating under the CAC followed the same principle.

Then too, urban redevelopment bore a comparatively direct and self-evident relationship to the personal or corporate prosperity of the Economic Notables. Business leaders might ignore the public schools or the political parties without any sharp awareness that their indifference would hurt their pocketbooks, but the prospect of profound changes in ownership, physical layout, and usage of property in the downtown area and the effects of these changes on the commercial and industrial prosperity of New Haven were all related in an obvious way to the daily concerns of businessmen. However much they might justify their apathy toward public schools and politics on the ground that they were not experts in these areas, redevelopment looked a good deal more like the kind of operation corporate executives, bankers, and utilities heads understood; it was, in a sense, business.

Finally, Economic Notables are busy men who, with only a few exceptions, have full-time business careers. Of course only a handful of the thousand public offices in question are full-time offices, and the part-time, often unpaid, offices are held primarily by men and women who have full-time jobs that leave them with no more time than the businessmen have to spend on public duties. However, it is not surprising that among any group of busy people only a few are willing to add participation in public affairs to the other demands on their time—even if, as is usually the case, the demand is only for a few hours a week. In their reluctance to give time to public affairs, the Economic Notables are not unique, for the orientation of American life to hedonistic and family satisfactions is a powerful pull against the gentle tug of public duty.

ROLE OF THE ECONOMIC NOTABLES IN RECENT DECISIONS

Sheer numbers are not always an index to influence. Even if the Economic Notables hold less than one out of twenty offices in the political parties, public education, and urban redevelopment (and presumably about the same proportion elsewhere, or less) one might argue that if one Notable serves as a kind of trustee for his fellow Notables, he might well prove to be very powerful. He might represent the aggregate power of all the Economic Notables.

In some such fashion one might seek to preserve the hypothesis that an economic elite of bankers and businessmen dominates New Haven. Yet any fair examination of the evidence must, I think, lead to the conclusion that this particular hypothesis, dramatic and satisfying as it may be to many people, is false. The temptation to fly from one falsehood to another at the opposite extreme is unfortunately one of the commonplaces of human existence; hence one might easily interpret the evidence as showing that the Economic Notables are virtually powerless: a conclusion surely equally unwarranted. Nor does it get us much closer to the truth to offer the vacuous evasion that the truth lies somewhere between the two extremes, for this is merely to reduce a social complexity to a loose and misleading metaphor.

The most impressive evidence against the hypothesis that the Economic Notables or their delegates completely dominate New Haven consists of a detailed examination of eight major decisions on redevelopment, eight on public education, and all nominations for elective office (most importantly for mayor) in both political parties for seven elections from 1945–57. These decisions have been reconstructed from records, newspaper files, and interviews with leading participants.[3]

To reconstruct these decisions is to leave little room for doubt that the Economic Notables, far from being a ruling group, are simply one of the many groups out of which individuals sporadically emerge to influence the policies and acts of city officials. Almost anything one might say about the influence of the Economic Notables could be said with equal justice about a half dozen other groups in the New Haven community.

Of the forty-eight Economic Notables participating officially in urban redevelopment, plus those who may have been participating unofficially, only seven seem to have exerted any leadership, according to the test suggested. (Table 6.8) Of these, only one was among the top seven; at least two others in the top seven exerted considerably more influence over the actual course of decisions than he did. There were, you will recall, no Economic Notables holding higher office in public education, and none were turned up as covert leaders. Only one Economic Notable was a leader in a political party, and he was something of an anomaly.

POLITICIAN OR NOTABLE?

This unique individual was John Golden, a Democratic party leader for a generation and a man whom most people in New Haven, if they happened to recognize his name, would have known only as the boss of the Democratic party.

Golden was, in some ways, a representative of an earlier era. As a

3. For a list of the decisions and a breakdown by major area of policy and by major occupation of persons interviewed, see Appendix B.

TABLE 6.8. *Economic Notables as leaders, 1950–1959*

	Party Nomina-tions N	Urban redevelop-ment N	Public education N	More than one sector N	Total, less duplications N
TOP LEADERS°					
Economic Notables	1	1	1	—	3
Others	8	6	8	2	20
Total					23
MINOR LEADERS°°					
Economic Notables	—	9	—	—	9
Others	4	10	7	3	18
Total					27
Totals	13	26	16	5	50

° Participants who were successful more than once in initiating or vetoing a policy proposal.

°° Participants who were successful only once in initiating or vetoing a policy proposal.

Source: For the method of constructing this table, see Appendix B.

political boss he was in the older tradition of urban politics. As a business-man he had this much in common with the entrepreneurs of the late nineteenth century: he had come a long way from modest beginnings.

He was born not far from New Haven in Old Saybrook, where his father was a station agent for the New Haven Railroad. Of Irish-Catholic stock, descended from a Democratic father and grandfather, he naturally became a Democrat too. About the time of the First World War, Golden went to work in the Greist Manufacturing Company where he rose to the rank of superintendent. He was evidently well thought of in business and banking circles. He was a member of the Rotary Club, helped to found the Community Chest, of which he later became chairman, and was active in civic affairs in other ways.

Like many people who later make their mark in politics, for as long as he can now remember Golden had been deeply interested in politics. He became Democratic chairman of his ward in 1924 (a post he still held a quarter of a century later). In 1931 he ran for the first and only time in his life as a candidate for elective office (as Democratic registrar of voters) and with the aid of the Depression, which turned 1931 into a Democratic year in New Haven, he won.

John Murphy, the newly elected mayor, was, like Golden, an Irishman and a Democrat; unlike Golden, he was not a businessman but a union official who felt he needed a reputable businessman as director of public works, a position particularly important to him because the city's credit was in a precarious condition. Murphy was bent on rigid economy, and the Department of Public Works was heavily involved in relief for the unemployed. Among others, Murphy turned for advice on Golden to James Hook, who owned the Geometric Tool Company across the street from the Greist firm and who, though a Republican, had supported Murphy for mayor. Hook knew Golden well and gave him strong support. Murphy offered the post to Golden, who accepted and resigned his job with the manufacturing company.

Not wishing to be dependent on the modest income from his city post, Golden started an insurance and bonding business. As he rose in politics, his business became highly lucrative. In due course he was made a director of the General Industrial Bank, a small commercial bank established by Jewish families in New Haven in response to the systematic exclusion of Jews from other banks; it was probably the only bank in New Haven since Andrew Jackson's day that might be called a "Democratic" bank rather than a "Republican" one.

By the time Murphy was defeated in his last try for office in 1945, Golden had become the real head of the Democratic organization. A moderately wealthy man by New Haven standards, he spent a healthy slice of his income on politics. His rule was occasionally challenged, but the challengers were regularly defeated. It was Golden who saw possibilities in a young member of the Board of Aldermen, Richard Lee, who ultimately was elected mayor in 1953 with Golden's strong support. As Lee's prestige, confidence, and authority grew, Golden and Lee shared control over the organization. By the end of the decade it was no longer possible to say which of the two would win in a showdown over control of the organization. But neither man stood to gain by a contest, neither sought one, and except for a brief conflict over charter reform (to be described in a later chapter) their coalition remained intact.

One could draw a pretty picture of the Economic Notables controlling Golden and Golden in turn controlling the Democratic party. But whatever else one might conclude about Golden's role in politics, it has been impossible to turn up any evidence to warrant the conclusion that he was an "agent" of the Notables. Like most successful politicians, particularly Democratic ones, he is not known to bear a profound respect for the political abilities of successful businessmen, and his style of life, outlook, and interests are more those of the political leader than the man of business. At the same time, many members of the business community who did not know him during his earlier business career look upon Golden with no little suspicion as an organization politician. (Because of their contacts with him on the Citizens Action Commission in recent years, some of the Economic Notables have developed a grudging respect for his shrewdness and judgment.) Moreover most of the Economic Notables are Republicans who usually support Republican candidates and oppose Democrats.

It might be thought that the Economic Notables have no need to "control" Golden since he is a successful insurance executive and bank director, and his views on policy questions must surely coincide with theirs. There is not only a profound truth in this observation but also an important distortion. If one searches for a massive divergence in opinion between Golden and New Haven business leaders, one will not find it. But if one looks for massive divergencies between Golden and almost any other group in the community, one will not find that either. If Golden's policies could be said to coincide substantially with those of the Economic Notables (in so far as the Notables agree among themselves) they could be said to coincide in the same sense with the policies of union leaders, school teachers, and factory hands. In short, in New Haven, as in the United States generally, the search for political conflict is likely to turn up differences that seem small measured by European standards or considered in the perspective of a revolutionary ideology (whether of the left or right) but that nonetheless may be thought by the participants to be quite great.

From the moon, viewed with the naked eye, the Rocky Mountains would seem little different from the plains, but the closer one draws to the Rockies the greater the difference becomes. So too in politics, differences shrink with distance. Many observers have viewed American local or even national politics as if they were standing on the moon looking at politics for signs of brutal class conflict and permanent cleavage; finding only scattered and unsatisfactory evidence, they nonetheless conclude that the rich and wellborn have in devious and mysterious ways imposed their policies on all the rest.

THE ASSETS AND LIABILITIES OF THE NOTABLES

Like other groups in the community, from Negroes on Dixwell Avenue to teachers in the public schools, sometimes the Notables have their way and sometimes they do not. As with other groups, the likelihood of getting their way is a complex function of many factors: the relevance to political influence of the resources at their disposal; the extent to which the group members agree; their application, persistence, and skill; the amount and kinds of opposition they generate; the degree to which their objectives are viewed as consistent with the political aims of elected leaders; and the extent to which their aims are consistent with widespread beliefs in the community.

The political assets of the Notables are imposing. First, they have two political resources of some value—money and social standing. Second, on all matters relating directly to business and commercial affairs, their views seem to carry special authority in the eyes of much of the community. Their authority is particularly great when policies impinge directly on business costs, earnings, investments, and profits, as many policies of local government do. Third, their financial stake in the city provides them with a strong and steady stimulus to participate in city decisions that bear immediately on their interests. Fourth, they are probably in more active communication among themselves than most other groups in the community. Their clubs, service organizations, business affairs, and central downtown location all make for frequent contact. Fifth, the goals of businessmen are legitimized by a system of beliefs widely shared throughout the community; among other things, this system of beliefs gives legitimacy to business itself as an essential and proper institution in American society.[4] Sixth, at the local level, the Notables have no persistent, organized public critics. Local issues have not, by and large, stimulated the active participation of groups or organizations whose leaders might frequently take a position counter to that of the Notables. Until recently, for example, trade union leaders have usually become involved in local affairs only on questions of the wages, security, and working conditions of city employees. In national affairs, the policies of the Economic Notables are frequently countered by proposals and criticisms from organized nonbusiness strata, including government agencies, but in local affairs in New Haven this rarely happens. Finally, the local newspapers are owned by a leading family in the Economic and Social Notability. The papers can always be counted on for a stanchly conservative defense of the rights and privileges of the Notability.

On the other side of the ledger, the Notables also incur liabilities that seriously reduce their influence. First, they suffer from the fatal defect of the patricians and entrepreneurs, the lack of sheer numbers. This defect, inherent in the structure of a modern socioeconomic system, has been compounded in New Haven, as in many other cities, by the tendency of the well-to-do to escape to the suburbs. Together with the descendants of the patricians and the entrepreneurs, the managers and executives of New Haven's corporations generally live outside the city. Industrialism, immigration, and population density have made New Haven less and less attractive as a residence; by contrast, the surrounding communities have retained the attractiveness of Connecticut's rolling wooded countryside, small-town Yankee atmosphere, and low taxes. When automobiles and good roads put the suburbs within easy commuting distance after the First World War, an exodus of the well-to-do began that has never

4. See *Big Business from the Viewpoint of the Public* (Ann Arbor, Survey Research Center, 1951).

ceased. Many of these business and professional emigrants, who might have participated in New Haven politics had they stayed, turn up in the suburban communities as party officials, selectmen, or members of the innumerable boards and committees characteristic of Connecticut town government. Though they keep their business and professional ties in New Haven, their political attention has shifted to the towns in which they live.

Second, the Notables are often in disagreement even on questions touching directly on their own interests. Local policies rarely affect all of them in quite the same way, and differences in background, age, temperament, attitudes, information, and corporate loyalties produce differences in the policies they espouse. These differences occur even in economic affairs, and are quite likely to exist in other sectors of government action, such as schools or welfare. The head of one of New Haven's largest firms exploded wrathfully against the publisher of the city's two newspapers:

> John Day Jackson's influence in town, as far as I'm concerned, is zero, which is an overstatement and I wish he didn't have as much influence as he did. I think he's one of the most undesirable elements in our whole community.

> *Why so?*

> Because John Day Jackson really epitomizes the 1880s in my opinion. You speak of reactionaries and selfish interests, that is John Day Jackson. He's against anything that means spending money and he's against anything that is not of direct benefit to the *Register.*

> *Why is he so much more against spending money than you are or other people?*

> Just a bug he has. He just feels the tax rate should be half what it is; we just spend money on a lot of useless things. I'm not saying that he's not right, but, my gosh, when he starts attacking putting up skating rinks for the kids and things like that, he's going too far.

Third, the authority with which the Economic Notables speak tends to be confined to matters bearing directly on the affairs of business. When merchants agree that a change to a one-way street has or will cut seriously into business, they receive the respectful attention of local officials. But when Mayor Lee wrung support for a proposed revision of the city charter from the Notables on the Citizens Action Commission, their backing seemed to carry little weight with opponents of reform, including John Golden, who covertly and successfully opposed the change. Indeed many critics, including some businessmen, felt that the Citizens Action

Commission went well beyond the range of its legitimate activities in expressing any opinion on the city charter at all.

Fourth, the Notables tend to participate only marginally in politics. Frequently, as we have seen, they live elsewhere. Then too their most important economic and social goals are not often *immediately* at stake in local decisions, particularly given the prevailing system of beliefs. They are busy men with full-time occupations. They are often unbelievably short on elementary political skills and information. Sometimes they fear that getting involved in issues on which the community is divided will be bad for business; they much prefer safely nonpartisan activities like the Community Fund.

A leading merchant summed up his attitudes toward politics this way:

> I have never become interested in the political arena. I can't tell you why.
>
> *Is it distasteful to you?*
>
> Well, not being of a political nature, I would rather not be in a position where I was ever going to hurt anyone. I'm willing to go along with anyone who is progressive in their thinking, anyone who will do good for other people, but I have never sought political office although I've been asked on occasions to accept a spot on the ticket here and there. . . . It just doesn't appeal to me. I'm not thick-skinned enough. . . . I should imagine that I would have a lot of sleepless nights if I were actively engaged in politics.

The president of a manufacturing corporation said:

> I think that's one trouble with my generation . . . we're not getting into politics as much as we should. . . . I think perhaps—speaking for myself and having observed other people—perhaps we're all scared. Any time we stick our nose into a political grindstone, we find that for every hour we can spend and for every dollar we can spend, the unions are right there with three times the number of people and three times the number of dollars. Ever since the New Deal, why, I feel that the businessman has been down the ladder of political influence and I think that it has unduly scared us. I've heard some of these old-timers like . . . say that we're a bunch of cream puffs in this political thing, and I think maybe he's right.

This Economic Notable had lived all his life in New Haven. He was a Republican. Yet he could not identify the man who for twenty years had been regarded as the Republican leader in New Haven:

What kind of a role in the Republican Party does Frank Lynch play?

Ted Lynch? [A manufacturing executive and one-time state senator]

No, Frank Lynch is not Ted Lynch.

I don't know. I've heard the name, Frank Lynch, but I haven't any idea. I don't know.

TAXES

In many issue-areas of public policy, the Economic Notables can hardly be said to have any direct influence at all, either because they do not agree or because they simply never enter the arena of policy. Their direct influence on public education and on political nominations, for example, is virtually nil.

Even on urban redevelopment, their record is a curious one. Few aspects of local policy could be more salient to the Notables than efforts to save downtown New Haven, yet the Economic Notables were able neither to agree on nor to put through a program of urban redevelopment even under a Republican mayor anxious to retain their support. When redevelopment came to New Haven the leadership for it came less from the Notables than from a Democratic mayor, whom most of them originally opposed and who as mayor had to wheedle, cajole, recruit, organize, plan, negotiate, bargain, threaten, reward, and maneuver endlessly to get the support and participation needed from the Notables, the small businessmen, the developers (who came principally from outside New Haven), the federal authorities, and the electorate. (See Chapter 10.)

Normally, except for redevelopment and concern over the diminishing prosperity of the city's heart, the main cutting edge of policy to the Economic Notables is taxation. Their individual and particular interests can in this case, as in many others, conflict somewhat with their collective interests. Like anyone else a Notable can keep his taxes down by means of a relatively low tax rate, a relatively low assessment, or both. If the Notables are to enjoy uniformly low taxes, either the general tax rate on real property must be reduced, or the gains of the Notables from reduced assessments must be offset by relatively higher assessments for other property owners. To an elected mayor, the possible advantages of favoritism to the Notables at the expense of other groups are minor compared with the possible costs, for the Notables cast a pitifully small fraction of the total vote at election time, and small property owners, who vastly outnumber the Notables, are no less sensitive to their assessments.

The greater numbers and equal sensitivity to taxes of small property owners helps account for the fact that they are underassessed in New Haven as compared with large property owners or with owners of business and nonresidential property. In recent years small single-family dwellings have been assessed at less than 40 per cent of their market value (as indicated by sales prices for comparable dwellings), whereas large single-family dwellings have been assessed at nearly 60 per cent and nonresidential properties at 60–80 per cent of their sales value. (Figure 6.1) Hence, if a Notable acting in his own personal or corporate

FIGURE 6.1. *Average assessed valuation as percentage of sales price, by kinds of property, 1954, 1955, 1957*

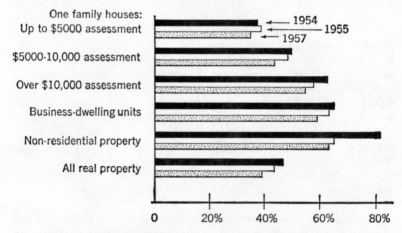

Source: New Haven Taxpayers Research Council, Council Comment, Mar. 9, 1959.

interest succeeds in having his assessment reduced, the effect is mainly to pass the bill to another Notable.

In 1959, Republican charges of scandalous practices by the Board of Assessors led to an investigation in which it was shown that on many occasions assessors had illegally reduced assessments—more often, it turned out, for friends and relatives of political figures than for the Notables or the large corporations. Large business firms, unhappy over their assessments, sometimes follow a more indirect practice if their efforts fail with the assessors themselves. There are certain tacit understandings in the local political culture that sophisticated participants can hope to rely on. If a firm protests its assessments and threatens to appeal to the courts, the city's attorneys may conclude that the reasonable course

—particularly in view of genuine uncertainty over whether the city's claims will hold up in court—is to reduce the assessment. Later, the firm's executives may contribute funds generously to the campaign of the incumbent administration.

An administration running close to the wind, however, may prefer a court fight to a loss in tax income from a settlement out of court, for in the case of a large firm a reduction sizable enough to make it worthwhile for the firm to engage in a court fight may also be big enough to throw the city's revenues out of whack. (In 1957, the ten largest owners of real estate in New Haven paid almost one-fifth of the total taxes levied by the city, and their taxes financed one-eighth of the city's total expenditures for that year.) Consequently, the city administration may prefer to contest the appeal.

Moreover the game of assessments can be played by both sides. A city administration lives in dread of raising the tax rate. A general increase in assessments, particularly on large firms, may do the trick instead. Celentano's Republican administration began an extensive reassessment program; Lee's Democratic administration continued it. The median assessed valuation of the fifty largest property owners in New Haven went from $838 thousand in 1948 to $1,640 thousand in 1957. (Table 6.9) During

TABLE 6.9. *Distribution of the fifty largest assessed valuations in New Haven, 1948 and 1957*

	1948 N	1957 N
$500,000–1 million	29	16
$1–2 million	9	14
$2–5 million	10	15
$5–10 million	1	2
$10–20 million	1	1
Over $20 million	0	2
Total	50	50
Median	$838,000	$1,640,000

the first five years of Lee's administration, revenues from property taxes rose by 35 per cent with no increase in the tax rate, largely as a result of vigorous reassessment.

The fact that Lee was anxious to avoid a higher tax rate reflected his belief that an increase could be turned by his opponents into a political liability. In part, no doubt, he was concerned over the predictable response of the local newspapers, in part over the effects on voters at large, and in part on the reactions of businessmen, large and small. For despite important differences of emphasis, the main policy thrust of the

Economic Notables is to oppose tax increases; this leads them to oppose expenditures for anything more than minimal traditional city services. In this effort their two most effective weapons ordinarily are the mayor and the Board of Finance. The policies of the Notables are most easily achieved under a strong mayor if his policies coincide with theirs or under a weak mayor if they have the support of the Board of Finance. Since the members of the Board of Finance, aside from the mayor himself and one alderman, are appointed by the mayor, the influence of the Notables on the budget is sharply reduced if the mayor exerts strong leadership and has policies differing from those of the Notables. Despite their waning numbers on the Board of Aldermen, businessmen have continued to play a predominant role on the Board of Finance. In the pro-business period of the 1920s, its members were not only drawn almost exclusively from business but they consisted mainly of the heads of larger firms rather than small independent businessmen. (Figure 6.2) In recent years the number

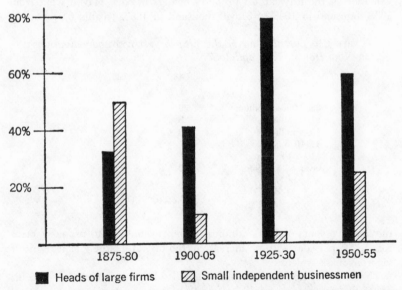

FIGURE 6.2. *Businessmen on the Board of Finance, as percentage of total membership (excluding ex officio members), 1875–1955*

of smaller independent businessmen on the Board has increased and the number of corporate chiefs has declined; nonetheless, New Haven mayors have continued to find it expedient to create confidence in their financial policies among businessmen by appointing them to the Board. By contrast, the increase in clerical and working-class participation has taken place almost entirely on the Board of Aldermen; their relative numbers increased only slightly on the Board of Finance. (Figure 4.2)

The steady pressure of the Notables against the expansion of public services and taxes undoubtedly has some effect, though it is impossible to say how much. Had their demands for public economy been in opposition to the demands of a large proportion of citizenry, the natural incentive of politicians to secure their own election surely would have resulted in policies designed to appeal to numbers rather than wealth. But it would be wrong to suppose that Economic Notables and business-men are in constant conflict with other significant groups over the policy of keeping taxes and expenditures low. Their essential strategy is a familiar aspect of American politics: to gain services and benefits from government and as far as possible to displace the costs from themselves to others. In the context of American ideology and perspectives, contests over taxes and services are evidently seen less as grand conflicts among social classes over relative shares in the public pie than as struggles by individuals or small constellations of individuals such as a family, a grocery store, a business firm, a neighborhood, or an ethnic or religious group. Even wage earners share this view. In the depths of the Great Depression a sociologist interviewing workers in New Haven concluded that:

> No abstract ideal nor current issue matters very much to the politically minded wage earner. He cannot afford to be concerned over such matters, because he looks upon the political party as a source of help in time of need, to get a job, to get one of his boys out of a court scrape, to show him how to fill out forms.[5]

Thus the policies of the Economic Notables have precipitated factional rather than class battles—if indeed they have caused any conflict at all, for it must be remembered that throughout much of this century, Demo-cratic and Republican mayors alike sought to outdo one another in their reputations for economy. Until the New Deal, the national leaders of the Democratic party, though less worshipful of business than the general run of Republican spokesmen, were no less keen on economy and budget-balancing. In Connecticut, even the Socialists were economy-minded; their "businesslike" administration in Bridgeport drew the admiration and political support of conservative Republican businessmen. The Demo-cratic mayor in New Haven during the Depression was a union official, the only person of nominally working-class status ever to be elected to the office of mayor in New Haven; yet he came into office in 1931 when the city's credit standing was so poor that it was difficult to carry on the city's

5. McConnell, *Evolution of Social Classes*, p. 156.

business; he took as his guiding objective the task of restoring the confidence of bankers and investors in the city's capacity to meet fiscal obligations. Ironically, his policy of strict economy was so rigidly enforced that his defeat by a Republican in 1945 after fourteen years in office was widely attributed to general discontent with the shabby state of the public services.

The fact is that the Economic Notables operate within that vague political consensus, the prevailing system of beliefs, to which all the major groups in the community subscribe. Even the limited influence the Notables possess over the level of taxes depends upon the extent to which their aims fit within the system of beliefs dominant in the community. Within limits, they can influence the content of that belief system; but they cannot determine it wholly. Like the American creed of democracy and equality, other aspects of the local belief system contain elements of both rigidity and great flexibility; the belief system has precise injunctions and vague mandates; and it is chock-full of inconsistencies. Skilled leaders, exploiting these various elements in the belief system (yet always imprisoned within its constraints) can manipulate the flow of local costs and benefits in different ways; some of these are inconsistent with the dominant concern of the Economic Notables over low taxes.

Even a Republican mayor, elected in 1945 on a campaign to improve the public schools and city services after a long period of starvation, had to increase taxes, and both he and his Democratic successor, as we have just seen, had to raise assessments. Over the decade from 1947–57, total city expenditures more than doubled; income from taxes rose by more than 70 per cent as a result of increases in the rate, in assessments, and in new construction. In this same period, the total assessments of the ten largest real property owners in New Haven rose by nearly 85 per cent.

The Social and Economic Notables of today, then, are scarcely a ruling elite such as the patricians were. They are, however, frequently influential on specific decisions, particularly when these directly involve business prosperity. Moreover, politicians are wary of their potential influence and avoid policies that might unite the Notables in bitter opposition. Fortunately for the politician, it is easy to avoid the implacable hostility of the Notables, for living conditions and the belief system of the community have not—at least so far—generated demands for local policies markedly antagonistic to the goals of businessmen and Notables. What would happen if such demands ever developed is not easy to predict. But judging from the fate of the patricians, competitive politics would lead in the end to the triumph of numbers over Notability.

7. *Overview:* From Cumulative to Dispersed Inequalities

In the United States as a whole, an industrial society followed an agrarian society. In New Haven, an industrial society followed a hierarchical urban society dominated by a patrician oligarchy. In the agrarian society, political resources were dispersed in an approximation to equality such as the civilized world had never before seen. In the old oligarchy of New Haven, political resources were concentrated in the familiar pattern of hierarchical societies. Against the background of an agrarian society, the institutions and processes of industrial society produced a concentration of political resources. Against the background of oligarchy in New Haven, the institutions and processes of industrial society produced a dispersion of political resources.

But this dispersion did not recapture the equalitarian distribution of political resources that existed in agrarian America. Industrial society dispersed, it did not eradicate political inequality.

In the political system of the patrician oligarchy, political resources were marked by a cumulative inequality: when one individual was much better off than another in one resource, such as wealth, he was usually better off in almost every other resource—social standing, legitimacy, control over religious and educational institutions, knowledge, office. In the political system of today, inequalities in political resources remain, but they tend to be *noncumulative*. The political system of New Haven, then, is one of *dispersed inequalities*.

The patrician-Congregationalist-Federalist elite that ruled New Haven prior to 1840 was a tiny group that combined the highest social standing, education, and wealth with key positions in religion, the economy, and public life. The entrepreneurs drove a wedge into this unified elite; social standing and education remained with the patricians, but wealth and key positions in corporate and public life went to the new men of industry. With the rise of the ex-plebes there occurred a further fragmentation of political resources. Rising out of the newly created urban proletariat, of immigrant backgrounds and modest social standing, the ex-plebes had one political resource of extraordinary importance in a competitive political system: they were popular with the voters. Popularity gave them office, and office gave them other political resources, such as legality and city jobs. Office, legality, and jobs gave the ex-plebes influence over government decisions.

Within a century a political system dominated by one cohesive set of leaders had given way to a system dominated by many different sets of leaders, each having access to a different combination of political resources. It was, in short, a pluralist system. If the pluralist system was very far from being an oligarchy, it was also a long way from achieving the goal of political equality advocated by the philosophers of democracy and incorporated into the creed of democracy and equality practically every American professes to uphold.

An elite no longer rules New Haven. But in the strict democratic sense, the disappearance of elite rule has not led to the emergence of rule by the people. Who, then, rules in a pluralist democracy?

Book II

THE DISTRIBUTION OF INFLUENCE

8. *Overview:* The Ambiguity of Leadership

One of the difficulties that confronts anyone who attempts to answer the question, "Who rules in a pluralist democracy?" is the ambiguous relationship of leaders to citizens.

Viewed from one position, leaders are enormously influential—so influential that if they are seen only in this perspective they might well be considered a kind of ruling elite. Viewed from another position, however, many influential leaders seem to be captives of their constituents. Like the blind men with the elephant, different analysts have meticulously examined different aspects of the body politic and arrived at radically different conclusions. To some, a pluralistic democracy with dispersed inequalities is all head and no body; to others it is all body and no head.

Ambiguity in the relations of leaders and constituents is generated by several closely connected obstacles both to observation and to clear conceptualization. To begin with, the American creed of democracy and equality prescribes many forms and procedures from which the actual practices of leaders diverge. Consequently, to gain legitimacy for their actions leaders frequently surround their covert behavior with democratic rituals. These rituals not only serve to disguise reality and thus to complicate the task of observation and analysis, but—more important—in complex ways the very existence of democratic rituals, norms, and requirements of legitimacy based on a widely shared creed actually influences the behavior of both leaders and constituents even when democratic norms are violated. Thus the distinction between the rituals of power and the realities of power is frequently obscure.

Two additional factors help to account for this obscurity. First, among all the persons who influence a decision, some do so more directly than others in the sense that they are closer to the stage where concrete alternatives are initiated or vetoed in an explicit and immediate way. Indirect influence might be very great but comparatively difficult to observe and weigh. Yet to ignore indirect influence in analysis of the distribution of influence would be to exclude what might well prove to be a highly significant process of control in a pluralistic democracy.

Second, the relationship between leaders and citizens in a pluralistic democracy is frequently reciprocal: leaders influence the decisions of constituents, but the decisions of leaders are also determined in part by

what they think are, will be, or have been the preferences of their constituents. Ordinarily it is much easier to observe and describe the
distribution of influence in a political system where the flow of influence
is strongly in one direction (an asymmetrical or unilateral system, as it is
sometimes called) than in a system marked by strong reciprocal relations.
In a political system with competitive elections, such as New Haven's, it
is not unreasonable to expect that relationships between leaders and
constituents would normally be reciprocal.

One who sets out to observe, analyze, and describe the distribution of
influence in a pluralistic democracy will therefore encounter formidable
problems. It will, I believe, simplify the task of understanding New Haven
if I now spell out some of the theory and assumptions that guided our
study of the distribution of influence.

THE POLITICAL STRATUM

In New Haven, as in other political systems, a small stratum of individuals is much more highly involved in political thought, discussion, and
action than the rest of the population. These citizens constitute the political stratum.

Members of this stratum live in a political subculture that is partly
but not wholly shared by the great majority of citizens. Just as artists and
intellectuals are the principal bearers of the artistic, literary, and scientific
skills of a society, so the members of the political stratum are the main
bearers of political skills. If intellectuals were to vanish overnight, a
society would be reduced to artistic, literary, and scientific poverty. If
the political stratum were destroyed, the previous political institutions
of the society would temporarily stop functioning. In both cases, the
speed with which the loss could be overcome would depend on the
extent to which the elementary knowledge and basic attitudes of the elite
had been diffused. In an open society with widespread education and
training in civic attitudes, many citizens hitherto in the apolitical strata
could doubtless step into roles that had been filled by members of the
political stratum. However, sharp discontinuities and important changes
in the operation of the political system almost certainly would occur.

In New Haven, as in the United States, and indeed perhaps in all
pluralistic democracies, differences in the subcultures of the political and
the apolitical strata are marked, particularly at the extremes. In the
political stratum, politics is highly salient; among the apolitical strata, it
is remote. In the political stratum, individuals tend to be rather calculating
in their choice of strategies; members of the political stratum are, in a
sense, relatively rational political beings. In the apolitical strata, people
are notably less calculating; their political choices are more strongly
influenced by inertia, habit, unexamined loyalties, personal attachments,

emotions, transient impulses. In the political stratum, an individual's political beliefs tend to fall into patterns that have a relatively high degree of coherence and internal consistency; in the apolitical strata, political orientations are disorganized, disconnected, and unideological. In the political stratum, information about politics and the issues of the day is extensive; the apolitical strata are poorly informed. Individuals in the political stratum tend to participate rather actively in politics; in the apolitical strata citizens rarely go beyond voting and many do not even vote. Individuals in the political stratum exert a good deal of steady, direct, and active influence on government policy; in fact some individuals have a quite extraordinary amount of influence. Individuals in the apolitical strata, on the other hand, have much less direct or active influence on policies.

Communication within the political stratum tends to be rapid and extensive. Members of the stratum read many of the same newspapers and magazines; in New Haven, for example, they are likely to read the *New York Times* or the *Herald Tribune*, and *Time* or *Newsweek*. Much information also passes by word of mouth. The political strata of different communities and regions are linked in a national network of communications. Even in small towns, one or two members of the local political stratum usually are in touch with members of a state organization, and certain members of the political stratum of a state or any large city maintain relations with members of organizations in other states and cities, or with national figures. Moreover, many channels of communication not designed specifically for political purposes—trade associations, professional associations, and labor organizations, for example—serve as a part of the network of the political stratum.

In many pluralistic systems, however, the political stratum is far from being a closed or static group. In the United States the political stratum does not constitute a homogeneous class with well-defined class interests. In New Haven, in fact, the political stratum is easily penetrated by anyone whose interests and concerns attract him to the distinctive political culture of the stratum. It is easily penetrated because (among other reasons) elections and competitive parties give politicians a powerful motive for expanding their coalitions and increasing their electoral followings.

In an open pluralistic system, where movement into the political stratum is easy, the stratum embodies many of the most widely shared values and goals in the society. If popular values are strongly pragmatic, then the political stratum is likely to be pragmatic; if popular values prescribe reverence toward the past, then the political stratum probably shares that reverence; if popular values are oriented toward material gain and personal advancement, then the political stratum probably reflects these values; if popular values are particularly favorable to political,

social, or economic equality, then the political stratum is likely to emphasize equality. The apolitical strata can be said to "govern" as much
through the sharing of common values and goals with members of the
political stratum as by other means. However, if it were not for elections
and competitive parties, this sharing would—other things remaining the
same—rapidly decline.

Not only is the political stratum in New Haven not a closed group, but
its "members" are far from united in their orientations and strategies.
There are many lines of cleavage. The most apparent and probably the
most durable are symbolized by affiliations with different political parties.
Political parties are rival coalitions of leaders and subleaders drawn from
the members of the political stratum. Leaders in a party coalition seek to
win elections, capture the chief elective offices of government, and insure
that government officials will legalize and enforce policies on which the
coalition leaders can agree.

In any given period of time, various issues are salient within the
political stratum. Indeed, a political issue can hardly be said to exist
unless and until it commands the attention of a significant segment of the
political stratum. Out of all the manifold possibilities, members of the
political stratum seize upon some issues as important or profitable; these
then become the subject of attention within the political stratum. To be
sure, all the members of the political stratum may not initially agree that
a particular issue is worthy of attention. But whenever a sizable minority
of the legitimate elements in the political stratum is determined to bring
some question to the fore, the chances are high that the rest of the
political stratum will soon begin to pay attention.

Although political issues are sometimes generated by individuals in the
apolitical strata who begin to articulate demands for government action,
this occurs only rarely. Citizens in the apolitical strata are usually aware
of problems or difficulties in their own circle; through word of mouth or
the mass media they may become aware of problems faced by people in
other circles. But to be aware of a problem is by no means equivalent to
perceiving a political solution or even formulating a political demand.
These acts are ordinarily performed only by members of the political
stratum. Within the political stratum, issues and alternatives are often
formulated by intellectuals, experts, and reformers, whose views then
attract the support of professionals. This is how questions as abstract and
difficult as the proper rate of growth in the Gross National Product are
injected into national politics; and, as we shall see, this is roughly the
route by which urban redevelopment came into the politics of New Haven.

However, in gaining attention for issues, members of the political
stratum operate under constraints set by party politicians with an eye
on the next election. Despite the stereotype, party politicians are not

necessarily concerned *only* with winning elections, for the man who is a party politician in one role may, in another, be a member of a particular interest group, social stratum, neighborhood, race, ethnic group, occupation, or profession. In this role he may himself help to generate issues. However, simply qua party politician, he not only has a powerful incentive to search for politically profitable issues, but he has an equally strong motive for staying clear of issues he thinks will not produce a net gain in his votes in the next election.

Because of the ease with which the political stratum can be penetrated, whenever dissatisfaction builds up in some segment of the electorate party politicians will probably learn of the discontent and calculate whether it might be converted into a political issue with an electoral payoff. If a party politician sees no payoff, his interest is likely to be small; if he foresees an adverse effect, he will avoid the issue if he can. As a result, there is usually some conflict in the political stratum between intellectuals, experts, and others who formulate issues, and the party politicians themselves, for the first group often demands attention to issues in which the politicians see no profit and possibly even electoral damage.

The independence, penetrability, and heterogeneity of the various segments of the political stratum all but guarantee that any dissatisfied group will find spokesmen in the political stratum, but to have a spokesman does not insure that the group's problems will be solved by political action. Politicians may not see how they can gain by taking a position on an issue; action by government may seem to be wholly inappropriate; policies intended to cope with dissatisfaction may be blocked; solutions may be improperly designed; indeed, politicians may even find it politically profitable to maintain a shaky coalition by keeping tension and discontent alive and deflecting attention to irrelevant "solutions" or alternative issues.

In his search for profitable issues, the party politician needs to estimate the probable effects various actions he might take will have on the future votes of his constituents. Although he is generally unaware of it, he necessarily operates with theory, a set of hypotheses as to the factors that influence the decisions of various categories of voters and the rough weights to assign to these factors.

The subculture of the political stratum provides him with the relevant categories—businessmen, Italians, wage earners, and the like. It also furnishes him with information as to the voting tendencies of these groups, e.g., their predisposition to vote Democratic or Republican. Given a category and its voting tendency, the party politician typically operates on the simple but sound assumption that human responses can be influenced by rewards and deprivations, both past and prospective. His task then is to choose a course of action that will either reinforce the voting tendency of categories predisposed in favor of him or his party, or weaken the voting tendency of categories predisposed to vote against him or his party. This he does by actions that provide individuals in these categories with rewards or the expectation of rewards.

SOME POLITICAL AXIOMS

Most of the people in the political stratum at any given moment take for granted a number of assumptions so commonplace in the political culture of the time and so little subject to dispute that they function as "self-evident" axioms. The axioms include both factual and normative postulates. In New Haven, the most relevant current axioms among the political stratum would appear to be the following:

1. To build an effective political coalition, rewards must be conferred on (or at least promised to) individuals, groups, and various categories of citizens.

2. In devising strategies for building coalitions and allocating rewards, one must take into account a large number of different categories of citizens. It would be dangerous to formulate strategies on the assumption that most or all citizens can be divided into two or three categories, for a successful political coalition necessarily rests upon a multiplicity of groups and categories. (In the early decades of the century a minority in the political stratum, leaders of the Social Democratic and Socialist Labor parties, pursued a strategy that reflected a confident belief in the existence of a bipolar socioeconomic structure in which political beliefs and actions were almost wholly determined by working-class or white-collar ways of making a living. But because this strategy failed to win elections, it has never been widely approved in the political stratum, least of all among the party politicians in the two major parties.)

3. Although a variety of attributes are relevant to political strategy, many different attributes can either be subsumed under or are sometimes overridden by ethnic, racial, and religious affiliations.

4. In allocating rewards to individuals and groups, the existing socioeconomic structure must be taken as given, except for minor details. (The local political stratum has not been strongly reformist, certainly not on social and economic matters. Except perhaps for socialists, local reform movements have concentrated on defects in the political system, not the socioeconomic structure of the society. And except for a few men who dreamed and spoke of changing the face of the city, until recently the political stratum has assumed that the physical and economic features of the city are determined by forces beyond their control.)

5. Although a certain amount of legal chicanery is tolerable, legality and constitutionality are highly prized. The pursuit of illegal practices on a sizable scale is difficult to conceal; illegal actions by public officials ordinarily lead, when known, to loss of public office; unconstitutional

action is almost certain to become entangled in a complex network of judicial processes. The use of violence as a political weapon must be avoided; if it were used it would probably arouse widespread alarm and hostility.

6. The American creed of democracy and equality must always be given vigorous and vociferous support. No one who denies the validity of this creed has much chance of winning political office or otherwise gaining influence on the local scene. Among other things, the creed assumes that democracy is the best form of government, public officials must be chosen by majority vote, and people in the minority must have the right to seek majority support for their beliefs.[1]

7. In practice, of course, universalistic propositions in the American creed need to be qualified. Adherence to the creed as a general goal and a set of criteria for a good government and a good society does not mean that the creed is, or as a practical matter can be, fully applied in practice. (Some elements in the political stratum are deeply disturbed by the gap between ideal and reality. Most people in the political stratum, however, are probably either unaware of any sharp conflict between ideal and reality, or are indifferent to it, or take the gap for granted in much the same spirit that they accept the fact that religious behavior falls short of religious belief.)

LEADERS AND SUBLEADERS

In any durable association of more than a handful of individuals, typically a relatively small proportion of the people exercises relatively great direct influence over all the important choices bearing on the life of the association—its survival, for example, or its share in such community resources as wealth, power, and esteem, or the way these resources are shared within the association, or changes in the structure, activities, and dominant goals of the association, and so on. These persons are, by definition, the leaders. It is the leaders in New Haven whom the following chapters seek to identify and describe.

The goals and motives that animate leaders are evidently as varied as the dreams of men. They include greater income, wealth, economic security, power, social standing, fame, respect, affection, love, knowledge, curiosity, fun, the pleasure of exercising skill, delight in winning, esthetic satisfaction, morality, salvation, heroism, self-sacrifice, envy, jealousy, revenge, hate—whatever the whole wide range may be. Popular beliefs and folklore to the contrary, there is no convincing evidence at present

1. On the extent of belief in this creed in two cities (Ann Arbor, Michigan, and Tallahassee, Florida) see James W. Prothro and Charles M. Grigg, "Fundamental Principles of Democracy: Bases of Agreement and Disagreement," *Journal of Politics*, 22 (1960), 276–94. See also Ch. 28 below.

that any single common denominator of motives can be singled out in leaders of associations. We are not compelled, therefore, to accept the simple view that Moses, Jesus, Caligula, Savanarola, St. Ignatius, Abraham Lincoln, Boss Tweed, Mahatma Ghandi, Carrie Chapman Catt, Huey Long, and Joseph Stalin all acted from essentially the same motives.

To achieve their goals, leaders develop plans of action, or strategies. But actions take place in a universe of change and uncertainty; goals themselves emerge, take shape, and shift with new experiences. Hence a choice among strategies is necessarily based more on hunch, guesswork, impulse, and the assessment of imponderables than on scientific predictions. Adopting a strategy is a little bit like deciding how to look for a fuse box in a strange house on a dark night after all the lights have blown.

Ordinarily the goals and strategies of leaders require services from other individuals. (Both Christ and Lenin needed disciples to increase and rally their followers.) To perform these services more or less regularly, reliably, and skillfully, auxiliaries or subleaders are needed. The tasks of subleaders include aid in formulating strategies and policies; carrying out the dull, routine, time-consuming or highly specialized work of the eternal spear bearers, the doorbell ringers, the file clerks; recruiting and mobilizing the following; and, in a country like the United States where there exists a strong democratic ethos, helping by their very existence to furnish legitimacy to the actions of the leaders by providing a democratic façade.

To secure the services of subleaders, leaders must reward them in some fashion. Here too the range of rewards seems to be as broad as the spectrum of human motives. However, some kinds of rewards are easier to manipulate than others. In business organizations, the rewards are mainly financial ones, which are probably the easiest of all to manipulate. In many other kinds of associations—and evidently to some extent even in business—either financial rewards are too low to attract and hold subleaders capable of performing the tasks at the minimum levels required by the leaders, or within a certain range other kinds of rewards are more important to the auxiliaries than financial ones. Leaders may therefore contrive to pay off their auxiliaries with nonfinancial rewards like social standing, prestige, fun, conviviality, the hope of salvation, and so on.

Thus the survival of an association of leaders and subleaders depends on frequent transactions between the two groups in which the leaders pay off the subleaders in return for their services. To pay off the subleaders, leaders usually have to draw on resources available only outside the association. Sometimes leaders can obtain these resources from outside by coercion, particularly if they happen to control the single most effective institution for coercion: the government. This is one reason—but by no means the only one—why government is always such an important pawn in struggles among leaders. Ordinarily, however, the association must produce something that will appeal to outsiders, who then contribute resources that serve, directly or indirectly, to maintain the association. Probably the most important direct contribution of these outsiders—let us call them constituents—is money; their most important indirect contribution is votes, which can be converted into office and thus into various other resources.

In some associations, subleaders themselves may be put to work on tasks that produce a surplus available, directly or indirectly, for allocation by the leaders. Political party leaders in New Haven, for example, appoint as many of their subleaders as they can to municipal jobs. The income from these jobs is a payoff to the subleaders for their party work. Subleaders in city jobs are in turn assessed at election time for campaign contributions; these contributions provide a "surplus" that may be spent to pay off subleaders who don't have city jobs.

Because every person's time is to some extent limited, every activity competes with every other. Therefore it is not enough for leaders merely to provide *some* rewards for subleaders; they must furnish rewards big enough to attract subleaders they want from other associations or from individual, family, friendly, neighborly pastimes like watching television, mowing the lawn, taking the family to the beach, playing cards, drinking beer in a tavern, reading the newspapers, and so on.

In a rough way, associations can be classified as either vocational or avocational. In vocational associations the subleaders have full-time jobs for which they are paid; in avocational associations they do not. To the extent that an association can produce services for which others will pay, as in the case of a business organization, auxiliaries can be given full-time employment. But many associations cannot or do not sell their services for money because to do so would be inconsistent with the leaders' goals or the loyalty of auxiliaries and followings. (The sale of indulgences, for example, helped generate the Reformation that split Protestantism from the Roman Catholic Church.) If an association also lacks other means of securing a large income, such as levying assessments on followings, it must necessarily remain avocational. Because it cannot lure subleaders away from other activities by paying them adequately, an avocational association often resorts to other kinds of rewards, such as prestige, social status, and conviviality.

POLICIES

To achieve their own goals, secure the services of subleaders, and obtain outside support from constituents, leaders usually find it a useful strategy to commit themselves (or appear to commit themselves) to certain choices they will make under some specified conditions. These commitments represent their policies—or at any rate their *promises* as to policy. For many reasons, not the least being the general uncertainty and constant flux of events, leaders frequently do not live up to their promises. But their proposed or actual policies often contain a direct or indirect, actual or expected payoff *of some kind* to subleaders and constituents. The attempt to satisfy the preferences of both subleaders and constituents by policies is one of the commonest sources of conflict that leaders of political associations encounter.

Despite some general theories of considerable persuasiveness, the precise reasons why an individual prefers one alternative to another are not so well understood that any general and comprehensive explanation for all preferences can be offered with confidence. (Part of the uncertainty arises because of persistent doubts that a white rat in a maze is exactly equivalent to a human being in a quandary.) Whatever the reasons may be, individuals do have preferences on matters of policy. Sometimes these preferences are extraordinarily strong, sometimes weak. Sometimes one's preferences can be explained by one's hopes that a policy will produce concrete benefits to oneself or to the people nearest one's center of life. In other cases (though I take it as axiomatic that any policy one approves of is expected to be rewarding in *some* sense) the benefits may be general or, if specific, may be conferred on individuals remote from oneself. I do not mean to suggest that what would ordinarily be called altruism plays anything like a dominant role in politics, but it would be misleading to exclude it altogether. Not everyone ceases to be interested in good public schools when his own children grow up; advocates of public housing usually turn out to be middle-class people who have no need for it themselves; individuals have pressed for compulsory smallpox vaccination even though they and their families were already immunized; dentists have generally supported the fluoridation of public water supplies. One could multiply the examples.

Policies are an important means, though not the only means, by which leaders attract the support they need from constituents. In fact, policies sometimes win over constituents who then identify themselves with the association more or less permanently and can be regularly counted on to support the association even when some of its leaders and policies change. These constituents make up the *following* of the association.

The policies that leaders promise to constituents and followings—I shall call them *overt* policies—are not always identical to, or indeed even consistent with, the covert commitments they make to their subleaders. From the point of view of a leader concerned with the task of building his following, it would be ideal if his subleaders were indifferent to his overt policies, for this would give him freedom to develop overt policies exclusively adapted to the desires of constituents and followings. But this kind of complete independence from the desired subleaders is almost impossible for a leader to attain. It could exist only where the flow of rewards for which subleaders gave their services did not depend at all on the overt policies of leaders. For example, such a situation might exist where a group of subleaders needed an excuse to justify the convivial activities generated by their service in the association and therefore happily contributed their services without regard to any policies of the leaders simply in order to maintain the camaraderie they experienced in the association.

By providing jobs, certain kinds of vocational associations may also come close to liberating the overt policies of leaders from the demands of subleaders, particularly if the role of the subleader as it is defined in the culture is confined simply to doing his job and receiving his wage or salary without caring about or having a right to participate in the shaping of the overt policies of the association. In business organizations, rank-and-file employees are usually assumed to have only slight interest in the overt policies of the business other than those touching on their own wages, hours, and working conditions.

However, political associations, at least in the United States and certainly in New Haven, are more nearly avocational than vocational. (For the leaders, to be sure, they are often vocational—although, paradoxically, the virtues of amateurism are so highly regarded that leaders whose major occupation and source of income is politics often try to disguise the fact in order to avoid the epithet "professional politician.") Political associations, unlike business firms, do not produce services or commodities that can be openly sold for a price. Indeed the laws of the state of Connecticut as of other states flatly prohibit transactions of this kind. In New Haven, the amount of income legally or illegally secured by an association engaged in politics is tiny compared with that of a business firm with an equivalent number of full-time and part-time workers. Nor are nonfinancial rewards easily obtainable. The esteem among persons of high social standing that political officials seem to have enjoyed in New Haven in the nineteenth century has probably declined. Even the amount of influence open to a subleader is usually slight. (One minor subleader encountered in New Haven in the course of our study displayed his influence by "fixing" parking tickets for his friends. On investigation, it turned out that he fixed the tickets by paying the fines out of his own pocket.)

Despite the avocational character of political associations in New Haven, two processes help to reduce conflicts between the overt and covert policies of political leaders and to produce a loyal corps of subleaders who, while concerned with covert policies, are often indifferent to overt policies.

First, a prerequisite to success for both the overt and covert policies of political leaders ordinarily is to win elections and thereby attain the rights and powers of office. Office is necessary if jobs, contracts, and other favors are to be dispensed to subleaders; office is also necessary if overt policies are to be executed. Hence subleaders are motivated to win elections and to support whatever overt policies are needed to win, as long as these do not threaten covert postelection commitments.

Secondly, even if a subleader is initially attracted into an association because of the overt policies of the leaders, participation generates new rewards. Because an association provides opportunities for conviviality, it can come to fill a normal human need for friendliness, comradeship, respect, and social intercourse. And a subleader who participates in an association may strengthen his identification with it so that it becomes an extension of his own personality; the victories and defeats of the association are then equivalent to victories and defeats for the subleader himself.

These two processes, however, do not always eliminate conflict between the overt and covert policies of political leaders. Conflict is likely to arise, for example, whenever large elements of the political stratum are developing stricter standards of political morality. In particular, if the middle- and upper-class segments of the political stratum increase in size, then demands for extending civil service requirements, professionalism, public review, fixed procedures, and neutrality are likely to become more widespread and more insistent. Bureaucratization and middle-class influence in local politics are likely to go together. Conflicts may also arise if overt policies with seemingly great popularity among constituents require structural changes in the organization of government that would make it more difficult to honor traditional kinds of covert policies. In New Haven, as we shall see, an attempt to reform the city charter produced just such a conflict.

In these and many other similar cases, political leaders face a painful dilemma, for they must either fight the "organization" or lose the support of some of their constituents and perhaps even hitherto reliable followings. Either choice may involve electoral defeat and possibly the end of a political career.

DEMOCRACY, LEADERSHIP, AND MINORITY CONTROL

It is easy to see why observers have often pessimistically concluded that the internal dynamics of political associations create forces alien to popular control and hence to democratic institutions. Yet the characteristics I have described are not necessarily dysfunctional to a pluralistic democracy in which there exists a considerable measure of popular control over the policies of leaders, for minority control by leaders within associations is not necessarily inconsistent with popular control over leaders through electoral processes.

For example, suppose that (1) a leader of a political association feels a strong incentive for winning an election; (2) his constituents comprise most of the adult population of the community; (3) nearly all of his constituents are expected to vote; (4) voters cast their ballot without receiving covert rewards or punishments as a direct consequence of the way they vote; (5) voters give heavy weight to the overt policies of a candidate in making their decision as to how they will vote; (6) there are rival candidates offering alternative policies; and (7) voters have a good deal of information about the policies of the candidates. In these circumstances, it is almost certain that leaders of political associations would tend to choose overt policies they believed most likely to win the support of a majority of adults in the community. Even if the policies of political associations were usually controlled by a tiny minority of leaders in each association, the policies of the leaders who won elections to the chief elective offices in local government would tend to reflect the preferences of the populace. I do not mean to suggest that any political system actually fulfills all these conditions, but to the extent that it does the leaders who directly control the decisions of political associations are themselves influenced in their own choices of policies by their assumptions as to what the voting populace wants.

Although this is an elementary point, it is critical to an understanding of the chapters that follow. We shall discover that in each of a number of key sectors of public policy, a few persons have great *direct* influence on the choices that are made; most citizens, by contrast, seem to have rather little direct influence. Yet it would be unwise to underestimate the extent to which voters may exert *indirect* influence on the decisions of leaders by means of elections.

In a political system where key offices are won by elections, where legality and constitutionality are highly valued in the political culture, and where nearly everyone in the political stratum publicly adheres to a doctrine of democracy, it is likely that the political culture, the prevailing attitudes of the political stratum, and the operation of the political system itself will be shaped by the role of elections. Leaders who in one context are enormously influential and even rather free from demands by their constituents may reveal themselves in another context to be involved in tireless efforts to adapt their policies to what they think their constituents want.

To be sure, in a pluralistic system with dispersed inequalities, the direct influence of leaders on policies extends well beyond the norms implied in the classical models of democracy developed by political philosophers.

But if the leaders lead, they are also led. Thus the relations between leaders, subleaders, and constituents produce in the distribution of influence a stubborn and pervasive ambiguity that permeates the entire political system.

SOME HYPOTHESES

Given these assumptions, one might reasonably expect to find in the political system of New Haven that the distribution of influence over important decisions requiring the formal assent of local governmental officials is consistent with the following hypotheses:

First, only a small proportion of the citizens will have much *direct* influence on decisions in the sense of directly initiating proposals for policies subsequently adopted or successfully vetoing the proposals of others.

Second, the leaders—i.e., citizens with relatively great direct influence —will have a corps of auxiliaries or subleaders to help them with their tasks.

Third, because a democratic creed is widely subscribed to throughout the political stratum, and indeed throughout the population, the public or overt relationships of influence between leaders and subleaders will often be clothed in the rituals and ceremonies of "democratic" control, according to which the leaders are only the spokesmen or agents of the subleaders, who are "representatives" of a broader constituency.

Fourth, because of the need to win elections in order to hold key elective offices, leaders will attempt to develop followings of loyal supporters among their constituents.

Fifth, because the loyalty and support of subleaders, followings, and other constituents are maintained by memories of past rewards or the expectation of future rewards, leaders will shape their policies in an attempt to insure a flow of rewards to all those elements whose support is needed. Consequently, in some circumstances, subleaders, followings, and other constituents will have significant *indirect* influence on the decisions of leaders. The existence of this indirect influence is an important source of ambiguity in understanding and interpreting the actions of leaders in a pluralistic system.

Finally, conflicts will probably occur from time to time between leaders' overt policies, which are designed to win support from constituents, and their covert policies, which are shaped to win the support of subleaders or other leaders. The keener the political competition, the more likely it is that leaders will resolve these conflicts in favor of their overt commitments.

To determine whether these propositions actually fit the political system of New Haven, I now propose to turn to three "issue-areas" where it is possible to examine decisions to see what processes of influence are at work. Decisions in two of these areas, public education and urban redevelopment, require the formal assent of local government officials at many points. The third, the process of making nominations in the two major parties for local elective offices, is only quasi-governmental, but I have chosen it on the assumption that whoever controls nominations might be presumed to occupy a critical role in any effort to gain the assent of local officials.

9. Leaders in Political Nominations

The ambiguous nature of leadership in a pluralistic system with sharp competition for elective offices is nowhere more evident than in the influence of party leaders over nominations.

THE LEGAL THEORY OF PARTY

What might be called the "legal theory of party" in New Haven provides for thoroughly democratic control over nominations by all those who, in the words of the election laws, are "enrolled adherents" of the party—the registered party "members," as they are often called, or as we might call them the "active party followings." Anyone legally entitled to vote may enroll in the party of his choice; though he cannot enroll in more than one party at the same time, he incurs no obligations by enrolling. Since any American citizen twenty-one years old or over must (with only a few exceptions) be admitted as a voter if he has lived a year in Connecticut and six months in the town where he seeks to vote, all save a tiny fraction of adults are legally free to enroll in one party or the other.

In the legal theory of party, control over nominations reposes solidly with the enrolled members. Although the rules of the two parties vary slightly within the permissible limits of the state election laws, roughly speaking the legal theory thrusts sovereignty into the hands of enrolled members voting secretly in primaries in their own neighborhoods, the wards. Thus the party members in each of New Haven's thirty-three wards gather in a primary every second year to elect their ward leaders. Republicans elect a ward committee, which in turn chooses a chairman and a vice-chairman. Democrats elect a chairman and a chairwoman who then appoint a nominating committee. The two leaders from each ward also constitute the city-wide governing council of the party, the town committee. The town committee in turn elects its own officers.

Nominations for public office, according to the legal theory, are made either directly or indirectly by party members. Nominations of candidates for positions on the Board of Aldermen (which consists of one alderman from each ward) originate in the nominating committees in the wards as recommendations to the town committee. If the town committee endorses the nominee for alderman presented by a ward, and if no opposing slate is submitted by any party members in that ward, the nomination recommended by the ward committee is automatically adopted. If an opposing slate is presented, the contest is decided by party members voting secretly in primaries in the particular ward. Republican party rules provide for a primary contest in all cases where "any registered Republican or Republicans of New Haven . . . submit a slate of nominees in opposition to those of the ward nominating committee." The rules of the Democratic party are silent on this point, but under the state election laws any faction that can muster the signatures of 5 per cent of the enrolled party members on a petition in behalf of their nominee can legally require a secret primary.

Candidates for city-wide offices—the mayor and thirteen other officials —are nominated indirectly by the rank-and-file adherents of the party. Democrats allow the town committee to nominate their candidates for city-wide offices; Republicans require a convention. The Republican convention usually numbers around two hundred delegates, all elected in wards in roughly the same way aldermanic candidates are nominated. Candidates for the state House of Representatives and Senate are also nominated in conventions made up of delegates from towns and senatorial districts; both in the legal theory and in actual practice the nomination procedure of these offices is about the same as that for mayor, but since they are not central to our story I shall say no more about them.

REALITY VERSUS LEGAL THEORY

Under the legal theory of party, then, rank-and-file members can control nominations by democratic means; to do so they need only to exercise their well-established legal rights. In fact, however, the process runs flatly counter to this pattern in three ways: (1) the enrolled adherents of each party are only a minority of the party followings; (2) the members who are active in caucuses and primaries are a minority of all the members; and (3) the whole paraphernalia of democratic procedures is employed not so much to insure control from below as to give legitimacy and acceptability to the candidates selected by the leaders. From a reconstruction of the events leading up to the nominations for mayor over the past two decades, based in large part on the accounts of leading participants, it appears typical that in each of the two major parties the mayoralty candidate is selected prior to the nominating convention by a handful of party leaders who usually but not always are also on the town committee. When the key leaders of a party agree, possibly at the end of a period of negotiation, their candidate is presented to the nominating convention and receives the nomination by acclamation. The number of persons who have participated in these decisive negotiations and influenced the outcome seems never to have been more than a half dozen in recent years; sometimes the number has been even smaller.

The distribution of direct influence on nominations for mayor and aldermen might be thought of in the shape of a triangle. The broad base consists of the voters. In the election for mayor in 1959, about 80 per cent of the registered voters went to the polls, and in an unusually lopsided election they split their votes about five to three for the Democratic candidate. (Table 9.1) The bulk of the voters had had virtually no *direct*

TABLE 9.1. *The political parties, 1959*

	Number	Percentage of all registered voters
DEMOCRATIC PARTY		
Voted Democratic (mayor)	36,694	50
Democratic followers[a]		
"strong" 14,700		20
"weak" 15,400		21
	30,100	41
Enrolled Democrats	21,850	30
Active Democrats[b]	11,700	16
Active in nominations[c]	4,400	6
Leaders controlling nominations	3–5	0.005
REPUBLICAN PARTY		
Voted Republican (mayor)	22,710	31
Republican followers[a]		
"strong" 8,750		12
"weak" 5,150		7
	13,900	19
Enrolled Republicans	7,600	10
Active Republicans[b]	11,000	15
Active in nominations[c]	1,500	2
Leaders controlling nominations	4–6	0.006

a. From survey data; excludes "independent" Democrats and Republicans. "Strong" or "weak" was determined by the following questions: "Generally speaking, do you usually think of yourself as a Republican, a Democrat, or what?" If the answer was Republican or Democrat, "Would you call yourself a strong Republican (Democrat) or a not very strong Republican (Democrat)?"

b. From survey data; includes only "strong" and "weak" Democrats and Republicans active in at least 5 ways—contribute money, attend meetings, try to persuade others, belong to a political organization, work for party or candidate.

c. From survey data.

influence on the process of nominations, yet their indirect influence was very great indeed, since the party leaders were anxious to present the candidate who had the greatest electoral appeal. Around 60 per cent of the total number of registered voters might be considered followers of one party or another; these are persons who usually think of themselves as Republicans or Democrats.[1] Like the voters in general, the followers have negligible direct influence on nominations, but leaders take into account the characteristics of their followings—particularly the ethnic characteristics—in trying to decide what kind of candidate will have the greatest appeal. Thus in 1959, when Mayor Lee was running for his fourth two-year term on the Democratic ticket and former Mayor Celentano refused to run on the Republican ticket, the Republican leaders settled on another candidate of Italian extraction, James Valenti; the choice was intended, among other things, to appeal to an important ethnic group in the Republican following.

A smaller group of citizens, about 40 per cent, were enrolled or registered as Democrats or Republicans. About three out of four of these were Democrats. In the legal theory of party, these citizens determine the nominations; in fact, their direct influence is small. Still, for the ward leaders, they are constituents; battles for the votes of enrolled party members sometimes take place in ward caucuses and primaries in contests for party offices or even for elective offices. Hence party leaders at ward and city levels cultivate the enrolled members in order to secure their votes in caucuses and primaries.

Many of the enrolled members are, of course, inactive. In 1959 about half the enrolled Democrats gave some signs of party activity; among Republicans, evidently some persons who were not enrolled nevertheless were active in behalf of the party in various ways. A much smaller proportion, however, seems to have been active to any significant degree in nominations: only about 6 per cent of the registered voters in our sample claimed some activity in Democratic nominations and about 2 per cent in Republican nominations.

In each party there are several hundred subleaders in party positions or elective office. Except for the leaders themselves, these men have the greatest influence on nominations; they work in the wards, get out the vote on election day, perform small favors, organize a ward following that can be counted on to support their candidates in caucuses and primaries, and form a potential source of opposition to incumbent leaders. A rising man in the party who seeks to win acceptance from the leadership, or even to overthrow it, ordinarily begins by building up a corps of loyal supporters among the subleaders; he expands his support from one ward to the next until finally he must be listened to on nominations. This, as we shall see in a moment, was the pattern followed by two men of Italian stock, George DiCenzo and William Celentano, who ultimately

1. In our survey of registered voters, the question was phrased: "Generally speaking, do you usually think of yourself as a Republican, a Democrat, or what?"

attained support in enough wards to constitute a powerful—for a time, indeed, the dominant—faction within the Republican party. When one assesses the relative influence of two party leaders over party actions —Golden and Lee, for example—in effect one must attempt to calculate how many subleaders in the wards would support one or the other in case of conflict.

Except for the rare instance of the subleader who seeks to challenge the top leadership, most subleaders are content to permit a few top leaders to negotiate and ultimately to decide on nominations. The function of the subleader in the typical case is to "go along" loyally and thus provide a suitable democratic façade for the actions of the party leaders.

PARTY DEMOCRACY: RITUAL

Indeed one way to interpret the whole process of nominations is to view it essentially as a creation and instrumentality of the leaders, shaped to their needs and purposes.

Until 1955, when the state legislature passed a law providing for direct primaries under certain specified conditions, it was in the interest of party leaders to confine enrollments to a small loyal band of easily controlled adherents. About three-fourths of the total adult population ordinarily take the trouble to register as voters in New Haven; although the turnout at elections varies, about 80–90 per cent of the registered voters usually go to the polls. But only about two-fifths of the registered voters are enrolled in one of the two parties, in part because in the past party leaders found it easier to control smaller numbers. The new law in 1955 undermined this postulate. In the event of a direct primary under this law, small party enrollment conceivably might be more of a liability to the party leaders than an asset. For one thing, certain dissident subleaders who were strong in some wards might find it easier to challenge the party leaders in a city-wide primary if the number of party members in the remaining wards was relatively small. In the Democratic party, the leaders were also concerned about the possibility of a state-wide primary over nominations for governor or U.S. senator. Nominations for state-wide offices had always been settled in party conventions at Hartford, but under the 1955 law an aspiring candidate who received 20 per cent of the votes on any roll call at the nominating convention could require a state-wide direct primary. The possibility that Mayor Lee himself might try to obtain the nomination for senator and precipitate a direct primary was by no means out of the question. Because of their small Democratic registration, the New Haven leaders could be seriously handicapped in a contest with other large cities where Democratic registrations were larger. Hence in 1959 the triumvirate leading the Democratic party in New Haven (John Golden, Mayor Lee, and Lee's director of public works, Arthur Barbieri) concluded that safety lay in numbers and reversed their long-standing strategy of keeping the party rolls down. Both the triumvirate and the opposing faction engaged in an intensive campaign to enroll Democrats. As a direct result of their efforts, Democratic enrollments in New Haven rose from 16,500 in June to nearly 22,000 in September when the primaries for local offices were held.

But even the enrolled party members rarely use their legal right to participate in nominations. The turnout for the caucuses and ward primaries at which ward leaders are elected is usually negligible; often only the ward leaders show up, accompanied perhaps by a few members of the nominating committee. Rank-and-file opposition to the nominations made by the leaders is virtually unknown; in the absence of a faction of dissident subleaders in the party, the rank and file are unlikely to participate at all in the nominating process. Even when leaders of rival factions create the opportunity, only a minority of the enrolled members participates. In 1959, when the most widely organized primary contest in memory took place in the Democratic party, less than half the registered Democrats turned out.

This contest in 1959 amply demonstrated the firm control wielded over Democratic nominations by the triumvirate. Their control was disputed by B. Fred Damiani, leader of the Twelfth Ward, a thorn in the flesh of the triumvirate, and a stubborn man on whom the usual techniques of pacification had not worked. The party leaders had even made him an assistant corporation counsel in the hope of quieting him down; then when Damiani's irritations and aspirations still proved to be unyielding, he lost his city job. But neither the carrot nor the stick worked. By 1959 he was determined to challenge the power of the triumvirate in open battle. He sought the nomination for mayor and created a rival slate of candidates for three other city-wide offices and for sixteen of the thirty-three positions on the Board of Aldermen. He was crushed in the primaries by a vote of more than four to one; his candidates for the three other city-wide nominations were beaten by even larger margins; and his aldermanic candidates lost in every ward except his own, where his man, the incumbent alderman from the ward, squeaked through with a bare majority of the primary votes.

The fact that Damiani lost, and that other dissident leaders had lost before him, did not mean of course that someday a rival faction might not win. But even if a new faction were to win, the almost certain consequence would be to replace one small group with another.

Control over nominations in the Republican party furnishes a good case in point. Since the days of the Ullmans there have been a succession of Republican leaders in New Haven. The Ullmans were defeated during the twenties by advancing age and the enormously powerful state boss,

J. Henry Roraback. Their mantle first passed to a Roraback henchman, Clarence Willard; after Roraback's suicide and Willard's disgrace in a series of notorious exposures known as the Waterbury scandals, local leadership was inherited by one of Willard's helpers, a genial Irishman, Frank Lynch. Lynch was, however, unable to stave off the rise of a new faction led by a young lawyer of Italian extraction, George DiCenzo, and an undertaker of high standing in the New Haven Italian community, William Celentano.

By the 1930s, as we have already seen, the Italians of New Haven were in the second stage of political assimilation, while the Irish held the key positions in the Democratic party and received most of the jobs in city hall. Discrimination against Italians by Irish Democrats was strongly felt; even today, a slight provocation is sufficient to cause humiliating memories and angry resentments to rise to the surface among many members of the older generation of Italians in New Haven. For a young Italian with political ambitions, the Republican party offered more opportunities than the Democratic, particularly in view of the work performed a generation earlier by the Ullmans and the fact that Republicans outnumbered Democrats in the state as a whole.

DiCenzo's rise in the Republican party is an excellent example of a successful challenge of incumbent leaders by a subleader. Like Celentano, DiCenzo represented the new Italian middle class. DiCenzo grew up in New Haven, attended the University of Maryland Law School, and returned to New Haven to practice law. He enrolled as a Republican and was active in the 1927 mayoralty campaign. The presidential campaign of 1928, however, affected him as it did many other Catholics; he became head of an Al Smith Club, participated vigorously in the campaign and even ran for justice of the peace on the Democratic ticket. When the election was over, however, he concluded that his future lay with the Republican party, in part no doubt because as a lawyer he was not unmindful of the patronage in the state judicial system, and the Republicans controlled the state courts.

Allying himself with the Roraback group led by Willard and Lynch, he set out to take over the six wards that comprised the Tenth Senatorial District. By means of state patronage, influence in the courts, enrolling friends and sympathizers on the party lists, legal aid, and other activities, DiCenzo built up a corps of followers in each ward. In a decade he controlled every ward in the district; by virtue of this control, he was automatically accepted among the smaller coterie of leaders who effectively chose the candidates for mayor. In 1939 DiCenzo had supported another newcomer in Republican politics, William Celentano; in 1941, partly because of DiCenzo's argument that a candidate of Italian extraction would have a hard time winning as long as Italy was considered a hostile country, Celentano did not run. Celentano and DiCenzo held to this strategy until 1945, when DiCenzo entered into an electoral coalition with Celentano. Together, they secured Celentano's nomination for mayor. Celentano won the election and remained in office through four terms until he was defeated by Lee in 1953. During this period, DiCenzo served as corporation counsel to the city and was Celentano's closest political ally and a powerful force in the party.

Though Lynch was less than enthusiastic about the key role DiCenzo and Celentano played in the party, he had no alternative but to go along with them. Of the four state senatorial districts into which New Haven is divided, DiCenzo carried one in his pocket and had great influence in a second. Lynch controlled a third; Lynch's well-to-do allies in effect controlled the fourth. As the most popular candidate the Republicans could muster, Celentano could have the nomination any time he wished, but despite occasional flirtations with the nomination, after his defeat in 1953 he invariably refused to run. In one case his refusal came so close to the election that Lynch's faction was caught unprepared, and after several hurried and unsuccessful attempts to pass the poisoned chalice to men whose prudence exceeded their heroism, the ill-fated nomination finally came to rest with an eager victim whom no one expected to win— an expectation that was roundly confirmed in the following election.

In both parties, nomination of the incumbent mayor by his own party is assured. The resources at a mayor's disposal are much too great for any dissident faction in his party to overcome; thus Damiani's fight against the renomination of Lee in 1959 was widely and accurately foreseen to be futile. In addition to patronage and a wide assortment of other favors and punishments available to the chief executive of the city, an incumbent mayor has already demonstrated his capacity to win at least one election. Party workers are unlikely to be impressed, therefore, by the prospects awaiting them if they support the leader of a rival faction. When a party is out of office, factionalism is more likely. Thus in 1949 when the Republicans were in power, the leadership of the Democratic party was seriously challenged; Golden was, as one of the participants put it later, fighting for his political life. But in 1959, as we have seen, with the mayoralty once more in the hands of the Democrats no one doubted that Golden, Lee, and Barbieri could easily crush the Damiani forces. Likewise when the Republicans were in power from 1945 to 1953 Celentano's renomination was taken for granted; certainly the Lynch faction made no serious effort to oppose him. After 1953, however, when the Republicans were out of office, the two factions constituted an uneasy and mutually suspicious coalition. Lynch sought to weaken the hold of his opponents on the Italian population by supporting **Henry DeVita** as town chairman, and the Lynch faction became the **Lynch-DeVita** faction. But because the Lynch-DeVita faction lacked a strong candidate, they were forced into a biennial ritual of sounding out Celentano, being rejected, turning to a willing but foredoomed victim, and suffering catastrophe in the election. Nonetheless, the leaders of the two factions have always managed to settle their differences in private, present the convention with a single slate, and receive the unanimous endorsement of the convention on the first ballot.

With only a few differences, aldermanic nominations are a small-scale replica of mayoralty nominations. Ordinarily the initiative for recruiting suitable candidates lies in the wards, but party leaders often intervene directly, and usually they have no difficulty either in getting their own candidates accepted by the ward committee or in denying nominations to hopefuls they find objectionable. Unless incumbent aldermen have alienated the party leaders or decline to run, they, like mayors, are automatically renominated. On rare occasions a ward leader may have enough strength in his own right to force an unwanted aldermanic candidate on the party leaders, as Damiani succeeded in doing in the Twelfth Ward in 1959. But a ward leader in this situation is in a position of inherent instability; either his strength must improve outside his own ward to the point where he is accepted into the inner circle, as with DiCenzo in the Republican party, or he is likely to be wholly isolated and ultimately cut down.

FUNCTIONS OF THE RITUAL

One might well wonder why party leaders bother to surround their control over nominations with such an elaborate democratic façade. There seem to be at least four reasons: (1) democratic ceremonials and codes help to clothe the decisions of the leaders with legitimacy; (2) they arouse and strengthen the loyalties of the subleaders; (3) they provide an orderly means of adjudicating disputes; and (4) they make it easier for new social elements to find a place in the party. Although much of the time the process is purely ceremonial, it *can* entail something more than ceremony; like the elaborate duelling codes developed in seventeenth-century France, the ceremonials are the surface manifestations of a code within which grim combat can take place. In a similar way, the nomination system provides for democratic *ceremonials* plus *a code of combat*.

The use of ritual, ceremonial, and pageantry to give legitimacy and propriety to important actions in the life of an association is so widespread in human societies that it should astonish no one to discover that modern democratic societies have also created their own ceremonials. Nor is it surprising that in a community where the democratic ethos is powerful and traditional the rituals take on predominantly democratic aspects rather than, say, the decorum and pageantry of a monarchy. It would be going too far to say that the rituals are entirely hollow and deceptive. As is often true with ceremonials in other areas of life, the meaning of political ritual to the participants is often ambiguous; in New Haven few participants appear to be wholly deceived about what goes on, but to many of them the *precise* nature of reality remains cloudy and even a little mysterious. In any case, without some such process the legitimacy of the leaders' control over nominations would surely dissolve as quickly as that of the Federalist patricians when they were confronted with citizens who no longer believed in the divine right of wellborn Congregationalists to dominate political institutions. Since the demise of the patricians as a ruling class, democratic ceremonials have come to be one of the conventional means for legitimizing leadership.

If leaders, subleaders, and followings all find democratic forms useful for gaining acceptability, the ceremonials also serve a second purpose important to the leaders. The whole symbolic process of participating in nominations helps to activate the subleaders for work in the forthcoming campaign. The ceremonies are in this respect not unlike the traditional tribal rites prescribed for warriors before battle. The interest of the subleader is stimulated, his loyalty is reinforced, his sense of self-esteem is enhanced, and his willingness to work for the election of his party's candidates is strengthened when he meets, observes, and listens to the leaders and participates with the party faithful in the critical task of nominating candidates.

A third function of the process is that it furnishes an orderly method for settling disputes among the leaders and thus helps to forestall disaster to the party. Since some conflict over nominations is probably unavoidable, unless means of adjudication were agreed on in advance by the leaders the party might soon degenerate into a state of hopeless factionalism. The elaborate ceremonial of nominations, with its ultimate ritualistic appeal to the convention or the town committee, serves as a framework within which disputes can be settled without tearing the party apart. The implicit code of rules is widely understood; if it is violated the dispute can be adjudicated by means of the explicit party rules and state statutes regulating the nominating process. Although the explicit rules are silent on questions of cohesion, loyalty, and unanimity, the implicit rules impose a taboo on any attempt to carry factional disputes beyond the court of last appeal, the convention or town committee. Indeed the whole nominating process is governed by a widely shared expectation in the political subculture of New Haven that no matter how bitter the quarrels may be, disputes will ordinarily be settled behind closed doors without appeal to convention or town committee; in the exceptional case when conflict does reach these bodies, once the decision has been made all the participants are expected to forget internal dissensions and unite to smite down the common enemy. Although dissident factions do not always accept decisions against them —do not, that is, adhere strictly to the unwritten code—the fact that the party leaders have resorted to the accepted method for resolving disputes is usually enough to guarantee that the loyalty of subleaders to the party remains unimpaired.

Finally, democratic ceremonials and implicit codes make it less likely that new social elements will be excluded from the party. In a competitive political system within a changing society, a party that neglects any important potential source of support decreases its chances of survival. Nothing in the ceremonies or in the codes according to which nominations are made completely precludes the possibility that a party will commit suicide; but the process makes it less likely—precisely because the common understandings include not *merely* ceremonial but implicit and explicit rules with varying degrees of authority and acceptability. Taken together, the ceremonials and rules increase the likelihood that as new social strata emerge, existing or aspiring party leaders will see and seize opportunities to enhance their own influence by binding these new elements to the party. The process may be peaceful, as it is likely to be when existing leaders reach out to new groups in the way the Ullmans deliberately sought out the Italian immigrants; or it may entail struggle and conflict, as it did when DiCenzo gradually built up his strength among second-generation Italians in his state senatorial district and thereby forced the existing party leaders to accept him as a coequal. One way or another, however, new social elements are likely to be recruited into one or both of the parties not only as subleaders but ultimately as leaders.

Doubtless the integration of new social elements into political parties could happen in other ways. But in the United States, and particularly in a city like New Haven where successive streams of immigration and internal migration have constantly created new social elements, the problem has been far more acute than in other countries. Elsewhere, parties have been organized around entire social strata, as in the case of socialist, labor, peasant, and middle-class parties in Europe. In the United States, new social elements have been rapidly integrated into the old parties. To a remarkable degree the existence of democratic ceremonials that give shape to the rules of combat has insured that few social elements have been neglected for long by one party or the other. While it would be too much to argue that the ceremonials and rules were deliberately conceived to fulfill this function, or that party leaders now knowingly maintain them for this reason, the rules and rituals might not have survived had they not fulfilled this function.

10. Leaders in Urban Redevelopment

Like the distribution of influence on political nominations, influence over redevelopment in New Haven takes a somewhat triangular shape. The people of New Haven acquiesce and approve; they have elected and re-elected a mayoralty candidate whose principal platform has been urban redevelopment. Yet the *direct* influence of the electorate on the key decisions involving redevelopment has been negligible compared with the direct influence of a few leaders. In origins, conception, and execution, it is not too much to say that urban redevelopment has been the direct product of a small handful of leaders.

Origins

Perhaps the most significant element in the modern history of city planning in New Haven is that very little happened until redevelopment became attached to the political fortunes of an ambitious politician. Redevelopment was not produced by a surge of popular demand for a new city nor was it produced by the wants and demands of the Economic Notables, even though many of them believed that changes in the physical pattern of the city were necessary to their own goals. The possibility cannot be ruled out that if the Economic Notables were much more unified, influential, skillful, and dedicated to redevelopment than they are in New Haven, they could provide the dominant leadership and coordination. But in New Haven their support was only a necessary, not a sufficient condition for the aggressive action by city officials required for comprehensive reshaping of the face of the city.[1] This will become clear as we examine the origins of the redevelopment program.

Enthusiastic advocates of redevelopment sometimes claim to see its genesis in the first settlement of New Haven in 1638 when the founders, under the leadership of John Davenport, a clergyman, and Theophilus Eaton, a businessman, carefully and deliberately laid out the town in

1. Up to the time of writing, New Haven's redevelopment program has not had many critics. What follows in this chapter, however, is not an appraisal of the desirability of the program but an attempt to understand the political forces that shaped it. Whether the program is eventually judged a brilliant effort or a ghastly mistake is irrelevant to the purposes of this book.

nine squares with the town Green at the center. But we need hardly carry the story to quite so remote a past. For the modern problems of New Haven began after it became an industrial city with slums, run-down areas, and an accretion of man-made features that reflected historical rather than current hopes and needs. In 1907 the mayor of New Haven appointed a New Haven Civic Improvements Committee (at the urging of a distinguished New Haven citizen, George Dudley Seymour) made up of thirteen of the city's most prominent residents, including the governor of the state, some of the most prosperous businessmen, a few of the largest real estate owners, and other worthies. The committee secured the services of Cass Gilbert, architect, and Frederick Law Olmstead, landscape planner, who in 1910 issued the first of several plans and reports that blueprinted a bright future of widened streets, more parks, harbor development, and other changes.[2] But, as was true later on, the net effect of the report was slight. A city plan commission was created in 1913 but was given neither funds nor a professional staff. In the late 1920s and 1930s, James W. Hook, a leading business figure in New Haven, pressed for action on a variety of fronts, but it was 1941 before the City Plan Commission was finally given enough money to hire professional help.

The following year, under the leadership of Angus Fraser, a prominent businessman (in 1943 he was the Republican candidate for mayor), the Commission hired Maurice Rotival, a well-known city planner, as a consultant. Rotival brought out a comprehensive scheme of development, but little was done about his proposals for ten years. In 1953 the Chamber of Commerce produced a "Ten Point Program" that reflected many of the suggestions contained in the earlier plans and reports, including Rotival's.

For three reasons, none of these proposals made headway. First, they were all expensive, and they provided no realistic solution to the problem of costs. Secondly, although they envisaged comprehensive rather than piecemeal alterations, they did not provide realistically for a political process that would secure agreement on a strategic plan. Thirdly, political officials whose support was necessary if action by the city was to be forthcoming saw no particular political gain and much political loss if they were to push hard on city planning and development.

A partial solution to the first problem was offered for the first time by Title I of the Federal Housing Act of 1949, which authorized the expenditure of one billion dollars in loans to cities for planning redevelopment projects and acquiring property to be cleared. An additional half billion dollars was made available in grants, the cities themselves being required to bear only one-third of the net costs of redevelopment projects.

2. Osterweis, *Three Centuries of New Haven*, pp. 390–92.

The grants were, in effect, a means of enabling a city to acquire and clear land and then sell it at a loss to redevelopers.

So far as it is now possible to determine, the possibilities created by Title I were first impressed on local political leaders by a man from academia. A young professor of political science at Yale, Henry Wells, who also happened to be the Democratic alderman from the First Ward and the aldermanic member of the City Plan Commission, had carefully studied the new act and concluded that both the city and the Democratic party might gain if the Democrats on the Board of Aldermen seized upon urban redevelopment as a program. Although the Democrats had won a slight majority on the Board of Aldermen in 1949, their candidate for mayor, Richard Lee, had lost to Celentano. To Wells, Title I seemed to offer an issue on which the Democratic majority might take the initiative away from the Republican mayor for the next two years.

Among others, Wells won over Lee and Norton Levine, a new alderman who had succeeded Lee as Democratic floor leader. The state had meanwhile passed a law permitting cities to establish redevelopment agencies. With Lee's approval, Levine talked to Mayor Celentano, who agreed not to veto a resolution establishing the agency if it were presented as a Republican measure. Subsequently, under the stimulus of Lee, Levine, and Wells, the Board of Aldermen passed a resolution in the summer of 1950 authorizing the mayor to create a redevelopment agency and appoint to it a board of unpaid citizens and a paid director.

Thus urban redevelopment in New Haven began, as Wells diagnosed it afterward, as "a power play—to take the ball away from Celentano, the Republican mayor. In other words, urban redevelopment helped solve *our* problem of political rewards—as it did Dick Lee's four years later."

Mayor Celentano's dilemma as Republican leader was serious. The local newspapers would probably oppose redevelopment as costly; along with most political figures in New Haven the mayor attributed to the papers great influence with voters. Many families might have to be displaced; certainly these people would fight the city administration. Redevelopment was untried; mistakes were probably unavoidable; they could be costly; and most voters would probably pin responsibility for mishaps on the mayor rather than on the Democratic majority in the Board of Aldermen. In 1950, redevelopment hardly appeared to possess great electoral appeal. Since the Democrats had only a three-vote majority, they could not override a veto. On the other hand, many members of the business community had long insisted that improvements in the city were indispensable if the downtown business district was to be preserved from decay; most of these businessmen were Republicans and contributors to the party. The Mayor himself personally favored redevelopment. Faced with this uncomfortable dilemma, Celentano chose to support redevelopment; on his urging the Republican minority on the Board regularly voted with the Democrats on redevelopment.

Thus in spite of its partisan origins, urban redevelopment soon acquired a nonpartisan aura that continued to surround it throughout the next decade. Ironically, this aura of nonpartisanship was to serve the political purposes of the Democrats and particularly those of Richard Lee.

Under Mayor Celentano redevelopment moved slowly ahead. In later years, redevelopment in New Haven became so closely fused with the image of Celentano's successor, Lee, that it is difficult now to provide a fair appraisal of Celentano's role. Both friends and critics agree that Celentano was politically somewhat timid and unadventurous. Moreover, though he supported redevelopment he never made it the central policy of his administration; probably only a mayor who did could move redevelopment ahead in the face of all the obstacles to it. The city agencies involved in the numerous aspects of redevelopment were autonomous and uncoordinated; it would require great force and zeal, as well as unusual political skill, to drive these diverse forces as a single team.

Nonetheless, in 1952 with Celentano's backing the Redevelopment Agency secured the approval of the Board of Aldermen for a proposal to raze fifteen acres of the worst slum area in the city on Oak Street. However, federal funds for the Oak Street project were still a long way off, and before plans proceeded very far the election of 1953 put Lee into the mayor's office.

Only thirty-seven when he was first elected, Lee already had long experience in New Haven politics. He came from a Catholic working-class family of mixed English, Scottish, and Irish origins (in public he chose to emphasize his Irish forebears), went to New Haven public schools, worked as a reporter on the *Journal Courier,* served as an officer in the Junior Chamber of Commerce, had a brief spell in the army, and from 1943 until his election as mayor was in charge of Yale's public relations. He had been a member of the Board of Aldermen, where he quickly became the Democratic minority leader; after an intra-party fight in 1945, in which he supported John Golden, he became a protégé of Golden.

Lee had become a skillful politician. After his two narrow defeats in 1949 and 1951, the last by two votes, he was unusually sensitive to the important consequences of minute shifts in the opinions, habits, or vagaries of voters. Possibly as much by temperament as by his experience of an electoral defeat that could be regarded only as sheer chance, he was prone to worry about the dangers of unexpected and uncontrolled events. For many years he suffered badly from ulcers, which sometimes sent him to the hospital at critical moments. He was a worrier, who spent much of his time laying plans to ward off incipient dangers.

He possessed a large repertoire of political skills and an unusual ability to perform a variety of different roles. His political skills included a talent for public relations that played no small part in developing his national reputation. He had an investment banker's willingness to take risks that held the promise of large long-run payoffs, and a labor mediator's ability to head off controversy by searching out areas for agreement by mutual understanding, compromise, negotiation, and bargaining. He possessed a detailed knowledge of the city and its people, a formidable information-gathering system, and an unceasing, full-time preoccupation with all the aspects of his job. His relentless drive to achieve his goals meant that he could be tough and ruthless. But toughness was not his political style, for his overriding strategy was to rely on persuasion rather than threats.

The Mayor had learned to move with outward ease in several sharply contrasting worlds. He bought his clothes at the best men's shops in New Haven, customarily wore tweed jackets to work, and with his bow ties, button-down shirts and crew-cut hair, he could pass for any well-dressed Yale alumnus. He was one of the few members of Mory's, Yale's undergraduate eating club, who had never attended Yale; and he was perhaps the only associate fellow in any of Yale's ten residential colleges who had never attended a college or university of any kind. He was on a first name basis with a large proportion of the Yale establishment from the president and deans to the headwaiter at the Faculty Club.

For a poor boy growing up in New Haven, life was not always so congenial, and it is clear that Lee's decade as director of public relations at Yale was an important period in his development. Lee's experiences at Yale extended his horizons and made him receptive to ideas that would have frightened a more run-of-the-mill politician. He learned there how to work easily with professional people and developed a sense of the need for expertness and intelligence in public affairs. He never hesitated, for example, in hiring the best talent the city could buy for redevelopment.

In a city where rancor between town and gown is never far below the surface, the Mayor's Yale associations could have been a severe handicap, but his political opponents found it difficult to change the image that Lee himself carefully cultivated of a local boy in the mayor's office, a home-grown Irishman, a family man, a devoted Catholic, a hard-working mayor and a friend to everyone in the city.

As Lee described it later, by 1953 he had arrived at the conclusion that the problem of "doing something about New Haven" was partly one of coordination. His unsuccessful 1951 campaign had taken him into the worst slums in New Haven:

> I went into the homes on Oak Street and they set up neighborhood meetings for me. I went into block meetings . . . three and four in one night. And I came out from one of those homes on Oak Street, and I sat on the curb and I was just as sick as a puppy. Why, the smell of this building; it had no electricity, it had no gas, it had kerosene lamps, light had never seen those corridors in generations. The smells . . . It was just awful and I got sick. And there, there I really began . . . right there was when I began to tie in all these ideas we'd been practicing in city planning for years in terms of the human benefits that a program like this could reap for a city. . . . In the two-year period [before the next election] I began to put it together with the practical application. . . . And I began to realize that while we had lots of people interested in doing something for the city *they were all working at cross purposes. There was no unity of approach.*

In the 1953 campaign he emphasized the importance of doing something about the condition of New Haven. He promised to appoint a committee of prominent citizens within sixty days after taking office, to work out a common program for the city. It is impossible to know whether his views and his promise had any effect on the outcome of the election, which was close. Indeed, in 1953 it was impossible to foresee the extent to which the emphasis on redevelopment would turn out to be politically profitable; Lee has since said that he himself did not anticipate the political harvest he would ultimately reap. Moreover, it is doubtful whether Lee or anyone else foresaw the kind of organization that was to develop in New Haven to coordinate the physical transformation of the city, nor did any one realize how rapidly urban redevelopment would burgeon into a major, perhaps the central activity of the mayor and his staff.

Lee had difficulty at first in carrying out his campaign promises. He approached a number of prominent people about the chairmanship of the citizens committee he had promised; a few turned him down flatly; others were reluctant. He even appointed a committee of several well-known citizens to help him in the search.

Instead of sixty days it was many months after the Mayor was in office before he got his chairman, a well-known bank president, Carl Freese, and it was nearly a year after the election before he was able to announce the creation of the Citizens Action Commission (CAC). It was not until February of 1955 that he began to build up a new staff at the Redevelopment Agency. Edward Logue was brought in as Development Administrator; Logue soon became the Mayor's right-hand man on redevelopment, a hard-driving, vigorous executive who coordinated the work of the Redevelopment Agency, the City Plan Commission, and all other agencies in so far as they touched on redevelopment. The incumbent director of the agency was fired, and until the fall of 1955 Logue served in fact if not in title as the executive director of the Agency. That fall a Massachusetts man, Ralph Taylor, was named director. The chairman of the Agency resigned and the Mayor appointed a new man, Frank O'Brion, another banker. Lee now had the core of his redevelopment team: himself, Logue, Taylor, Freese, O'Brion.

Under Lee, the whole pace of redevelopment gradually altered. By the end of his first term Lee had made redevelopment the central policy of his administration. Then the election of 1955 gave him solid grounds for concluding that the political appeal of redevelopment far exceeded any other conceivable issue within his grasp. After having been narrowly defeated twice by Celentano and having won by a margin of less than 2 per cent in 1953, Lee polled 65 per cent of the vote in 1955 against a somewhat inexperienced candidate of Italian extraction (Celentano having decided to bide his time). In the preceding century, no candidate for mayor had ever won that large a percentage; even Roosevelt had carried New Haven with only 63 per cent in 1936. When Lee went on in 1957 to win again with 65 per cent of the vote, the spectacular political appeal of redevelopment seemed proven. At first the unknown mayor of a minor American city Lee (with some help on his part) began to attract national attention. Articles about redevelopment in New Haven, in which Lee featured prominently, appeared in *Harper's*[3] and the *Saturday Evening Post*;[4] Lee became chairman of a Democratic Advisory Committee subcommittee on urban problems; in 1958 he was widely mentioned as a possible candidate for U.S. senator though he declared he would not seek the nomination because he had to see redevelopment through as mayor of New Haven.

For a city of its size, New Haven soon had an urban redevelopment program unmatched in the country. By the end of 1958, New Haven had spent more federal funds per capita for planning its redevelopment projects than any of the country's largest cities, more than any other city in New England, and more than any other city of comparable size

3. Jeanne R. Lowe, "Lee of New Haven and His Political Jackpot," *Harper's Magazine*, Oct. 1957.

4. Joe Alex Morris, "He is Saving a 'Dead' City." *The Saturday Evening Post*, Apr. 19, 1958.

except one. Only one city in the country, the nation's capital, had received more per person in capital grants, and no other city had so much reserved for its projects. (Figure 10.1) By 1959 much of the center of the city was razed to the ground.

FIGURE 10.1. *Federal expenditures and obligations for redevelopment and renewal, on a per capita basis, as of Dec. 31, 1958*

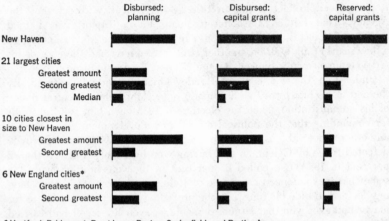

* Hartford, Bridgeport, Providence, Boston, Springfield, and Portland.

Source: U.S. Housing and Home Finance Agency, Urban Renewal Administration, Urban Renewal Project Directory, Dec. 31, 1958 (Washington, D.C.)

THE DISTRIBUTION OF INFLUENCE

In its annual report for 1958, the Citizens Action Commission presented a chart showing the organization of city development agencies. (Figure 10.2) Like most charts displaying the formal skeletal features of an organization, this one reveals nothing about the relative influence of the people occupying the various boxes.

Depending on the preconceptions one brings to the matter, a reader of the annual reports of the CAC might reasonably arrive at one of several conclusions. A reader with strongly optimistic and democratic attitudes might draw comfort from the fact that the CAC committees shown on the chart consist of nearly five hundred citizens and from the statement in the 1957 report that

> The CAC and its Action Committees are in the best sense "grass roots" organizations which include a cross section of community life with all its rich and varied character. The knowledge of the program goals and their support by these representative men and women are

FIGURE 10.2. *Organization of city development agencies*

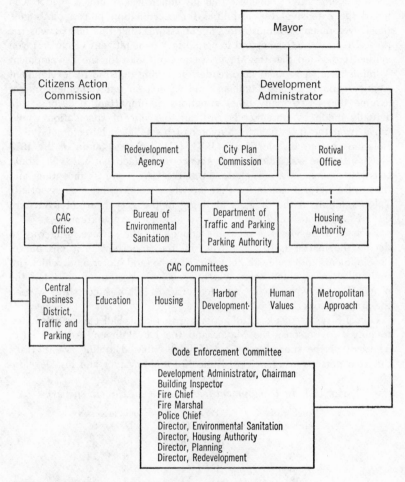

Source: New Haven Citizens Action Commission, Annual Report, 1958, p. 6.

the democratic foundation on which the success of urban renewal in New Haven depends.[5]

Because the top committee, the twenty-five-man Citizens Action Commission, included the heads of large utilities, manufacturing firms, banks,

5. New Haven Citizens Action Commission, *Third Annual Report, 1957* (New Haven, 1957), p. 1.

and other businesses, a reader expecting to find the hidden hand of an economic elite might conclude that his hunch was sound. A reader who noted the extensive responsibilities for coordination placed on Logue, the Development Administrator, might assume that this official was the power behind the throne, and in actual fact some citizens of New Haven evidently decided that the Mayor was a front man for the Development Administrator. A sophisticated reader, observing that the Redevelopment Agency contained the technicians and experts on redevelopment, might assume that as in many other situations all important decisions were actually made by bureaucrats. Still another line of speculation would move from the fact that the Mayor had been Yale's Director of Public Relations before his election in 1953, to the charge made in the 1955 election that he was Yale's stooge, thence to the fact that Yale's President Griswold had been a vice-chairman of the CAC from its inception, and thus to the natural conclusion that the whole undertaking was essentially Yale's solution to the dangers of living in the very heart of a modern city. An ingenious mind could contrive still other explanations.

Each of these views is plausible enough on the surface. One way to decide the matter is to reconstruct all the important decisions on redevelopment and renewal between 1950–58 and determine which individuals (or in some cases which agencies) most often initiated the proposals that were finally adopted or most often successfully vetoed the proposals of others.

Out of fifty-seven successful actions of this kind, half can be attributed to only two persons: the Mayor and the Development Administrator. The rest of the successes were widely distributed among twenty-three different persons or agencies. (Table 10.1) The Mayor and his Develop-

TABLE 10.1. *Redevelopment leaders in New Haven: successes*

Number of successes	Persons N	%	Total successes N	%
1	18	72	18	32
2	4	16	8	14
3	1	4	3	5
13	1	4	13	23
15	1	4	15	26
Total	25	100	57	100

ment Administrator were more often defeated than other participants (Table 10.2), but an examination of these defeats is revealing. The seven cases in which the Mayor failed to get some proposal of his adopted were these: in two instances leading business executives declined to serve as

TABLE 10.2. *Redevelopment leaders in New Haven: defeats*

Number of defeats	Persons		Total defeats	
	N	%	N	%
1	5	63.5	5	26
2	1	12.5	2	11
5	1	12.5	5	26
7	1	12.5	7	37
Total	8	100.0	19	100

chairman of the CAC; in two cases important business firms, one in New Haven and one outside, rejected invitations to participate in redevelopment projects; in the remaining three cases other governmental units (a federal agency, a state agency, and the state courts) made unfavorable decisions. All of these rebuffs reflected not so much a lack of influence over the participants in urban redevelopment as an inability to control certain aspects of the outside environment.

TABLE 10.3. *Some characteristics of leaders in redevelopment*

	Successes		Defeats	
	N	%	N	%
OFFICIALS				
Local	39°	67	12	63
State	2	3		
Federal	4	7		
Total	45	77	12	63
OTHERS				
Notables and large corporations	7°	12	4	21
Developers	3	5	2	11
Retailers	2	3	2	5
Neighborhood groups	1	2		
Total	13	22	7	37
Grand total	58°	99.0°°	19	100.0

° Includes one Economic Notable who was head of Citizens Action Commission, appointed by Mayor; his action was counted both under "Officials" and "Others."

°° Less than 100.0% because of rounding.

A breakdown of the characteristics of the redevelopment elite also shows that the initiative in the program has lain much more with public officials than with private individuals or groups. (Table 10.3) However, there were important differences—sometimes gross, sometimes subtle—

in the kind of influence exerted by the most important leaders in urban redevelopment. These differences stemmed partly from divergent skills and temperaments and partly from the nature of the offices, skills, and resources available to different leaders.

THE VARIETIES OF INFLUENCE

Four different though interrelated tasks in the formation and execution of policy had to be shared: (1) setting the general direction of policy, which is partly a matter of determining (explicitly or implicitly, by action or inaction) what kinds of policies would be emphasized and how much in resources would be poured into them; (2) developing specific proposals; (3) negotiating agreements on the specific proposals; and (4) carrying out the policies when enough agreement was negotiated.

Every administration assumes some posture that furnishes participants with clues as to what kinds of policies are most likely to be pushed or opposed and how much of resources in energy, time, skills, and money are likely to be available for different policies. The posture of a "do-nothing," "avoid risk," "save money" administration is soon obvious to all. So is the weakness of an administration that gives away its initiative to all comers. If schools are treated as a favored area, or public works contracts as a protected one, the matter is soon known to all those who need to calculate what they are most likely or least likely to get done in accordance with their own desires and hopes. If an administration publicly favors and privately fears redevelopment, participants soon know it. If an executive lacks energy and drive and his policies wither on the vine, the participants soon adapt their strategies to this particular fact of life.

What Lee did as mayor was to push redevelopment and renewal to the center of focus and to hold it there year after year. He determined that a large share of energy, time, skills, and money would go into redevelopment. He devoted most of his own time and attention to it. He saw the need for a Citizens Action Commission and an extensive system of subcommittees, knew what kind of men he wanted for the CAC, persuaded them to accept membership, brought in Logue, induced him to abandon his attempt to start a law practice in order to work full-time on redevelopment, identified himself fully with redevelopment, and made it into a major issue of his unceasing campaign for re-election. A mere preference for a better city would hardly have been sufficient to maintain his energetic commitment to redevelopment; though he may have been in doubt as to its political payoff during his first term, from his re-election in 1955 onward it was clear that in redevelopment he had managed to identify himself with a program of enormous political potentiality that in time might make him a serious contender for higher office.[6]

No one but the Mayor could have given redevelopment the priority it received. In another administration, the Development Administrator could have been frustrated and helpless. In Lee's, the Development Administrator's furious drive and energy found infinite outlets in redevelopment. Probably more than anyone else, the Development Administrator worked out the proposals that became the policy-goals of the administration and determined the specific forms that redevelopment and renewal were to take.

Edward Logue, the development administrator, graduated in 1942 from Yale, served on seventeen missions as a bombardier with the Fifteenth Air Force in Italy, and returned to New Haven to graduate from the Yale Law School. As a law student, he attracted the attention of the Yale community by organizing the maintenance and service workers of Yale in a CIO union. Shortly after Logue's graduation from law school, Chester Bowles was elected governor, and Logue soon joined the liberal reformer in Hartford as a legal advisor, in which post he began to acquire administrative seasoning. He admired Bowles, in whom he found a political leader congenial to his own strong impulses toward reform, and when Bowles (who was defeated for re-election after a cyclonic single term of innovation in state policies) was appointed ambassador to India by President Truman, Logue accepted an invitation to accompany him as his chief administrative assistant. When Bowles was replaced in 1953 after Eisenhower's victory, Logue came back to New Haven to begin a law practice and at once found himself heavily involved in Lee's political fortunes, first as an active leader of a Citizens for Lee committee and then as the Mayor's chief assistant and counselor on redevelopment. This activity gradually absorbed his entire time, and he gave up the attempt to practice law in order to take over first as acting Director of the Redevelopment Agency and later as Development Administrator.[7]

After determining in a general way where the Mayor wanted to move next, the Development Administrator usually supervised the development of a specific proposal. In this stage, the Development Administrator served as a stand-in for the Mayor; his word was in effect the Mayor's word. Essentially what he did was to bring the skills of his associates and subordinates to bear on the task of working out a particular proposal.

6. A detailed analysis of the various techniques and relations involved and the parts played by the various participants will be found in the forthcoming companion volume by Raymond Wolfinger, *The Politics of Progress.*

7. In 1961, Logue left New Haven to head Boston's redevelopment program.

In doing so, he relied heavily on three people and their staffs: Ralph Taylor, the director of the Redevelopment Agency, Norris Andrews of the City Plan Commission, and Maurice Rotival, whose firm of city planners served the city in a consulting capacity. Each of these men, of course, drew in turn on the technical skills of his own staff.

To develop a proposal is not necessarily to invent it. As every historian knows, it is often impossible to determine precisely who first thought of the ideas that shape events. As we have seen, certain general ideas about the city had been floating around New Haven for half a century. In the Oak Street area, the Lee administration carried through an idea already in the planning stage under Mayor Celentano. With Church Street, it was the Development Administrator himself who, after months of consideration, discussion, and preliminary planning, sat down late one night and drew on a city map the boundaries he then proposed and the Mayor accepted—boundaries that in their economic and social implications seemed so bold and daring that for months the exact nature of the proposal was kept in secrecy as the Mayor, the Development Administrator, and the Redevelopment Director tested it for feasibility and acceptability.

In so far as one can ever locate a source of ideas, probably Maurice Rotival was as much the ultimate fount as any living person. As we have noted, Rotival was the author of a master plan for New Haven in 1941. He was an imaginative Frenchman, a professional city planner who spun off ideas as a pin wheel throws off sparks. And, like sparks, his ideas often vanished into the darkness. But his presence in New Haven, where he headed a firm of city planning consultants with a world-wide clientele, insured that his ideas would be heard. In a few places, the sparks fell on tinder, smoldered, and finally burst into flame. Like many inventors, Rotival saw his ideas seized and executed by others in ways he did not altogether approve.

But none of Rotival's proposals, nor those of anyone else, were self-enacting; to pass from idea to reality every proposal required an expenditure of critical resources—money, time, energy, attention, skill, political support. The Development Administrator's influence rested in part on the fact that it was his responsibility to assess the costs and gains—economic, social, political—of the various possible proposals generated by himself, his associates, and his subordinates, to arrive at a judgment about the few that seemed worthwhile, to explore these with the Mayor, and to develop the ones that met with the Mayor's approval to a stage where the Mayor could begin securing the necessary support and approval from others. The Development Administrator could not have discharged this task if he had not had the Mayor's confidence; he could not have retained the Mayor's confidence if he had not been

loyal to him and sensitive to his political needs, prospects, and hopes.
The Mayor's judgment was final, the Development Administrator's preliminary; but the two men were so close that the Development Administrator's preliminary judgment was unlikely to diverge consistently
from the Mayor's final judgment.

The main burden of negotiating support for a proposal was divided
among the Mayor, the Development Administrator, and the Director of
the Redevelopment Agency. It is only a slight oversimplification to say
that it was the Mayor's task to get the support of the major political
interests in the community, the Development Administrator's to insure
the participation of developers, and the Redevelopment Director's to
win the consent of the federal agencies.

The Mayor sought support for his redevelopment proposals from as
strange a coalition as had ever existed in New Haven. This coalition included the other leaders of his own party, who were skeptical of redevelopment until the election of 1955 convinced them of its political
potency; the DiCenzo-Celentano wing of the Republican party; public
utility heads, bankers, manufacturers, and retailers who were Republicans
almost to a man; the Yale administration; the liberal Democrats among
the Yale faculty; the working-class and lower-middle-class ethnic groups,
particularly Negroes and Italians, and their spokesmen; trade union
leaders, educators, small merchants, the League of Women Voters, the
Chamber of Commerce; and enough voters to win elections by a margin
so impressive that it guaranteed not only the continuation of redevelopment but Lee's own long-run political prospects. For the most part, the
Mayor met a receptive audience and won the support and acquiescence
he needed without serious or prolonged conflict.

The Development Administrator negotiated with potential developers
to induce them to come into projects on terms acceptable to the city, and,
if they agreed, worked out the specific terms of the understandings and
the contracts. At first he also negotiated with the federal authorities,
mainly the regional office of the Housing and Home Finance Agency in
New York. But after Ralph Taylor became director of the Redevelopment Agency in 1955, he began to take over this function.

Taylor came to New Haven to fill a post made vacant when the Mayor
and Logue concluded that the incumbent director lacked the drive and
zeal they wanted. Like Logue, Taylor was not a native New Havener;
he came from a Jewish family in Somerville, went to Harvard, was in
Italy with the army, returned to Harvard to earn his M.A. at the Littauer
School of Public Administration, and took over in Somerville as the head
of a redevelopment program that proved to be substantially abortive.
He had not been in New Haven long before it became clear that he
matched Logue in energy, resourcefulness, and dedication, and the two

quickly formed a closely knit team. The Director had one great asset the Development Administrator and the Mayor necessarily lacked; he was considered a professional by his peers throughout the country, many of whom he knew well. As the New Haven program began to attract attention, respect for the Director soared among his professional colleagues, including those in the federal agencies. Thus he took on more and more of the task of negotiating with the "Feds"; he knew how to cut through the interminable delays characteristic of bureaucratic agencies, and he exploited statutes and rules to gain concessions for New Haven that cut down the actual cash contribution the city was required to make. Consequently, although the city was supposed to bear one-third of the cost, its actual cash outlay was very much less than this; in one case, even self-liquidating parking garages were included as part of the city's contribution. The city was able to move far partly because its agents moved fast; at a time when most cities were still debating whether to apply for federal funds, New Haven had already secured a disproportionate share of what was available.

If policies are not self-enacting, neither are they self-executing. It is possible to win agreement on a particular proposal and lose it during the execution. The task of driving policies through and securing the coordination needed among a diversity of political officials and city agencies fell chiefly on the Mayor and his Development Administrator. As we shall see in Chapter 17, the political structure of the city government was converted from a highly decentralized to an executive-centered order, partly for the purpose of coordinating redevelopment activities. This transformation was largely the work of the Mayor; the day-to-day coordination was largely the responsibility of the Development Administrator.

DEMOCRATIC RITUALS: THE CITIZENS ACTION COMMISSION

What was the function of the Citizens Action Commission? Lee described the CAC this way:

> We've got the biggest muscles, the biggest set of muscles in New Haven on the top C.A.C. . . . They're muscular because they control wealth, they're muscular because they control industries, represent banks. They're muscular because they head up labor. They're muscular because they represent the intellectual portions of the community. They're muscular because they're articulate, because they're respectable, because of their financial power, and because of the accumulation of prestige which they have built up over the years as individuals in all kinds of causes, whether United Fund, Red Cross, or whatever.

The members had been shrewdly selected to represent many of the major centers of influence or status in the community. Its membership included three bankers: Freese, O'Brion, and a third who was president of the New Haven Chamber of Commerce; two men from Yale: President Griswold and Dean Rostow of the Law School; John Golden, the Democratic national committeeman and hitherto the acknowledged leader of the New Haven Democratic party; (Lynch, the aging Republican party leader was approached but refused); the president of the State CIO Council and the secretary-treasurer of the State Federation of Labor; four of the city's most prominent manufacturers; the president of an investment firm; the board chairman of the leading power company; the manager of a large chain store; the Italian-American president of a construction company; an elder statesman of the Jewish community; a partner in one of the leading law firms; and four individuals who had special status in housing, welfare, education, and industrial development. In addition to the Citizens Action Commission itself, there were six special committees; these in turn had nearly thirty subcommittees. Altogether the Commission and the committees had over four hundred members, drawn mainly from the educated, activist, middle-class segments of the community, the very people who ordinarily shunned direct participation in partisan politics.

Except for a few trivial instances, the "muscles" never directly initiated, opposed, vetoed, or altered any proposal brought before them by the Mayor and his Development Administrator. This is what the men on the Citizens Action Commission themselves said:

A banker said:

> Well, I think the decisions would be brought up first by the technical staff to the Mayor. The Commission would pass them on the general policy level . . . then the decision would be made by the Board of Aldermen on the recommendation of the Mayor.

> *Did you have to modify their proposals very often?*

> Well, they usually came up pretty well developed, but we oftentimes would slant the way we felt the business community would react to certain things and the way we felt the approach should be made. I think that our function was to—*we were a selling organization.*

The president of a large industrial firm said:

> The CAC helps set the atmosphere in the community so they're receptive to these things the city administration is trying to do. So, therefore, the city administration is not shoving things down the

community's throat. It's selling them to the community, through the CAC.

Have you, for example, done any selling?

Oh yes, oh yes . . . Talking to friends of mine, talking at meetings of the Manufacturers' Association . . .

Do you talk individually or do you give speeches, or what?

Mostly individual. I've never given a speech on the subject.

An executive in a utilities firm:

Have there been any cases where the CAC has modified the proposals that have been put forth since you've been on it?

I can't recall any.

A lawyer:

Who would you say was important in making that decision? [To extend the Oak Street Connector]

Well, the matter was taken up by the Mayor at a meeting of the Citizens Action Commission. It was discussed and debated around and we agreed with the Mayor. He got his information, of course, from the traffic commission, from the engineers, from the Redevelopment Agency and all the others and he passed it on to us. We represent the group through which these decisions are filtered. I've often felt that the group as a group is inadequate in the sense that *we don't really initiate anything as far as I can recall. We haven't yet initiated anything that I know of.* We discuss what has been developed by the Redevelopment Agency or the City Planning Commission or one of the other groups. The Mayor or somebody from one of these groups presents it to us and we discuss it, we analyze it, we modify some of it, we change—

Could you give me an example of some case where you modified or changed some proposal?

Well, I don't think that I can give you an example of anything where I can say that the Commission actually changed a proposal.

A lawyer:

Do you know of any cases where proposals that have been brought forward from the city administration have been altered by the CAC or the people on the redevelopment agency?

No I can't say that I do. I can't think of any that would fall into that description.

The contributions of members of the CAC tended to be minor or, if important, of a technical nature. For example, a leading lawyer, Morris Tyler, whose firm also served as legal counsel to the city on redevelopment matters, discovered in 1955 that under existing state legislation the power of eminent domain permitted the city was wholly inadequate for redevelopment purposes; at the request of redevelopment leaders in New Haven the statute was changed by the state legislature. To see the members of the CAC and its action committees as policy-makers is, however, to miss their real role. The elaborate structure of citizen participation, it must be remembered, did not grow up spontaneously; it was deliberately *created* by Mayor Lee. Its functions in urban redevelopment seem to have been roughly equivalent to those performed by the democratic rituals of the political parties in making nominations for public office; citizen participation gave legitimacy and acceptability to the decisions of the leaders, created a corps of loyal auxiliaries who helped to engender public support for the program and to forestall disputes.

The importance of the CAC in assuring acceptability for the redevelopment program can hardly be overestimated. The mere fact that the CAC existed and regularly endorsed the proposals of the city administration made the program appear nonpartisan, virtually nullified the effectiveness of partisan attacks, presented to the public an appearance of power and responsibility diffused among a representative group of community notables, and inhibited criticisms of even the most daring and ambitious parts of the program as "unrealistic" or "unbusinesslike." Indeed, by creating the CAC the Mayor virtually decapitated the opposition. The presence of leading bankers, industrialists, and businessmen—almost all of whom were Republicans—insured that any project they agreed on would not be attacked by conservatives; the presence of two of the state's most distinguished labor leaders and the participation of well-known liberal Democrats like the Dean of the Yale Law School meant that any proposal they accepted was not likely to be suspect to liberals. To sustain a charge of ethnic or religious discrimination would have required an attack on distinguished representatives of these groups.

A Republican banker on the CAC summed up a prevalent view among the members of the CAC itself: "It [the CAC] has to exist to get the combined community in back of something of this nature. In other words, if the city administration tried to put this over as a political effort it would meet, obviously, right away, serious objections, because it would become a political football." The aura of nonpartisanship helped to gain acceptance for redevelopment and its consequences—not all of which were immediately beneficial—and at the same time did no harm to the political career of Mayor Lee. The leaders of the Republican party were presented with a dilemma which they never quite knew how to meet.

Because the Mayor was building his political career on the success of redevelopment, the Republicans could not damage him without attacking either redevelopment or his role in it, but because everything in the redevelopment program was endorsed by Republican notables to attack the Mayor was to alienate established sources of Republican electoral and financial support.

The appointment of over four hundred people to the various action committees gave urban redevelopment a broad and heterogeneous set of subleaders it might otherwise have lacked. The members of these committees initiated no key decisions; they were auxiliaries. They were recruited because they were thought to be favorably predisposed toward certain aspects of redevelopment and renewal; they were counted on to form a group of loyal supporters who would help enlist a community following. Like the main CAC itself, the action committees drew on diverse segments of the community. There was an action committee on industrial and harbor development consisting mainly of businessmen, architects, and lawyers, and a second on the central business district, traffic, and parking, that was drawn from the same sources; there was one on housing, and another on health, welfare, recreation, and human relations, made up in great measure of social workers, liberals, clergymen, Negro leaders, housing officials, and religious leaders; a fourth on education consisted mainly of teachers, members of the Board of Education, school administrators, PTA heads, and housewives; and a small committee on the metropolitan area consisted of leading lawyers, town planners, and architects. Most of the action committees rarely met; many members failed to attend the few meetings there were. The actual effects of membership on the CAC or on action committees is unknown, but it seems reasonable to conclude that many people who might otherwise have been apathetic or even opposed to the program were provided with at least a weak tie of loyalty. One member of the CAC, a lawyer, commented as follows:

> *Who do you see as the people who are primarily responsible or influential in making these decisions?*
>
> Well, I think there that the question indicates to me an error on your part. At least I think it's an error in that it implies the CAC in fact had anything to do with the decision [on Church Street redevelopment]. I think it would be more accurate to say the CAC is again a major stroke of brilliant policy on the part of the regular municipal administration to set up an organization which has its basic function getting so many people that are communally tied to New Haven that once they are sold, their area of influence in the aggregate would be so large that you can get a substantial portion of the

thinking public behind these projects, not only the ones we've been discussing, but all the others in mind.

It would be carrying the parallel with political parties too far to say that the democratic ritualism of the CAC and its action committees provided a means for the orderly settlement of conflicts among the leaders for, as we have seen, no significant conflicts ever arose within the CAC or between the CAC and the city administration. Yet the fact that no conflicts appeared is itself significant. For the men on the CAC were too important in their own right, too knowledgeable, and too independent to be merely tools of the Mayor. The interviews leave little doubt that they genuinely believed in the value of redevelopment; they believed in it on grounds that made sense according to their own predispositions. There is no indication in the interviews that the Mayor and the redevelopment officials significantly altered or even tried to alter the kinds of criteria the men on the CAC brought to their judgments; probably the most the Mayor and redevelopment officials could do was to show how, given these criteria, the proposals made sense. One of the most conservative Republicans on the CAC, a banker, evidently saw no inconsistency between redevelopment, which of course depended on federal funds, and his opposition to "giveaway programs," foreign aid, and social security.

I think there's altogether too much money given away and I don't know where it's going to come from as this thing snowballs. . . . We are undermining the moral fibre of the whole country. Nobody has to do anything, and I've never seen a country yet, or read of one, that didn't fall apart after they went so far, and that's where I think we're headed.

But as for redevelopment the same respondent said that the Chamber of Commerce

felt that something had to be done here, it couldn't be done by private interest, it couldn't be done by public entirely, and it couldn't be political. And as a result of that, when Mayor Lee did come into power, he took this over and he's, I think, done a marvelous job with it. . . . I'm thoroughly convinced that if we're going to have a city, and it's going to be a shopping area, that something had to be done. Something is being done now. . . . Here's a dream that we've had for a long time and we're very happy to see it be culminated in this final action that's been taken.

Another banker said:

If taxes are going to remain high and there is going to be a social program in the United States and if . . . there's no other way—if we can't stop it—if personal income taxes cannot be reduced, why there's only one thing to do and that is to devise ways and means so that we can share in it. That's pretty selfish. I'm not interested in building a highway through Montana or . . . a TVA down South, and I'd like to see some of those dollars come back into Connecticut so that we can enjoy some more benefits.

A labor leader who emphasized the "universal support" of union members and officials for the program was asked whether there had been "any criticism or concern over the large role of the business interests in the program." He replied:

No . . . nobody seems to be bothered by that because I think everybody wants a prosperous community and because in the long run I think everybody feels—that is, most everybody feels—that they benefit in one way or another by a prosperous community, even if it just means a better economic atmosphere. . . . And there's another factor here that's probably important. The building trades, the most conservative element in the labor movement, even more conservative than the teamsters . . . the building trades benefit directly from the program, and so they are enthusiastic towards it and have even made contributions to the CAC committee itself. . . . On the other end of the scale from the conservative building trades, the more sophisticated trade union leaders (and they don't number as many as they did some years ago, when idealism was much stronger than it is today) have been completely taken with the program because of the concern of the program leaders with the human relations aspect of it. So, for different reasons, we have a pretty good cross section of real interest of the labor leadership and of the labor movement in general.

It would be unrealistic in the extreme to assume that these men could have been persuaded to lend their support to just any proposal. The task of the Mayor and the Development Administrator was to persuade them that a particular proposal satisfied their own criteria of judgment, whether these were primarily the criteria of businessmen concerned with traffic and retail sales, trade union leaders concerned with employment and local prosperity, or political liberals concerned with slums, housing, and race relations.

Thus, properly used, the CAC was a mechanism not for *settling* disputes but for *avoiding* them altogether. The Mayor and the Development Administrator believed that whatever received the full assent of the CAC would not be strongly opposed by other elements in the community. Their estimate proved to be correct. And the reason was probably not so much the direct influence over public opinion of the CAC collectively or its members individually, as it was that the CAC *was* public opinion; that is, its members represented and reflected the main sources of articulate opinion in the political stratum of New Haven. The Mayor and the Development Administrator used the CAC to test the acceptability of their proposals to the political stratum; in fact, the very existence of the CAC and the seemingly ritualistic process of justifying all proposals to its members meant that members of the administration shaped their proposals according to what they expected would receive the full support of the CAC and therefore of the political stratum. The Mayor, who once described himself as an "expert in group dynamics," was particularly skillful in estimating what the CAC could be expected to support or reject. If none of the administration's proposals on redevelopment and renewal were ever opposed by the CAC, the explanation probably lies less in the Mayor's skill in the arts of persuasion than in his capacity for judging with considerable precision what the existing beliefs and commitments of the men on the CAC would compel them to agree to if a proposal were presented in the proper way, time, and place.

Constituents: The Organized Interests

In initiating and coordinating the redevelopment of the city, then, the leadership was chiefly official, and the most important center of direct influence was the Mayor and his redevelopment team. As individuals, certainly, the Mayor and his team exerted more direct influence on redevelopment decisions than any other individuals in New Haven.

But in redevelopment as in other issue-areas the relation of leaders to constituents is reciprocal. The collective influence of the political stratum would have been sufficient to end redevelopment at any moment. Indeed, if the political stratum had been sharply divided over redevelopment, the program could never have moved so rapidly or covered so much of the city's area. Hence the most influential leaders constantly struggled to shape their proposals to fall within what they conceived to be the limits set by their constituents.

The important constituents were of two kinds. One consisted of the organized and often institutional interest groups in New Haven, the other of the voters.

Although the organized interest groups were too weak and divided to carry on the task of initiating and coordinating redevelopment, they were strong enough so that their vigorous opposition might easily have blocked a proposal. As we saw, the Chamber of Commerce could not do much to speed up redevelopment under Mayor Celetano; in the absence of a clear test, we cannot say exactly what would have happened if they had opposed redevelopment, but at a minimum Lee and his redevelopment team would have had much harder going. This was also true of other organized interests—the banks, for example. The First National had to be persuaded by Lee and Logue to back redevelopment; had the directors of the bank concluded that redevelopment was not in the bank's interests, the widening of Church Street, which was an important element in the redevelopment of the central business district, would probably have been out of the question. If all the banks in New Haven had opposed redevelopment, it could hardly have moved forward even under the skillful auspices of Lee, Logue, and Taylor.

Yale furnishes an even better example. Although the university is sometimes regarded by suspicious citizens of New Haven as an obscurely powerful force in local politics, in fact it is in a weak political position. Like academic people everywhere, Yale faculty members are politically heterogeneous and jealous of their individual autonomy; they can be counted on to raise a cry of academic freedom at the first suggestion from an incautious university administration that they are expected to hew to a single political line on anything. Certainly no administration in recent years has even hinted at the existence of a Yale party line. Although a few individual faculty members are involved in New Haven politics —the last three Democratic aldermen from the First Ward have been young Yale faculty members—most Yale people are much less interested in the politics of New Haven than in the politics of Yale, their professional associations, the nation, or the international arena. And more of Yale's faculty and other employees live outside New Haven than in the city. Finally, although the university is one of the largest property owners in New Haven, it also happens to be far and away the largest owner of tax-free property; hence Yale officials are highly sensitive to community hostility and fearful of any action that might embroil the university in local controversy.

On the other hand, Yale had a big stake in redevelopment. Although the university could not initiate and coordinate a program of redevelopment and renewal, its cooperation was useful; its opposition could have been formidable. Many leading citizens in business and the professions are old Blues, and old Blues are famous for their loyalty to Yale. A program that actually threatened the future of the university could be counted on to mobilize a coalition of faculty and townspeople powerful enough so that no politician in his right mind would contemplate the prospect with equanimity.

Thus the men who were most influential in redevelopment constantly struggled to shape their proposals to fall within what they conceived to be the limits imposed by the attitudes and interests of various elements in the community. They took the major outlines of the socioeconomic structure as given: the banks, the industries, Yale, the labor organizations, the Negro community, and so on. With respect to the physical pattern of the city, the redevelopment leaders were radical; with respect to the socioeconomic structure they were—by comparison with proponents of the New Deal, for example—conservative.

CONSTITUENTS: THE VOTERS

Neither in 1950 nor in later years was there anything like a discernible popular demand for measures to reverse the physical and economic decay of New Haven, though citizens were evidently discontented with the city in various ways. In late 1956, in a survey of over a thousand residents of the greater New Haven area, 40 per cent reported that they were shopping downtown less often as compared with a few years before while only 12 per cent said they were shopping more often. In Hamden, where a new Sears Roebuck store and a large shopping center had gone up, the figures were 56 per cent and 4 per cent respectively. There were the usual irritations over parking and traffic. About 52 per cent of the sample said parking was a disadvantage to shopping in downtown New Haven, and 13 per cent cited traffic. Of those who had cars, 81 per cent said parking facilities were inadequate. Over 60 per cent felt there was need for a new hotel, and 51 per cent felt there was need for a new department store. The results of the survey also revealed general concern over slums. At that time, when the Oak Street slum clearance project was the most salient feature of redevelopment, 71 per cent rated the redevelopment program as "excellent" or "pretty good"; of these about two-thirds cited as reasons that it was getting rid of slums, providing good housing, creating a decent place to live, and the like.

It is impossible to say with confidence how important these worries over New Haven were to its citizens, but it is reasonable to suppose that for most people they were at a low level of urgency. Thus the feeling that something had to be done about New Haven was latent; it was potential rather than existing; agreement on a strategic plan had to be created. It would be wrong to suppose, then, that politicians were pressed into action by public demand. On the contrary, they had to sniff out the faint smell of distant political success, generate the demands, and activate the latent consensus.

Nonetheless, if the citizens of New Haven had not been largely predisposed in favor of the different aspects of redevelopment—if redevelopment threatened to hit them adversely on what they felt to be matters of importance—then they might have voted against Lee in 1955. Had they done so, the ambitious program that unfolded in later years would in all likelihood have died at birth, for the election of 1955 was a decisive turning point. It was a smashing electoral victory for Lee, and because

Lee had made redevelopment his central policy his victory was inter-preted, rightly or not, as public approval of redevelopment. The results of the elections of 1957 and 1959 were interpreted in much the same fashion.

What voters did was to vote for or against Lee in elections. A majority vote against Lee would have amounted to a veto on redevelopment. A close vote would have left the choice risky and ambiguous. A large vote, twice repeated, was seen as a green light. In effect, the role of the electorate was not to demand redevelopment, to initiate it, or directly to influence concrete decisions, but at two-year intervals to vote for or against a leader identified with redevelopment and so to express what would be interpreted as support for, or disapproval of, the program.

If the Mayor and his redevelopment team were more successful than any other individuals in initiating proposals for redevelopment and re-newal that were later adopted, their success rested on their capacity for anticipating what the organized interests, the political stratum, and the voters in general would tolerate or support.

11. Leaders in Public Education

Though leadership in the public school system has many of the characteristics of leadership in the political parties and in urban redevelopment,
there are also significant differences. Like the parties but unlike urban
redevelopment, the school system has existed for a long time. Policy-making in the schools is far more routinized than in redevelopment; it is far
more professionalized—one might say bureaucratized—than in the parties,
in the sense that almost all of the people who make day-to-day decisions
about the schools meet certain professional standards and have a strong
sense of their own professionalism. The schools are more insulated from
electoral politics than are the parties, of course; as with redevelopment,
leaders in the schools maintain an aura of nonpartisanship.

As in urban redevelopment and party nominations, there are a number
of diverse elements in the political stratum whose educational wants and
concerns the leaders attempt to conciliate, anticipate, and satisfy. In so far
as they are organized into self-conscious associations, these elements, the
public school interests, are somewhat like the subleaders in the political
parties. As in redevelopment, the public school interests possess a strong
concentration of purpose. Moreover, most of the associations active in
school affairs are specialized around the politics of the public schools and
play a minor part in the political parties and in urban redevelopment.

Origins

Three years after New Haven Colony was founded, a town meeting
ordered "thatt a free schoole shall be set up in this towne." [1] Historians
have debated whether the term "free school," a term commonly used in
colonial Connecticut meant free in the modern sense of relief from tuition

---

1. The quotation is from Osterweis, *Three Centuries of New Haven*, p. 34. See
also his comments, p. 38. Osterweis indicates that the "free school" subsequently
established in New Haven was "free in that any one could go who would pay the
tuition" (p. 38). For the view that "when the colonists of Connecticut used the term
'free school' in their laws and educational practices, *they meant a school free from
tuition charges*," see A. R. Mead, *The Development of Free Schools in the United
States, as Illustrated by Connecticut and Michigan* (New York, Teachers College,
Columbia University, 1918), pp. 42–43. However, in the case of Ezekiel Cheever's
"Free School" in New Haven, according to Osterweis, "The pupils were required to
pay a fee for attending and the public treasury also contributed funds" (p. 38).

or free merely because anyone who paid the tuition could enter. But there is no debating the fact that the Puritans looked upon knowledge of the word of God revealed in the Scriptures as a necessary condition for Christian living. Christian living was, in their view, a necessary condition for salvation and therefore the central and proper objective of social institutions. Without enough education to read or at least to understand the Scriptures, Christian living was impossible. It followed then that education was a necessary and proper concern of the community.

Two full centuries passed, nonetheless, between the resolution of the town meeting in 1641 and the establishment of free, compulsory, public education in New Haven. To be sure, the convictions of the Puritans meant that a sizable part of the population was always given some kind of education. When Tocqueville visited the United States in 1831, he even went so far as to conclude that "primary instruction is within the reach of everybody." In fact, however, the development of widespread public education in the United States followed rather than preceded Tocqueville's journey. Indeed, had Tocqueville's travels brought him in touch with the members of a committee of New Haven citizens appointed to investigate the city's schools during the very year he was in America, he could have learned that in 1831 nearly two-thirds of all the children in New Haven between the ages of four and sixteen attended no school at all. The modern public school system of the city dates from the decade before the Civil War, when the first "all graded school" was opened, a public high school was established, and a Board of Education replaced the old district and society school committees that had previously supervised schools under a quaint intermingling of public and private funds and authorities.[2] It was not until 1869 that Connecticut finally passed a law compelling all towns to maintain free public schools.[3]

Now, nearly a century later, under the laws of the state everyone over seven and under sixteen years of age must attend public school unless the parent shows that "the child is elsewhere receiving equivalent instruction during such hours and terms in the studies taught in the public schools." The public school system of New Haven consists of thirty-five elementary schools, four junior high schools and two high schools. In addition, within the city or its immediate environs there are ten Catholic parochial schools and seven nonsectarian private schools.

The public schools are a large operation. Annual outlays for the public school system run from a quarter to a third of all city expenditures and constitute far and away the biggest item in the budget. (By comparison the police and fire departments together amount to only one-fifth of total

2. Osterweis, *Three Centuries of New Haven*, pp. 33–39, 226–30.
3. Mead, *Development of Free Schools in the U.S.*, p. 69.

city expenditures; health and welfare are between one-twentieth and one-tenth.) In 1959 the regular school system employed about 1,250 people, including 924 teachers, 98 administrators, 43 clerks, and 184 janitors, repairmen, etc. In addition, programs in adult education and summer recreation employed over 200 persons. Altogether one out of every two persons employed by the city government worked in the school system.

The responsibilities placed on the public schools by law, custom, and popular expectations are heavy. The schools are, of course, expected to provide a minimum level of knowledge for all except the mentally retarded and a much higher level for the increasing proportion of students who aspire to higher education. The schools are, and from the time of their establishment have been, expected to prepare the student for a useful calling. In addition, the schools have always been assigned a heavy responsibility for helping to form the character, moral sensibilities, and civic attitudes of the student. In a city of immigrants like New Haven, the last task has necessarily assumed a position of key importance.

Considering the nature of the tasks assigned to the public schools, it is hardly surprising that control over the schools is seen as worth fighting for by leaders of many different groups.

THE SPLIT: PUBLIC VERSUS PRIVATE

One factor that bears heavily on local decisions about the public schools and on the nature of leadership in school affairs is that a large number of parents send their children to Catholic parochial schools, to private nonsectarian day schools in the greater New Haven area, or to

TABLE 11.1. *Children enrolled in public and private schools in New Haven, 1926–1955*

	In public schools N	In private schools N	In private schools %
1926	30,444	4,796	13.5
1931	30,377	4,900	13.9
1936	27,010	3,976	12.8
1941	21,398	4,774	19.0
1946	17,783	5,027	22.0
1951	20,604	5,949	22.4
1955	19,995	4,634	18.7

Note: Ages of children included are 4–16 from 1926–46, 7–15 for 1951, and 6–17 for 1955.

Sources: *New Haven's Schools*, p. 23; M. J. Ross, *The Relationship of Public and Non-public Schools in Connecticut* (Connecticut State Dept. of Education, Research Bulletin No. 6, 1956); and Bureau of Research and Statistics, State Dept. of Education, Hartford.

boarding schools. This separation between public and private school population, which is common in other cities along the Eastern seaboard and almost unknown in the Middle West and Far West, is highly significant in New Haven, where about one child out of five attends a private school. (Table 11.1)

Unfortunately for the public school leader, some of the private schools draw off the students from the more prosperous and better educated elements in the community, as James S. Davie showed in a study of children sixteen or seventeen years old in 1949 whose parents were legal residents of New Haven. Using a six-fold classification of residential areas (based on income, nationality, occupation, delinquency, dependency, social club membership, and inclusion in the social register), Davie found that only about one child out of ten in the three lower residential categories was sent to a private school. In the two intermediate residential categories, one out of five went to a private school. But in the highest category—children from "Class I" neighborhoods—four out of ten children were in private schools.[4] (Figure 11.1)

FIGURE 11.1. *Percentages of children in public and private secondary schools in six ranked residential areas*

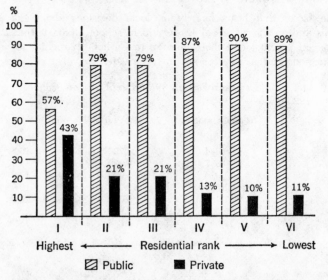

Source: James Davie, "Education and Social Stratification" (Doctoral dissertation, Yale University, 1951). The percentages cover all school children 16 or 17 years of age whose parents were residents of New Haven. The classification of residential areas is based on income, nationality, occupation, delinquency, dependency, social club membership, and inclusion in the social register.

Among private school children, however, there is a marked difference between those who go to Catholic parochial schools and those who go to nonsectarian private schools. Children in "Class I" neighborhoods go overwhelmingly to nonparochial schools; in the three lowest ranking neighborhoods, on the other hand, a child who does not attend a public school is almost certain to go to a parochial school. (Figure 11.2) It

FIGURE 11.2. *Where the social strata educate their children: the better the neighborhood, the higher the proportion of private school children in nonparochial schools*

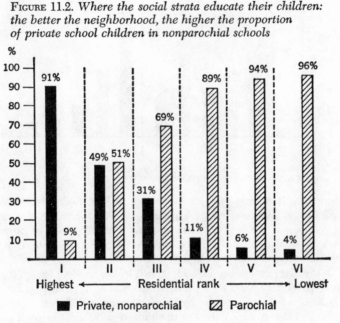

Source: Davie, "Education and Social Stratification."

follows that the private nonparochial schools consist mostly of students from only the better neighborhoods; in 1949, Davie's data show, three-fourths of the students in private secondary schools came from Class I and Class II neighborhoods. By contrast, nearly three-fourths of the students in the parochial secondary schools lived in the three lowest ranking neighborhoods. (Figure 11.3)

The split between private and public schools in New Haven has two

4. James S. Davie, "Education and Social Stratification" (Doctoral dissertation, Yale University, 1951). See also his article "Social Class Factors and School Attendance," *Harvard Educational Review, 23* (1953), 175–85.

FIGURE 11.3. *Where the private school students live: most parochial school students live in the poorer neighborhoods; most nonparochial students live in the better neighborhoods*

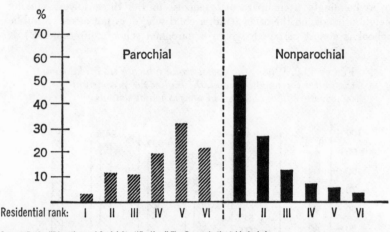

Source: Davie, "Education and Social Stratification." The figures in the table include all school children 16 or 17 years of age whose parents were residents of New Haven.

consequences. It reduces the concern among the better educated elements in New Haven for standards of excellence in the public schools, and it creates among about a fifth of the parents a double load of costs for education—local taxes and private tuition—that generates latent opposition to increasing the outlays on public schools.

As to the first point, when an educational leader in New Haven tries to mobilize parents to press for better public schools, he finds that his own standards of adequacy—not to say of excellence—are likely to be higher than those of the average parent with children in public schools. To meet his own standards, then, a leader must push for better educational facilities and services than many parents would insist on if left to themselves. It is not so much that parents make demands on leaders for better schools as that leaders try to win the support of parents.

Of course the standards of excellence used by any professional group are frequently higher than those satisfactory to a layman. To meet the standards articulated by the various professional groups in any modern community would exhaust the total available resources many times over. But in the field of public education in New Haven the discrepancy between standards is particularly acute because the average parent of a public school child has had considerably less formal education than is now compulsory. In 1950 half the people twenty-five years of age or over in New Haven had not gone beyond the ninth grade. Only a little more than a third had completed high school. In eighteen wards, or more than half, the average (median) person had stopped just short of the ninth grade. In seven more wards, the average person had gone beyond the ninth grade but had not finished high school. In only eight wards, or not quite one-fourth, had the average adult completed high school. Many of the better educated parents, who might normally be expected to support high standards in the public schools, are likely to give their attention instead to the private schools where their own children are enrolled.

As to the second point, parents bearing a double load of costs for education are joined in latent opposition to increasing expenditures on public schools by the business firms, corporations, and individuals with extensive property holdings who pay a large share of the taxes. But they represent a relatively small proportion of the voters and are greatly outnumbered by the parents of public school children.

The net effect of the private schools, parochial and nonparochial, is to reduce enthusiasm for expenditures on the public schools among various strata in the population whose interests would not ordinarily coalesce. In contrast to a community located in the Middle West or the Far West where a leader concerned with excellence in the public schools can often count on the support of the better educated and more prosperous people in the city, in New Haven he has to seek support elsewhere. Because the standards of educational excellence accepted by the great bulk of the population are low, and because the parochial schools in any case draw off some of the enthusiasm that might otherwise be generated among the less educated and less well-to-do, any effective educational coalition is likely to be composed for the most part of the better educated people in the middling strata of the community, with a tiny sprinkling of Social and Economic Notables who for various reasons feel a commitment to a good public school system even though they may send their own children to private schools.

THE CHURCH

In some quarters in New Haven it is strongly held that the Roman Catholic church exercises a good deal of surreptitious control over the public school system. The fact seems to be, however, that the church exerts little *direct* influence on decisions involving public schools, although at the same time certain aspects of the school system inevitably reflect the elemental fact that over two-thirds of the people in New Haven are Roman Catholic.

Many people in New Haven seem to have heard rumors of actions by the church on public school matters, but assiduous efforts to track down information leads one to few facts. A well-informed Protestant, who knew the city well, suggested that the Irish Catholics in the school system tended to act with considerable cohesion on certain issues, but he had no evidence bearing on influences by the church as such:

> It [Irish Catholic cohesiveness] may be a kind of ethnic solidarity very common in American politics?
>
> That's right. It's something very like that, plus mutual favors, you know.
>
> Has there ever been any instance that you know of where the church, as such, has intervened in decisions?
>
> No. But there was, there was a situation that hung over from the long past which I never completely understood.

The "situation that hung over from the long past" proved to be a matter of public record, involving the Hamilton School, which had originally been built by the church in 1868 as a parochial school for children of Irish immigrants. Around the turn of the century as the Irish were moving out of the area and the Italians—many of whom spoke little English—were moving in, the city rented the school from the church while nuns, some of them evidently Italian-speaking, continued to teach as paid appointees of the Department of Education. No one seems to have given much attention to this curious and constitutionally dubious arrangement until 1947, when a school survey conducted by a professor of education from Cornell noted the situation and recommended that as the nuns retired they should be replaced by lay teachers.[5] Some non-Catholics responded vigorously; and a few Catholic leaders in the field of public education, who felt that both the church and the school system were vulnerable to criticism as long as the anomaly persisted, urged that the arrangement be terminated. The Board of Education, which had continued to rent the school from the church, was not disposed to put up a new building, but it did adopt the recommendation advanced in the school survey. Over the next decade retiring nuns were replaced by lay teachers. A similarly anomalous arrangement with the Highland Heights Orphanage was treated in the same fashion.

Aside from these cases, charges of direct influence on school decisions by the church proved to be unsubstantiated. An unusually tough-minded informant, who was not a Catholic, responded to a question about church influence as follows:

> I have not seen any evidence [of] any organized influence. That is, interference by the church as such. I've seen, now and then, some evi-

5. New Haven's Schools: An Investment in Your City's Future, Report of a Survey of the Public School System 1946–47 (New Haven, 1947), p. 9. The director of the study was Julian E. Butterworth, Professor of Educational Administration at Cornell University.

dence of bigotry on the part of individuals; but for that matter, I would suggest that there might be just as much bigotry on the part of non-Catholics as on the part of Catholics. . . . I have not had any experience with any issues where it [religion] makes any difference. There could be issues. The use of the school for religious purposes. There is a kind of limited use of the schools which nobody bothers with. I mean it doesn't matter a great deal, but it could grow serious. . . . Nor have I seen any issues that you could call racial or religious issues. I haven't seen any evidence of that problem. I've heard a great deal of concern expressed by some people but I simply have not seen any evidence that a problem exists.

In so far as the Catholic church can be said to have an influence on the schools, it is more a matter of cultural climate and the impact of parochial schools than of direct influence. The fact that two-thirds of the citizens of New Haven are Catholics means that the political and administrative institutions of the city are to a great extent staffed by Catholics. For a generation every mayor has been Catholic; a majority of the members of the Boards of Aldermen, Finance, and Education are Catholic. In recent years the Board of Education, an appointed body, has had three to four Catholic members. For at least thirty years, the superintendent of schools has been a Catholic. In 1959, three assistant superintendents were Catholics, most of the principals were Catholics, and a majority of the teachers and the pupils were Catholics.

The church makes its indirect influence felt most heavily by inducing many Catholics to send their children to parochial schools; the consequences of this, as I have suggested, are to decrease citizen support for expenditures on the public schools. But even here the matter is more complicated than it might appear at first glance, for as we shall see shortly the public schools have become an important avenue of advancement for persons of immigrant and therefore often Catholic background. The very fact that the largest religious group among the administrators and teachers in the public schools is Catholic means that the prestige, income, and careers of a significant segment of the Catholic community are bound up with the prosperity of the public school system. Moreover, far more Catholic families send their children to public schools than to parochial schools.

From the simple fact, then, that a majority of the citizens of New Haven are Catholics, one cannot safely conclude that the political leadership will not give vigorous support to the public school system. If no private and parochial schools existed in New Haven, the support would probably be much more steadfast and the political consequences for a laggard mayor might more quickly reveal themselves. But as long as many Catholic parents send their children to public schools, and the public school system provides career opportunities for young people of the Catholic faith, the Roman Catholic population will not be of one mind on the relative importance of public and parochial schools, and a politically significant section of the Catholic community can be counted on to support the public schools.

THE DISTRIBUTION OF INFLUENCE: THE LEADERS

An examination of eight different sets of decisions taken between 1953 and 1959 indicates that there are three main centers for initiating or vetoing policies involving the public schools. These are the mayor, the Board of Education, and the superintendent of schools.

In New Haven, the seven members of the Board of Education are appointed for four-year terms by the mayor, who is ex officio an eighth member. Appointments are staggered; hence by the end of his first term in office a mayor will usually have had the opportunity to appoint a majority of the members to the Board.

Because the local norms prescribe that the schools should be insulated from politics, a mayor who attempted to press his own policies directly on the school system through the Board or the superintendent would antagonize the segments of the political stratum most keenly interested in the schools. Consequently, the mayor ordinarily influences school policy only indirectly through his appointments to the Board. Even then, the mayor does not have a free hand. By tradition, members are reappointed as long as they are willing to serve; because of this tradition, it is not always simple to ease out a Board member whom the mayor would prefer not to reappoint. Moreover, some ethnic, religious, and professional distribution is assumed to be necessary. In recent years, the Board's appointive members have included three Catholics, two Protestants, and two Jews. Among the Catholics were one man of Irish stock and another of Italian stock. Mayor Lee appointed the state head of the AFL-CIO to the Board; fear of trade union resentment may henceforth require a trade union man on the Board. In response to rising demands from Negroes, Lee also appointed a Negro; probably no future mayor will fail to follow his lead.

Once the mayor has appointed his members, his direct influence is limited. The Board members are unpaid. They have careers, goals, and standards of their own. Membership on the Board is time-consuming and even onerous. Board members do not feel particularly beholden to the mayor. Hence the most a mayor can do is to choose people in whom he has confidence and then give them his strong backing when they call for help.

The superintendent of schools is a major official. In 1960 his annual salary of $16,300 was the highest of any official in the city except for the mayor himself. Once appointed, a superintendent is difficult to remove, not only because he builds up his own following among the public school interests but because he can invoke the support of national professional groups if his removal does not seem to be based on considerations of professional adequacy.

Because of all the constraints on the mayor and the Board of Education, a superintendent in whom they have confidence can be expected to acquire a major, perhaps even decisive, influence on policies relating to essentially internal school matters—that is, policies that do not require extensive negotiations with elements in the political stratum not primarily concerned with the public schools. If the mayor and the Board lack confidence in the superintendent, then the direct influence of Board members on decisions is likely to increase, as Board members substitute their own judgment for his. Finally, if the situation of the schools generates a series of proposals and decisions that require extensive negotiations outside the public school system, then the direct influence of the mayor is likely to increase. Consequently the relative influence of the mayor, the Board, and the superintendent tends to be different at different times and with different kinds of decisions.

Consider now the following scoreboard. In eight different sets of decisions between 1953 and 1959, there were twenty-seven instances in which the initiation or veto of a policy alternative could be attributed to a particular individual, group, or agency. The successful actors included eight individuals, a group of three members of the Board of Education, three official agencies (in cases where the action could not be attributed to any particular individual), and the Teachers' League. Of the twenty-seven instances of successful action on policy, all except three were traceable to participants officially and publicly involved in the school system. Fifteen, or more than half, were traceable to the mayor or officials who were members of his educational coalition. All the rest were scattered among a variety of individuals and agencies, from the Board of Finance and the Board of Park Commissioners to the superintendent of schools and the president of Yale.

One might suspect the validity of crude measures of this sort, but the conclusions they suggest fit with the qualitative evidence. Taken together, the qualitative and quantitative evidence seems to support three propositions. First, the number of citizens who participate directly in important decisions bearing on the public schools is small—just as it is in the other areas of public life we have examined. Second, direct influence over decisions in public education seems to be exerted almost entirely by public officials. Third, in recent years the chief center of direct influence has been the mayor and his appointees on the Board of Education, rather than the superintendent.

As with urban redevelopment and political nominations, however, it would be a serious error to assume that the individuals and groups with the greatest *direct* influence on decisions are autonomous. On the contrary, they consider the reactions of a number of different public school interests who can, if aroused, make themselves felt in various ways—not least through elections.

The most important of these public school interests are the administrators, the teachers, and the parents of the children in the public schools.

School Administrators

In New Haven, for every nine teachers there is an administrator of some sort—a superintendent, assistant superintendent, supervisor, assistant supervisor, or principal. The school administrators rather than the teachers are the elite of the American public school system.

The ambitious teacher, particularly if he is a man, soon learns that greater income and power are to be found in an administrative career; if he remains in teaching, the terminus is plainly visible and not overly attractive. In New Haven in 1959, the official upper salary limit for a public school teacher was $7,000 (a decade earlier it had been $3,600). The average teacher's salary was about $5,450. By comparison, principals were on the average paid half again as much; the highest salary a teacher could receive was over a thousand dollars less than the average salary paid to a school principal. Three of the four assistant superintendents were paid twice as much as the average teacher. The superintendent was paid three times as much.

Once a teacher obtains a "school of his own" as a principal or moves into the administrative hierarchy as a supervisor, he belongs to an elite group within the school system. In New Haven this is symbolized by the right to belong to a separate association, the Principals' Club.

But to succeed in his new career, the school administrator must obey the First Commandment of the public school administrator: "Thou shalt not alienate teachers, parents, superiors, or professional colleagues." In making his way according to this rule, he brings with him doctrines about education, teaching, and administration that he has learned at his teachers' college, doctrines that he may continue to acquire in annual installments at summer school until he has earned his Ph.D. in education. He also brings his own temperament, experiences, idiosyncrasies, and even neuroses.

The school administrator is faced with two great problems. On the one hand he depends heavily on the cooperation of others to get the resources he needs to run the schools in a fashion that will insure his professional recognition and advancement. On the other hand, to maintain his professional standards and reputation he must oppose outside interference in the school system, particularly by politicians. Sometimes it is impossible to reconcile these two needs.

The school system gives away education to its pupils (and their parents) and pays for it out of public funds. In New Haven, unlike many other places in the United States, funds for the public schools are appropriated by the city government out of general revenues obtained from taxes, state grants, and loans. Because the city government is subject to a great variety of demands, the views, aims, and strategies of political leaders usually do not coincide entirely with those of citizens and administrators concerned with the schools. The adequacy of school appropriations therefore depends in part on the effectiveness of various leaders, including school administrators, in mobilizing the support of the other public school interests and in part on how important the views and actions of these interests are in the calculations of the men who make the decisions on city revenues and expenditures. The teachers, of course, are one key group who can sometimes be mobilized.

TEACHERS

If the public school system is an important instrument in the Americanization of the immigrant, and if the education provided by the public schools is the first step in a social ladder leading to social respect and self-respect according to American standards, to become a *teacher* is to take a still higher step. Jobs in the school system have been one of the main avenues to assimilation. When an ethnic group is in its first stage, some of its members become janitors in the schools. Later, as the ethnic group moves into its second stage, school teaching is a wedge that permits the group to expand its white-collar segment. Then, in the third stage, members of the ethnic group begin to receive appointments as school administrators.

For this process of assimilation to function effectively, two prerequisites are necessary. First, the training required for teaching must be inexpensive and easily available. Second, teachers from immigrant backgrounds must be free to enter into teaching without discrimination. Normal schools satisfy the first requirement; city elections eventually guarantee the second. Under the prodding of leaders in the public school movement like Henry Barnard, free teachers' institutes were created in Connecticut in 1848. The State Normal School was established the next year.[6] From that time forward a boy or girl with limited means and a high school diploma could become a public school teacher. When city elections began to be won by ethnic candidates, the likelihood of discrimination declined.

6. Mead, *Development of Free Schools in the U.S.*, p. 48.

Thus the rate at which an ethnic group is being assimilated can almost be determined from the proportion of its members who are public school teachers. Judging from their names, about two out of three teachers were of Yankee or English stock in 1900; about a quarter were Irish; there were no Italians. Over the next two decades the proportion of Irish teachers rose as the proportion of Yankee teachers fell. But the time of the Italians had not yet arrived either in politics or in school teaching. Even in 1930, the Russians—mainly Russian Jews—outnumbered the Italians. In 1939, however, William Celentano was nominated for mayor; within one generation, 20 per cent of the teachers bore Italian names. (Figure 11.4)

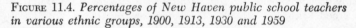

FIGURE 11.4. *Percentages of New Haven public school teachers in various ethnic groups, 1900, 1913, 1930 and 1959*

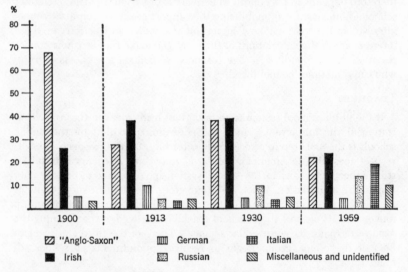

Source: Percentages are based on an examination of all names listed on the roster of teachers for the given year.

In 1947, a report on the New Haven school system described "the median, or typical teacher," as

> about 45 years of age. She was born in New Haven and attended local schools. After graduation from high school, she took her professional training at New Haven State Teachers College graduating . . . from the two-year course. Immediately upon graduation she entered the local system without teaching experience elsewhere and has been teaching here ever since.[7]

7. *New Haven's Schools*, p. 33.

Altogether, teachers make up the largest group of municipal employees—nearly one-third of the total. They are organized in two professional associations, the New Haven Teachers' League and the American Federation of Teachers. The Teachers' League is older and larger, claiming two-thirds of the teachers as members; principals are also eligible for membership and are often chosen as presidents. In orientation, the League is a professional association rather than a trade union and is affiliated with the Connecticut Education Association; because it has worked closely with the last two superintendents, it has been called a "company union" by its critics. The smaller, more union-oriented Teachers' Federation is affiliated with the AFL-CIO, accepts only teachers as members, and is less warmly received by the school administration. As a result of an ill-conceived set of recommendations on discipline submitted a few years ago by the Federation, critics have sometimes called it "irresponsible" and "crack-pot." The close ties with the school administration enjoyed by the leaders of the Teachers' League have permitted it to perform functions denied to the Federation, and in general the League has played a more prominent role in important decisions.

The most influential leaders on questions involving public education —the mayor, members of the Board of Education, the superintendent —are constrained in their choices by what they think will be acceptable to the teachers. In 1955, the opposition of the Teachers' League was, as we shall see in Chapter 17, a major factor in the unexpected defeat of a proposed reform of procedures on appointments and promotions.

DEMOCRATIC RITUAL: THE FOLLOWINGS

The greatest ambiguity in the relations of leaders and constituents stems from the fact that individuals who seem to have the greatest direct influence on decisions are themselves influenced in their choices by the need to gain and retain popular support. This ambiguity is further compounded by the fact that leaders do not merely respond to demands; they also help to generate them. In public education, as we have noted, differences in the objectives of leaders and parents induce leaders to develop methods of generating new demands among parents and other citizens. One of these methods is the creation of special associations. Just as the numerous action committees provide a democratic façade and a body of subleaders and followings for leaders in redevelopment and renewal, and the party functionaries and convention delegates furnish auxiliaries for party leaders, so certain citizen organizations provide subleaders and followings for leaders in public education. The PTA's fit most obviously into this role.

Ostensibly, of course, a Parent-Teachers' Association is a democratic organization of parents and teachers associated with a particular school, brought into being and sustained by their joint interests. In practice, a PTA is usually an instrument of the school administrator. Indeed, an ambitious principal will ordinarily regard an active PTA as an indispensable means to his success. If no PTA exists, he will create one; if one exists he will try to maintain it at a high level of activity.

The functions of the PTA are rather like those of party subleaders. The PTA supplies a group of people whose loyalty and enthusiasm can occasionally be mobilized for educational purposes important to the leaders. Thus an energetic principal of a New Haven school in a low-income neighborhood described how he had organized a PTA in order to improve the facilities of the school. He went to an important neighborhood leader, he said, and persuaded her that "the kids in the neighborhood needed help." Together they started a PTA. In order to involve the parents even more heavily, they then induced the PTA to endorse a hot lunch program; this required PTA members to raise funds and even to hire kitchen help. As participation in the PTA increased, the principal began to work for a new school to replace the old one. When obstacles were raised by the city administration, the principal called a meeting of PTA members and other neighborhood leaders and "gave them a rousing speech asking for their help. Within twenty-four hours they were on the phone and in other ways bringing pressure on the administration. The problem was solved."

It is a rare PTA that ever opposes the wishes of a principal, and its mere existence helps to give a certain legitimacy to the otherwise hierarchical structure of the school system. As long as the principal keeps the active PTA members moderately satisfied, he will appear to have the "backing of the parents" for his programs and policies.

But a PTA is also useful to head off or settle conflicts between parents and the school system. A shrewd principal often uses the PTA to find out what problems are in the parents' minds; he then brings about some adjustments in the school's program or perhaps allays the concern of parents simply by discussing the problem with them. PTA meetings also create an atmosphere of friendliness and conviviality that blunts criticism. For many women, in fact, the PTA is obviously an outlet for social needs; PTA meetings furnish opportunities to escape from the home for a few hours, meet neighbors, make new friends, gossip, talk about children, partake of coffee and pastry, and achieve a fugitive sense of social purpose. Some female Machiavellians even look upon PTA activity as a way of assuring favorable treatment for their own children. And they may be right, for the experienced principal or teacher learns from PTA meetings who the most interested parents are, who the "troublemakers" might be, who makes demands on the school system, and who does not. If he is politically sensitive, the principal is likely to conclude that it is safer to ignore the difficulties of a child whose parents are not interested enough to participate in the PTA than the problems of a child whose mother is a PTA activist.

The PTA is also a legitimate channel through which potential leaders may enter into the school system, test themselves, gain experience, and pass into the ranks of the leaders. It is a remarkable fact that three recent appointees to the New Haven Board of Education all became involved in the politics of the public schools via the PTA. To be sure, each of these men had already possessed a strong prior interest in education. But it was when the education of their own children was at stake that they became active in their PTA. One of them recalled later:

> I became President of the PTA out there. They make it a habit to have men, most schools have women, and the supply of men is short and so they ask around. That's how they got on to me. So I started my stint, and I had children in school of course at the time, three of them. Well, I noticed right away, when I started going into the school in any kind of detail, it was in really dreadful condition. . . . And so . . . we got together a committee of parents consisting of a doctor and an engineer and so on and we went over the school together and drew up a report emphasizing all the things that needed to be done, and emphasizing in particular all the things that were actually danger-ous. . . . We sent this out to all the parents and we had a mass meeting at the school PTA meeting and, of course, we got a lot of support. So we went down to the Alderman and persuaded him that we had lots of support. Well, we took about fifty people down and it was getting on by that time toward campaign for Celentano. We made all the capital out of that we could, so the result was we did get results. Quite fast. They put, oh I don't know, $50,000 in the kitty and started repairing the school. Well, I suppose it was because of this that I was appointed to the CACE [Citizens Advisory Com-mittee on Education] thing. . . . And the next thing was, of course that there came a showdown on the School Board [and two members were not reappointed]. That's how I got involved in the Board—very simple.

Another member whose route to the Board was almost identical re-called:

> The first [PTA] meeting I attended . . . was one in which the school building program was discussed. This committee reported, that's why I went, and I had some things to say that night and one thing led to another, and . . . the first thing that happened in that district I was asked to be a president of the PTA. The principal called me one night and they were having a meeting and I was quite taken

by surprise. I had never had anything to do with PTA before. . . .
My wife usually went to the meetings. But prior to that, you see, our
children had been small, and we didn't have any particular interest in
PTA before they enrolled in school. So the first thing I knew, I was
appointed—or elected—president of the PTA, and as president of the
PTA I had a good deal more to say than I ever had to say about
educational affairs [before].

He was subsequently appointed to the Citizens Advisory Committee on
Education.

I am an outspoken cuss. At the first meeting which I attended, the
discussion of construction of new schools was up—high schools . . .
I thought the doggone resolution which was being offered was much
too mild, and I had a good deal to say.

Later he became chairman of the CACE and a few years after that he
was appointed to the Board of Education.

These are the exceptional cases. Ordinarily a PTA president is a
housewife who lacks the time, experience, interest, and drive to move
into the real centers of educational influence. Moreover, the focus of the
individual PTA is narrow, since parents are more interested in the
current education of their own children than in enduring problems of
the educational system as a whole. It is probably for these reasons that
the individual PTA's and the New Haven Council of Parent Teachers'
Associations have not played a prominent role in important decisions.

It was because of the limitations of the PTA's that Mayor Lee created
the Citizens Advisory Committee on Education (CACE) in 1954. The
CACE was originally outside the framework of the CAC, largely because many business leaders felt that redevelopment ought to be kept
distinct from education, but at Lee's insistence the CACE was finally
incorporated into the CAC as a special subcommittee. Thus the CACE
furnished a new corps of auxiliaries in the field of public education.

The CACE illustrates nicely the way many citizen committees fit
the needs of leaders. The first chairman, John Braslin, was an educator
who worked in New York and lived in New Haven; he had been chairman of the PTA at a school located in one of the best residential areas
of New Haven. Before World War II, he had taught French at Hill-
house High; he was an old friend of the Mayor—they had even been in
the same platoon in basic training during the Mayor's brief stint in the
army—and the Mayor turned the task of organizing the committee over
to him. Braslin said later,

What I did was to make a list of about 150 names of people . . .
many of whom I knew through Junior Chamber work, through work

prior to the war . . . air raid wardens, and activities of that sort. And then I asked representatives of various organizations like the labor unions and the merchants downtown, the League of Women Voters, the PTA council, to recommend names to me who would be members of the CACE and act as liaison with these various civic, social, and service groups in the city. . . . I whittled the list down to 100 names . . . I wanted a large representative group that would really cover a broad section of the city.

The first task of the CACE and probably its most important one was to help arouse support for new public high schools. But it had other jobs to do, too. Braslin said,

In order to keep this large committee as a functioning group, what I did was to break it down into seven subcommittees and I first appointed a governing board as an executive board composed of fifteen members. . . . I figured . . . I'll pick these people because these are the ones that I will have to work with, that I will be openly responsible for, and on whom I will depend to lead and encourage and arouse the other members of the over-all committee. So from among these fifteen I was able to draw a chairmanship for each of the seven subcommittees. Then, the executive board first decided on and we picked seven areas of study: personnel, finance, building, school population, and publicity, public relations, and the like.

The leaders then sent out a note to the members asking them to indicate the area each was most interested in; they placed the members on sub-committees according to their interests.

From its inception, then, the CACE was an instrument of its leaders for generating support for schools. How effective it was it is difficult to say. There is little doubt that it helped to generate support for new high schools at a time when the mayor badly needed support. It pressed for higher teachers' salaries. It sponsored an improved program for testing the vision of school children that was finally adopted by the Board of Education.

RITUAL AND REALITY

But as in party nominations and redevelopment, the distinction between the ritual and the reality of power in public education is obscured by reciprocal relationships between leaders and constituents through which constituents exert a good deal of *indirect* influence on the decisions of leaders. This reciprocal relation is illustrated by events surrounding the mayoralty election of 1945.

In education, as I have suggested, latent discontent with the achievements of the schools is generally not widespread among the parents of school children; hence it is more difficult for leaders to stimulate demands for schools than it has been for redevelopment. However, in 1945 dissatisfaction *was* widespread, and leaders took advantage of the discontent to generate demands. Just as the election of 1955 proved to be decisive for redevelopment, because it seemed to confirm the existence of widespread support for it, so the election of 1945 created in the local political stratum a belief in the potency of school teachers and parents when they are aroused.

During the long administration of Mayor Murphy, from the first years of the Great Depression to the close of the Second World War, the public schools shared the fate of most other municipal services in New Haven. They declined. Murphy was elected in 1931 on a platform that promised to restore the city's unfavorable credit standing. The public schools entered hard times. Teachers' salaries, which had never been high, remained low. School buildings deteriorated. In 1930 more than a third of New Haven's elementary schools were already at least half a century old. Yet they were destined to grow older, for despite the vast surge of Public Works Administration construction that dotted the rest of the nation with new school buildings, not a single public school nor a single addition to a public school was built in New Haven between 1929 and 1947. At the depth of the Depression in the school year 1933–34, annual expenditures per pupil dropped in New Haven to $80, compared with $115 in Hartford. Of seventeen cities with populations between 110,000 and 325,000 in New England, New York, New Jersey, and Pennsylvania, New Haven was third from the bottom in expenditures per pupil in 1937–38 and in 1943–45.[8]

In 1945, as the war approached an end, as wartime shortages no longer served as an adequate justification for not building schools, and as the inflation induced by the war economy continued to bite into teachers' salaries, resentment rose among teachers and parents. To DiCenzo and Celentano, who had decided that Celentano should re-enter politics after his wartime withdrawal, the disaffection of the teachers and other city employees was a happy stroke of fortune. They therefore approached the teachers (and other city workers), entered into an electoral compact with them, and helped them to organize. They privately promised a few of the leaders among the teachers special consideration in the event of a Republican victory and agreed to improve the schools. The Teachers' League and the League of Women Voters took the lead in pointing up the deficiencies of the school system. Although ostensibly nonpartisan (and although most of its leaders were, like Murphy, Irish Catholics and

8. Ibid., p. 322,

probably Democrats), the Teachers' League openly placed the blame for the deterioration of the schools on the city administration in a pamphlet that appeared before the election that year. The League charged,

> For some time New Haven has been going backward. . . . The chief reason is this: Those who have been administering the city do not believe in progress. . . . They believe it is inevitably going to decay. Their only policy, therefore, is one of economy. . . . This view they have evidenced in many things, but in nothing more than in their policy toward the public schools.

In graphic terms and heavily inked drawings they detailed the charges: deterioration, danger, dirt, ill-lighted buildings, out-of-date textbooks, insufficient playgrounds, excessive clerical and other demands on teachers' time, low salaries, poor working conditions, high turnover of teachers, loss of pupils to private schools. The teachers and parents were strongly supported by the League of Women Voters.

Celentano's decisive victory, in which he carried twenty-three of the city's thirty-three wards, was widely attributed among professional politicians to his support not only from the city's Italian population but also from city employees and from teachers and parents aroused over the state of the schools. After his election, Mayor Celentano appointed a Citizens Advisory Committee of distinguished citizens. He hired a professor of educational administration from Cornell to conduct a survey of the public school system with the aid of a staff of nearly fifty people. (The survey, completed in 1947, recommended the independence of education from politics, more effective professional leadership, more expenditures on the schools, and "as soon as building prices appear to be somewhat stabilized, an extensive program of rebuilding and remodeling." [10]) A new superintendent was appointed. School expenditures went up, along with a general increase in the city budget. Teachers' salaries were raised. Two new elementary schools were constructed, and a third was on the way by 1953. And some of the teachers who had worked most actively for Celentano's election in 1945 were suitably rewarded; one even became a high school principal.

The relations of influence between leaders and constituents in this struggle involving the schools were pervaded by ambiguities. A few people, the leaders, evidently exerted great direct influence on a series of decisions about teachers' salaries, appointments, appropriations, buildings. But some of these leaders were elected to office because parents and teachers expressed their discontent with existing policies by voting against the incumbent. The winning candidate, together with other

10. *New Haven's Schools*, p. 4.

leaders, helped to activate and channel discontent; had they not done so, it might have lain smoldering much longer, even indefinitely, or fizzled out in bootless enterprises. These leaders probably would have had neither the resources nor the skill to manufacture such a politically potent issue had there been no latent predispositions stemming from an accumulation of experiences neither created nor influenced by the leaders.

12. *Overview:* Direct Versus Indirect Influence

The six hypotheses set out at the end of Chapter 8 seem to be consistent with the processes for making decisions in New Haven, at least in the three issue-areas examined in the preceding three chapters. If one analyzes the way in which influence in these three issue-areas is distributed among citizens of New Haven, one finds that only a small number of persons have much *direct* influence, in the sense that they successfully initiate or veto proposals for policies. These persons, the leaders, have subleaders and followers. Because of widespread belief in the democratic creed, however, overt relationships of influence are frequently accompanied by democratic ceremonials, which, though ceremonial, are not devoid of consequences for the distribution of influence. The choices made by constituents in critical elections, such as those in New Haven in 1945 and 1955, do have great *indirect* influence on the decisions of leaders, for results of elections are frequently interpreted by leaders as indicating a preference for or acquiescence in certain lines of policy.

Assuming one could measure the amount of influence each adult in New Haven exerts over decisions in a given issue-area, the distribution of *direct* influence would look something like Figure 12.1. Many con-

FIGURE 12.1. *A schematic diagram of the distribution of direct influence on decisions*

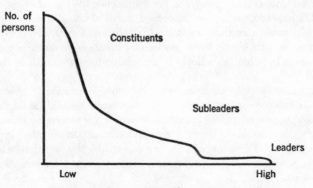

No. of persons

Constituents

Subleaders

Leaders

Low   High

Amount of influence over decisions in a given sector

stituents have no direct influence at all; most people have very little. Subleaders of course have much more; the influence of the most powerful subleaders merges imperceptibly into that of leaders. Only a tiny group, the leaders, exerts great influence.

If one were to illustrate *indirect* influence, the distribution would look something like Figure 12.2. A few citizens who are nonvoters, and who for

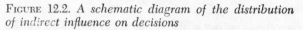

FIGURE 12.2. *A schematic diagram of the distribution of indirect influence on decisions*

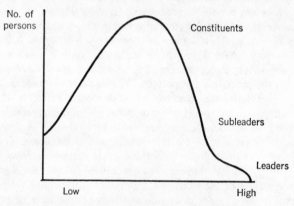

some reason have no influential contact with voters, have no indirect influence. Most citizens, however, possess a moderate degree of indirect influence, for elected leaders keep the real or imagined preferences of constituents constantly in mind in deciding what policies to adopt or reject. Subleaders have greater indirect influence than most other citizens, since leaders ordinarily are concerned more about the response of an individual subleader than an individual citizen. Finally, leaders exert a great amount of indirect influence on one another, for each is guided to some extent by what he believes is acceptable to some or all of the other leaders.

Unfortunately, one cannot measure influence so precisely; although the diagrams are convenient illustrations, they leave us with ambiguities in the relations of leaders and constituents which are extremely difficult and probably impossible to resolve satisfactorily at present by appeal to direct evidence. These ambiguities are created by the fact that leaders do not merely *respond* to the preferences of constituents; leaders also *shape* preferences.

Suppose the leaders in every issue-area are substantially identical and agree on the policies they want. One may even suppose that although not identical they are all drawn from a single homogeneous stratum of the community and therefore possess identical or complementary objectives—which is rather as it must have been in the days of the patrician oligarchy. The capacity of leaders to shape the preferences of citizens would surely be relatively high in either case. Ordinary citizens would depend on a single, unified body of leaders for information and cues about policies; they would have relatively little opportunity to pick up information about other alternatives. Moreover, if leaders in all issue-areas were substantially alike and agreed on objectives, they could combine their political resources to induce citizens to support their policies through many different techniques of coercion and persuasion. Leaders could, and presumably would, *aggregate their resources* to achieve common objectives.

Suppose, on the other hand, that leaders differ from area to area and disagree among themselves, and that because of their disagreements they actively seek for support from constituents. Then the capacity of leaders to shape the preferences of citizens would—other things remaining the same—be lower. Citizens would have alternative sources of information, and the techniques of coercion and persuasion employed by one group of leaders could be countered to some extent by other leaders.

Clearly, then, in order to answer the question, "Who rules in New Haven?" we need to know more than the *distribution* of influence. We need also to know something about *patterns* of influence. Four questions are particularly relevant.

First, from what social strata are leaders and subleaders in different issue-areas drawn?

Second, to what extent are they drawn from the same strata?

Third, to what extent do leaders and subleaders in the same or different issue-areas agree on objectives?

Fourth, to the extent that they disagree, how do leaders and sub-leaders in different issue-areas resolve disagreements?

Book III

PATTERNS OF INFLUENCE

13. Specialization of Influence: Subleaders

Probably the most striking characteristic of influence in New Haven is the extent to which it is *specialized;* that is, individuals who are influential in one sector of public activity tend not to be influential in another sector; and, what is probably more significant, the social strata from which individuals in one sector tend to come are different from the social strata from which individuals in other sectors are drawn.

This specialization shows up most clearly among the subleaders, whose characteristics will be examined in this chapter. In the next, evidence will be presented bearing on the specialization of the top leaders.

SIMILARITIES AMONG SUBLEADERS

Considered as a group, the subleaders in the three issue-areas studied earlier—party nominations, urban redevelopment, and public education—possess certain similarities that tend to distinguish them from the average registered voter.

First, subleaders stand somewhat above their fellow citizens in financial position, educational attainments, and social status. (Table 13.1) In a society where public life is still widely thought to be a man's world and where men rather than women are generally expected to occupy the positions of responsibility, it is not surprising that two-thirds of the subleaders are men. But they are distinguished by more than merely the conventional privileges of American manhood. Subleadership in New Haven is skewed toward the middling strata. Subleaders tend to live in better than average residential areas. The majority hold white-collar jobs. Even within the white-collar category itself, there are three times as many professionals, proprietors, and managers among the subleaders as among registered voters. The subleaders have received considerably more education. They earn more money. They are more likely to own their own homes.

Considering the electorate of New Haven, the working classes are numerically underrepresented and the middle strata numerically overrepresented among the subleaders. Just over half the sample of registered voters regard themselves as belonging to the working class; although we asked no comparable question of subleaders it seems doubtful that many more than the 9 per cent who were skilled or semi-skilled manual em-

TABLE 13.1. *Subleaders are a somewhat select group*

	Subleaders[a] 1958 %	Registered voters[b] 1959 %	Population 1950 %
40 years of age or over	73	63	53 [c]
Males	66	49	49 [c]
Live in Class I, II, and III residential areas	57	31	36 [d]
White-collar occupations	69	37	42 [e]
Educated beyond high school	54	19	14 [e]
Annual income over $10,000	30	6	3 [e]
Own own homes	63	42	32 [f]

Notes:

a. Data on subleaders in this and other tables unless otherwise noted are from a 1958 survey sample of 297, consisting of 136 subleaders in the Democratic and Republican parties, 115 in urban renewal and redevelopment, and 46 in public education. See Appendix B.

b. Data on registered voters in this and other tables unless otherwise noted are from a 1959 survey of a sample of 525 registered voters. See Appendix B.

c. Percentage of population over 20. U.S. Census Bureau, *Population Census, 1950*, Vol. II, Part I, p. 143.

d. From an unpublished table, "New Haven Residential Areas by Predominant Characteristics," based on interviews with a 5% sample of heads of households of the New Haven metropolitan area during 1950–51, Department of Sociology, Yale University.

e. *Population Census, 1950*, Vol. II, Part I, Table 44, p. 1–96, Table 53, p. 1–104, and Table 57, p. 1–104.

f. U.S. Census Bureau, *County and City Data Book, 1956*, p. 365.

ployees would call themselves members of the working class. But in an affluent and complex society where the terms "middle class" and "working class" have increasingly less exact meaning, it might be more informative to say that by almost any measure the subleaders, on the average, stand one or two social levels higher than the voters, who are themselves of slightly higher social and economic position than the adult population as a whole. For example, if occupations are divided into seven categories ranging from major professionals and higher managers at the top to unskilled laborers at the bottom, the average voter will be found at the margin between the fourth category (clerical and sales employees and technicians) and the fifth (skilled manual employees) whereas the average subleader falls at the margin between the second category (managers, proprietors, and lesser professionals) and the third (administrative employees, small businessmen, etc.).

One might conjecture that the subleaders are an ambitious lot who from beginnings like those of the average voter have moved farther and more rapidly. But this seems not to be the case. A high degree of social and economic mobility is a characteristic of American life, as it probably is in any country that undergoes rapid industrialization and economic growth. Yet, judging from admittedly rather incomplete data, the subleaders do not seem to have advanced themselves more than others; they simply began at a somewhat higher level. To be sure, half the leaders who gave us information on their fathers' occupations were in occupations of higher status than their fathers, but so were half the voters. About four out of ten had moved from less desirable neighborhoods to their present residences, but so had four out of ten voters. Why then do the subleaders seem to end up better off in these respects than the voters? Mainly, it seems, because they began with a head start. Slightly more than half the subleaders reported that their fathers had worked in white-collar occupations compared with about one-fourth of the voters.

Second, despite these advantages, subleaders are much more similar to the voters than to the Social and Economic Notability of New Haven. For example, only about four out of every ten subleaders have completed college; although this is enough to distinguish them from the voters, among whom only about one out of ten has finished college, it also marks them off from a Notability in which a college diploma is taken for granted. Moreover, only 4 per cent of the subleaders attended a private day school; another 4 per cent attended a private boarding school. Nearly 80 per cent attended public high school; and a tiny group—about 2 per cent—attended a parochial high school.

Consider other marks of social position. Take residence, for example: if residential areas are ranked in six categories according to various criteria of social standing,[1] only one out of six subleaders lives in a Class I neighborhood, and only a third live in the top two categories. Or take income: one-fifth of the subleaders reported a family income under $5,000 a year. Just as the voters did, nearly two-fifths of the subleaders reported incomes between $5,000 and $10,000. Ninety-three per cent said that their principal source of income was their job or husband.

The subleaders are most assuredly not an interlocking business elite. Four out of five have no business affiliations other than their jobs; only 7 per cent have more than one additional business affiliation; only 3 per cent have business affiliations outside New Haven. Only one out of ten is a director of a bank or other business firm; almost without exception the directors were subleaders in urban redevelopment, and their firms were local rather than national corporations.

This similarity to the voters rather than the Notables is perhaps most sharply revealed by the fact that the subleaders are predominantly of

1. See Appendix C.

recent immigrant stock. Very few are Yankees by origin. Four out of ten in our sample were born outside New Haven; one out of three was born outside New England; about one out of twelve was born in Europe, mainly in Italy or Eastern Europe. It might be thought that at least those born in New Haven are Yankees. But this is not the case. The fathers of 70 per cent of the subleaders were born outside New England. In fact the fathers of over half were born in Europe, and the fathers of another fifth were born in the United States but outside New England. Only one-fifth of the subleaders claimed that any one of their four grand-parents was born in New England; in fact, seven out of ten had at least one grandparent who was born in Europe.

A third characteristic of the subleaders is that they are joiners. (Table 13.2) One might suppose that the propensity of subleaders for joining

TABLE 13.2. *Subleaders are joiners*

Number of organization affiliations°	Subleaders %	Voters %
None	—	1
One or two	15	70
Three or four	36	22
Five or more	47	7
No answer	3	1
Total	101	101
N	281	525

° For both subleaders and voters, religion is automatically counted as one affiliation.

organizations is no more than a reflection of the general fact that par-ticipation in organizations, like political participation, is a function of status, income, and education. But this explanation fails to account for the special avidity with which subleaders join organizations, for even when income and education are taken into account the difference be-tween subleaders and voters is still very marked. Among college graduates, for example, 61 per cent of the subleaders in our sample belong to five or more organizations compared with only 14 per cent of our sample of voters. Among high school graduates, 70 per cent of the voters belong to only one or two organizations compared with 19 per cent of the subleaders; more than four times as many subleaders belong to five or more organizations. The difference between voters and sub-leaders in joining organizations also remains striking when income is taken into account.

The subleaders are not only joiners; they actually attend meetings and serve as officers—or so they claim. Sixty per cent said they usually attended the meetings of their clubs and organizations. Seventy per cent have been officers or committee members at one time or another, compared with only 15 per cent of the registered voters.

Fourth, it is hardly surprising to find that the subleaders indicate considerably more interest in public affairs than the voters. (Table 13.3) Doubtless many citizens are in positions of subleadership precisely

TABLE 13.3. *Subleaders are interested in public affairs*

| | Subleaders | | |
	National affairs %	Local affairs %	Voters %
Very interested in public (local and national) affairs	63	77	23
Somewhat (fairly)	31	18	47
Not interested at all (Not so interested, uninterested)	4	4	28
No answer	1	2	1
Total	99	99	99
N	281	281	525

Note: Questions were slightly different for the two groups. Words in parentheses were used for subleaders.

because they do have relatively intense interest in some aspect of public policy. Indeed, given the general indifference of the mass of voters, the innumerable opportunities, and the insatiable needs of leaders for a corps of auxiliaries, almost anyone who publicly expresses a high degree of interest in public affairs is likely to be invited sooner or later to join some civic organization. No doubt the process works the other way around at times, and individuals who become auxiliaries for other reasons may in the course of their experiences develop a heightened interest in public affairs.

Again, one might suppose that the greater interest expressed by subleaders than by voters is merely a function of their education, but this seems not to be the case. Among the college graduates in both groups, a considerably higher proportion of subleaders say they are very interested in public affairs; among the high school graduates the difference is four to one. Indeed, among the subleaders a slightly higher proportion of high school graduates than of college graduates express a keen interest in public affairs. Nor does the higher average income of subleaders account for the difference in level of interest, for subleaders with lower incomes seem to be just as interested as subleaders with higher incomes.

As might be expected of people interested and involved in public affairs, subleaders are avid newspaper readers. Judging from our sample, virtually every one of them reads one of the local newspapers; about 70 per cent read at least one out-of-town paper and nearly a third claim to read two or more; half read the *New York Times*. Half also read a picture magazine like *Life* or *Look*, and slightly under half read a news magazine like *Time* or *Newsweek*. Only 5 per cent reported that they read one of the "liberal" magazines like *The Nation*, *New Republic*, or *The Reporter*. About four out of five watch television more than an hour a day; one-sixth reported watching it as much as three hours a day.

DIFFERENCES AMONG SUBLEADERS

So far, the subleaders have been treated as a single group. Do they, however, differ among themselves? Are the subleaders who participate in political nominations drawn from the same segments of the community as the subleaders in redevelopment and education? Are they perhaps even the same individuals?

The fact that the subleaders are predominantly "middle class" in their characteristics suggests that one of three possible patterns may describe their relationship.

First, the subleaders in one issue-area may be the same individuals as the subleaders in other areas. The existence of this pattern would strongly support the hypothesis that a single cohesive middle-class group of leaders and subleaders exercises predominant influence over the major public policy decisions in New Haven.

Second, the subleaders in each area may be different individuals and yet share essentially the same interests and social characteristics. This pattern would support the hypothesis that a cohesive middle-class group of leaders and subleaders dominates decisions in New Haven although its members specialize among themselves in order to cover the major areas of policy.

Third, subleaders in different areas may be different persons with significantly different interests and social characteristics. This pattern would lend evidence to the hypothesis that the leaders and subleaders who influence decisions in New Haven are not members of a cohesive group at all but reflect the interests and concerns of different segments of the population.

The first pattern definitely does not exist in New Haven. Convincing evidence is displayed in Tables 13.4 and 13.5, which show the overlap in the "leadership pools" in the three issue-areas. The pools consist of the names of all leaders and subleaders involved in a particular issue-area. Out of 1,029 leaders and subleaders in the three pools, only thirty-

TABLE 13.4. *Multiple leadership in New Haven, 1958*

	Number in leadership pools		
		More than one	
Issue-area	One issue-area only	issue-area	Total
Urban redevelopment	406	29	435
Political nominations	477	20	497
Public education	114	17	131
Total	997	66	1,063
Total, less duplication	997	32	1,029
As % of total	97%	3%	100%

two—or 3 per cent—are engaged in more than one issue-area. (Table 13.4) Only two persons are involved in all three. (Table 13.5)

Or consider the overlap between any two sectors. (Table 13.5) Since the pools are of different sizes the maximum possible overlap would exist if all the members of a smaller pool were also members of a larger pool. Yet only 2 per cent of all the leaders and subleaders in public education are involved in political nominations. Only 9 per cent are involved in urban redevelopment—and it is worth noticing that most of these are included as members of the urban redevelopment pool only

TABLE 13.5. *Overlap among the leaders and subleaders in three issue-areas, 1958*

	Urban redevel- opment and nominations	Urban redevel- ment and education	Education and nominations	All three
Maximum possible overlap	435	131	131	131
Actual overlap	15	12	3	2
Actual as % of possible	3%	9%	2%	1.5%

by virtue of their membership on the Citizens Advisory Committee for Education, which, as we saw in the last chapter, was made a subcommittee of the CAC. Only 3 per cent of the leaders and subleaders in urban redevelopment are involved in political nominations.[2]

What of the second possibility? Are the subleaders in different issue-areas merely specialized representatives drawn from essentially the same social strata? The evidence points strongly against this hypothesis and in favor of the view that the subleaders in different issue-areas are

2. I am grateful to Nelson Polsby for compiling these figures. The same data are set out and discussed in his "Three Problems in the Analysis of Community Power," *American Sociological Review, 24* (1959), 796–803.

drawn from and reflect the divergent interests of different strata in the community. For example, the subleaders involved in party nominations bear many of the characteristics of the average registered voter; the subleaders in urban redevelopment, by contrast, are very different from the average registered voter; and the subleaders in public education are a middling group between the other two. At the risk of great over-simplification, one might say that the subleaders in urban redevelopment are drawn from the upper and the upper-middle strata; the subleaders in public education are drawn exclusively from the middle strata; and the subleaders in the political parties are drawn from the lower-middle and the upper working strata.

Consider, for example, the neighborhoods, occupations, and incomes of the subleaders. A much larger proportion of the subleaders in urban redevelopment live in the best neighborhoods, are top managers or professionals (lawyers, doctors, dentists, etc.) and earn $10,000 a year or more. (Table 13.6) In fact, about one out of four subleaders in urban redevelopment lives in one of the best neighborhoods; one out of three is a professional man or higher executive; and about one out of two has an income of $10,000 or more.

The subleaders in public education are concentrated more than the others in the middling strata of the community. About six out of ten live in Class II and Class III neighborhoods, work as managers, proprietors, lesser professionals, administrative employees, or small businessmen, or have incomes between $5,000 and $10,000 a year.

The subleaders in political nominations furnish a nice contrast with those in redevelopment and in education, for a much higher proportion come from the lower white-collar and wage-earning strata. They are very much more likely than other subleaders to live in Class IV, V, or VI neighborhoods, to work as clerks, technicians, and wage earners, and to have incomes under $5,000 a year. In fact nearly two-thirds of them live in the bottom three ranks of neighborhoods compared with about one-fourth of the subleaders in education and one-eighth of those in urban redevelopment. Only a negligible proportion of the subleaders in urban redevelopment or in education are clerks, technicians, or wage earners, whereas 42 per cent of the subleaders in political nominations fall into these occupational groups. Four out of ten subleaders concerned with nominations report incomes of less than $5,000, compared with only tiny fractions in the other two groups. In all these respects, as a careful inspection of Table 13.6 will show, the subleaders involved in the nomination system are remarkably similar to the voters.

The one respect in which this untidy social ranking does not prevail is in formal educational attainments, where the subleaders in public education rank fully as high as the subleaders in urban redevelopment—

TABLE 13.6. *Subleaders in different issue-areas are drawn from different social strata*

Characteristics	Subleaders in: Redevelopment %	Public education %	Parties %	Registered voters %
RESIDENTIAL AREAS				
Class I	26	12	7	5
Class II and III	49	60	30	26
Class IV, V, and VI	12	27	62	67
No answer	13	3	1	2
Total	100	100	100	100
OCCUPATION				
Major professionals, higher executives, etc.	32	12	12	5
Managers, administrators, small businessmen	46	59	24	20
Clerks, wage earners	7	5	42	60
No answer	15	24	22	15
Total	100	100	100	100
INCOME				
Above $10,000	54	22	12	6
$5,000–$10,000	30	66	34	39
Below $5,000	6	2	39	47
No answer	10	10	15	8
Total	100	100	100	100
N	115	120	46	525

a fact not altogether surprising. Both groups of subleaders, on the other hand, have notably more formal education than the subleaders in political nominations, who once again are rather similar to the rank-and-file voters. Whereas two out of three subleaders in development and education have completed college or have even gone on to graduate and professional school, two out of three subleaders in political nominations have never gone beyond high school.

A profile of each of the three groups might run something like this. An urban redevelopment subleader is an executive in a large or medium-sized firm, a professional man (or the wife of an executive or professional man), who owns his own home and lives in one of the "good" or even one of the "best" neighborhoods. He earned at least $10,000 a year in 1958. He is probably either a Protestant or a Jew and was not born in the New Haven area. He came from middle-class parents both of whom had been born in the United States; he went to college; and judged by widely prevailing standards he has moved up in the world since his childhood.

The subleader in education is likely to be a professional man or professionally engaged at some time and in some way with education—a school administrator, a teacher, or an ex-teacher. He owns his own home and lives in a neighborhood that is considerably better than average though not one of the best. He earned between $5,000 and $10,000 in 1958. He is probably Catholic, or perhaps Jewish, and he was born in New Haven or the New Haven area. His father was probably a small businessman or white-collar worker born in the United States. He himself went to college and started out in a white-collar job—quite possibly as a school teacher. Considering his background and career so far, by the usual standards he has advanced considerably beyond his beginnings.

The subleader involved in political nominations might strike many people as the epitome of the average man. He is a white-collar worker, probably a salesman or clerk or perhaps a small businessman who left school during or after completing high school. He rents or owns a home in an average neighborhood. In 1958 his income was between $3,000 and $7,500. He is a Catholic who was born in New Haven. His father was probably a wage earner who was born outside the United States; almost certainly both his grandparents were immigrants.

THE DYNAMICS OF RECRUITMENT

It is not difficult to account for this pattern of specialized subleadership. In order to mobilize the support they need, leaders look for subleaders well adapted to the characteristics of a particular set of constituents. But the supply of recruits in a given segment of the population is strongly influenced by its peculiar social and economic environment, for this helps to determine the sorts of things one is interested in and therefore the extent to which one is willing or even eager to work as a subleader. The needs of leaders determine the demand; the interests of citizens determine the supply.

Considered from this point of view, it is altogether natural that the characteristics of subleaders in political nominations would approximate rather closely those of the average voter, for not only do political leaders need subleaders who are not too sharply distinguished from the voters, but citizens who are interested in holding positions as party functionaries are likely to be men and women of rather average attainments. Party leaders must have organizations in the poor wards as well as the rich, among the immigrant and foreign-speaking voters as well as the Yankees, among the ignorant as well as the educated. In the poor ward the party functionary is more likely to be poor than rich; in the Italian ward he is more likely to be of Italian than of Yankee extraction; in a ward where few people have gone beyond the eighth grade, the ward leader is not likely to hold a Ph.D. in political science. (In 1959 the only alderman who had a Ph.D. represented the First Ward—where Yale is located. The degree, incidentally, *was* in political science and it was earned, of all places, at Harvard.) Although political leaders need representatives who work easily with constituents and therefore are not too sharply set off from the voters, at the same time they do not necessarily want mere nonentities. A man with some standing in his neighborhood is likely to influence more votes than a nonentity. Hence the thrust of the recruiting efforts of leaders is toward a man who stands out a little from his neighbors but not so much that he seems remote and unapproachable.

The supply of recruits is limited, however, by the relatively low attraction of politics. When registered voters were asked, "If you had a son just getting out of school, would you like to see him go into politics as a life work?" 57 per cent of our sample of voters gave an unqualified no, and only 28 per cent gave an unqualified yes. For most people the primary activities of family and occupation push politics out to the periphery of interest, concern, and activity. Moreover, party politics does not carry much prestige. The defeat of the patricians by the new men of business and these in turn by ex-plebes who commanded the fealty of the immigrants reduced the prestige of politics among people of standing. Today, as we saw, Social and Economic Notables are scarcely to be found anywhere in public life. Businessmen in particular and the middle classes in general avoid partisan roles—at least in public—and prefer nonpartisan activities like the Community Fund that create few enemies. Hence the only persons who stand to gain much in the way of prestige by taking a position of subleadership in one of the parties are those of lower standing.

Once prestige went out of politics, little was left to attract people into subleadership positions. For the ordinary auxiliary in the parties, the material rewards are, like those of power and prestige, too slight to hold any attraction for people of means. Party functionaries are unpaid, as are aldermen, and except for a few top positions the pay in city jobs is modest. For this reason also, many people in the middling strata shun politics.

Thus factors both of demand and supply converge to recruit individuals of average attainments into political party activities.

In a similar way the strategies of leaders and the interests of particular strata of the population converge to provide a set of auxiliaries in urban redevelopment who are well above the average voter in attainments. As we saw, the leaders who designed the CAC deliberately sought to attract a collection of subleaders to redevelopment and renewal who would lend prestige and nonpartisanship to the program and help sell it not only to the community at large but to certain groups in particular—business, industry, professionals, middle-class do-gooders, egg-head liberals, the trade unions, and others. The implications of redevelopment guaranteed that these groups would be the most interested; hence it was not difficult to recruit the kinds of people the leaders wanted.

The fact that public education is a city-wide function forces geographical and social dispersion among its subleaders; but the nature of public education means that better educated individuals are likely to be concerned with and interested in this issue-area. The number of potential recruits from better educated levels is reduced, however, because well-to-do professional and business men are inclined to send their children to private schools. Thus we find that public education draws subleaders from the middling groups in the community—people who are below the top but definitely above the bottom social, economic, and educational levels.

It is not surprising, perhaps, that when subleaders in public education were asked to name the local problem they considered the most important, two-thirds mentioned education and only one-third mentioned redevelopment. Among the subleaders in redevelopment, by contrast, slightly over half mentioned redevelopment while less than a third mentioned education. No doubt the causal connection runs both ways; individuals who are most interested in a particular area of policy are most likely to be recruited, and the interest of those who are recruited is reinforced by participation.

14. Specialization of Influence: Leaders

The specialization that characterizes the subleaders is also marked among the leaders. With few exceptions any particular individual exerts a significant amount of direct influence in no more than one of the three issue-areas studied.

Of the various decisions examined in redevelopment, twenty-six actors (persons or groups) succeeded in initiating a policy or vetoing a proposed policy. In party nominations, thirteen actors were successful—four in the Democratic party and nine in the Republican party. In public education, sixteen actors exerted direct influence. (Table 14.1) Eliminating duplica-

TABLE 14.1. *Leadership in three issue-areas*

Number of actors successful:	Redevelopment	Party Nominations Democratic	Republican	Public education	Total, including duplications
One time	19	0	4	7	30
Two or three times	5	2	2	8	17
Four or more times	2	2	3	1	8
Total	26	4	9	16	55

tions, fifty different individual actors initiated or vetoed policies in all three.

However, only three leaders initiated or vetoed policies in more than one issue-area. These were Lee, Logue, and Celentano.

Of the remaining forty-seven leaders, twenty-seven, or more than half, exerted direct influence in only one instance. Seventeen exerted direct influence in two or three instances in only one issue-area. And three exerted direct influence in four or more instances in only one area. These three were Golden, DiCenzo, and Frank Lynch, who were, as we have seen, dominant in political nominations. (Table 14.2)

Altogether, six leaders successfully initiated or vetoed proposals four times or more in at least one issue-area. These were Lee, Logue, Golden, Celentano, DiCenzo, and Lynch. Of these, only two—the two mayors, Celentano and Lee—exerted direct influence in all three. Logue, one of the top leaders in redevelopment, also initiated one proposal in public education. Despite their very great influence on political nominations,

TABLE 14.2. *The scarcity of multiple leaders*

Level of influence°	N
Low: one success in one issue-area, none in others	27
Intermediate: two or three successes in one issue-area, none in others	17
High:	
Four or more successes in one area, none in others	3
Four or more successes in one area, one in another	2
Four or more successes in all three issue-areas	1
Total	50

° Some combinations are not shown because there were no cases.

Golden, Celentano, DiCenzo, and Lynch played no significant role in decisions on public education and redevelopment.

Doubtless greater overlap could be found in other sectors of policy—for example, in party nominations, patronage, and city contracts. It would be injudicious to conclude that Golden's influence in the Lee administration, or DiCenzo's in the Celentano administration, was in fact limited strictly to political nominations. Despite these qualifications, however, the extent of specialization of influence is striking. In New Haven, it would appear, only the mayor is in a position to exercise much direct influence on more than a few sectors of public policy.

Direct influence is not only specialized. To a great extent it reposes—or at any rate it has in recent years—in the hands of public officials. Of twenty-five persons with high or intermediate influence, sixteen were public officials. (Table 14.3) The one highly influential Notable was John Golden, whose position we examined in Chapter 6.

TABLE 14.3. *Sources of leadership*

Level of influence	Public officials	Notables or corporations	Others	Total
Low	11 °	8 °	8	27
Intermediate	12 °	4 °	3	19
High	4	1	1	6
Total	27	13	12	52 °°

° An individual who was both an official and a Notable was counted in both columns.
°° Includes two individuals who were counted both as officials and Notables.

To what extent are the leaders drawn from a single homogeneous stratum of the community? Of the fifty different actors, fifteen were agencies, groups, or corporations; they acted in situations where it was impossible to ascribe the initiation or veto of policy to a particular person. Of these fifteen collective actors, four were business firms, three were citizen groups, and eight were federal, state, or local government agencies. Of the thirty-five individual persons, seven were Social or Economic Notables and the remaining twenty-eight were not. Sixteen of the individual persons were of Yankee, English, or Scotch-Irish stock; six were of Irish stock; four were of Italian stock; and nine were of various European origins, other than Ireland, Italy, or the British Isles. Seventeen were Protestants, thirteen were Catholics, and five were Jews.

As with the subleaders, the issue-area in which a leader's influence is specialized seems to be a function of durable interests or concerns. These interests can usually be traced initially to professional or occupational goals and strivings. Leaders in redevelopment are with a few exceptions officially, professionally, or financially involved in its fate. Most of the leaders in the public schools have a professional connection of some kind with education. The occupational ties of party leaders are more complex. Usually, however, there is a reciprocal benefit: party connections advance the leader in his occupational goals, and occupational success in turn enables him to enhance his influence in the party.

Thus the answers to two of the questions set out at the end of Chapter 12 are furnished by the phenomenon of specialization:

First, a leader in one issue-area is not likely to be influential in another. If he is, he is probably a public official and most likely the mayor.

Second, leaders in different issue-areas do not seem to be drawn from a single homogeneous stratum of the community.

The other questions remain. To what extent do leaders in different issue-areas agree on a common strategy? And how do they settle their conflicts? In short, how are the actions of different leaders with specialized influence over decisions in different issue-areas integrated?

15. Five Patterns of Leadership

The number of theoretically possible patterns of integration is almost infinite. However, because of their familiarity and generality, five possibilities were considered in our study of New Haven. These were:

1. Covert integration by Economic Notables.
2. An executive-centered "grand coalition of coalitions."
3. A coalition of chieftains.
4. Independent sovereignties with spheres of influence.
5. Rival sovereignties fighting it out.

The first of these, covert integration by the Economic Notables, is a common answer suggested by studies of a number of other cities. In this pattern the top leaders consist of a unified group of private citizens who arrive at agreements about policies by covert negotiations and discussions carried on in the privacy of their clubs, homes, business firms, and other private meeting places. Leaders gain their influence from their wealth, high social standing, and economic dominance. Usually the leaders are wealthy executives in important business firms; if this pattern fitted New Haven, presumably the top officers of Yale would be included because the university is one of the largest property owners and employers in the city.

A revealing aspect of this hypothesis is its insistence on the essentially clandestine or covert exercise of influence by the "real" leaders. Why? Because in most cities today the overt, public incumbents in the highest official positions—the mayors and other elected politicians, city officials, party chairmen, and so on—are rarely drawn from the ranks of wealth, social standing, and corporate office. By contrast, the patricians of New Haven were an *overt* political elite. They made no bones about their dominance. They not only openly occupied key positions in the religious, educational, and economic institutions of New Haven, but they also held a visible monopoly of all the important public offices. This, as we have seen, is indisputably not so today. If individuals of wealth, status, and corporate position dominate politics, evidently they *must* do so covertly.

The hypothesis of covert control by the Economic Notables is both widely popular and strongly supported by many scholarly studies, from the Lynds' monumental examination of Muncie, Indiana in the twenties and thirties to Floyd Hunter's more recent analysis of the "power structure" of Atlanta.[1] Indeed the term "power structure" has so much passed into the vocabulary of the informed man that it has become a current bit of jargon among educated inside-dopesters. Although careful analysis has shown that the conclusions about influence contained in the academic studies often rest upon dubious evidence and even that some of the data found in the works themselves actually run counter to the conclusions,[2] some communities do seem to have conformed to this pattern in the past and some may today. Certainly some citizens of New Haven believe firmly in the existence of a covert elite and offer plausible evidence to support their view.

I believe the evidence advanced in previous chapters is sufficient to warrant the rejection of the hypothesis that this pattern applies to New Haven. In every city where Economic Notables are alleged to rule covertly, it is important to note, evidently they do so by means sufficiently open to permit scholars and newspapermen to penetrate the veil; indeed, an inspection of the information contained in descriptions of these cities indicates that the job of probing into the clandestine structure of power has presented few barriers to the assiduous researcher. It is all the more improbable, then, that a secret cabal of Notables dominates the public life of New Haven through means so clandestine that not one of the fifty prominent citizens interviewed in the course of this study—citizens who had participated extensively in various decisions—hinted at the existence of such a cabal; so clandestine, indeed, that no clues turned up in several years of investigation led to the door of such a group.

To abandon the hypothesis of covert integration by Economic Notables does not mean that the Economic Notables in New Haven are without influence on certain important decisions. In Chapter 6 I have tried to describe the scope and limits of their influence; in chapters to follow I shall return to certain other aspects of their influence, particularly to the problem of explaining the paradox that a stratum of the community with seemingly superior economic and social resources has only limited direct influence on the decisions of local government. I shall take up this matter in Book V, where I try to account for the distribution and patterns of influence that exist in New Haven. Meanwhile, what the evidence seems to establish rather conclusively is this: if one wants to find out how

1. Lynd and Lynd, *Middletown* and *Middletown in Transition*; Hunter, *Community Power Structure* and *Top Leadership, U.S.A.*

2. For a detailed analysis of this point, see the forthcoming companion volume by Nelson W. Polsby, *Community Power and Political Theory*.

policies of different leaders are coordinated in New Haven, one must consider some pattern other than covert integration by Economic Notables.

A second pattern is envisioned in an alternative hypothesis: that today the top leaders are more likely to comprise a coalition of public officials and private individuals who reflect the interests and concerns of different segments of the community. In this view, a coalition is generally formed and the policies of the coalition are coordinated largely by elected leaders who draw on special skills and resources of influence that leaders without public office are not likely to have. This pattern of integration is usually associated with vigorous, even charismatic elected chief executives; presumably it was characteristic of the presidencies of FDR and Truman.[3]

In its implications the hypothesis of an executive-centered coalition is radically different from the first possible pattern. Where covert domination by Economic Notables reflects relatively stable social and economic factors, the executive-centered coalition may be more ephemeral; the coalition may fluctuate greatly in strength and even dissolve altogether when the coalition's leaders can no longer reconcile their strategies and goals. Moreover, in the pattern of covert domination, influence derived from public office and popularity with the electorate is completely subordinate to influence derived from wealth, social standing, and corporate position; in the executive-centered coalition, the prerogatives of public office, legality, legitimacy, and electoral followings are independent sources of influence with a weight of their own. Finally, the hypothesis of a covert elite logically leads to a certain pessimism about popular government. If government officials and elected politicians are merely handmaidens of the upper classes, one cannot expect much in the way of peaceful reform via politics. Change must come about either through the gradual action of outside factors, like changes in industrial organization or technique, or else through a revolutionary seizure and transformation of the state by leaders of social segments who for some reason cannot win elections and attain public office. The hypothesis of integration by an executive-centered coalition, by contrast, allows for the possibility that reformist or radical coalitions (as well as conservative ones) may, by peacefully winning elections, obtain control of the powers of government and introduce durable changes in the distribution of access to influence, wealth, education, and social standing.

The third pattern is seen as integration of policies in different sectors by a coalition of chieftains. Something like it fits the various party and

3. See Arthur M. Schlesinger, Jr., *The Coming of the New Deal* (Boston, Houghton Mifflin, 1959), Part VIII; James M. Burns, *Roosevelt: The Lion and the Fox* (New York, Harcourt Brace, 1956); Richard Neustadt, *Presidential Power* (New York. John Wiley, 1960).

nonparty coalitions that control policy-making in Congress and particularly in the Senate.[4] The difference between the second pattern and this
one is of course only one of degree; in marginal cases it would be
impossible to say whether a particular pattern of integration should be
called executive-centered or a coalition of chieftains.

A coalition of chieftains, like the executive-centered coalition, is consistent with the hypothesis that nowadays top leaders are likely to be
public officials and private individuals who reflect the varying and even
conflicting interests and concerns of different segments of the community.
In the executive-centered coalition, integration of policy is achieved
largely by means of the skills and resources of an elected leader; in a
coalition of chieftains, integration takes place mainly by negotiations
among the chieftains that produce exchanges of information and even-
tuate in agreement. The executive-centered pattern contains a sizable
degree of hierarchy in the distribution of influence among the leaders. The
chief executive is at the center of a "grand coalition of coalitions"; in the
extreme case he is the only leader with great influence in *all* the allied
coalitions, perhaps the only leader who even *participates* in all of them.
Moreover, his special resources mean that every other leader in the
grand coalition is more dependent on the executive for perpetuation of
his influence than the executive is dependent on him. In a coalition of
chieftains, on the other hand, if hierarchy appears, it is weak and may
rest almost exclusively on a central position in the network of communications occupied by a particular leader or set of leaders. Thus, although a
few chiefs may be somewhat more influential than others, they are all
highly dependent on one another for the successful attainment of their
policies. There is some specialization of influence by issue-areas; a chief-
tain in one area may be deferred to on matters lying in his domain, and
he in turn defers to other chieftains in matters lying in theirs. But the
chiefs actively coordinate their policies through extensive interchange of
information and reciprocal favors. An awareness that their most important
policy goals do not conflict and a predisposition for similar strategies
provide a basis for agreement on strategies.

Since a coalition of chieftains depends almost entirely on likeminded-
ness, reinforced by the arts of negotiation and compromise, the life of a
coalition may be short or long depending on the state of agreement and
the negotiating capacities of the chiefs. A coalition may reflect persistent

4. Recent observers describe Congress in terms that would fit the pattern here,
although each offers highly important differences of emphasis and interpretation.
Cf. David B. Truman, *The Congressional Party* (New York, John Wiley, 1959), Ch.
4; William S. White, *Citadel, The Story of the U.S. Senate* (New York, Harper,
1956), Chs. 8 and 14; Roland Young, *The American Congress* (New York, Harper,
1958), Ch. 3.

goals held among durable social and economic segments or the ephemeral goals of social elements in flux.

With some reservations as to historical accuracy, the fourth and fifth patterns might be regarded as analogous to a system of independent city-states or petty sovereignties. This is the pattern of congressional action dominated by virtually autonomous committees that was described by Woodrow Wilson in his classic *Congressional Government*. It is approached in some ways by what two recent observers find to be the pattern of decision-making in New York City.[5] In this system of petty sovereignties each issue-area is controlled by a different set of top leaders whose goals and strategies are adapted to the particular segments of the community that happen to be interested in that specific area. As long as the policies of the various petty sovereignties do not conflict with one another, the sovereigns go about their business without much communication or negotiation. When policies do conflict, the issue has to be settled by fighting it out; but since the sovereigns live within a common system of legal norms, constitutional practices, and political habits, "Fighting it out" means an appeal to whatever processes are prescribed, whether voting in a legislative or administrative body, decision by judges, executive approval, or elections. The practice of fighting it out increases the likelihood of appeals to the populace for support, and hence the extent to which leaders shape their policies to what they think are the predominant preferences of the populace. However, since fighting it out is mutually costly and the results are highly uncertain, strong spheres of influence may develop with a relatively clear understanding as to the limits of each sphere; in this case, fighting it out is avoided, appeals to the populace are less likely, and policies are shaped more to meet the goals of leaders, subleaders, and special followings.

Thus the way in which petty sovereignties integrate their policies tends to assume one of two patterns, depending on the extent to which the policies of the one sovereign are consistent with those of the other. If the petty sovereigns perceive their policies to be strictly inconsistent, in the sense that a gain for one means an equivalent loss to the other, then conflict is unavoidable and fighting it out is likely to be the method of settlement. This is the case, for example, if the sovereignties are two highly competitive parties, both intent on winning office for their candidates.

However, if the petty sovereigns perceive their policies to be consistent or even complementary, in the sense that a gain for one entails no loss for the other and may even produce a benefit, then fighting it out is likely to be avoided. Possibility of conflict is minimized by mutually accepted

5. Herbert Kaufman and Wallace Sayre, *Governing New York City, Politics in the Metropolis* (New York, Russell Sage Foundation, 1960), Ch. 19.

spheres of influence, combined with a strong presumption that the status quo must be adhered to; it is also understood that if disagreements arise they are to be resolved by implicit, or occasionally explicit, bargaining among the petty sovereigns without an appeal to the populace or other external authorities.

These five patterns of coordination seemed to us most likely to cover the range of possibilities in New Haven, though the likelihood of finding still other patterns could not be excluded a priori. During our investigation of New Haven two possible variations on the five patterns became obvious. First, the prevailing pattern might vary with different combinations of issue-areas. For example, the pattern of integration applying to nominations and elections might not be the same as the pattern applying to education and redevelopment. Second, patterns of integration might vary over time. The variations might be long-run changes, such as the decline of the patrician oligarchy; they might be short-run changes; conceivably, one might even encounter more or less regular fluctuations in integrative patterns associated with, say, periodic elections.

Except for the first pattern (covert integration by Economic Notables), which it now seems safe to reject, all of these possibilities appear to be entirely consistent with the evidence so far. In the chapters that follow I shall demonstrate, from an examination of particular decisions, that all of the remaining four patterns have actually existed in New Haven in recent years. Before 1953 there existed a pattern of independent sovereignties with spheres of influence, which I shall call Pattern A. This gave way briefly to a coalition of chieftains and then, under Mayor Lee, to an executive-centered "grand coalition of coalitions," which I shall call Pattern B. Standing quite apart, the pattern of integration with respect to the political parties has been that of rival sovereignties fighting it out, which I shall call Pattern C.

16. Pattern A: Spheres of Influence

The characteristic pattern of integration in New Haven before Lee's victory in 1953 seems to have been one of independent sovereignties that managed to avoid severe conflict by tacit agreements on spheres of influence. Because the boundaries were by no means perfectly defined, conflicts and disputes sometimes had to be settled by negotiation. But with the exception of the political parties, most of the time each of the petty sovereignties went its way without much interference from the others.

For example, under Mayor Murphy (1931–45) once the basic decision on school appropriations had been made, the public school system was substantially autonomous and largely under the control of the superintendent. Under Mayor Celentano, appropriations were increased and a new superintendent was appointed, but the decentralized pattern continued, and the locus of power remained in the hands of the superintendent. Zoning was substantially autonomous; in practice it was hardly coordinated at all with the work of the City Plan Commission or the Redevelopment Agency. Appointments to the Board of Zoning Appeals were among the most coveted political prizes in the city, since the capacity to grant or refuse variances to zoning regulations could be used to induce payoffs of various kinds. The Board of Fire Commissioners, the Parking Authority, the Housing Authority, the Department of Health, the Department of Public Works and the Building, Plumbing, and Housing Inspectors were each in a different part of the forest.

There was no dominant center of influence over these agencies. The Mayor and the Corporation Counsel constituted whatever center of coordination and control existed. When conflict occurred these two men were usually drawn sooner or later into the negotiations, and their wishes carried weight. But Celentano was not an executive who sought to develop his full influence over the various departments. He was disturbed by public criticism and highly sensitive to the views of the aging owner of the city's two newspapers. Hence after a brief flurry of reform in the school system following his election, the Mayor did not exercise and did not seek to exercise a decisive role in the decisions of the various petty sovereignties that made up the official and unofficial government of New Haven.

Survival of the system of independent sovereignties was aided by three factors. First, because most citizens are indifferent about public matters unless public actions encroach upon their own primary activities (which is not often or for long), control over any given issue-area gravitates to a small group which happens to have the greatest interest in it. Second, because political resources are fragmented (as we shall see in subsequent chapters), no one except the mayor has enough resources at his disposal to exert a high degree of influence over all the issue-areas. In short, given the distribution of resources, if the mayor cannot or does not coordinate policy, then no one else can do so by the deliberate and direct exercise of influence. Thirdly, in this case the Mayor evidently believed that interference with the decisions of properly constituted agencies was undesirable; hence he saw no reason to exploit his available resources to the full in order to gain influence over their decisions. The petty sovereignties, then, enjoyed a large measure of autonomy.

Under some conditions the pattern of petty sovereignties might have produced such total deadlock or such a rapid increase in city outlays for various agencies as to be politically self-destructive. For several reasons, however, the pattern was relatively durable; indeed, New Haven may well revert to the pattern again. Because there is little basic disagreement over policies, the political parties do not divide the community into two warring sets of bitter-end partisans. On the contrary, attitudes among the voters, the active participants, and the subleaders usually pile up so much in one direction that leaders in both parties must struggle to present themselves as the true believers in the only policy that nearly everyone seems to agree on.

One recurring source of disagreement, to be sure, is the proper level of expenditures a particular agency is to be allowed. On this matter the petty "sovereignties" were not sovereign and disagreements had to be settled by *ad hoc* negotiations among the leaders, the most important of whom were the mayor and the members of the Board of Finance. Even then, however, because the largest element in legitimacy is precedent no matter how accidental or seemingly irrational the relevant precedent may be, agreement is relatively easy if an agency is prepared to accept without increase whatever appropriation it had during the preceding year. When other conflicts arose, as they occasionally did, these too were settled by *ad hoc* negotiations.

The system worked by negotiation, then, because the costs of an attempt to enlarge any one domain of influence appeared greater than the highly uncertain gains that might accrue. The system tended to a natural equilibrium in which each of the sovereigns was relatively well contented with his sphere of influence and unwilling to jeopardize his position by seeking to extend his sphere or curtail that of another. It was to this equilibrium that the system returned after a disturbance brought on by a brief controversy.

THE PATTERN DISPLAYED: THE METAL HOUSES

Since our investigation did not begin until 1957, concrete evidence on how the system of independent sovereignties worked is rather fragmentary. Fortunately, however, a case study made in 1953 of a political incident that occurred that year provides us with a vivid picture of the system in operation.[1] The story is worth telling here not only for the light it throws on the pattern of political coordination but because it illustrates many other aspects of the system as well.

In the winter of 1953, Benjamin and Milton Lebov, two brothers who had grown wealthy from a junk business located at the foot of Truman Street in the Hill section of New Haven, bought some metal houses from the New York Housing Authority, which sold them for scrap. The Lebovs did not intend to use the houses as scrap. Earlier that winter they had obtained a permit from the office of the New Haven Building Inspector to put up sixty-five metal houses in an area not far from the junk yard that was zoned for industry and had no restrictions on the structures that might be erected.

The Lebovs seriously misjudged the response of the neighborhood. The residents of the Hill, which was the heart of the state senatorial district in which George DiCenzo had established his control over the Republican party, were predominantly Italian and of the working classes. The Sixth Ward, where the Lebovs proposed to erect their metal houses, might easily have been mistaken by hasty observers for a run-down and disintegrating area. Ninety per cent of the Sixth's labor force consisted of manual laborers, skilled artisans, service workers, and a few clerks and salesmen. Only seven other wards out of the city's thirty-three had so few white-collar workers. The average person over twenty-five had not completed the eighth grade; in the number of college graduates, the Sixth was third lowest in the city. A fifth of the population was foreign-born; of these half had been born in Italy and about a fifth had been born in Russia. The Italians were, of course, Catholics. The Russian-born residents were largely Jewish. The Eighth Ward, adjacent to the Sixth, had about the same characteristics. Here, the hasty observer might easily conclude, was a likely spot in which to find the politics of a mass society.

Despite surface appearances, however, neither ward was a slum area.

1. Originally written as a senior honors essay at Yale, the case study later appeared in considerably shorter form as one of the Cases in Public Administration and Policy Formation of the Inter-University Case Program: William K. Muir, Jr., *Defending "The Hill" Against Metal Houses*, ICP Case Series, No. 26 (University, Ala., University of Alabama Press, 1955).

The average family income in both wards was a little above the median for the city. The population was relatively youthful, vigorous, hard-working. The two wards contained almost no Negroes. The residents were by no means defeated or spineless. They took pride in their homes, in their work, in their children, and in their neighborhoods. In the residential area in the vicinity of Truman Street near the spot where the Lebov brothers intended to put up their metal houses, the largely Italian population maintained a strong and vigorous community life that made it possible to mobilize the neighborhood when the residents felt themselves threatened, as they did when they began to hear about the metal houses.

The proposal to erect the metal houses, parts of which began to appear in the junk yard, seemed to nearby residents to constitute a clear threat to the neighborhood. The cheap unorthodox housing seemed to imply slums, an influx of Negroes, a decline in property values, a sharp change in an area in which many of the residents had lived their entire lives. In short, their primary concerns were adversely affected by men whose actions they could not hope to influence—except perhaps through politics. And so these essentially apolitical people turned briefly to political action to avert the danger they thought confronted them.

In 1953, as a result of ticket splitting in the 1951 elections, the city executive was in the hands of Republicans while a slender majority of the thirty-three aldermen were Democrats.

The Sixth was a Democratic ward. For years it had given lopsided majorities to Democratic candidates, local, state, and national. When Celentano ran the first time for the mayoralty in 1939, the ethnic loyalties of the Italians overpowered their partisan loyalties, and the ward split almost exactly even. When Celentano ran again in 1945 and was elected, the Sixth supported him; thereafter it returned to the Democratic fold in mayoralty elections. In 1953 its alderman was a Democratic Irishman named James Slavin.

The Eighth, which had been as overwhelmingly Democratic as the Sixth, went for Celentano in 1945, for his Italian opponent in 1947, and then for Celentano again in the next two elections. Its alderman was an Italian Republican named Montalto who had managed to slip into office in 1947 and had won by narrow margins in the subsequent three elections.

Miss Mary Grava, a spinster who had lived all her life on Truman Street and was outraged at the prospect that the metal houses would change the character of the neighborhood, took the lead in fighting against the Lebov brothers. Although she had never been active in politics, as a lifetime resident of the ward she had some acquaintance with her alderman, James Slavin. When she phoned Slavin and protested about the houses, he agreed to get together with Montalto to see what could be done.

After examining the city charter, Slavin and Montalto finally prepared an amendment the effect of which was to prevent houses of unusual materials, including metal, from being erected in New Haven without the permission of both the City Plan Commission and the Board of Aldermen. Early in May the amendment went to the Committee on Legislation of the Board of Aldermen.

Meanwhile the Lebovs had decided to seek another permit to build more metal houses in a nearby residential area. Because this neighborhood was zoned for residence and the plans for the metal houses did not meet zoning standards, the Lebovs were turned down by the Building Inspector. They appealed to the Board of Zoning Appeals. At the meeting of that Board in late May, Miss Grava, other residents of the neighborhood, and four aldermen, including Montalto and Slavin, appeared in opposition to the request for a variance from the zoning regulations. The Board unanimously rejected the Lebovs' application. The Lebovs had lost the first round.

But the danger to Miss Grava and her neighbors in the vicinity of Truman Street remained alive as long as the Lebovs were free to proceed with their project at the site they had originally chosen in the area zoned for industry. Political activity on Truman Street mounted; Alderman Slavin was subject to endless telephone calls; Montalto, in desperation, took to fleeing the city on weekends or remaining hidden inside his house; and "Miss Grava herself was everywhere, dropping words of warning, or the latest rumor of some alleged Lebov malfeasance, in stores, on street corners, from her porch, or on the telephone." [2]

Early in June the Committee on Legislation of the Board of Aldermen met to consider the charter amendment proposed by Slavin and Montalto. The Committee was made up of two Democrats and a leading Republican, all of whom were sympathetic to the protests of the neighborhood. Moreover, in executive session the Director of the City Plan Commission testified to the undesirability of cheap metal houses; after all, the New York Housing Authority had never intended the metal houses to last more than three to five years and they were in danger of turning into slums almost from the start. The Committee decided, however, that no amendment to the charter was necessary, since the existing charter gave the Board of Aldermen ample power to prevent the construction of the houses if they so wished.

One week later, despite a promise to the contrary the Lebovs' lawyer had made at the Committee hearing, the Lebovs began construction. The Chairman of the aldermanic Committee of Legislation immediately filed a resolution demanding that the license issued by the Building Inspector be revoked.

2. Ibid., p. 12.

At this point, however, the Lebovs ran up some fresh battalions, consisting of no less than Mayor Celentano and his corporation counsel, George DiCenzo. In response to a request from two Democratic aldermen on the Board who were sympathetic to the Lebovs, on July 3 DiCenzo announced it as his considered legal opinion that "the Board of Aldermen does not have the legal power to order abatement of existing metal houses on the ground that they constitute a nuisance." The Lebovs had won Round Two.

On the night of July 5, twenty-five Democratic and Republican aldermen assembled in an unofficial meeting at which most of them agreed to support the resolution against the Lebovs, despite the opinion of the Corporation Counsel. On the following hot summer evening, over two hundred anxious and excited citizens from the threatened neighborhood gathered in the aldermanic chambers at City Hall for the regular monthly meeting of the Board of Aldermen at which the crucial vote was to be taken. After caucusing separately for several hours while the tension mounted among the sweaty and anxious citizens in the hot aldermanic chambers, the Democrats and Republicans finally descended from their caucus rooms to vote. The resolution passed over the opposition of a minority of three aldermen—all of them Democrats. The neighborhood had won the third round.

They had not yet won the fight however. The Lebovs could still win if the Mayor were to veto the resolution and if the opposition on the Board could be increased enough so that the veto would not be overridden. If twelve aldermen could be persuaded either to stay away or to vote in support of the Mayor, the veto would stand. The Lebovs sought to decrease the number of their opponents on the Board in two ways: by threatening to sue the aldermen individually for allegedly "illegal" action and by appealing to liberal opinion on the ground that their project promised housing for Negroes, who were notoriously subject to discrimination in their search for better homes.

Aware of these dangers, Miss Grava worked to improve the position of herself and her neighbors. She called upon one of the leaders in the New Haven League of Women Voters who, being anxious to broaden the narrow upper- and middle-class membership of the League, responded with a promise to support Miss Grava's efforts; later the leader in the League even offered a thousand dollars to help the neighborhood retain a lawyer to represent both the neighborhood and the aldermen in any legal actions that might take place. Miss Grava also got in touch with Richard C. Lee, who had been defeated in his second try as Democratic candidate for mayor two years earlier and was now the most likely Democratic candidate in the mayoralty election just four months away. Lee counseled Miss Grava to keep up the pressure on the members of the Board of

Aldermen, to organize, and to maintain a steady flow of favorable publicity. The lead in organizing a neighborhood association was taken by
Miss Grava's sixty-three-year-old brother, Dominic Grava. Although he
had prospered and moved away from the Hill to a middle-class neighborhood, he still maintained his affections for his old neighborhood—in addition to which he owned several houses there. He had known the Mayor
since Celentano's boyhood; he was, in fact, both Celentano's godfather
and his neighbor, and the Mayor had appointed him to the Capital Projects Programming Commission. Grava became the organizing spirit
behind the Hill Civic Association; he saw to it that the officers and the
Board of Directors, of which he himself was chairman, were suitably
balanced among Italian and Jewish residents of the neighborhood. (The
Lebovs were Jewish, and it was obviously important that the battle should
not turn into an ugly ethnic conflict that might split the neighborhood and
weaken the public standing of those who fought the Lebovs.) One of the
first acts of the Association was to hire a lawyer, Joseph Koletsky, who
agreed to serve for a fee of a thousand dollars; that the sum was collected
within five days from the residents of the embattled neighborhood is
testimony to the passion of the citizens.

Meanwhile, however, the residents lost the fourth round in the continuing battle. In mid-July, the Mayor vetoed the aldermanic resolution.

For a brief moment, it looked as if the residents had suffered a grave,
perhaps even a decisive blow. But their intense political activity, their
passion, their organization, and their appeal to home and neighborhood
against the deliberate invasion of social decay and slums, all now began
to have their effects. The Lebovs' victory, like the Mayor's veto, was
ephemeral. Within two weeks the tide of battle turned forever against
the Lebovs and their allies.

A sign that the tide was turning was furnished by the support the
residents now won from Henry DeVita. DeVita was the Republican
minority leader on the Board of Aldermen and (as we saw in Chapter 9)
leader of a faction of the party hostile to the domination of DiCenzo and
Celentano. Though he did not come from the Hill, DeVita was of Italian
stock; the base of his influence in the party lay in another area of the city,
around Wooster Square, which was even more densely populated by
working-class Italians. He may have felt that the conflict presented him
with the possibility of undermining DiCenzo's control over the Tenth
Senatorial District. Moreover, when Celentano was first elected in 1945
the Mayor had opposed the choice of DeVita as majority leader, ostensibly
on the ground that it would give a too Italianate aspect to the party;
Celentano was rebuffed by the Republican aldermen, and DeVita won
the post. Whatever DeVita's motives may have been, he now announced
that he was wholly opposed to DiCenzo's opinion. His action was a major

victory for the residents, for Celentano and DiCenzo could no longer count on any votes from the Republican minority on the Board of Aldermen.

Because of a procedural contretemps, at a special meeting of the Board of Aldermen in July the Mayor's veto was not overridden. But at the next regular meeting of the Board in August, the veto was overturned 25-2 by a bipartisan coalition.

Though the Lebovs continued to press their case in the courts and in the press, for all practical purposes they had lost. The houses were never built. In time the rusting parts met the fate the New York Housing Authority had originally intended for them—they were turned into scrap.

Aware that they had suffered a major defeat with an election a few months away, the city administration sought to recover some of the ground it had lost. After a fire set by an arsonist turned one of the "fire proof" metal houses into a twisted frame the Fire Inspector promptly withdrew his approval. At the height of the mayoralty campaign in October, the Mayor announced that he would never allow the Lebov houses to come into the city. Even DiCenzo reversed himself. "I have come to the conclusion," he said, "that the Lebov Corporation . . . had not proceeded in accordance with the law . . . I will resist the development of this metal house project in this area by every legal means."

A few weeks later, Celentano lost the mayoralty election to Lee. The contest over the metal houses probably had little to do with the outcome, for it involved only a few hundred people. Even in the Sixth and the Eighth Wards, Lee's vote was only one per cent higher than it had been in 1951; Lee won in the Sixth and lost in the Eighth, just as he had in 1951. It is possible, however, that the publicity about the conflict in the local press created the impression among some wavering voters that the Celentano administration suffered from a lack of drive and coordination.

Some Observations on the Incident

The struggle of the people on the Hill against the metal houses illustrates several aspects of the political system.

To begin with, it displays three *durable* characteristics of the system. First, the residents of the Hill became active politically not from a sense of duty nor out of a sustained interest in politics but only because primary goals at the focus of their lives were endangered, and political action was thought to be the only way to ward off the danger. The metal houses directly threatened a variety of values basic to the residents of the neighborhood around Truman Street—or so, at least, they thought. Few of them had participated much in politics before; after the threat disappeared, few of them did anything again.

Second, even in this case where the primary values of several hundred citizens were involved, leadership quickly developed. What at first consisted mostly of spontaneous responses to a threat and uncoordinated direct actions by different residents soon changed in character as the struggle went on. Leaders began to give guidance and coordination; leaders recruited subleaders; and subleaders were carefully recruited from among both Italians and Jews in order to conform to the most salient characteristics of the constituents whose support was needed. The Association, though ephemeral, had already taken on by the time the aldermen voted in August most of the characteristics of political associations that have become familiar to us in the course of this study.

Third, conflict of this intensity is a rarity. Ordinarily, political decisions move along in an atmosphere of apathy, indifference, and general agreement. Even in this case, the conflict may have resulted largely from a serious miscalculation by the Mayor and his Corporation Counsel as to the amount of support available to the Lebovs, for the final coalition that defeated the Lebovs was overwhelming and seems to have rested on a very broad base of support. The community, it appears, was never really split, for among these leaders, subleaders, and active participants, support piled up almost wholly on one side; the rest of the community probably did not much care.

Although these characteristics of the system seem to be highly resistant to change, the pattern of integration that prevailed was more ephemeral. It displayed many characteristics of the pattern of petty sovereignties with spheres of influence. Yet open conflict could not be averted, and the course of the conflict suggests three important characteristics of the pattern of petty sovereignties.

First, despite the absence of great cleavages in New Haven, to avoid conflict altogether requires a very high level of political information and skill. Mayor Celentano and Corporation Counsel DiCenzo evidently made a strategic miscalculation when they supported the Lebovs, a miscalculation they tried to correct after the fight had already gone against them. A higher level of skill and more information might have enabled them to ward off the conflict before it got out of control: probably they need have done no more than to adopt at first the very policy that in fact they finally felt they had to adopt anyway.

Second, there was no clear center of dominant influence in the order. No single group of unified leaders possessed enough influence to impose a solution. There was not even a unified coalition with that much influence. The coalition that finally won was created *ad hoc;* it represented the temporary convergence on a common policy of different leaders drawn from a number of different centers of influence. That winning coalition fell apart as soon as victory was secure.

Both the winning and the losing coalitions were unstable compounds.

The losing coalition consisted mostly of two wealthy junk dealers; the Republican Mayor and his Corporation Counsel; the Mayor's appointee, the Building Inspector; and several Democratic aldermen. It also had the wavering support of the local press. The winning coalition consisted of several hundred residents of the Hill; leaders of a rival Republican faction; Lee, a Democratic leader; the Board of Zoning Appeals; and the remaining aldermen, both Republican and Democratic.

Third, the pattern of independent sovereignties with spheres of influence was incapable of providing centralized, deliberate coordination over a wide range of city activities—and hence was unsuited to the task of carrying through urban redevelopment and renewal on a massive scale. The relatively slow pace of urban redevelopment under Mayor Celentano was at least in part an inevitable result of the decentralized political mechanism through which the mayor had to operate. If the size and pace of redevelopment and renewal were to be stepped up, the political order itself would have to be changed.

17. Pattern B: The Executive-Centered Coalition

During Mayor Lee's first term the political order was swiftly transformed. The pattern of petty sovereignties he had inherited soon gave way to another of the five patterns mentioned earlier, a coalition of chieftains. However, this pattern proved to be transitional, and we need not concern ourselves with it here. The executive-centered coalition that followed proved to be more durable. In this pattern, only the Mayor was a member of all the major coalitions, and in each of them he was one of the two or three men of highest influence.

Important parts of this story have already been narrated in previous chapters. In Chapter 9 we saw how Lee first came into office as a protégé of John Golden, the Democratic leader; how he formed a coalition with Golden and another Golden man, Arthur Barbieri, the town chairman of the party; and how this coalition substantially decided nominations in the Democratic party. In Chapter 10 we saw how Lee inherited a sprawling collection of agencies and processes that determined the physical and social patterns of the city; how he formed a new redevelopment coalition; and how this coalition enabled him and his collaborators in redevelopment to assume influence over local policies on redevelopment and renewal. In Chapter 11 we saw that out of some twenty-seven instances of successful action on policies bearing on the public schools in the years between 1953 and 1959, fifteen were traceable to the Mayor or to officials who were members of his educational coalition, while all the rest were scattered among a variety of individuals and agencies.

During Lee's tenure as mayor, control over urban redevelopment became much more highly centralized in the hands of the mayor and his redevelopment team than it had been in the previous administration. Control over public education became slightly more centralized, though the pattern was, as we shall see, rather complex. Control over nominations in the Democratic party actually became somewhat more decentralized, for Golden's one-man rule gave way, as we saw, to a triumvirate in which Golden shared his power with Lee and Barbieri. To a considerable extent, the growth of the new mayor's influence in the Democratic party and in public education was a function of his influence in redevelopment and renewal. It was the need for redevelopment that created the need for an executive-centered order, and it was widespread agreement on the need for redevelopment that generated widespread acquiescence in the creation of an executive-centered order.

Urban Change and Patterns of Influence

The pattern of petty sovereignties is perfectly adapted to piecemeal changes, which are typically produced by one or several intensely interested individuals who believe they stand to gain from some relatively small alteration in the physical pattern of the city. The number of people involved varies. The alteration may be sought by a single dentist who wants to convert a residence into a dental office, a family seeking to put up a neighborhood store, or an alliance of builders and merchants who want to construct apartments and shopping facilities. Because these people stand to gain, they are charged with energy: they scheme, plan, negotiate, haggle, bring pressure, make illicit payments, and otherwise use their influence to get what they want. Sometimes they encounter only light resistance because everyone else is apathetic or indifferent. At other times there is sharp skirmishing with other small, unified, hostile groups. In these short, tense battles the side less well-organized, less numerous, less resourceful, less affluent or otherwise less effective gets defeated. If the antagonists are more or less equal, there may be a stalemate or a compromise.

A city constantly undergoes change of some sort. But piecemeal changes often merely reduce some tensions while they generate others. As in the classic case of the onset of an economic depression, when the actions each individual businessman takes to save his own skin by laying off employees and living off inventories only speeds the depression on its way, so in the case of the city, the sum total of piecemeal actions may end up creating a city that very few people would choose to design if they were capable of anticipating a wider range of consequences and had some means of avoiding these consequences without immediate loss.

Because changes in the physical organization of a city entail changes in social, economic, and political organization, the larger the area altered the greater and more varied are the effects: on housing, neighborhoods, schools, shopping areas, churches, property ownership, incomes, employment, taxes, social standing, ethnic relations, business opportunities, and political influence. Rapid, comprehensive change in the physical pattern of a city is a minor revolution.

In the political context of a city like New Haven, such a revolution requires a distribution of costs and benefits nicely adjusted so as to command the support of a powerful coalition. There is no reason to suppose that such a happy balance of costs and benefits exists, even in principle, in every city. Moreover, even if this broad combination of actions, this strategic plan, does exist in some abstract sense, it must be discovered, formulated, presented, and constantly reinterpreted and reinforced. The skills required for discovering and formulating the grounds on which coalitions can be formed, the assiduous and unending dedication to the task of maintaining alliances over long periods, the unremitting search for measures that will unify rather than disrupt the alliance: these are the tasks and skills of politicians. It is obvious too, that in order for comprehensive action to succeed, the influence over the decisions of the city government exerted by the coalition that supports the broad strategic plan has to be greater than the influence of any opposing coalition. Consequently, no matter what their official positions may be, if indeed they have any at all, the leaders of an alliance capable of large-scale alteration in the physical shape of a city must be, by definition, among the de facto political leaders of that community.

When Lee took office in January 1954, there was evidently latent agreement within the political stratum of New Haven on the need for redevelopment. In ways discussed in an earlier chapter, Lee converted this latent agreement into active support for a huge program; in this effort the creation of the CAC was an inspired act.[1] But the program that the political stratum almost unanimously supported could not be executed under the old highly decentralized pattern of petty sovereignties. In effect, then, Lee converted support for redevelopment into acquiescence in a new pattern of influence, the executive-centered order.

Thus the executive-centered order was legitimized by the need for coordinating decisions on redevelopment. And since redevelopment touched so many aspects of the life of the city, few public agencies and associations wholly escaped the demand for more coordination and control. To take a single example, operating under the old ground rules the Board of Zoning Appeals could slowly undermine in fact some of what was agreed on in theory in any strategic plan of redevelopment. Now, for the first time, representatives from the City Plan Commission and from redevelopment were heard when a zoning variance was requested. Behind them stood the Mayor, persuading, insisting, threatening. In February 1959, he finally appointed a completely new Board of Zoning Appeals composed of leading citizens who could be counted on to reject variances at odds with the basic objectives of the city plan. (Paradoxically, by appointing members who could not be pressured, the Mayor lost much of his *direct* influence over the Board; but perhaps he felt he no longer needed it.)

However, although the Mayor became highly influential over many

1. See above, Chapter 10. Some of the techniques used in gaining support are described in detail in Raymond Wolfinger's forthcoming volume, *The Politics of Progress.*

sectors of policy, it would be a mistake to interpret the executive-centered coalition as a completely hierarchical arrangement. Perhaps most integrative mechanisms that appear strictly hierarchical on first view would prove on closer examination to be much looser, less neatly patterned, more riven by internal contests over authority, frequently disordered by ambiguous and uncertain relations of influence, and subject to a good deal of internal negotiation and bargaining. In any event this was true of the executive-centered order in New Haven.

In urban redevelopment, the constraints on centralization were weak. In public education, they were much stronger; the area of latent agreement was less inclusive, the opposition was more powerful, and decisions were marked by extensive negotiation, conciliation, and bargaining. In the remainder of this chapter I shall illustrate, by means of some decisions on educational policy, the differences between the older pattern of petty sovereignties and the newer executive-centered order.

CHIEF EXECUTIVE OR CHIEF NEGOTIATOR?

The extent to which the mayor of New Haven can safely intervene in decisions involving the public schools is ambiguous. No doubt everyone in the political stratum takes it for granted that a mayor may legitimately have an important influence on the level of appropriations and expenditures. He will also influence the level of teachers' salaries and school construction, as mayors have done in New Haven for the last thirty years. He is necessarily involved, too, in major appointments. On the other hand, intervention on minor appointments and promotions would antagonize many of the citizens most interested in the schools; when mayors and other party leaders intervene in minor appointments and promotions, therefore, they usually do so covertly. Traditionally a mayor maintains a hands-off attitude on problems of curriculum and internal organization. However, the mayor is ex officio a member of the school board; and his support for one proposal or another can be decisive not merely because of his vote but because some members can usually be counted on to follow his lead. Hence different factions on the Board of Education will sometimes turn to the mayor for support. In this way he can be drawn into gray areas where the propriety of his intervention is unclear.

Different mayors interpret their role in different ways. We have seen how Mayor Celentano, after his election in 1945, supported an increase in school appropriations, in teachers' salaries, and in school buildings, and made sure that some of his key supporters in the school system received satisfactory jobs. In one significant respect, however, the system remained substantially unchanged. In the school system that Celentano inherited, control was evidently parceled out in three ways. School appropriations were the province of the mayor. Educational policies were the province of the superintendent. Appointments and promotions were subject to negotiation between politicians and school administrators. Amid these forces, the school board appointed by the mayor was little more than an instrument of the superintendent. With slight modifications these spheres of influence continued under the Celentano administration.

Under Lee, however, the pattern was altered. Control over key decisions of all kinds came to rest more and more with the mayor and his new appointees on the Board of Education and correspondingly less with the superintendent (who was held over from the Celentano administration) and other leaders in the old system.

This change in the locus of control was achieved in two ways. First, new appointments to the Board made it possible for the mayor's appointees to dominate the Board; second, the Board gradually increased its influence over the superintendent and school administrators. Even in Lee's administration, however, a division of labor existed. When decisions had to be made involving leaders *within* the school system, the new Board members took charge, knowing they could call on the mayor to back them up if they needed it. When decisions involved negotiations with leaders *outside* the school system, the mayor took charge, knowing that he could count on his appointees on the Board to back him up if he needed it.

In this respect leadership on school matters mirrored the general pattern. The mayor was the only individual who was highly influential in all the coalitions, in education, urban redevelopment, political nominations, welfare, police, and others. If it were possible to single out any one person as the leader of the "grand coalition of coalitions," the mayor was unmistakably that man.

Yet it would be grossly misleading to see the executive-centered order as a neatly hierarchical system with the mayor at the top operating through subordinates in a chain of command. The mayor was not at the peak of a pyramid but rather at the center of intersecting circles. He rarely commanded. He negotiated, cajoled, exhorted, beguiled, charmed, pressed, appealed, reasoned, promised, insisted, demanded, even threatened, but he most needed support and acquiescence from other leaders who simply could not be commanded. Because the mayor could not command, he had to bargain.

The centrifugal forces in the system were, in short, persistent and powerful; the fullest and most skillful use of all the resources available to the mayor added barely enough centripetal thrust to keep the various parts from flying off in all directions. Or, to change the image again, the system was like a tire with a slow leak, and the mayor had the only air pump. Whether the executive-centered order was maintained or the system reverted to independent sovereignties depended almost entirely, then, on the relative amount of influence the mayor could succeed in extracting from his political resources.

Sometimes his resources were too slender, and despite his efforts he was unable to create or sustain a grand coalition; he tried and failed, for example, to obtain a new city charter.[2] More often, however, his bargaining produced roughly the results he sought. The building of the high schools will serve to illustrate the mayor's role as the chief negotiator in the executive-centered coalition.

STRUGGLE OVER THE HIGH SCHOOLS

After Lee was elected in 1953, but before he was fully caught up in redevelopment, he may have intended to make the rebuilding of the school system the dramatic central action of his first term. If so, the high schools were a good place to start. There were three of them—one academic, one commercial, one for manual arts—and they all sat tightly together on a little island engulfed by Yale. The school survey sponsored by Mayor Celentano in 1947 had recommended that two of the buildings be torn down, that if possible the third should be sold to Yale, and that two new high schools should be built on new sites.[3] The Board of Education subsequently agreed on a building program providing for one new high school about 1960; nothing was said about a second.

When Lee entered office, as we have seen, one of his first acts was to create a Citizens Advisory Commission on Education. The mission assigned to the CACE by the Mayor, a leading member later recalled, was "to look into the school situation and advise the Board of Education and arouse the community interest in better schools for New Haven." The first chairman, you will remember, took great pains to organize the CACE as an effective pressure group. Meanwhile the Mayor appointed two new members to the Board of Education. In 1954–55, as the CACE and the League of Women Voters engaged in a vigorous campaign to generate public support for new high schools, the Board of Education—where the Mayor's new appointees were beginning to exercise their influence—revised its earlier building plans in order to speed up the day when new high schools would be built.

Yet there was one crucial limit to the Mayor's freedom of action— financial resources. The Mayor was firmly convinced that political success depended on his ability to reach his policy objectives without raising taxes. To follow this strategy and at the same time to build new high schools, the Mayor had to solve three problems: he had to find a source

2. An extensive account of the rejection of the revised charter will be found in the forthcoming volume by Wolfinger, *The Politics of Progress.*
3. *New Haven's Schools,* Ch. 13.

of funds outside the tax structure, turn up two low-cost building sites, and keep construction costs within modest limits.

In meeting the first problem, Lee was aided by circumstances. ("I think it may be true," Machiavelli once wrote, "that fortune is the ruler of half our actions, but that she allows the other half or thereabouts to be governed by us.") Over the years the governing authorities at Yale had come to regard the high schools as a blight in the midst of the university. Moreover, the university needed land for expansion. And if these were not already good and sufficient reasons, the daily migration of a horde of New Haven high school students through the Yale campus created frictions.

The Mayor had known the new president of Yale in the days when the one was director of public relations for Yale and the other was a history professor. The Mayor had invited the President to serve as vice-chairman of the Citizens Action Commission; the President had agreed; now they encountered one another frequently at these meetings. One day the Mayor casually broached the idea of selling the high schools to Yale. The President was intrigued. Encouraged, the Mayor subsequently came forward with a definite proposal. The President accepted. Soon only the price remained to be settled.

Both sides were anxious to consummate the deal. To the Mayor, Yale's offer to purchase the old schools was a heaven-sent source of funds which he could use to build two new high schools; hence he could ill afford to push the price so high as to scare Yale away. To the authorities at Yale, the chance to buy the schools was more than they had ever really hoped for; therefore they dared not insist on driving a bargain so hard that the Mayor might find it politically unpalatable. The compromise figure the two sides finally agreed on—$3 million—was higher than Yale's appraisal of the value of the buildings; one of the Yale officials involved in the final negotiations on the price said later, "As the university sees it . . . we paid the city more for those schools than either they were worth intrinsically or than the city could have got from any other purchaser." Yet the difference of a few hundred thousand dollars was less important to Yale than the possession of the land and buildings. As for Lee, despite the accusation in the next mayoralty campaign that he had sold out to Yale, and despite a persistent if politically unimportant body of citizens who held firmly to the belief that the city had indeed sold the schools too cheaply, probably he gained in political stature from the exchange, for now he could proceed with the high schools.

It was the Mayor, you will note, who carried on all the negotiations with Yale. It was the Mayor who persuaded the Board of Finance and the Board of Aldermen to accept Yale's offer. And a few months before the sale was completed, it was the Mayor who informed the Board of Education of the plans afoot. There was never much doubt that the various Boards would accept what he arranged, though in his negotiations with Yale he used the difficulties he might run into in getting the deal accepted by the various other city authorities as part of his argument for a higher price than Yale had wanted to offer.

Now that Yale's cash brought the new high schools within reach, the Board turned to the question of sites. The only way to obtain low-cost sites, and thereby comply with the Mayor's over-all strategy, was to build the schools on city-owned property—which in effect meant park land. The authors of the 1947 school survey had, in fact, proposed two sites for new high schools in parks on opposite sides of the city. The Board now made this proposal its own.

But the members had not allowed for resistance from the Board of Park Commissioners. This Board, one of two anachronistic political institutions in New Haven,[4] consisted of eight unpaid members and the mayor ex officio. Under a section of the city charter passed three-quarters of a century earlier when the entrepreneurs were dominant, three commissioners were permanent members; two of these filled the vacancy caused by the resignation or death of the third. Three commissioners were appointed by the mayor for three-year terms; at the time of the conflict over school sites two of these were holdovers from the preceding administration. Finally, two commissioners, one from each party, were chosen for one-year terms by the Board of Aldermen.

To the consternation of the Mayor and the Board of Education, the Park Commissioners rejected both of the proposed sites. Because the three permanent members and the Republican appointees to the Board were in a majority, obviously the Mayor had to negotiate.[5] The Park Commissioners proposed two alternative sites. Although several of the Mayor's appointees to the Board of Education were anxious to fight out the issue in the public press, the Mayor himself urged caution. One of the alternative sites proposed by the Park Commissioners was in a redevelopment area; hence some costs might be shifted to the federal

4. The other was a committee of the "Proprietors of Common and Undivided Grounds" that dated from 1641. Cf. p. 66, above.

5. A few years after the conflict described here, one of the permanent members of the Board resigned. One of the other two permanent members happened to be in Europe and unable to return immediately; under a hitherto unused section of the charter, the absence of a quorum of two made it possible for the Mayor to appoint a permanent member. His appointment was a descendant of neither the patricians nor the manufacturing entrepreneurs but a man of Italian ancestry who had been very active on the Board as an appointed member.

government. The Mayor assured his appointees on the Board of Education that if the Board accepted that site he could probably persuade the commissioners to accept the Board's first choice for the other school.

The Board's first choice, however, was a site in East Rock Park, a handsome area of woods, trails, cliffs, and a high bluff of red sandstone that is the city's most striking landmark. The park is a favorite and easily accessible spot for walking, a view of the city, family picnics, and lovers' trysts. Its excellent winding roads to the top enable the visitor to drive to the summit for a fine view of the city. One of the roads, English Drive, was paid for by one of the nineteenth-century entrepreneurs encountered in an earlier chapter, James English.

Philip English, his grandson, was now a permanent member of the Board of Park Commissioners. English may have felt a special personal interest in maintaining East Rock Park intact, and he was supported by the other permanent members and several of the appointive ones. The Mayor had to bargain, but he had little to bargain with. The alternative site proposed by the Park Commissioners was in an area of increasing industrialization which the Mayor and the Board of Education firmly believed was unsuitable for a high school. The haggling dragged on month after month during a period when construction costs were rapidly climbing. Finally, the Mayor and the Park Commissioners both yielded. The site they agreed on was in the Park, as the Board of Education wanted; it was well situated not far from what sociologists (and real estate agents) classified as a Class I residential neighborhood. But it was on low, marshy land that could not be made suitable without vast amounts of fill and piling—and hence additional, unanticipated expenses.

The Park Commissioners had therefore enormously increased the Mayor's third problem—keeping costs low enough so that Yale's cash payment for the old high school buildings would cover most of the cost of the new high schools.

The Mayor's original estimate of costs had been, to say the least, preliminary—"a kind of wishful underestimate of the cost by Dick himself," one of the Mayor's supporters described it later. The inadequacy of those estimates, the costly preparation of the sites, and the extended delay during a period of rapidly rising building costs now converged abruptly toward one stark conclusion: if the Mayor was to adhere to his political strategy and avoid a tax increase, the outlays for building and equipment required under the Board of Education's plans would have to be slashed. The Mayor took the members of his educational coalition into his confidence and assigned to his Development Administrator the task of finding economies. The Mayor's supporters were convinced, as one of them put it, that with some savings turned up by the Development Administrator through the substitution of materials which they "had every reason to believe were of the same quality but in some cases cost a third less" and some cutting "from the ideal proportions that had been set according to the wishes expressed by heads of departments, principals, and so on," they "could still have good schools and so there didn't seem to be any alternative at all." Possibly the other members of the Board, as one participant later suggested, never "really caught on quite to what the score was." Anyway, the cuts were made. In the end, however, the schools cost nearly twice as much as the city received from Yale and it took a good deal of budgetary juggling to prevent a rise in taxes.

The Mayor, then, was the central figure in the negotiations over the schools. But he was a negotiator rather than a hierarchical executive. He could rarely command, but he could apply his political resources and skills to the task of negotiating and bargaining. Given the distribution of political resources in New Haven, perhaps he achieved about as much centralization as the system would tolerate.

Victory and Defeat

If the Mayor was the chief negotiator when decisions required the integration of policies in several different issue-areas, he followed the course of his predecessors and deliberately adopted a more passive role on internal educational questions. Aware that his direct intervention might be politically dangerous, he relied on the judgment of his new appointees—who in any case were men of stature hardly willing to take orders even if he had been so inept as to issue them. The Mayor's first appointee to the Board, in 1954, was Maynard Mack, professor of English at Yale and the first Yale faculty member appointed to the Board in generations. That same year the Mayor also appointed Mitchell Sviridoff, state head of the CIO (later of the merged AFL-CIO) and the first trade union man ever appointed to the Board. In 1956 he appointed John Braslin, who had been the first chairman of the CACE. The Mayor himself was an eighth member, ex officio; hence he and his new appointees had half the votes if they needed them. In addition, whenever the Mayor made his position known, the new appointees could count on William Clancy, the chairman of the Board. Though she stood outside the coalition, Mrs. Harry Barnett, wife of an executive of a downtown department store, usually agreed with Mack, Sviridoff, and Braslin.

The Mayor could have had no way of knowing how easily his appointees would work together. Mack, Sviridoff, and Braslin had never met before they were appointed. Except for a determination to improve the schools, which they all shared, when they were appointed they had no plans, no definite policies. As for the Mayor, one of them later re-marked, "all that he ever said to me was that he wanted good schools and would back us."

By accident, then, rather than design, it turned out that Mack, Sviridoff, and Braslin worked in harmony. Believing that the Board had abdicated its legitimate influence to professional administrators, they were determined to restore the Board to what they felt was its rightful place in the determination of educational policy. They admired Lee and liked his policies. Although they sometimes needed his authority as a backstop, he needed their prestige, their political untouchability, and their vigor, if his administration was to develop and carry out a school program that would win approval from teachers and parents, whose support, the elections of 1945 had shown, was as vital to a candidate for mayor as their hostility was dangerous. One of the new appointees reflected later on the working partnership that developed:

> It was not organized in advance. It had no agreed program. It just evolved. By the like-mindedness of two people, to whom a third was eventually added of *their* own choice, it *became* a coalition, by its own volition rather than the Mayor's, and was never in any sense the Mayor's instrument except in so far as he would consent to back what *we* wanted: we were never a coalition in the sense of backing what *he* wanted unless we wanted it, too.

The Board's earlier status was nicely symbolized by the fact that no agenda was circulated before it met. Hence members came unprepared, allowed the superintendent and the chairman of the Board to determine what was to be taken up, and acted on information supplied almost exclusively by the very administrators the Board was supposed to super-vise. Although that arrangement was altered without much difficulty after the new appointees came on the Board, their attempt to influence other policies met greater obstacles.

Squeezed among competing factions, the Board itself lacked allies among administrators and teachers, was sometimes deliberately mis-informed as to what actually transpired in the schools, and could not be sure that its own policies would be faithfully executed throughout the system. The heart of the Board's difficulty was that promotions and appointments were used to build up factions, loyalties, and dependencies in the school system. Many teachers took it for granted that advance-ment depended entirely on "pull." In 1957 one of the members of the Board told the following story:

> My kid came home one day . . . and told me that in their guidance class they were discussing careers. This was a seventh or eighth grade class and one of the girls got up and said she was

interested in a teaching career and particularly in becoming a principal. And how do you become a principal? And the teacher said—and she wasn't joking, "Well, you have to know the mayor." This was the common view and still is the problem.

A direct attack on promotions and appointments, however, would challenge two formidable sets of forces. To leaders in the Democratic party, an increase in the Board's influence over major appointments must only produce a diminution of their own. To Superintendent Justin O'Brien, an appointee of the previous mayor, the implications were probably more subtle. By the professional standards of a school administrator, it would be desirable if the Board reduced outside political influences on appointments and promotions within the school system, but such a step might also curtail the Superintendent's own influence and even weaken the coalition he had built up to counter factions still hostile to him.

The issue first confronted the Board directly in 1955 when an opening occurred for an assistant superintendent for elementary education. Mack and Sviridoff settled on Miss Mary White. A member of the New Haven school system for forty years, she had been Sviridoff's sixth-grade teacher. Now she was the highly respected principal of the laboratory training school at the State Teachers College, a post she was not anxious to leave as she looked forward to her imminent retirement. Miss White was Irish, Catholic, and a Republican.

Lee's Democratic cohorts, Golden and Barbieri, backed a junior high school principal, James Valenti. Valenti was Italian, Catholic, and an independent Democrat. Although Valenti was an old friend of Barbieri, Golden and Barbieri probably were animated by objectives more complex than mere amiability. Valenti's appointment would provide a handsome gesture to the Italian community, quiet Valenti's political aspirations, and provide Golden and Barbieri with an ally in a high position within the school system.

The Superintendent, who technically had the power of appointment subject to the Board's approval, had his own candidate. So did the Chairman of the Board. There were half a dozen other applicants, none of whom had much backing though many of them tried to create support. Of one of the applicants a Board member recalled later: "Even the guy who sells me gasoline was, I remember, urging me to take a beneficent view of his candidacy. These people get around. How he ever knew where I got my gasoline, God only knows, but anyway there it was."

Though the Superintendent indicated his hostility to the other candidates, he hesitated to press his own. (Soon his own reappointment would

be coming up.) Hence the battle narrowed down to a contest between
Miss White and James Valenti. The Mayor, who was hospitalized because of his ulcers during much of the controversy, was caught in a
position of great delicacy: Miss White was his first choice, but by
supporting her he would oppose the candidate of Golden and Barbieri.
At the critical meeting of the Board when the first vote was taken, the
Mayor was in the hospital, and no candidate received a majority. Confronted with a stalemate when he emerged from the hospital, the Mayor
made the decisive choice. He called the Chairman of the Board of
Education and expressed his support for Miss White. At its next meeting
the Board voted unanimously for Miss White. (Four years later Valenti
was the Republican candidate for mayor against Lee. He lost again.)

With this victory in hand, the Mayor's new appointees next launched
a frontal attack on one of the major sources of factional influence by
trying to neutralize the process of promotions. Now, however, they were
playing on their own. "We never asked for his [the Mayor's] aid," one of
them said later; "It never occurred to us, for we were frankly green,
that it would be required, or useful." Whether, in a pinch, they could
have obtained the full support of the Mayor on this matter as they had
on the appointment of Miss White is uncertain; complete neutrality on
promotions was not necessarily an unmixed blessing to the Mayor. In
any case, after leaving the hospital the Mayor was preoccupied with an
accumulation of pressing problems, and the dispute over promotions
was not one of them.

In essence, the proposal developed under the auspices of Mack and
Sviridoff involved two critical changes. The procedures used in promotions to the rank of principal or higher were to be clarified and made
explicit; and all candidates for promotions were to be screened by a
special committee, which would then make its recommendations to the
superintendent. The membership of the screening committee was carefully spelled out; in addition to the superintendent and several other
specified officials, it was to include several members of the Board—and
also a teacher.

In preliminary meetings the proposal evidently evoked wide enthusiasm—not least, it seems, from the official representative of the
Teachers' League. Only the Superintendent expressed doubts. Nonetheless, between a Saturday morning, when the proposal was enthusiastically
approved in committee, and the following Monday night, when the
Board met to consider it, the Teachers' League shifted from support to
opposition. An explanation offered by some participants in the struggle
is that the Superintendent of Schools and the leaders in the Teachers'
League got together and concluded that to preserve their joint influence
from the threat of erosion they had better oppose the proposal. The

Superintendent's interpretation is that the leaders of the Teachers' League finally concluded over the weekend that one teacher serving on a committee to recommend the promotion of another teacher would be embarrassing to everyone concerned.

At a Board of Education meeting well attended by representatives of the diverse organizations concerned with school policy, only the representative of the Teachers' League spoke in opposition. In spite of the League's opposition, the proposal passed the Board unanimously.

Yet the policy was never put into effect. Later, the Teachers' League was joined in its opposition by the Principals' Club. Members of the Board began to get cold feet. Finally the entire proposal was tabled. Five years later the Board was still considering the idea of codifying procedures on promotions, but the proposal for a screening committee was dead. One of the supporters of the plan concluded later,

> We were defeated more because we were green at the game, not anticipating the kinds of influence that could be brought to bear over a weekend . . . than for any other reason. I think too, with hindsight, that our plan had the demerit of not being simple: it was somewhat complex, therefore extremely easy to misunderstand and to misrepresent. Finally, if anybody let us down, it was the teacher groups: if they had had the courage to stand up for these reforms, which in private they had insisted they wanted, nobody could have withstood them, or would have dared to politically.

Why did the Mayor's coalition win on the appointment of Miss White and lose on promotions procedures?

Mainly, it appears, because of the way the Mayor employed his influence. In the matter of Miss White's appointment he had made his stand clear and had put his influence behind her appointment. In the matter of promotions, he neither opposed the members of his coalition nor gave them his unequivocal support. There is little doubt that if he had vigorously insisted on the promotions policy they sought, the Board would have stood its ground; if the Board had remained firm, the Superintendent would have complied.

Had he failed to support Miss White the Mayor might have permanently alienated important support: the candidate of Golden and Barbieri would have been appointed; their influence within the schools and within the party would have increased relative to his own; and his highly favorable public image would probably have been damaged. The proposal on promotions was a different story. This time the Mayor's appointees made no effort to invoke his authority; they too were dismayed by the opposition their proposal had stirred up among the teachers. The Mayor was a busy man; he could not be expected to intervene every time his appointees on the Board ran into a snag; if he did so too often he might easily step over the ill-defined boundaries beyond which his intervention would appear to many persons as illegitimate political interference in the school system.

Thus, although the executive-centered order of Mayor Lee had drastically curtailed the independence of the old petty sovereignties and had whittled down the relative influence of the various chieftains, that order was no monolith. The preferences of any group that could swing its weight at election time—teachers, citizens of the Hill, Negroes on Dixwell Avenue, or Notables—would weigh heavily in the calculations of the Mayor, for the executive-centered coalition was not the *only* important pattern of influence in New Haven. The unending competition between the two political parties constituted another pattern of influence; thanks to the system of periodic elections, the Mayor and his political opponents were constantly engaged in a battle for votes at the next election, which was always just around the corner.

18. Pattern C: Rival Sovereignties

The leadership of the two political parties presents a pattern strikingly different from those that have prevailed in other parts of the political system in New Haven.

Within both the Republican and Democratic parties, it will be recalled, nominations for local office have for years been tightly controlled by very tiny sets of leaders. In describing control over nominations, I have also said something of the relations among the leaders *within* each of the two parties. But what of the relations between the leaders of each of the two parties?

In brief, the pattern that prevails in New Haven is one of petty sovereignties in periodic conflict in campaigns and elections. The men who control the nominations and manage campaigns in the Republican party are ordinarily a somewhat different set from those who control nominations and manage campaigns in the Democratic party. The two parties are to a great extent independent and competitive. Probably the competition between them has always been rather vigorous. Although rotation in office is not decisive proof of competition, in the past three-quarters of a century only once, during Mayor Murphy's fourteen-year span from 1931–45, has a single party held the office of mayor for more than a decade. In that same period there have been only four occasions when one party has held the mayor's office for as long as eight years; there have been two six-year periods of control by one party and two four-year stretches. In all the other elections, or almost exactly half, the incumbent party was defeated after only a single two-year term in the mayor's office.

The Grounds of Party Competition

In the years following the defeat in 1953 of the Republican mayor, William Celentano, competition between the two parties was somewhat weakened. The defection of many Republican business leaders to Mayor Lee deprived the Republicans of a traditional source of campaign funds and provided Democrats with larger financial contributions than they had ever before enjoyed. The shifting loyalties of the larger businessmen may in turn have temporarily softened the opposition of Celentano and Di-

Cenzo to the administration of Mayor Lee. But there were other, probably more telling considerations. Celentano evidently felt that he could not defeat Lee; at the same time (so it was said by his critics within the Republican party), he did not wish anyone else to make so big a showing against Lee as to become the party's natural choice to run if and when Lee finally declined in popularity or moved on to the governor's mansion or the Senate. Hence, according to his critics, his support of Republican candidates against Lee was sometimes little more than perfunctory. As for DiCenzo, his ties with the Lee administration grew closer as the chances of a Republican victory waned. In 1957 he was appointed by Lee as chairman of a commission to revise the city charter, a task in which he endorsed most of the proposals suggested by Lee's lieutenants; in 1959, when a new system of state circuit courts was created, he was appointed by Governor Ribicoff, a Democrat, as a judge of the Circuit Court of Connecticut; subsequently he resigned from his position as state central committeeman for the Tenth Senatorial District and avowed his determination to cut all ties with partisan politics. Thus an influential opponent was out of the way.

Even so, party competition continued. The Lynch-DeVita wing of the Republican party ran mayoralty candidates who sharply attacked Lee's record. The Republicans on the Board of Aldermen, though a tiny minority, maintained a barrage of criticism in lengthy speeches written for the benefit of the newspapers by Henry DeVita, the Republican town chairman. Republican leaders kept up a steady fire through the local press. If they failed to make much of a dent in Lee's popularity at the polls, it was not altogether through want of trying.

The battlegrounds of competition during these years could be classified under three headings; unfortunately for the Republicans, Lee and the Democrats were considerably better off than the Republicans in every category.

The first was an appeal to ethnic loyalties and interests. The Republicans sought to attract Italian voters by nominating candidates of Italian background. In this they attained a fair degree of success, as Table 18.1 shows. The Democratic triumvirate (one of whom, Arthur Barbieri, was particularly well cast to handle appeals to the Italian voter) sought to counter this strategy by offering appointments, patronage, contracts, a comprehensive plan of urban redevelopment and renewal in DeVita's stronghold (the Wooster Square neighborhood), and extensive plans for rehabilitation of the Hill area, where DiCenzo had held sway; all of these benefits helped the Democrats to gain support among the Italians. By 1959, as Table 18.1 suggests, voters of Italian origin split about evenly between Lee and his Republican opponent, James Valenti. As we saw in Chapter 4, the Democrats maintained a considerable following

TABLE 18.1. *Support for Republican candidates for mayor among Italians, 1953–1959*

Election	Republican candidate	Ethnic background	Percentage of Italian vote cast for Lee
1953	Wm. Celentano	Italian	39
1955	P. Mancini, Jr.	Italian	43
1957	Edith V. Cook	Yankee	59
1959	J. Valenti	Italian	47

Source: Adapted from a table in Donald E. Stokes, *Voting Research and the Businessman in Politics* (Ann Arbor, Mich., Foundation for Research on Human Behavior, 1960), p. 14. Stokes based his table on surveys by Louis Harris and Associates, New York City.

among all the other major ethnic groups except the small minority of Yankee Protestants. Thus on New Haven's traditional battleground of party competition—ethnic loyalties and interests—the Democrats managed to secure an advantage despite lingering Republican predispositions among the largest ethnic group, the Italians.

The second ground of competition has just been alluded to, namely, covert policies relating to jobs and contracts. On this ground, the party that controls local government has a clear advantage—as the bosses of political machines in many American cities demonstrated for generations. Just as the Republicans had the advantage when they controlled local government from 1945 to 1953, so from 1953 the Democrats benefited from their capacity to channel city jobs and expenditures to their supporters. In New Haven, outright illegality in disposing of jobs and contracts seems to be rare.[1] The great bulk of what is done covertly by political leaders in New Haven is not illegal; within the code of professional politicians concerned with maintaining party organizations and electoral coalitions most of their covert policies are not even reprehensible, though many of them would offend the sensibilities of a large number of citizens, particularly those who possess what are sometimes called middle-class morals. When political leaders reward friends and punish enemies, it is not so much a conflict with law as a conflict with normal moral standards that encourages them frequently to act circumspectly in order to avoid public disclosure.

The third ground of competition was, of course, overt policies. By giving prominence to his program of urban redevelopment and renewal, on which, it was suggested earlier, there existed widespread latent agreement, Mayor Lee made it difficult for Republican opponents to compete with him on overt policies. Either they had to attack a highly popular

1. This point will be taken up again in Ch. 21, p. 239.

program or they had to capture attention on issues far less dramatic and infinitely less interesting to the voters. Neither alternative was workable, and time and again the Republicans found themselves contesting with Lee where he was least vulnerable. The best they could reasonably hope for was that economic disaster, undue delay, or scandal would occur in the redevelopment program, but during the period covered in this study, at least, none of these occurred. Under the circumstances, probably any other strategy would also have failed, as Celentano no doubt foresaw when he cautiously rejected Republican overtures to run for mayor against Lee.

THE EFFECTS OF POLITICAL COMPETITION

To what extent did competition for votes between leaders and parties at periodic elections actually matter in the determination of the policies and actions of local government during these years? This question, as I have shown at many points in this book, poses formidable problems of observation, measurement, and analysis. It is therefore tempting to adopt the simplifications embodied either in optimistic interpretations of democracy according to which elected leaders are hardly more than agents of the electorate or in pessimistic or hostile interpretations that portray elected leaders as the agents of a small ruling elite. The evidence and analysis introduced so far strongly argue that neither of these furnishes a satisfactory description of New Haven.

The extent to which political competition at elections actually influences policies is evidently a function of a number of closely interrelated and rather complex factors, of which four are particularly important:

1. *The extent to which elections, political competition, and the desire for elective office (whatever may be the psychological basis of such a desire) tend to produce political activists whose strategy is to win office by shaping their overt and covert policies in whatever ways they think will gain the greatest number of votes at some future election— usually the next one.* In New Haven the number of such activists, the professional politicians, is moderately large.

2. *The extent to which this effort on the part of competing politicians actually leads to policies that reflect more or less accurately the political values of large numbers of voters and thus produces a measure of "democratic control" over policies.*

This is a function of many different factors.[2] One is the extent to which citizens vote, a proportion in New Haven local elections that runs around

2. I have deliberately chosen to use somewhat loose language at this point to deal with an exceedingly complex problem. I have discussed some of these complexities in greater detail in *A Preface to Democratic Theory* (Chicago, University of Chicago Press, 1956).

50–60 per cent of the adult population. Another is the extent to which those who vote differ in their values and interests from those who do not vote.[3] Additional factors are the extent and intensity of approval or disapproval of various policies among citizens and the extent to which these attitudes are activated, articulated, channeled into action, and perhaps even changed by new experiences. The political leaders themselves play a critical role in activating, channeling, and sometimes in changing latent attitudes. Thus Celentano and DiCenzo helped the Teachers' League and the League of Women Voters to reinforce feelings of discontent among parents and teachers over the state of the public schools, and they succeeded also in channeling the expression of these attitudes into votes against the incumbent mayor and for Celentano. Likewise, with the help of the CAC, Lee managed to activate widespread but largely latent feelings of discontent about the state of the city and latent attitudes of approval toward redevelopment; he channeled these attitudes into support for him at the polls.

The extent to which the policies of competing politicians reflect voters' preferences is also a function of one other highly critical factor—the way in which the outcome of an election is interpreted by members of the political stratum, particularly the professional politicians. The relation between an election outcome and the preferences of voters can be highly complex, and interpretations can—perhaps often do—err. If so, then voters do indeed influence policies—but not necessarily in ways they intend.

3. *The extent to which competing elected leaders actually succeed in determining the policies of government.* Their success depends on their influence over government policies in comparison with the influence of officials who are not elected, Social and Economic Notables, small pressure groups, and others. The relative influence of elected officials is in turn a function of their political resources, the rate at which they use their resources, and their political skills.[4] As we have seen, under Mayor Lee the influence of the chief elected official, the mayor, was considerably higher than it was under Celentano.

4. *The extent to which the policies of government affect important rather than merely trivial values of citizens.* This in turn depends upon the role government plays in the life of the community. Some aspects of a community that many citizens would agree were highly important—employment, for example, or the distribution of incomes—lie pretty much beyond the reach of local government. Then too, in the United States most goods and services are provided by nongovernmental rather than governmental agencies. Nonetheless it is probably true that directly or

3. Both of these matters are discussed further in Ch. 25.
4. I shall return to this point in the next chapter.

indirectly, by action or inaction, the policies of local governments have significant consequences for an extremely wide range of values. Thus the fact that the city of New Haven does not own and operate factories, department stores, or hospitals clearly does not mean that its policies have not had some impact on local factories, department stores, and hospitals.

What can we conclude about the specific effects of political competition in New Haven?

First, the elected officials of New Haven have had a significant influence on many policies—on schools and redevelopment, for example. And whatever may be the relation between elections and the preferences of citizens as to local policies, elections do determine—sometimes by an exceedingly small margin of votes—*who* is elected to office. Thus even if recent elections in New Haven were interpreted only as a choice of individuals to hold elective office, the effects on some policies were considerable.

Second, political competition and elections, at a minimum, lead to the rejection of a great range of possible policies, some of which may be discussed in campaigns but many of which are never discussed at all. Thus the assumption, referred to in Chapter 8, among members of the political stratum that the essential characteristics of the socioeconomic system should remain substantially unchanged means in effect that every election is an implicit rejection of all policies that would entail sweeping changes in the social or economic structure of New Haven.

Third, the attempt of political leaders to win the votes of the various ethnic groups in New Haven has had a sizable effect on many policies that are not openly discussed in campaigns—on the ethnic and social characteristics of the men and women nominated for public office and on decisions concerning appointments, contracts, and other public expenditures. Two important side effects of these efforts to appeal to ethnic groups have probably been (1) to speed assimilation, transmit political skills, and gain acceptability among them for the American creed of democracy and equality, and (2) to inhibit the growth of distinctive working-class political identifications, ideologies, and political parties.

Finally, from time to time elections clearly have had a decisive effect on specific policies. Rightly or wrongly—but probably rightly—the election of Celentano in 1945 was interpreted throughout the political stratum as a vote in favor of spending more money on the schools. Rightly or wrongly—but probably rightly—the re-election of Lee in 1955 was taken as a sign that the voters had given overwhelming approval to urban redevelopment.

In short, New Haven is a republic of unequal citizens—but for all that a republic.

PLURALIST DEMOCRACY: AN EXPLANATION

Book IV

THE DISTRIBUTION OF POLITICAL RESOURCES

19. On the Species *Homo Politicus*

We have now discovered and exposed the anatomy of political influence in New Haven. We have described the long-run changes from oligarchy to pluralism; we have analyzed the distribution and patterns of influence; we have traced the short-run changes from spheres of influence to an executive-centered order. We know now *how* the system works. Can we explain *why?*

Let us start with man himself: with his opportunities and resources for gaining influence and the way he exploits—or more often neglects to exploit—his political potentialities.

Homo Civicus

Civic man is, at heart, simply man; man is the child grown up; the child is the human species after millions of years of evolution. In spite of ideas and ideals, the human organism still relentlessly insists on its primordial quest for gratifications and release from pain. The child and the youth learn various forms of gratifying experience; they learn of love, and food, of play, work, and rest, of the pursuit of curiosity, the perception of order and pattern, sex, friendship, self-esteem, social esteem. Throughout man's life, experiences like these channel his efforts, his energies, his attention. They represent his hungers, his needs, his wants.

The child, the budding civic man, learns all too soon that he cannot indulge himself without stint. Constraints are imposed on his liberty to gratify himself, both by nature herself in the form of physiological, mechanical, and psychological limitations and also by other individuals —his family, to begin with, then playmates, teachers, and later a host of others. The child struggles, resists, and is caught, more or less firmly, in a net woven by himself and his society.

He learns how to delay his gratifying experiences; because of the various barriers imposed on him, the routes he now chooses to his goals are frequently complex and time-consuming, sometimes boring, occasionally painful, at times dangerous.

He discovers that just as others constrain him in his efforts to achieve his primary goals, he too has resources that he can use to influence others to gain his own ends. At first these resources are closely attached to his own person and consist of simple, direct actions and reactions like affection, friendliness, anger, hostility, crying, destructiveness. But the world, as he gradually learns, contains many resources that can be used more indirectly. In our own culture, for example, he soon finds that money has a magical power to induce the compliance of many different people for many different purposes.

Thus *homo civicus* begins to develop strategies, ways of using his resources to achieve his goals. Even in choosing strategies, he discovers, he does not enjoy complete freedom. Some strategies are banned, some are permissible, others are encouraged, many are all but unavoidable. Schooling and a job are presented to him as compulsory strategies; it is made clear that any attempt to depart from these paths will be visited not only by a great loss in his capacity to attain his goals but possibly even by outright punishment. Schooling is considered instrumental in gaining knowledge, and knowledge is a resource of widespread applicability; a job is instrumental in acquiring income and social standing, resources that are important for a variety of ends.

Young *homo civicus* learns that his choices are constrained by laws enforced by the police, by courts, and by many other officials. He learns of clusters of institutions and men called governments, toward some of which he develops sentiments of loyalty or cynicism. He may accept the constraints on his choices flowing from the actions of these governments, or he may try to evade them, but in either case he gradually learns that the range of permissible strategies in dealing with governments is a good deal wider and includes many subtler alternatives than he had first assumed. Among his resources for influencing officials, *homo civicus* discovers the ballot. Although the prevailing public doctrine of American society places a high value on this resource, and *homo civicus* may himself give lip service to that doctrine, in fact he may doubt its value and rarely if ever employ it, or he may vote merely out of habit and sense of duty. Or he may see the ballot as a useful device for influencing politicians.

Homo civicus has other resources, too. For example, he can forego a movie or two in order to make a contribution to a political campaign; he can forego an evening of television in order to distribute propaganda for a candidate. But the chances are very great that political activity will always seem rather remote from the main focus of his life. Typically, as a source of direct gratifications political activity will appear to *homo civicus* as less attractive than a host of other activities; and, as a strategy to achieve his gratifications indirectly, political action will seem considerably less efficient than working at his job, earning more money, taking out insurance, joining a club, planning a vacation, moving to another neighborhood or city, or coping with an uncertain future in manifold other ways.

Sometimes, however, the actions or inactions of governments may threaten the primary goals of *homo civicus* (as in the cases of Miss Grava and her neighbors when they were threatened by the metal houses, or the New Haven school teachers threatened by declining salaries and poor schools). Then *homo civicus* may set out deliberately to use the resources at his disposal in order to influence the actions of governments. But when the danger passes, *homo civicus* may usually be counted on to revert to his normal preoccupation with nonpolitical strategies for attaining his primary goals.

Homo civicus is not, by nature, a political animal.

HOMO POLITICUS

Despite several thousand years of richly insightful speculation, not much can be said with confidence about the factors that shape *homo politicus* out of the apolitical clay of *homo civicus*. Presumably, in the course of development some individuals find that political action is a powerful source of gratifications, both direct and indirect. If and when the primary goals that animate *homo civicus* become durably attached to political action, a new member of the genus *homo politicus* is born. Political man, unlike civic man, deliberately allocates a very sizable share of his resources to the process of gaining and maintaining control over the policies of government. Control over policies usually requires control over officials. And where, as in the United States, key officials are elected by voters, political man usually allocates an important share of his resources to the process of gaining and maintaining influence over voters. Because the acquiescence of *homo civicus* is always a necessary condition for rulership, and to gain his consent is often economical, in all political systems *homo politicus* deliberately employs some resources to influence the choices of *homo civicus*. Political man invariably seeks to influence civic man directly, but even in democratic systems civic man only occasionally seeks to influence political man directly.

Like civic man, political man develops strategies that govern the ways in which he uses the resources at his disposal. Like civic man, political man chooses his strategies from a narrowly limited set. In some political systems, the limits imposed on *homo politicus* are broad; in others the limits are relatively narrow. In pluralistic, democratic political systems with wide political consensus the range of acceptable strategies is narrowed by beliefs and habits rooted in traditions of legality, constitutionality, and legitimacy that are constantly reinforced by a great variety of social processes for generating agreement on and adherence to political norms. Whoever departs from these acceptable strategies incurs a high risk of defeat, for the resources that will be mounted against the political deviant are almost certain to be vastly greater than the resources the political deviant can himself muster. Even *homo civicus* (under the prodding of rival political leaders) can be counted on to rise briefly out of his preoccupation with apolitical goals and employ some of his resources to smite down the political man who begins to deviate notice-ably in his choice of strategies from the norms prescribed in the political culture.

RESOURCES

The resources available to political man for influencing others are limited, though not permanently fixed. For our purposes in this book, a resource is anything that can be used to sway the specific choices or the strategies of another individual. Or, to use different language, whatever may be used as an inducement is a resource.

How one classifies resources is to some extent arbitrary. It would be possible to list resources in great detail, distinguishing one from the other with the utmost subtlety or to deal in very broad categories. One could search for a comprehensive and logically exhaustive classification or simply list resources according to the dictates of common sense. One could employ elaborate psychological categories derived from theories of modern psychology, or one could use more commonplace terms to classify resources. To the extent that we can explain the patterns of influence in New Haven, it will do, I think, to use categories dictated by common sense; to do more at this stage of our knowledge would be pseudoscientific window dressing.

Some resources can be used more or less directly as inducements. Or, put another way, the kinds of effective and cognitive experiences men-tioned a moment ago as peculiarly fundamental and universal depend rather directly on some kinds of resources and more indirectly on others.

A list of resources in the American political system might include an individual's own time; access to money, credit, and wealth; control over jobs; control over information; esteem or social standing; the possession of charisma, popularity, legitimacy, legality; and the rights pertaining to public office. The list might also include solidarity: the capacity of a member of one segment of society to evoke support from others who identify him as like themselves because of similarities in occupation, social standing, religion, ethnic origin, or racial stock. The list would include the right to vote, intelligence, education, and perhaps even one's energy level.

One could easily think of refinements and additions to this list; it is not intended as an exhaustive list so much as an illustration of the richness and variety of political resources. All too often, attempts to explain the distribution and patterns of influence in political systems begin with an *a priori* assumption that everything can be explained by reference to only one kind of resource. On the contrary, the various manifestations of influence in New Haven described in earlier chapters can be explained, as we shall see, only by taking into account a number of different political resources.

Although the kinds and amounts of resources available to political man are always limited and at any given moment fixed, they are not, as was pointed out a moment ago, permanently fixed as to either kind or amount. Political man can use his resources to gain influence, and he can then use his influence to gain more resources. Political resources can be pyramided in much the same way that a man who starts out in business sometimes pyramids a small investment into a large corporate empire. To the political entrepreneur who has skill and drive, the political system offers unusual opportunities for pyramiding a small amount of initial resources into a sizable political holding. This possibility will prove to be highly important, as we shall see, in accounting for changes in influence in New Haven.

HYPOTHESES

In Book I, we saw how the monopoly over public life enjoyed by the Congregational patrician families of New Haven was destroyed, how the entrepreneurs without inherited social position and education acquired the prerogatives of office, and how these men were in their turn displaced by ex-plebes who lacked the most salient resources of influence possessed by their predecessors: hereditary social status, wealth, business prominence, professional attainments, and frequently even formal education beyond high school. The change in the New Haven political system from the election of Elizur Goodrich in 1803 to John W. Murphy in 1931—the first a descendant of a sixteenth-century Anglican Bishop, a Yale graduate, a Congregationalist, a lawyer, a judge, congressman, Federalist; the second a descendant of Irish immigrants, a Catholic, a Democrat, and a union official in Samuel Gompers' old Cigar Makers International Union—represented nothing less than an extended and peaceful revolution that transformed the social, economic, and political institutions of New Haven.

This change in New Haven is fully consistent with three of the key hypotheses in this study. First, a number of old American cities, of which New Haven is one, have passed through a roughly similar transformation from a system in which resources of influence were highly concentrated to a system in which they are highly dispersed. Second, the present dispersion is a consequence of certain fundamental aspects of the social, economic, and political structures of New Haven. Third, the present dispersion does not represent equality of resources but fragmentation. The revolution in New Haven might be said to constitute a change from a system of *cumulative inequalities* in political resources to a system of noncumulative or *dispersed inequalities* in political resources.

This system of dispersed inequalities is, I believe, marked by the following six characteristics.

1. Many different kinds of resources for influencing officials are available to different citizens.

2. With few exceptions, these resources are unequally distributed.

3. Individuals best off in their access to one kind of resource are often badly off with respect to many other resources.

4. No one influence resource dominates all the others in all or even in most key decisions.

5. With some exceptions, an influence resource is effective in some issue-areas or in some specific decisions but not in all.

6. Virtually no one, and certainly no group of more than a few individuals, is entirely lacking in some influence resources.

If, as we have just hypothesized, New Haven is a system of dispersed inequalities possessing the six characteristics of such a system, how does this help us to account for the patterns of influence described in earlier chapters?

One way to answer the question is to look at the ways in which resources are distributed in New Haven. It would be tedious to examine in detail *all* the kinds of resources existing in the community. Keeping in mind the great variety of political resources listed a moment ago, we can proceed to consider a list of resources short enough to be manageable and yet long enough to permit us to test some alternative explanations for the distribution, patterns, and changes of influence in New Haven. This shortened list of political resources will consist of social standing (discussed in the next chapter), access to cash, credit, and wealth (Chapter 21), access to certain resources at the disposal of elected leaders, such as the legal powers of public office, popularity, and jobs (Chapter 22), and control over information (Chapter 23).

20. Social Standing

Unfortunately, both as a term and a topic, "social standing" is plagued with confusions, two of which confront us at once. First, the term itself is often a source of confusion, for though "social standing" is a widely used expression, as a concept it is hard to pin down. What I have in mind by referring to social standing in a given circle is the extent to which members of that circle would be willing—disregarding personal and idiosyncratic factors—to accord the conventional privileges of social intercourse and acceptance among equals; marks of social acceptability include willingness to dine together, to mingle freely in intimate social events, to accept membership in the same clubs, to use forms of courtesy considered appropriate among social equals, to intermarry, and so on. To the extent that individuals and groups accord one another these privileges, they may be said to enjoy equal social standing. If, on the average, individuals who have some quality in common are willing to accord the privileges of social equality to individuals classified by some other criterion, but the converse is not true, then it is reasonable to say that individuals in the first group have lower social standing than those in the second. Since my purpose is to explain patterns of influence and not to explore sociological concepts, a greater degree of precision will have to depend on the context; extended efforts at formal definition would not, I think, either strengthen or weaken my argument.

A second confusion arises from a failure to distinguish social standing as a resource for influencing *governmental* decisions from the effects of a system of social status on other behavior of individuals. Nothing in what follows should be interpreted as denying that the system of social standing in New Haven has important and widespread effects on behavior. From evidence presented in earlier chapters, I have drawn only two conclusions of a narrower range, namely that individuals of highest social standing in New Haven do not exercise a high degree of influence over governmental decisions, and that those of high influence tend to be from middling social levels. These facts and certain concomitant circumstances are all I wish to account for here.

To do this, I offer several interrelated explanations. First, there exists a social threshold beyond which low standing is a severe handicap in gaining high influence over key governmental decisions; this threshold occurs

approximately at the line dividing white-collar from blue-collar occupations. Second, high social standing is difficult to exploit as a resource of
influence because of a number of important institutional limits. Third, individuals of high social standing do not in fact employ their social standing in order to acquire influence. Fourth, the fact that, below the highest
levels, influence itself is a source of social standing accounts for much of
whatever correlation between social standing and influence exists in the
middle social strata.

Exclusion of the Wage Earner

Every one of the fifty leaders in Tables 14.2 and 14.3 who were found
to have some significant influence on decisions in the three issue-areas
examined in this book have white-collar occupations. Moreover nearly
70 per cent of the subleaders in these three areas also pursue white-collar
callings. (See Table 13.1) Although the subleaders in the political parties,
as we saw, most closely mirror the general population, and although over
60 per cent of them live in the three "less desirable" categories of neighborhoods, even their ranks contain few men and women in laboring occupations. In fact, although skilled, semiskilled and unskilled employees
comprise around 45 per cent of the registered voters, only 19 per cent of
the subleaders in the political parties are drawn from these various categories of wage earners. (Table 20.1)

TABLE 20.1. *Politicians and voters: Political subleaders are more
likely than voters to have white-collar occupations*

Occupations of heads of households	Political subleaders %	Registered voters %
Executives, proprietors, managers, professionals	18	12
Small businessmen, minor professionals, clerks, salesmen, technicians, etc.	41	28
Skilled, semi-skilled, unskilled employees	19	45
Retired, housewives, no answer, etc.	23	16
Total	101 *	101 *
N	121	525

* Percentages add to more than 100% because of rounding.

A wage earner is rarely appointed or elected to any of the city's leading
offices. An examination of the previous or outside occupations of 124

Democrats in office under Mayor Lee in 1957 shows that only one out of five was a wage earner; of 116 Republicans in office under Mayor Celentano in 1950, only one out of ten was a wage earner. (Table 20.2)

TABLE 20.2. *Nongovernmental occupations of Democratic and Republican city officials*

Occupations	Republicans 1950 %	Democrats 1957 %
Executives, proprietors, managers, professionals	47	47
Small businessmen, minor professionals, clerks, salesmen, etc.	40	29
Skilled, semi-skilled, unskilled employees	10	20
Retired, housewives, no answer, etc.	4	5
Total	101 °	101 °
N	116	124

° Percentages add to more than 100% because of rounding.

The marked underrepresentation of wage earners in the ranks of the influential is explainable both by their social standing and the whole style of life that tends to accompany it. The very occupation of the wage earner typically narrows his opportunity to engage during his working hours in the kinds of activities essential to the acquisition of political influence. Yet this by no means is the whole answer. As we shall see in Chapter 26, the wage earner makes fewer attempts to exert influence than the white-collar worker; he votes less often, is less likely to participate in campaigns, and is very much less likely to get in touch with a political official about a problem. Much of his seeming indifference can be traced to his limited education; political activity and interest both increase with greater education, as we shall see in detail later on. Education in turn is related in a complex way to social standing for educational background is usually taken directly into account in estimating social standing, and education also has a powerful indirect bearing on most of the other factors that enter into social standing, from speech and dress to occupation and income.

But the effects of the general life situation associated with different levels of social standing run even deeper. On the one hand the process of recruiting leaders and subleaders works against individuals of lower social standing. A leader who recruits auxiliaries to work even in a predominantly working-class ward is not likely to want individuals whose social standing in the ward is low; a leader is far more likely to look for someone with enough standing to command the respect of as large a group of voters as possible. There is probably an optimum range above the average standing of a given group within which the favorable effects of social standing are at a maximum. If a leader or subleader falls much below this optimum, he loses the esteem of the upper sections of the group; and if he stands socially too far above the optimum he may seem to be alien and unsympathetic.

In addition, political skills are in many respects middle-class skills; the tasks of political officials are white-collar tasks; hence no matter where he may have started in life a political official necessarily pursues a calling more akin to that of a white-collar worker than that of a laborer. Though a political official occupies a world in which a trade union official may move easily, his world, like that of the trade union official himself, is somewhat outside the life orbit of the wage earner.

The wage earner lives in a subculture marked by attitudes and values different from those of white-collar workers, businessmen, and professionals. To be sure these differences may be breaking down, but evidently

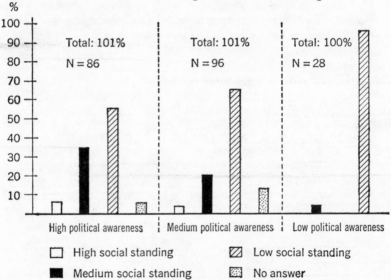

FIGURE 20.1. *Political awareness and social position among voters who have attended high school but not college*

Note: Political awareness score derived from 7 questions about local, state, and national affairs; social standing derived from a 2-factor weighted index of social position, using occupation and residence.

they are far from extinct. In the subculture of the wage earner and others of lower social standing, familiarity with politics and people who move in political circles is decidedly less likely than it is among higher social strata, even when differences in education are taken into account. Thus among voters who have attended high school but not college, those whose political awareness is lowest are drawn almost entirely from the "lower" social strata; the proportions drawn from these strata decrease as political awareness increases. (Figure 20.1)

The net effect of all these factors is to reduce enormously the chances that a person of low social standing will make any steady effort to exert *direct* influence on the decisions of government officials. In part, then, wage earners, service workers, and others of lower social standing simply remove themselves from the contest for leadership in the various issue-areas.

Nonetheless, it would be wrong to conclude that the activities and attitudes of people in these strata have no influence on the decisions of government officials. Though wage-earners lack social standing, they are not without other resources, including the ballot, and what they lack as individuals they more than make up in collective resources. In short, although their direct influence is low, their indirect collective influence is high. This is a point I shall return to later on.

POLITICAL HANDICAPS OF THE SOCIAL NOTABLES

At the other end of the social scale we find the Social Notables also having remarkably little direct influence on government decisions. There are two closely related reasons, to which I have already alluded. First, several factors make it difficult for the Social Notables to exploit their high social standing as a source of influence. Second, the Social Notables do not in fact try to use their resources. I shall discuss the first point in this section and take up the second in the next.

An inescapable consequence of any system of social standing is that the number of individuals at the apex must be relatively small. A charmed circle that everyone can step into rapidly loses its magic. In New Haven the Social Notability consists of several hundred families who keep their numbers down by applying a few highly restrictive criteria of acceptability.

Conceivably, under certain circumstances, the social gatekeepers at the top could manipulate political decisions by granting or withholding social acceptability. But obviously widespread suffrage and free elections enormously complicate the tasks of the social gatekeepers. For example, if the gatekeepers in the most exalted ranks were to use their social standing to win political officials over to policies unpopular with the unprivileged electorate, officials would soon have to choose between social acceptability among the Notables and electoral victory. If the gatekeepers at the top sought to avoid this dilemma by controlling the electorate itself, they could succeed only if social standing were a dominant value to a majority of the individuals in the community and the social pyramid were so neatly hierarchical that individuals at one level would mold their political activities according to the pleasures of the gatekeepers at the next social level above.

To suggest such a social design for modern New Haven is to indicate its absurdity. Indeed, even the days of the patricians were numbered after the franchise expanded and an organized opposition appeared; yet the patricians had access to a concentration of resources, of which social standing was only one, that far surpassed the political resources of today's Social Notables. Aside from a fatal inflexibility, the major weakness of the patricians, like that of the Notability today, was their tiny number.

In a political system with universal suffrage, then, the Notables face a peculiar dilemma if they seek to maintain their influence. Either their policies and candidates must please the populace, or power begins to slip from their hands. But if they must be deferential to the populace, why seek influence?

Since the days of the patricians, developments have further impaired the capacity of the Social Notables to use their social standing as a political resource. The more high social standing becomes a matter of inheritance rather than achievement, the less strength it has as an incentive. And the less powerful the incentive, the less useful social standing is as a political resource. Whole segments of the New Haven community are automatically debarred from admission into the Notability by their ethnic origins or religion; the capacity of the Notables to gain influence over local officials is peculiarly handicapped because those who are most effectively barred are precisely the ex-plebes who occupy public office.

In 1952 a sociologist concluded that New Haven's "current social structure is differentiated *vertically* along racial, ethnic, and religious lines, and each of these vertical cleavages, in turn, is differentiated *horizontally* by a series of strata or classes that are encompassed within in. Around the socio-biological axis of race two social worlds have evolved—a Negro world and a white world. The white world is divided by ethnic origins and religion into Catholic, Protestant and Jewish contingents. Within these divisions there are numerous ethnic schisms." [1]

Meanwhile, many avenues to a middling social standing have opened up that are far beyond the capacity of any single set of gatekeepers to control. The middling groups have even invaded many of the old domains

1. A. B. Hollingshead, "Trends in Social Stratification: A Case Study," *American Sociological Review, 17* (1952), p. 685.

of the Notables, who have had to flee to ever more private quarters, far removed from the public gaze.

Even the clubs could not hold out forever as virgin preserves of the Yankees. Shortly after the First World War, a bearer of one of the most renowned family names in New Haven is said to have remarked in the locker room of the Lawn Club that he no longer sympathized with the admission policies of the Club; he resigned his membership and never rejoined. In the 1950s a few carefully screened persons who were neither Yankee nor Protestant were admitted to the Lawn Club and the Junior League. The change was more evident in the old stronghold of upper-class conviviality and intellectuality, the Graduate Club, a preserve of Ivy League graduates. In the 1930s a terrific furor developed when a Yale anthropologist of international standing was denied admission because he was a Jew; two decades later the Graduate Club was in effect open to anyone of decent character who had a respectable college diploma and enough money for dues.

It would not do to exaggerate the point. Ethnic, racial, and religious barriers still tend to divide the community vertically. Nonetheless, the manifold opportunities to achieve social standing in the middling ranges reflect far-reaching transformations in New Haven, and indeed in the United States itself, that make it impossible for any single group in the community to serve as gatekeepers to *middle-class* social standing.

For one thing, sheer growth in population has made it impossible for the citizens of New Haven to identify more than a small fraction of their fellow citizens by name, origins, achievements, and occupations. The names of the authentic old New Haven families are all but unknown to the general public. Older, more hierarchical societies met the problem of anonymity by overt signs of social rank—by pedigrees, titles, costumes, and the like—that could be counted on to keep out the impostor (most of the time) and to secure the appropriate degree of deference due to one who occupied a given station in life. But of course American society provides for no official marks of rank, and the unofficial ones are necessarily subtle and imitable.

Moreover, the widespread opportunities for an education, including in recent years access to colleges and universities hitherto the domain of a small segment of American society, have greatly undermined if not altogether destroyed the exclusive character of what had been one of the most important marks of social standing. In 1810 the city of New Haven, in the midst of which Yale had existed for a century, must have contained fewer than fifty college graduates—perhaps no more than thirty —out of a total city population just under six thousand, or something below one per cent of the total. In 1950 nearly 9 per cent of the total population reported to the U.S. census takers that they had attended college; and almost 5 per cent had gone four years or more. The absolute numbers and proportions of college-educated citizens were of course rapidly increasing. Although the ratios are not comparable with those just mentioned, in our survey in 1959 nearly one out of every five registered voters reported some college education; one out of ten reported four years or more.[2]

If the spread of education has disseminated one conventional mark of social rank among a much wider segment of the population, and thereby blurred its significance, a high and rising material standard of living and numerous avenues to wealth in an expanding economy have brought about a further blurring. In an economy that permits a large fraction of the population to engage in leisure activities that were once the privilege of the wealthy and to indulge in extensive expenditures on highly standardized commodities, differences in the patterns of leisure, consumption, and display by the various segments of the community are increasingly difficult to maintain. Sailing, skiing, riding, and fly-fishing become the pastimes of clerk and butcher's helper, and the man with the new swimming pool turns out to be a carpenter with a working wife. When criteria that served the *cognoscenti* a year ago prove obsolete today, distinctions based upon consumption and display must become increasingly subtle. But subtlety is precarious, too, for the mass media insure a rapid transmission of information about the new styles of life; even conspicuous nonconsumption is imitable.

A final factor in the change is the increased complexity of the occupational structure. In his survey of New Haven in 1811, Timothy Dwight listed considerably fewer than a hundred callings; even an amateur census taker today would surely list ten times that many occupations; the census code lists thousands. The callings listed by Dwight are easily classified into artisans, commerce, and the professions. The outlines of a lower class, a middling group, and an upper class must have been rather easily distinguished simply by occupations; the middling group was small. Today the enormous variety of occupations makes for fine distinctions

2. Estimates of college graduates for 1810 are based on Dwight's contemporary listing of 32 clergymen, lawyers, physicians, and surgeons in New Haven and the total population of the city; Dwight also lists 16 schools, some of whose masters were college men. There were 5 professors at Yale, in addition to the president, and a "medical institution" with 3 professorships had been established though it had not yet opened. Dwight, *Statistical Account of New Haven*, pp. 33, 40, and 59. The 1950 figures are from the population census, which counts the number of school years completed only for persons 25 years old and over. The 1959 figures are from our survey of 525 registered voters, whose educational level is probably slightly higher than that of adults as a whole, and necessarily higher than the level for the entire population.

and ambiguities, particularly with respect to the large number of occupations intermediate between the very top and the very bottom in public esteem.[3]

THE SELF-DISFRANCHISEMENT OF THE SOCIAL NOTABLES

In the face of an increasingly intolerable situation, the Social Notables simply withdrew from the political arena. Rather than deal with politicians of alien stock and dubious manners, engage in a new kind of politics that lacked the dignity and style of the old, and suffer the danger of impaired reputation, they abandoned the local political arena to the newcomers.

It is difficult to date their withdrawal, but it seems to have occurred between the beginning of this century and the end of the First World War. The attitude of the Social Notables toward public affairs today was summed up by an upper-class participant in civic life who spoke scathingly of the "people who have always gone to the Assemblies since they were little and who have always gone to the Sargents' Frolic. I am sorry to say," he went on, "my notion is that some of them whom I wouldn't give standing room to, consider that it is beneath them to engage intensively in the civic and political area." Another put it this way:

> The statement that the Yankees ran the place was probably true up through about 1904, 1905, 1906, around there, and then it began to disappear right away. Part of it surely is due to the fact that the old Yankees don't have any children or if they do, they just don't

3. A survey by the National Opinion Research Center reported in 1947 produced many anomalies. A nation-wide cross-section was asked to evaluate a list of 90 occupations by giving "your own personal opinion of the general standing that such a job has: 1. Excellent standing. 2. Good standing. 3. Average standing. 4. Somewhat below average standing. 5. Poor standing. X. I don't know where to place that one." In this pre-sputnik era, 51% said they did not know where to place a nuclear physicist. There was considerable disagreement as to whether the standing of many occupations of middling rank was "excellent," "good," or merely "average." Other examples of this wide dispersion were:

	Excellent %	Good %	Average %
Building contractor	21	55	23
Public school teacher	26	45	24
County agricultural agent	17	53	28
Railroad engineer	22	45	30
Official, international labor union	26	42	20
Radio announcer	17	45	35

National Opinion Research Center, "Jobs and Occupations: A Popular Evaluation," in *Class, Status and Power, a Reader in Social Stratification*, R. Bendix and S. M. Lipset, eds. (Glencoe, Ill., The Free Press, 1953), pp. 412–13.

have the pezaz. In other words, if you stop for a moment and ask yourself where the Davenports are, where the Etons are, where the Hillhouses are, and now where the Danas are, the answer is they're right under the sod. . . . Either Yankees have failed in their industries, they've been taken over by absentee owners, or the industry itself has gone out because it hasn't changed with the times. . . . And now there are remaining youngsters who trouble me some, because . . . I don't know what . . . they do, but they certainly don't seem to be pulling their weight. . . . They go to work and they come home—literally. . . . They just don't do anything!

The monopoly enjoyed by the middling white-collar strata over public life in New Haven is sufficiently explained, then, by the fact that while low standing and occupation are disadvantages to the wage earner, the high standing and occupation of the Social Notable do not confer corresponding advantages. In addition, political influence and public office are themselves sources of social standing. If the white-collar worker has a better chance than the wage earner to become a leader, it is also true that when he becomes a leader he often acquires additional standing in the eyes of his fellow citizens. A wage earner who makes his way in politics usually does not remain a wage earner.

The relation between social standing and political influence illustrates some points that in varying degrees apply to other resources as well. Thus a *threshold* is not uncommon with respect to other resources too; for example the man who tries to be mayor of New Haven with less than $20,000 in campaign funds might just as well stay home. Likewise, beyond a certain level an increase in resources is not always associated with increased influence; indeed, if the effect is to mark off an elite group as excessively privileged or potentially dangerous, greater resources may lead to diminished influence. Then, too, in the world of politics, as elsewhere, the use of resources beyond a certain point leads to diminishing returns. Moreover, to have a resource does not mean that it will be used to the full simply to gain influence over government officials and their decisions. Doubtless the Social Notables could somewhat increase their influence in politics if they were prepared to grant social acceptability to key politicians in return for influence, but in their view the costs would exceed the returns. In addition, collective influence may offset individual influence. A collection of individuals can combine their political resources; a large number of individuals, each with meager resources, can in this way exercise greater collective influence than a very small number with large resources. Thus the votes of the immigrant groups swamped the Social Notables and drove them out of public life. Finally, influence itself can be used to gain other resources.

21. Cash, Credit, and Wealth

Like other resources, cash, credit, and wealth are distributed unevenly in New Haven. From the 1950 census one learns that while half of the nearly 60,000 families and "unrelated individuals" in New Haven reported incomes under $2,714, a more fortunate 2.5 per cent reported incomes of $10,000 or more. Although the level of income has risen since 1950 the shape of the distribution probably has remained pretty much the same. (See Figures 21.1 and 21.2)

Although these data show the existence of considerable inequality in

FIGURE 21.1. *Distribution of family personal incomes in New Haven, 1949, and in the U. S., 1950 and 1956*

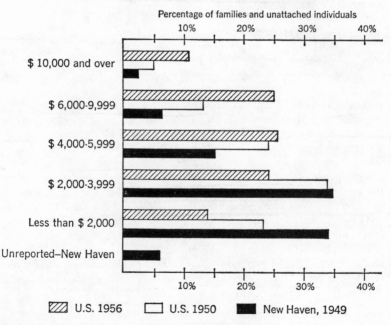

Sources: For New Haven, see U.S. Census, 1950, based on a 20% sample in 1949.
For U.S., see U.S. Dept. of Commerce, U.S. Income and Output, pp. 41, 161.

incomes, they do not tell us how various income groups share in the total income—how the pie is cut up. However, some inferences can be made from figures for the nation as a whole. In 1949, the median family income reported in New Haven was just over $2,700. This was considerably lower than the median family income for the whole country, which in both 1947 and 1950 (the two closest years for which data are available) was over $4,000. As might be expected, there were proportionately more low-income families and fewer high-income families in New Haven than in the

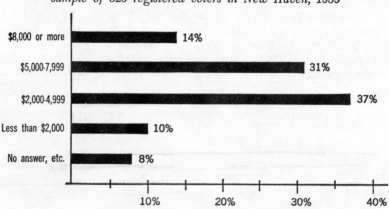

FIGURE 21.2. *Distribution of family incomes among a sample of 525 registered voters in New Haven, 1959*

nation as a whole. (Figure 21.1) As the central city in a large metropolitan complex, New Haven suffers from the fact that the wealthy often move to the surrounding suburbs while the poor remain behind. Nonetheless, although the typical family was evidently worse off in New Haven than in the country as a whole, it seems reasonable to suppose that the way the income pie is cut up in New Haven is not greatly dissimilar to that for the United States as a whole. If this is the case, then the top 5 per cent must receive close to 20 per cent of the income, and the top fifth must receive nearly half the income.[1] Even after taxes, probably close to one-fourth of the income goes to one-tenth of the families in New Haven as it did in the United States in 1956. (Figure 21.3) To the extent that financial resources can be used to obtain influence over public officials, then, a few families in New Haven—the Economic Notables—are in a much better position than the average citizen.

1. U.S. Dept. of Commerce, *U.S. Income and Output* (Washington, D.C., U.S. Government Printing Office, 1958), pp. 44–45.

FIGURE 21.3. *Distribution of family incomes (after taxes) in the U.S., 1956*

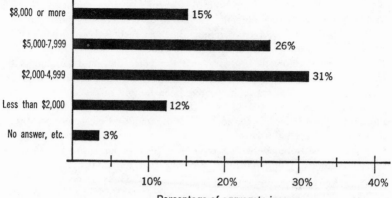

Source: See Fig. 21.1.

THE USES OF MONEY

Money can be used to obtain political influence directly in three principal ways: financial pressure, corruption, and political contributions.

A few observers of the New Haven scene are convinced that bankers exert financial pressures on politicians in some clandestine way. However, in the course of this study we found no one who had any evidence to support this hypothesis, nor even an informant who could describe very realistically what the nature of the transaction was supposed to be. We found no evidence that bank loans, mortgages, or other credit were used as financial pressures or inducements on individual politicians in New Haven. The city's borrowing is not even handled by local banks; New Haven is not a large financial center and its facilities are inadequate for marketing the city's bonds, which until 1958 were mainly handled by a Boston firm and since then by a Hartford bank.

In other times and other places, elections have been bought; if elections cannot be bought, politicians sometimes can. Thus an elite of wealth has sometimes used its resources to compensate for the handicap of size by converting cash into political influence; and for their part, politicians have converted popularity and the legal power pertaining to office into cash. In New Haven, however, corruption is petty rather than gross and does not involve the Economic Notables; it is confined mostly to small-time politicians and hangers-on; it consists of a commerce in individual favors rather than public policies. In the mayoralty election of 1959, Republicans charged that city tax assessors had illegally reduced certain tax assessments; upon investigation the charge proved to be true. The beneficiaries were a mixed bag—friends and relatives of the assessors, minor politicians, and relatives of party officials, including a relative of Barbieri. The assessors were removed from office, Barbieri resigned as public works director, a committee was appointed to make recommendations, and a reorganization followed. In years past the votes of certain members of the Board of Zoning Appeals were alleged to be obtainable at a price. Occasionally even aldermen may have been bought off.

Although some citizens of New Haven interpret these examples as merely the visible part of the iceberg, and conclude that great corruption must lurk beneath the surface, the fact that over the years only petty corruption and minor venalities have ever been exposed in the course of hotly fought campaigns strongly suggests that the invisible part of the iceberg is not much different from the visible. There is no evidence to suggest that favorable decisions on important matters of policy can be obtained by corrupt means. After a decade of large-scale transactions in urban redevelopment, no scandals had been brought to light.

Probably the most important use of financial resources in New Haven is for political contributions. These flow in two stages, from donors to political leaders and from political leaders to auxiliaries and voters. Political leaders need contributions primarily for campaigns, which grow more and more expensive. Accounting for campaign expenditures is too loose to allow precise estimates, but taking reported and unreported outlays into account a decent campaign for mayor will cost each party at least $50,000; it may run a good deal higher. In the calculus of politics it would be foolhardy beyond words to expect electoral popularity to flow from a spontaneous welling up of favorable sentiments among the voters as they enter the voting booth on election day. As in the entertainment world (with which politics has much in common), popularity in a political leader is treated as a depreciable asset requiring funds for growth, maintenance, and renewal. A large and probably increasing share of campaign funds goes into all the trappings, new and ancient, of publicity and propaganda. Another share lubricates the party organizations; party leaders refresh the loyalty and enthusiasm of ward leaders by generously passing out cash at election time. Ostensibly this cash is for campaign expenses incurred by the ward leaders. But no accounting is required and some ward leaders are known to pocket the money in lieu of a fair wage for a day's work. Political leaders also incur expenses throughout the year. They are expected to contribute heavily to their party's campaigns, and thus set a high standard for others to strive for. Their strategy calls for generosity: pick up the check at a restaurant, tip heavily, buy drinks for all, pass out a bonus to TV crews for their cooperation, and engage in the classic services and favors by means of which American urban politicians win gratitude and support. All this may easily cost a top party leader $5,000 a year—which is one reason why men with large incomes remain successful party leaders.

If these activities are a part of the strategy of gaining electoral support, potential or actual electoral success is a lever for prying campaign contributions from donors. Because the most reliable donors are the members of the party organization, the party in office has an extra advantage, for it can and does assess every individual who holds an appointive position. In doing so, the parties adhere to a widely admired theory of taxation and base their assessment on the size of the salary attached to the job.

Because even the party in office finds it impossible to finance a campaign solely from contributions by members of the party organization, the parties are forced to turn to outside sources. The extent to which the powers of office and popularity can sometimes be used as a basis for fundraising is illustrated by the changing sources of campaign contributions for the two parties in New Haven. Traditionally the Republican party in New Haven has received substantial campaign contributions from the Economic Notables, a pattern that continued through Lee's first two elections. However, after Lee had won twice and had successfuly identified himself as a key factor in the renewal of the downtown business area, during his third and fourth campaigns many Economic Notables shifted their contributions from the Republican candidate to Lee. For the first time in recent history, the Democrats were flush with campaign funds while the Republicans fell upon hard times. Whether Lee's successor in the Democratic party could inherit this business support is, however, highly problematical.

THE INTERRELATION OF MONEY AND INFLUENCE

Thus wealth and income bear somewhat the same relation to political influence as social standing does. The individual of low income is not without resources, but lacking money he does lack one resource of considerable importance. He may be able to compensate for lack of money by using other resources such as his time and energy more fully or skillfully, and as a group, the influence of the aggregate votes of the poor may more than offset the influence of the aggregate wealth of the rich. Nonetheless, man for man an individual of low income is likely to have fewer total resources than a person of higher income.

At the other end of the scale, money is a resource of diminishing effectiveness. From the point of view of the politician interested in electoral success, a coalition of wealth and numbers, being virtually unbeatable, would be very nearly perfect. But such a coalition is possible only when policies acceptable to both the few and the many do not markedly diverge. Lee was able to create such a coalition by building a program around urban redevelopment and renewal. Because of federal largesses and the skill of men like Logue and Taylor in dealing with federal officials, neither the few nor the many incurred any significant costs from the redevelopment program. Those who suffered directly were a handful of small businessmen and several hundred slum dwellers without much political influence. There was then no ground for conflict between the few and the many over the allocation of the costs of redevelopment. Had there been, Lee's coalition would have been impossible. But the phase of costless programs, which is paradise for the politicians who have created the coalition and political perdition for their opponents, cannot endure forever. If the program of downtown redevelopment were to fail, or if it were to succeed and attention shifted to renewal of run-down residential areas, it would become increasingly difficult for any politician, Democratic or Republican, to hold the urban redevelopment coalition together.

In so far as they can act collectively at all, the Economic Notables have a choice between two alternative strategies. They may make campaign contributions to both parties, or they can concentrate on one. In New Haven, as in the United States generally, they have followed the second strategy; they have contributed mainly to the Republican party. But this strategy automatically generates a counter-strategy on the part of Democrats, who, unable to count on the financial support of the few, seek the electoral support of the many. Because the policies acceptable to the many as well as to the wealthy few generally do not diverge very much on the local level, the differences between the policies of leaders in the two parties are never very great; nonetheless, the financial role of the wealthy inevitably has placed them somewhat outside the highest councils of the very party most likely to win local elections.

Moreover, political influence, like social standing, is an avenue to money. Influence is a source of income in any number of ways, from jobs to contracts. With a salary of $18,000, the mayor of New Haven is automatically among the top five per cent or so in income. That the insurance and surety firm of Golden, O'Neill, and Gebhardt has prospered over the last three decades is surely not unrelated to Golden's key position in New Haven politics. The undertaking business of William Celentano is said to have grown greatly during his term in office. This result would surely come as no surprise. Since time out of mind, American politicians have made a point of attending funerals. But Mayor Celentano did even more; to many a bereaved New Haven family it was a source of pride that the departed member was sent on his way with proper decorum by the mayor of New Haven himself.

Thus money and influence have a certain interdependence. The poor man is not likely to gain high influence; but if he does, somehow along the way he is no longer a poor man. He is not likely to become rich— Golden is an exception—but he is likely to attain at least a middling income.

22. Legality, Popularity, and Control over Jobs

Like the patricians the Social and Economic Notables illustrate a problem that confronts every elite. An elite is inherently deprived of the advantages of numbers. Hence if an elite is to attain a high degree of influence over government, its members must make up in other resources what they lack in numbers. Even if resources are distributed unequally, in a political system with universal suffrage, regular elections, and competing parties, this strategy is often difficult to execute.

THE VIRTUES OF LEGALITY

One of the most important political resources needed by elites everywhere, particularly in countries with established legal traditions, is legality. By this I mean conformity with the law, as the law is prescribed, interpreted, and enforced by government officials, including judges.

In all areas where the law is not neutral or silent, whoever seeks to impose his will on others without legality lacks legitimacy and challenges the state to invoke its peculiar and powerful sanctions. For an individual to flout the law is outlawry; for a group, revolution. An individual may succeed and the government remains; when a group succeeds, it wins a revolution. Thereafter the victorious group writes its own laws.

In the United States the tradition of legality is venerable, strong, and widely accepted—not so much perhaps as in some countries but more than in most. To inquire why this is so would take us far beyond the confines of this book. Let us accept the fact.

No group of people in the United States has ever succeeded in imposing its will on other groups for any significant length of time without the support of law—without, that is to say, the acquiescence of government officials and the courts. One might say, without undue exaggeration, that the Civil War resulted from an argument over legality. The South lost the war, but within less than a generation it won the battle of legality. White supremacy rested on legal foundations that extended from county courthouse to the Supreme Court of the United States. When in 1954 the Supreme Court sought to strike down segregation in the schools, the white South reached for legal weapons, for Southern leaders knew they could not win by naked terror. The robber barons who milked the public domain in the post-Civil War orgy of uninhibited social Darwinism, the Boss Tweeds and the rings of franchise owners, speculators, and grafters with their hands deep in city tills, even the criminals who advanced from individual depredations to organized crime and national "syndicates"—all in one way or another have had the law on their side, the law, at any rate, as interpreted and enforced by certain government officials.

Legality then is a political resource. Any group of people having special access to legality is potentially influential with respect to government decisions. The individuals who have the most direct access to legality are government officials. A noted chief justice of the Supreme Court, speaking with unusual candor and a little oversimplification, once said that the Constitution is what the judges say it is; he might have mentioned that what is legal at any given moment is what government officials enforce as legal with the sanctions officially available to them.

Even though officials have a special access to legality they are inhibited by constitutional, legal, and political norms from acquiring a monopoly over it. Legality requires the collaboration of various officials who diverge in obligations, loyalties, professional standards, and ambitions. Moreover, one set of officials—judges—can in some circumstances remove the mantle of legality from the policy of another set of officials and confer it on the actions of private citizens. One New Haven merchant, Robert Savitt, whose jewelry store on Church Street was slated for demolition and who was offered a price for his property less than he felt entitled to, fought his case to the Supreme Court of the State. Arrayed against him was the whole urban redevelopment coalition: the mayor, his aides, the Citizens Action Commission and all its "muscles," the First New Haven National Bank (the city's largest) which was to acquire a slice of Savitt's property, and, at a distance, Roger Stevens, a New York financier of wealth and national connections. The Supreme Court affirmed Savitt's right to introduce new evidence bearing on the legality and constitutionality of the condemnation of his property by the Redevelopment Agency. In the winter of 1959, while Savitt dickered for a better settlement with the Agency from his new position of strength, and demolition crews knocked down acres of building, Savitt's jewelry store stood, like some lucky survivor of an aerial bombing, unharmed amidst the rubble. In the end, the city paid more for Savitt's property than its leaders had intended. Savitt may not have had the big muscles on his side, but he had the law.

In the days of the patricians, the individuals who held political office, economic leadership, and highest social standing tended to be one and the same. Because officialdom and elite were identical, a socioeconomic elite could count on the acquiescence of government officials—to wit, themselves. As office became the prerogatives of the ex-plebes, however, elites could legalize their policies only with the acquiescence of government officials who were not themselves members of the socioeconomic elites. By virtue of their direct access to legality, the ex-plebes had a resource the elites both lacked and needed. Hence it became possible for ex-plebeian officials to bargain and negotiate with members of the socioeconomic elites and even to bring them into mutually profitable coalitions.

It happens, however, that certain government officials whose legal authority is strategically important to the elites acquire their offices, and hence their privileged access to legality, by winning elections. In a system where elections play a critical role in conveying correct access to legality, every socioeconomic elite, automatically outnumbered at the polls, confronts a puzzling choice of strategies. Either it must seek to win elections by pleasing a majority of voters with its policies more than any rival elite can do, or else it must displease a majority of voters, yet seek by arguments and inducements to detach officials from the very majorities that elect legislators and chief executives. No great problem arises if the policies preferred by the elites coincide with those that please the populace. But if the policies preferred by elite and populace should diverge, then both strategies are risky. If elites enter into competition for electoral support, they will have to trade some of the policies they would otherwise prefer for alternative policies that please the populace. Alternately, if they seek to please politicians and displease the populace, sooner or later they will encounter a politician who wants to get on in politics, who is debarred from the Notability anyway, who has goals, commitments, loyalties, and policies of his own, who prefers the votes of the many to the socioeconomic rewards of the few, and who is popular.

Popularity and Solidarity

One important way to gain direct access to legality is to be elected to public office. One way to win elections is to be widely known and liked —in short, to be popular.

Popularity is related in a complex way to legality. Though popularity can give access to legality, a leader who can clothe his policies with legality can also enhance his popularity. As with other resources, it is possible for a man who starts with a little popularity to pyramid his resources into a political empire. Countless politicians have done so in the past; countless more will do so in the future. The politician starts by converting small favors into popularity, popularity into votes, votes into office, office into legality, legality into more and sometimes bigger favors —and these into greater popularity. In the process the politician may also perform favors for himself and thereby improve his own income—which he can then use to grant more favors.

A party leader in New Haven described his career in these terms:

I first chose friends who were politically minded. This was a natural thing to do, making friends with people who have the same interests as you do. And I almost immediately joined the ward committee in my ward. . . . Soon I became ward chairman. You don't have any competition if you're ambitious. . . . If you do the work, people will let you do it. . . . Of course, I didn't do it because it was a burden. I *like* it. Work in politics is like a fraternal order, you meet a lot of people. You have to be liked. . . . I do a lot of things for people. I keep working at it. . . . People come to see me, call me at my home at night. For instance a woman calls me, her husband has gone out and got drunk, and he's been arrested for drunken driving. She can't meet bail. She calls me up and I go down and bail him out. Or a colored fellow gets in trouble, uses some of his employer's money; I go to his employer and write out a personal check covering the loss so the employer won't press charges. I just keep piling up good will. . . . I'm always building up loyalty. People never forget. Anyone can do these things, but most won't do it. . . . You gotta enjoy it.

But favors and legality are not the only foundations on which to pyramid resources. One of the most important potential sources of popularity in New Haven is, as we saw in Chapter 4, ethnic and religious solidarity. The solidarity of ethnic groups helped the many to offset by their numbers what they lacked in the resources possessed by the few. But at the same time it prevented the many from combining their numbers in the way that Marx had foreseen; for if Irishmen felt solidarity with Irishmen, it was also true that Italians felt solidarity with Italians, and neither felt it with the other. As proletarians, the wage earners of New Haven were an overwhelming majority; as Irishmen or Italians or Negroes, each of the ethnic groups was a minority. Hence electoral victories necessitated coalitions in which the leaders of one ethnic group bargained with those of another for the prizes and prerequisites of office. An ethnic group that might be unified around policies intended to benefit only its own members was not large enough to win elections; and any group large enough to win elections could not be unified around policies beneficial only to the members of one ethnic group.

Nonetheless, popularity in one ethnic group and a pervasive resentment and envy of the Yankees among the other evidently provided a firm basis on which many an aspiring politician could begin his climb to office. He could then use his powers of office and his popularity not only to improve his own income and social standing but also to bargain with the Notables on matters of policy. The more remote he was from their world, the more dependent he was on popularity in his own. The closer he came to their world, the more resources he had to bargain with. Thus the distribution of political resources made a unified hierarchical political system all but impossible; and it made a pluralistic bargaining system all but inevitable.

CONTROL OVER JOBS

Because most families are dependent on jobs for income and status, control over jobs is obviously a primary resource of great potential importance.

Probably the most relevant fact about jobs in New Haven is that no single employer dominates the job market. In New Haven proper during the 1950s only eleven manufacturing concerns had more than five hundred employees and only four had more than one thousand. About a third of the labor force was employed by the eight largest employers in the city; these were four manufacturing firms, the New Haven Railroad, the Southern New England Telephone Company, Yale University—and the City of New Haven. The largest employer in the city, Olin-Mathieson Chemical Corporation, employed slightly more than 5,000 workers or around 7 per cent of the labor force. As a firm, its political activities did not even make a ripple on the surface of New Haven's politics. Yale, the Railroad, and the Telephone Company were rivals for second place with 3,600–3,700 employees apiece, or around 5 per cent of the labor force each. Thus no single employer can hope to dominate New Haven through control over his employees. And collectively the large employers are too disparate a group for common action. Moreover, because of the secret ballot, unionization, professionalism, and powerful taboos against employers interfering with their employees' right to vote freely, private employers have little *direct* control over the choices their employees make at the polls.

Probably the most effective political action an employer can take is to threaten to depart from the community, thus removing his payroll and leaving behind a pocket of unemployed families. If the threat is interpreted seriously, political leaders are likely to make frantic attempts to make the local situation more attractive.

In the political climate of New Haven it is hazardous for political leaders to use tax assessments as an inducement for a firm to stay in New Haven. But redevelopment has provided a legal and acceptable alternative of great political utility. Thus when the Telephone Company contemplated moving its headquarters away from New Haven, the city speedily provided the company with a more favorable location in the Oak Street redevelopment area. Later, when Sargent and Company—a hardware manufacturer and seventh largest employer in the city—let it be known that it intended to sell the obsolete factory building that had been a landmark in New Haven for generations, city officials offered elaborate and ultimately successful counter-proposals to insure that Sargent would remain. The mayor and his redevelopment coalition supported legislation under which industrial property was eligible for redevelopment; the Wooster Square project, although motivated in large part by a desire to reverse residential decay in an Italian residential area, was also conditioned by the need to acquire the Sargent land and factory at a price high enough to make it profitable for the firm to remain in the city; developed land was provided for Sargent on another site; and the firm could expect to end up with a new factory built at a cost lower than it could have managed elsewhere. The threat to leave is a tactic, however, that once used cannot easily be repeated; and if an employer's investment in existing buildings and equipment is sufficiently large—as it is with Yale, the Railroad, and now the Telephone Company and Sargent—political realists would probably interpret a threat to shut down and leave the community as little more than a bold but harmless maneuver.

If private employers find it difficult to use their control over jobs as a regular political weapon, politicians are much less constrained. Indeed, probably nothing has done more to enhance the political resources of politicians than their control over municipal jobs. Writing in 1886 an historian observed that:

> An estimate of the entire number of men employed in any capacity, principal or subordinate, occasionally or continuously, in the local public service, places the sum at twelve hundred. About one in every fifty-eight of the people of New Haven is guarding the common interests of the municipal bodies politic, and is encamped upon the common pocket book.[1]

Today, with over 3,000 employees, the city is the fifth largest employer in New Haven; in fact nearly twice as many people work for the city as for the next largest employer, A. C. Gilbert, the toy manufacturer. The great bulk of the city employees are concentrated in the Departments of Education, Police, Fire, and Public Works. The Department of Public Works, with over five hundred employees, remains today the principal center of unadulterated low-level patronage. In addition there are a large number of boards and commissions; in the year 1959, for example, around seventy-five positions had to be filled on boards and commissions. An appointment to one of these, even if it carries no salary, can be used to create a sense of obligation to the incumbent mayor or to some other political leader.

Aside from maintaining a core of loyal voters and party workers, the most important use of jobs is to create a pliable Board of Aldermen. In 1958, out of thirty-three members of the Board of Aldermen only a few

1. Levermore, *Republic of New Haven*, p. 310 n.

appeared to be entirely free of some obligation to the city administration. Eighteen aldermen received income from the city; fourteen of these were employed by the city and four sold to it. Four more members had close relatives who worked for the city. Eight more members had been appointed by the mayor either to the Board itself or to some other board or commission. (Table 22.1) The Democratic alderman from the Twenty-

TABLE 22.1. *How members of the Board of Aldermen incur obligations for city jobs, contracts, and appointments*

Nature of the benefit	For self N	For close relatives N
Full-time job	6	3
Part-time job		
Over $4,000 a year	2	
Under $1,000	6	1
Contracts, sales, etc.	4	
Appointive positions		
Board of Aldermen	5	
Other	3	
Total	26	4
None	3	
Total		33

second Ward, it was discovered, was not only an inspector in the Department of Public Works but also held a full-time job in a cleaning establishment. It is an interesting and significant fact that when he was fired from his city job after receiving considerable publicity and criticism over his two jobs, he began to oppose many measures backed by the city administration. (He was denied renomination in 1959 by his ward committee and was defeated in the direct primary that followed.) Similarly, the alderman from the Third Ward was secretary and treasurer of a printing firm that usually printed the aldermanic journal at a price of $4,000 to $5,000 a year. A provision of the city charter requiring jobs of more than a thousand dollars to be put out to bid was ignored until 1960, when the City Purchasing Agent finally decided to invite sealed bids; the low bidder, it happened, was not the alderman from the Third Ward.

When a city administration needs votes it shows no reluctance to use its favors as both carrot and stick. Thus although a majority of the aldermen were privately opposed to the new city charter proposed by the administration in 1958, the Board nevertheless voted 29–4 to approve. Interviews with the aldermen strongly indicated that they voted against their private convictions out of fear of losing present or future benefits from the city—benefits they were in many cases sharply reminded of by spokesmen for the administration before the crucial vote occurred.[2]

In New Haven, however, as in American society generally, the long-run trend is clearly away from employer control over jobs to security of tenure protected by labor unions, professional associations, and law. This trend, which is noticeable in both private and public employment, is exemplified by the unionization of the janitors in the schools and the victory of the Machinists' Union in Olin Mathieson. The school janitors, or custodians as they prefer to be known, were the first city employees to be unionized; they were organized during Mayor Murphy's administration, which may seem fitting in view of the fact that Mayor Murphy himself was a union official. Paradoxically, however, the janitors were amenable to unionization in part because Murphy steadfastly refused to accede to their wage demands; in the 1945 election their leaders, and presumably many of the janitors and their families, opposed Murphy and supported Celentano. Since that day, grievance machinery has been established to handle individual cases; and union leaders appear before subcommittees of the Board of Education and the Board of Finance to press their negotiations for higher wages.

If the organization of the janitors represented the beginnings of unionization in public employment, a union victory in 1955 represented the end of an era in private employment. For nearly a century from its founding as the New Haven Repeating Arms Company through its transformation into Winchester Arms, its acquisition by Olin Industries and the merger of the national Corporation into the giant Olin Mathieson Company, the oldest, largest and best known firm in New Haven had been nonunion. At the end of 1955, the International Association of Machinists (AFL-CIO) won an NLRB election among employees by a vote of over four to one, and thereby earned the legal right to represent the workers in bargaining negotiations.

Today three dozen labor organizations have members in New Haven. In our sample of registered voters, 22 per cent were union members and another 14 per cent had someone in the immediate family who was a union member. Many city employees are members of labor unions or professional associations. As we have seen, the teachers have two organizations, one affiliated with the AFL-CIO, the other with the Connecticut Education Association. The school principals have their own association. The unionization of the janitors was followed by unionization of the firemen and policemen. If the Department of Public Works continues to use

2. Most of the material in this and the preceding paragraph is from an unpublished seminar paper by Bruce Russett, "The Role of the Board of Aldermen in the Defeat of the Proposed New Haven City Charter" (1959).

old-fashioned patronage methods, an important reason is that in many of its operations it uses casual unskilled laborers who lack a union or a professional association.

Thus a new group of leaders has recently emerged in local politics, the leaders of trade unions. So far they have barely begun to make their weight felt on the local political scene, for they and their members largely pursue the characteristically American trade union practice of concentrating on immedite bread and butter questions and eschewing political involvement. If the trade union group has had much less influence on political decisions than consideration of sheer numbers might suggest, this is partly because the leaders and the members have had no clear-cut image of the functions unions should perform in local politics—or, indeed, whether unions should have any role in local government at all.

Nonetheless, the political importance of trade union leaders does manifest itself in three ways. First, the election of 1945 created in the folklore of the politician the firm conviction that city employees are an election force of significant proportions. Caught between the electoral hazards that are believed to lurk in a tax increase and the dangers of political retaliation by angry city employees if their demands for higher wages are rejected, political leaders must resort to fancy footwork; in any case, it is no longer possible for them to ignore the claims of union leaders to be heard on the wages of their members. Second, union treasuries and assessments are a source of campaign funds, and union members are sometimes available as campaign workers. (However, union leaders concentrate their energies and interest more on national than on state and local elections.) Third, the support of trade union leaders probably helps political leaders to acquire or maintain legitimacy for their policies and popularity among some sections of the public.

In recent years, therefore, the trade union leaders have been increasing in prominence and influence. Mayor Celentano appointed the head of the Teamsters' Union to the Redevelopment Agency. Mayor Lee appointed both the president and the secretary of the State Labor Council (AFL-CIO) to the Citizens Action Commission. The president of the State Labor Council, as we have seen, was also one of Lee's first appointees to the Board of Education and one of its most influential members. In 1960 a group of younger trade union leaders won control over the Central Labor Council of New Haven; they were expected to play a more active part in local affairs than their predecessors had done.

There is then no unified group of individuals in New Haven with exclusive control over jobs. Private employers cannot use jobs as a direct influence on voting; the fact that politicians *can* has undoubtedly been one of the most important resources available to the political leader in his negotiation with Economic Notables. Private employers can occasionally acquire a strong bargaining position vis-à-vis politicians by threatening to leave the city, but this is necessarily a one-time strategy infrequently available to a few private employers, of whom even the largest controls only a relatively small fraction of the job market. Moreover, in recent years control over jobs by both private and public employers has been further restricted by unionization, professionalization, job security, and the rise of a new group, the trade union leaders. The resources of this group in terms of numbers, treasury, and organization are sufficient to guarantee that many private employers and most politicians and city administrations will bargain with them on matters important and relevant to their role as trade union leaders.

23. Control over Sources of Information

The media of mass communications—newspapers, radio, television, and magazines—enjoy a unique immediacy and directness in their contact with citizens. They regularly and frequently enter the homes of citizens: newspapers once or twice a day, magazines once a week, television and radio several hours a day. They do not force their way in; they are invited. They receive the willing and friendly attention of the household; they are, presumably, welcome guests.

The mass media are a kind of filter for information and influence. Since few citizens ever have much immediate experience in politics, most of what they perceive about politics is filtered through the mass media. Those who want to influence the electorate must do so through the mass media.

Control over the content of the mass media is thus a political resource of great potential importance. Dictators and democratic leaders alike recognize this fact, the one by establishing, the other by trying to prevent a monopoly of control over the mass media.

INFLUENCE: POTENTIAL

In New Haven, probably the most important means of mass communication on local politics are newspapers. There are two local newspapers, the morning *Journal Courier* and the *Evening Register*. Throughout the nineteenth century, New Haven's newspapers spoke with different voices. There were generally three or four of them. The *Connecticut Journal* was strongly Federalist, then Whig, and finally Republican. The *Register* was an unyielding advocate of the Democrats. After John Day Jackson acquired the *Register* in 1907 and began editing it himself, its editorial policies more and more unambiguously supported the Republicans. Later, when Jackson also acquired the *Journal Courier* and competing newspapers went under, New Haven was left with two newspapers both owned by the same man, both Republican in politics, both sharply etched with the convictions of the owner.

With over three-quarters of a million dollars in assessed valuation on his property, Jackson was one of the largest property owners in New Haven; in 1948 he ranked twenty-eighth; in 1957, forty-seventh. Jackson was more than merely a wealthy Republican; he was a devout conservative who steadfastly opposed practically all public policies enacted under reform administrations from Wilson's New Freedom onward, and he was particularly sensitive to all measures that threatened to increase local, state, or national taxes. Even the news columns of his paper conspicuously reflected Jackson's special brand of conservatism—so much so, in fact, that twice in a decade, reporters resigned in outrage over what they believed were deliberate falsifications of political news. As Jackson entered the tenth decade of his life, control over the papers passed gradually to his sons. In 1950 Jackson was still a force to be reckoned with; by 1960 he was too infirm to exert much personal control; in 1961, he died. However, the sons made few changes in the political attitudes fostered by the newspapers.

It is difficult to assess the influence of the Jackson newspapers on political decisions in New Haven. Certainly no other local political spokesman enters so many New Haven households so regularly. Almost everyone in New Haven reads at least one of the two newspapers. In our sample of subleaders, 50 per cent said they read one; another 41 per cent said they read both. Nine out of ten people in our sample of registered voters read the *Register*. The *Register* is the standard family newspaper throughout the New Haven area; its readers buy it for a great variety of purposes that have no particular relation to politics. On the other hand, the *Journal Courier*, which has a modest reputation for better coverage of politics, is widely read by people who are active and interested in politics. In fact, the more politically active an individual is, the more likely he is to read the *Journal Courier* as well as the *Register*. (Table 23.1)

TABLE 23.1. *In New Haven practically everyone reads the* Register, *and politically active people also read the* Journal Courier

	Most active[*] %	Moderately active %	Somewhat active %	Moderately inactive %	Completely inactive %
Read the *Register*	90	90	92	90	85
Read the *Journal Courier*	40	35	28	22	17
N	32	82	261	111	29

[*] Index of campaign participation. For basis of the index, see Appendix D.

Despite their incredible opportunity, one cannot say with confidence exactly what or how much effect the newspapers have. Because of John Day Jackson's conservative ideology, the political goals of the newspapers have usually been negative rather than positive. A more progressive and adventurous publisher might have sought ways and means of mobilizing public opinion; Jackson was more interested in immobilizing it. To achieve his purposes he did not have to initiate new policies; he had only to veto policies initiated by "spendthrift politicians" and "pressure groups."

INFLUENCE: ACTUAL

The newspapers have probably had some degree of influence on decisions in three ways. First, the negativism and hostility to innovation expressed in editorial policy together with the way political news is reported may reduce the level of political information, understanding, concern, and activity on the part of ordinary citizens somewhat below a level attainable with a different sort of newspaper. Yet it would be wrong to place very much blame on the newspapers, for indifference to politics flows from sources far too deep for easy cures. If political apathy in New Haven were induced solely by reading the local newspapers, then political activity would be lowest among those who read the local papers, and people who read *both* local papers would be less active than those who read only one. But we have already seen that the frequency of *Register* readers is virtually the same among the more active as among the less active citizens. And as for the *Journal Courier*, the more active a citizen is the *more* likely he is to read it. (Table 23.1) In fact, several different measures of political activity point in the same direction: the more active a citizen is in politics, the more likely he is to read both the local newspapers. (Table 23.2)

TABLE 23.2. *The more politically active a citizen is, the more likely he is to read* both *local newspapers*

	Most active %	Moderately active %	Somewhat active %	Moderately inactive %	Completely inactive %
Read both newspapers					
Participants in campaigns and elections*	40	31	26	21	17
Participants in campaigns, elections, and local policy-making**	38	37	22	27	22

* Index of campaign participation.
** Index of local action. For basis of this index, see Appendix D.

Second, the newspapers may influence the attitudes of their readers on specific policies. However, the capacity of newspaper accounts or editorials to influence specific attitudes is highly complex and variable. With all their advantages of easy entry into New Haven households, the Jackson papers suffer from the distinct handicap of being widely regarded as politically biased and even eccentric. This view of the papers is particularly strong among leaders and subleaders, who are opinion-

makers in their own right. In our interviews, leaders regularly denied
that the local papers had any influence on their views or those of their
friends. Their denials were usually accompanied by a reference, even
among Republican businessmen, to the archaic policies of the elderly
owner. Although these denials do not prove that the papers are ineffectual, they do indicate that the Jackson papers tend to lack one of the
important prerequisites of successful persuasion, confidence in the source.

The third way in which the newspapers may and probably have influenced decisions is by acting directly on the calculations of politicians.
Political leaders usually make their decisions in an atmosphere charged
with uncertainty; among the questions they are most uncertain about are
the attitudes of the voting public. In this kind of environment, if politicians
are convinced that the newspaper can influence "public opinion," a publisher can exercise a fair measure of control over the choices politicians
are likely to make. The more uncertain a politician is about the state of
public opinion or the more firmly he believes in the "power of the press,"
the more reluctant he will be to throw down the gage to a newspaper
publisher—especially to one who controls the only two newspapers in
the city.

There is a good deal of evidence that John Day Jackson's presumed
capacity for influencing public opinion gave him a strong leverage on
several of the recent mayors of New Haven. Well-placed informants insist that until Lee was elected it was common practice for the mayors
of New Haven to meet in weekly sessions with Jackson to hear his views
on public matters. The reports are denied as vigorously as they are
asserted. Even if the reports are true, they do not mean that a mayor
invariably hewed close to Jackson's policies. Whatever the truth of the
matter, friends, associates, and critics of Mayors Murphy and Celentano
tend to agree that both were acutely sensitive to Jackson's opinions and
highly attentive to the editorial policies of the newspapers. Mayor Lee's
attempt to carry out his programs without raising taxes probably also
reflects a belief that taxes are a latent issue the newspapers could whip
into an active one.

However, the influence of the newspapers on politicians depends on a
belief by politicians in the actual or potential influence of newspapers on
voters. A politician skeptical of a newspaper publisher's influence on the
attitudes of voters or confident of his own capacity to offset editorial
criticism is therefore more likely to chance a fight with the newspapers.
In this respect, Mayor Lee came into office with some advantages his
predecessors lacked. As we have seen, he had been a reporter for the
Journal Courier, and later, as director of the Yale News Bureau, he had
developed a sophisticated sense of public relations and a confidence in
his own appraisal of public opinion. Moreover, unlike his predecessors,

he liked to test the attitudes of voters directly, by means of sample surveys; under his prodding, the Democrats often hired Louis Harris, the well-known professional pollster, to take soundings of the electorate. Lee did not ignore the possibility that the newspapers might stir up opposition, but he used what was unquestionably a more realistic estimate of their capacity to do so. If the weekly meetings with the publisher had actually taken place before, now they definitely came to an end. Whether Lee would have been re-elected by even larger majorities with the support of the *Register* and the *Journal Courier* will never be known, but he definitely proved, as Roosevelt had a generation earlier, that a political leader can roll up enormous majorities in spite of the opposition of the press.

LIMITS: MULTIPLICITY OF SOURCES

How can one account for the fact that a newspaper publisher with a monopoly over the local press cannot defeat a mayor whose policies he opposes? There are two reasons, both highly relevant to our appraisal of control over information as a political resource. First, as owner and publisher of the city's only two newspapers the Jackson family does not in fact have anything like a monopoly over political information. Even the newspapers themselves are not monolithic. Some of the key editors and many of the reporters are pro-Democratic or personally friendly to Lee. In fact, during Lee's administration Republican leaders complained that news stories favorable to Lee were usually given prominent display while stories critical of him or favorable to Republicans were buried in the back sections; at one point, several Republican party leaders took their complaints to Jackson himself. Moreover, lacking adequate staff the papers often print news releases almost verbatim—a fact well known to anyone as experienced in planting news releases as Lee is. Then too, partly because of editorial traditions and partly because of genuine rivalry, a story appearing in the *Journal Courier* in the morning is often ignored or buried by the *Register* in the evening. Knowing this, sophisticated politicians occasionally time unfavorable releases to hit the smaller circulation *Journal Courier* and thus avoid prominent display in the *Register*.

Moreover, the more politically active a citizen is, the more likely he is to read an out-of-town newspaper. Very few citizens read *only* an out-of-town paper, but nearly four out of ten of the most active citizens read either the *New York Times* or the *New York Herald Tribune*. (Table 23.3)

Even if the newspapers were more monolithic than they are, they would be prevented from monopolizing information on political matters because of the variety of political sources. (Figure 23.1) Only about four persons

TABLE 23.3. *The more active a citizen is politically,*° *the more likely he is to read the* New York Times *or the* New York Herald Tribune

	Most active %	Moderately active %	Somewhat active %	Moderately inactive %	Completely inactive %
Read the *Times* or *Tribune*	38	15	18	14	7
N	29	68	89	148	188

° Index of local action.

out of ten in our sample of registered voters said they got more information about political affairs from newspapers than from other sources. About two in ten said they got more from radio or television, and almost as many relied on talking with other people.

Of these three alternative sources, radio and television are clearly the most important. The city has three radio stations (not counting Yale's student-run WYBC) and one TV station. There is little love lost between the newspapers and the broadcasting stations; presumably in an effort to reduce the appeal to advertisers of the new-fangled technique of radio broadcasting, John Day Jackson steadfastly refused to permit his newspapers even to list the programs of the local radio stations. As Franklin D. Roosevelt demonstrated with radio, TV and the radio provide a political leader who is opposed by the newspapers with an opportunity to reach

FIGURE 23.1. *New Haven citizens rely on a variety of sources for political news*

"Would you say that you get more information from newspapers, magazines, radio, television, or from talking with people?"

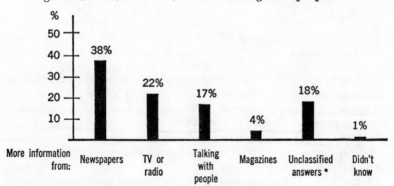

* Mainly people who gave more than one source of information.

Source: Our sample of 525 cases.

directly into the homes of the voters. Lee has made heavy use of both media in all his campaigns. How many people actually listen to these political broadcasts is difficult to say. The number who listen to local news via the air waves is, however, undoubtedly quite large. A fourth of the registered voters say that they get more of their political news from TV or radio than from any other source, and one-third list TV or radio as a better source of information than newspapers or magazines.

Finally, word of mouth and personal experience are highly important sources of information that remain to a substantial extent beyond the reach of top leaders. Although only one person out of six says that he gets more of his political information by talking with people than in other ways, word of mouth communication is actually more important than this figure indicates. Part of its importance rests on the fact that active people rely rather heavily for their political information on talking with others. In fact, among those who are *most* active in campaigns and elections, word of mouth is as important a source as the newspapers. (Table 23.4)

TABLE 23.4. *The percentage of persons who say they get more information about politics from talking with people is higher among politically active citizens than among inactive citizens*

	Most active %	Moderately active %	Somewhat active %	Moderately inactive %	Completely inactive %
Participants in campaigns and elections*	31	15	17	15	7
Participants in campaigns, elections, and local policy-making**	24	24	16	20	11

* Index of campaign participation.
** Index of local action.

The extent to which an individual gains his information from other people rather than from the mass media is partly a function of his own experience. In some issue-areas, many citizens have *direct* experience; what happens there is happening to *them,* in a rather immediate way. In others, only a few citizens have any direct experience; at best the others have only derivative or vicarious experience. The more that citizens have direct experience, the more they seem to rely on talking with other people as a source of news; the more vicarious or indirect their experience, the more they seem to rely on the mass media.

Direct experience is a persuasive teacher; often, too, it is a stubborn enemy of manipulative propaganda. The school teachers and city employees who revolted in 1945 against low pay and insecurity would not have been easy targets for a campaign to persuade them that they really had nothing to be concerned about. The citizens on the Hill whose neighborhood was menaced by the metal houses in 1953 were confronted with a palpable threat well within the range of their own experience and understanding.

The public schools are another obvious example of an activity that many citizens experience directly. Most citizens have been to school; many have school-age children. By contrast, a revision of the city charter touches the lives of very few citizens in any direct way; for most citizens the questions involved are necessarily abstract, technical, and remote. Even political nominations and the internal struggles of the political parties are, as we have had occasion to see, outside the range of immediate experience for most citizens.

Hence it is reasonable to expect that in order to keep informed about public schools, citizens draw heavily on their own experiences and talking with others, but in obtaining information about party politics or charter reform which is remote from their lives, they rely more on the mass media. This in fact seems to be the case. More registered voters in our sample keep themselves informed about the schools through their children, PTA's, talking to parents and teachers, and the like, than by the newspapers and other media. But more of them keep informed about the parties and charter reform through the newspapers and other media. (Table 23.5)

TABLE 23.5. *Sources of information for New Haven voters*

	On the public schools %	On the political parties %	On charter revision %
Talking with people, first-hand knowledge	39	15	10
Newspapers	21	42	38
Other media	1	8	13
No particular way	36	33	29
Don't know, etc.	2	2	11
Total	99	100	101

One final and highly important source of information outside the control of the local newspapers is *expert* opinion and knowledge. Experts are not always available; when they are available they are not always used; but in many areas of policy the views of experts have considerable legitimacy and persuasiveness. The mayor, the CAC, and the Redevelopment Agency do not depend on the mass media—least of all on the newspapers—for information about redevelopment and renewal, clarification of alternatives, costs, estimates of practicality, and the like. They turn to their own experts. To be sure, a great many citizens do not have access to expert knowledge and opinion, or do not know how to use it. But policy-makers usually do. And expert judgment is not confined to men in city hall. Yale is an important source of expert knowledge and professional information. Some civic organizations like the League of Women Voters and the New Haven Taxpayers Research Council also make systematic use of expert knowledge.

Limits: Apathy

In addition to the existence of alternative sources of information, a second critical limit on the influence of the newspapers is the relatively low salience of politics in the life of the individual. Despite the great quantity of information about politics pressing in on all sides, the average citizen is remarkably deaf and blind to everything not of vital interest to him. Although practically everyone knows the name of the mayor and nine out of ten know the name of the governor, in our sample of registered voters only one out of four citizens could name his representative in Congress or his alderman, and only one out of ten could name the chairman of the local Democratic or Republican party. (Table 23.6) Political indifference surrounds a great many citizens like impenetrable armor plate and makes them difficult targets for propaganda.

The campaign to revise the charter in 1958 provides a good illustration of the way in which a great flood of propaganda channeled through the mass media diminishes to a thin trickle when it encounters the desert of political indifference in which most citizens live out their lives. In 1958 Lee hoped to provide a more enduring legal basis for his executive-centered administration by revising the old charter, which imposed a number of troublesome legal restraints on the city's chief executive. Charter revision was a major topic of political news in the summer and fall of 1958; when the Charter Commission appointed by Lee completed its work, a Citizens Charter Committee was formed to gain public support for the revision. The chairman of the Committee wrote over a hundred letters to prominent citizens asking them to endorse the new charter and to contribute funds; the names of forty-nine persons who responded favorably were then added to the Committee's already impressive letterhead. The chairman wrote to another four or five hundred people asking for support and contributions. Altogether, the Committee collected over $8,000. An informal speaker's bureau was set up; advocates of charter revision spoke to various civic groups and appeared on television.

TABLE 23.6. *Most registered voters know the names of chief office-holders but not lesser politicians*

	Mayor	Governor	Congressman	Alderman	Party chairman Democrat	Party chairman Republican
	%	%	%	%	%	%
Correct name	98	92	27	24	13	11
Wrong name	—	1	16	10	16 °	6
Don't know	2	6	57	66	71	83
No answer	—	—	—	1	—	1
Total	100	99	100	101	100	101

° 12% gave the name of Golden, the unofficial party leader. This might be regarded as a tolerably well-informed answer.

Mayor Lee strongly supported the revised charter. His ally, John Golden, covertly opposed it—as most of the ward leaders and aldermen knew. After much consideration, the League of Women Voters decided neither to oppose nor to support the charter. A favorable vote was obtained from the Citizens Action Commission. The New Haven Taxpayers Research Council opposed it. Although George DiCenzo was the chairman of the Charter Commission and favored the proposal, all other leading Republicans condemned it.

The newspapers were hostile. During the month before the November election at which the charter was to be voted on, the chairman of the Citizens Charter Committee was able to place only five items in the *Register* and only three in the *Journal Courier*. In that same month nine unfavorable stories appeared in the *Register* and two in the *Journal Courier*. In addition, the *Register* carried eight unfavorable editorials, one on the front page, and one hostile cartoon; one moderately critical editorial appeared in the *Journal Courier*.

The Citizens Charter Committee ran seven large advertisements in the *Register* ranging from a little more than half a page to several that filled an entire page. Beginning on Saturday noon, November 1, and continuing until noon on the following Tuesday—the day of the election —once every hour radio station WAVZ ran a 20–25-second paid announcement favoring the new charter. Another station, WELI, ran about a dozen paid announcements. On October 27th the Mayor and the chairman of the Charter Commission appeared on a fifteen-minute television program in behalf of the charter. The Committee also arranged for twelve TV announcements during the weekend before the referendum. The opponents of charter revision paid for three fifteen-minute programs on TV during the best evening hours.

The Committee also distributed fliers in the wards; in some wards, in fact, people were hired to go from door to door to present the case for charter reform and to leave fliers.[1]

In spite of all this effort, however, few citizens ever paid much attention to the hot battle over charter reform that took place among the small coterie of leaders and subleaders. Only 45 per cent of those who voted in the regular election bothered to vote on the charter. Of those who voted on the charter, 65 per cent voted against it.

A month after the election a sample of 192 registered voters were interviewed. Only 35 per cent knew that the *Register* was against the charter. Half did not know what the paper's position was; the rest actually believed that the *Register* was neutral or for the charter. Four out of ten voters said they did not know whether the Democratic party favored the charter—an answer that in view of Lee's open support and Golden's tacit opposition was reasonable though unsophisticated. Less than one out of ten knew that the Democrats were divided; the rest thought the party was opposed to the charter. Significantly, these proportions were virtually the same among Democrats, Republicans, and independents. Although the official Republican position was unambiguous, six out of ten people in our sample said they did not know whether the Republican party favored or opposed the charter. Only a third said the Republicans were against it. Again, there were only slight variations in these proportions among Democrats, Republicans, and independents. Twenty-nine per cent did not know whether Lee was for or against the charter. Almost no one knew anything about the positions of the League of Women Voters, the CAC, or the Taxpayers Research Council.

Thus the revision of the charter was not a salient issue for most citizens, however important it seemed to many leaders and subleaders. And the vote on the charter hardly reflected any deep underlying commitment on the part of the voters. This situation both increased and decreased the influence of the newspapers. Precisely because the charter was not an issue of great salience for most voters, and because their decision to support or oppose it (or to ignore it entirely) was not anchored in well-established attitudes, for those who paid any attention at all to the views of the *Register* their editorials might have had some impact. Had the Democratic party organization faithfully supported the charter in the wards, the outcome might have been different. But in the absence of a clear-cut sense of direction provided by the Democratic organization, the attitude of the *Register* may have carried some weight among the minority who knew what it was. Although the question cannot be settled satisfactorily with the fragmentary data at hand, among those in our post-election survey who knew of the *Register*'s opposition, twice as many

1. The preceding paragraphs draw on information in an unpublished seminar paper by Richard Merritt, "The 1958 Charter Revision Commission" (1959).

voted against the charter as among those who did not know how the paper stood. This held true even among Democrats.

With some oversimplification one might hazard the guess that the influence of the local newspapers is likely to be a good deal less on issues that attract the interest and concern of large numbers of voters than on issues over which they are unconcerned. But if they are unconcerned, the voters are also amenable to influences other than the local press, including those of politicians and other notables filtered through other forms of mass media or through various organizational channels.

Book V

THE USE OF POLITICAL RESOURCES

24. *Overview:* Actual and Potential Influence

One of the most elementary principles of political life is that a political resource is only a *potential* source of influence. Individuals with the same amounts of resources may exert different degrees of influence because they use their resources in different ways. One wealthy man may collect paintings; another may collect politicians.

Whenever an individual chooses not to use all of his resources in order to gain influence, it is plausible to conclude that his actual present influence is less than his potential future influence. However, the idea of potential influence, which seems transparently clear, proves on examination to be one of the most troublesome topics in social theory. I shall not even try here to remove all the difficulty connected with the concept but only so much as is indispensable to our analysis. Let me begin by imagining a dialogue between two observers in New Haven.

A. I believe I can explain the various patterns of influence observed in New Haven by the hypothesis that the greater the political resources a group of individuals possesses, the greater its influence. I do not mean to say, of course, that I can always decide which of several groups possesses the greater political resources, for no common unit of measure exists to which various resources like money, social standing, legality, and popularity can all be reduced. Consequently, I cannot infer whether individuals with a great deal of money will be more, equally, or less influential than individuals with high social standing or the best access to officiality and legality, or the greatest popularity. But I can and do infer that the rich will be more influential than the poor, the socially prominent more influential than the socially obscure, and so forth.

B. I'm afraid there are several difficulties in your explanation. For one thing, you speak of extremes—the rich and the poor, the socially prominent and the socially obscure, and so on. But are you confident that smaller differences in resources would lead to the same conclusion? For example, would you expect the rich to be more influential than the moderately well off? Second, when you say "more influential"—more influential with respect to *what?* I assume you are talking about government decisions. But do you mean to say that the rich will be more influential than, say, the moderately well off with respect to *every* kind of decision made by government—for example, even decisions about which the rich care nothing and others care a great deal? This leads to my third point: suppose that—for whatever reason—the individuals with the greatest resources don't *use* them for political purposes? Finally, suppose they use their resources but do so in a blundering and ineffectual way?

A. I am not necessarily speaking of the actual influence of a group on all government decisions, as measured by their past or present perform-ance, for it is true that people with great resources may be indifferent about what happens in some area of public policy. I do say, though, that whenever individuals choose to employ their resources to whatever extent is necessary to gain their ends, then a group well off in resources will succeed despite the objections of others with lesser resources.

B. I see that you are referring to *potential* influence. But surely if you wish to be at all precise when you speak of the potential influence of a particular group of individuals, you must specify the circumstances you have in mind. In particular, you will have to specify not only the par-ticular area of policy, but the amount of resources the group actually will use and the skill or efficiency its members will display in using their resources.

A. I wonder if your approach doesn't rob the idea of potential influence of all its usefulness. After all, by specifying the circumstances properly, we could speak of the wealthy as potentially dominant in a given area of policy, or the proletariat, or the electorate, or the trade unions, or the bureaucrats—in fact, all sorts of groups.

B. Exactly! I believe, however, that the concept of potential influence is not really made meaningless simply by being made precise. On the contrary. Surely our analysis will gain in clarity if we can reduce some of the ambiguity that generally plagues discussions about power and in-fluence. If you want to refer to the potential influence of a particular group of individuals, all I ask is that you specify certain conditions—in particular the *level* at which members of this and other groups *use* their resources, and also your assumptions as to how *skillful* or *efficient* they are in employing them. It is quite true, of course, that under certain conceivable conditions almost any group at all could dominate some area of policy. The problem, however, is not only to specify what these conditions are but to predict the train of events that would bring them about, and to estimate how likely the train of events is.

A. I now restate my hypothesis to say that if, on the average, the mem-bers of group X have more of a given resource than the members of group Y, and if both use the same proportion of their resources with equal efficiency in order to gain influence over decisions in some given area, then group X will surely have more influence over decisions in that area than group Y.

B. Admirable! But note how different that is from your original state-ment. And I must point out one highly important error in what you have just said. According to your assumptions, if everyone used one-tenth of his income to gain influence over decisions in some area, then two millionaires would be more influential than any number of people of lesser income, assuming that no other kinds of resources were employed. But surely this is absurd. The aggregate outlay of a hundred millionaires who spent $10,000 apiece on politics would be equaled by the total contributions of a hundred thousand persons who spent $10 apiece.

A. I now see that when I speak of collective influence I must specify the *aggregate* resources used by a group. It seems to me that this makes the matter much more complicated. In order to predict whether a group of individuals will in fact combine their resources to support a common strategy, I must know something about the likelihood that they will act on some issue, rather than merely stand aside. Even if they do act, they may conflict in their strategies. To predict whether some collection of individuals—Republicans, millionaires, trade unionists, farmers, or what-ever—will actually agree on strategies, one needs to make some assump-tions about their attitudes with respect to a given area of policy. More-over, because there are other individuals in the political system, it is not enough to specify all these conditions for one group, but—at least in principle—for all the other groups as well. I must say, all this presents me with a task of such formidable proportions that from now on I shall hesitate to speak of potential influence at all!

Sources of Variation in Resource Use

It is clear that if individuals do vary in the extent to which they *use* their resources to gain influence, this variation might be fully as important in accounting for differences in influence as variations in the resources themselves. It is a fact of prime importance that individuals *do* vary, and vary enormously. For example, the extent to which individuals use their resources to gain influence over government decisions varies:

1. Over the life cycle of the individual. It is negligible among the young, is highest in the prime of life, and generally decreases among the aged.

2. As different events take place and different issues are generated in the political system. Most people employ their resources sporadically, if at all. For many citizens, resource use rises to a peak during periods of campaigns and elections. Some citizens are aroused by a particular issue like the metal houses, and then lapse into inactivity.

3. With different issue-areas. As we have seen, the individuals and groups who spend time, energy, and money in an attempt to influence policies in one issue-area are rather different from those who do so in

another. For example, in New Haven, business leaders have been much more active in redevelopment than in education or party nominations.

4. With different kinds of individuals. For example, professional politicians use the resources at their disposal at a very high rate; at the other extreme are individuals with no interest in politics.

Although one can find good explanations for many of the variations among individuals in their use of political resources, some differences are difficult to explain and remain the subject of speculation and research. The more obvious reasons why individuals vary in their use of political resources are:

1. Because of variations in access to resources. On the average, in a large population, it is reasonable to expect that the more resources one has, the more resources one would use to gain influence. For example, if everyone simply used the same proportions of his resources for political purposes, obviously the greater resources one had the more one would use.

2. Because of variations in political confidence or estimates as to the probability of succeeding in an attempt to influence decisions. A person who is pessimistic about his chances of influencing government policies is less likely to use his resources than one who is optimistic.

3. Because of differences in alternative opportunities for using one's resources in order to achieve other goals. For example, a young unmarried lawyer with few clients is likely to spend more of his time on politics than an older lawyer with a family, a large clientele, and an active social life.

4. Because of differences in estimates as to the value or "reward" of a successful effort. The higher the value one expects from a favorable outcome the more likely one is to invest resources. The value expected from a favorable decision need not be in the form of money, of course; it might be any one or a combination of a great variety of things that different human beings search for—security, personal prestige, social standing, the satisfaction of being on the winning side, specific liberties, justice, votes, popularity, office, and so on. The list is endless.

Why do individuals vary in these four respects? There are several important *subjective* reasons. First, individuals vary in their goals or the standards of value they use to appraise different events and possibilities. Second, individuals vary in their predispositions. For example, pessimism or optimism is often more than a transitory view of a particular political situation; frequently it is a persistent, generalized, stable orientation toward politics or even toward life-situations of all sorts. Third, individuals vary in their information about the political system—how it operates, the decisions being made, what the outcomes are likely to be, how probable this or that event is, and so on. Fourth, individuals vary in the ways they identify themselves with others: the people who matter most to one person are almost certain to be different from the people who matter most to anyone else.

There are also important variations in the *objective* situations of different individuals. It is useful to distinguish differences in objective situations according to their generality. Some objective differences are relatively specific to a given situation. The Hill neighborhood directly adjacent to the metal houses was a specific neighborhood composed of specific individuals. The merchants on the west side of Church Street who had to relocate their businesses were specific merchants. It is in no way mysterious that the people who reacted most strongly to the metal houses were families in the Truman Street neighborhood, nor is it surprising that the merchants who organized an association to protect their interests were on the west side of Church Street rather than the east side. Some objective differences, on the other hand, are general to a wide variety of situations: being poor or rich, well educated or uneducated, a professional man or an unskilled laborer, living in a slum area or a middle-class neighborhood—these are differences in objective situations of a more persistent and general sort that are likely to show up in a variety of different ways over a long period of time.

Because of these specific and general differences in the objective situations in which individuals are placed, different actions of government affect different people in different ways and to different degrees. To be sure, differences in objective situations take on meaning for an individual only as they are translated into the kinds of subjective factors mentioned above, such as values, predispositions, information, and identifications. Consequently, individuals in the same objective situation may not respond in the same way because they have different subjective interpretations of the situation. Nonetheless, the objective differences in individual situations are frequently so great that they largely explain why subjective differences arise.

But they do not wholly explain why, for it usually turns out that no matter what kinds of objective characteristics one uses to classify people, everyone in the "same" objective situation does not happen to respond in the same way. Because some variations in human behavior are always left unexplained by factors in the objective situation, one must conclude that the subjective life of the individual has a style and pattern often connected only in loose fashion to his "objective" situation.

25. Citizenship without Politics

How do citizens of New Haven vary in the extent to which they use their political resources? How do these variations help to account for the patterns of influence discovered in the course of this study?

Although it is difficult to answer these questions directly, we can do so indirectly by examining the extent to which different citizens participate in various ways in local political and governmental activities. The first fact, and it overshadows almost everything else, is that *most citizens use their political resources scarcely at all.* To begin with, a large proportion of the adult population of New Haven does not even vote.

After universal suffrage was established and the parties organized the electorate, voting rose to a high peak following the Civil War, when about three-quarters of the adult male population regularly voted in presidential elections. Even then, however, only about half voted in elections for mayor. With the tide of immigrants the proportions plummeted, because many immigrants were not citizens and many who were had slight interest in political affairs. The decline reached a low point with the introduction of women's suffrage in 1920. Since then the curve has risen again. (Figure 25.1) During the last decade the number of nonvoters has varied from a quarter of the adult population in presidential elections to a half in some mayoralty elections. (Table 25.1)

Even those who vote rarely do more, and the more active the form of participation, the fewer the citizens who participate. Consider, for example, participation in campaigns and elections. (Table 25.2) Only a tiny minority of the registered voters undertakes the more vigorous kinds of campaign participation. One finds (Figure 25.2) that only about one out of every sixteen citizens votes and also engages in five or more of the activities listed in the table; about one out of six votes and engages in three or four activities; one out of two votes and engages in one or two activities; and one out of five only votes. (Because our sample was drawn from the voting lists, the number of nonvoters was of course much smaller than it would be in a sample of the whole adult population; because we classified as not voting only those who had not voted in two out of the last three elections, the proportion is lower than it would be for any single election.)

FIGURE 25.1. *Percentage of citizens 21 years old and over voting in presidential and mayoralty elections, 1860–1950*

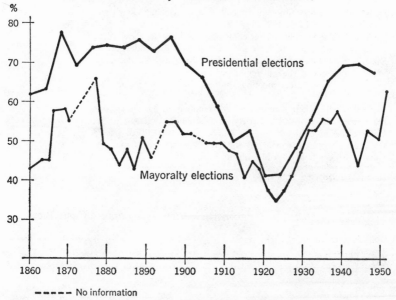

1860-1920: Males only   1920-1950: Males and females

Presidential elections

Mayoralty elections

- - - - - No information

It might be thought that citizens participate more actively outside campaigns and elections—for example, by getting directly involved in some way with the problems of local government. But just as with campaign activity, most people do very little beyond merely talking with their friends. Although nearly half the registered voters in our sample said they talked about New Haven politics and local affairs, only 13 per cent claimed they had done anything actively in connection with a local issue. (Table 25.3) Moreover, as with campaign activities, the number of persons who perform more than a few kinds of actions in local affairs is very small. At one extreme nearly 40 per cent of our sample said they had done

TABLE 25.1. *Voters in elections for president, governor, and mayor, 1949–1959*

	Number	Percentage of population 21 years old and over°
Actual voters	58,000–86,000	51–76
Registered voters	73,000–92,000	65–82

° Based on the 1950 census.

Table 25.2. *Campaign participation, by kinds of activities*

	Yes	
	%	N
Does anyone from either party call you up during campaigns or come around and talk to you?	60	320
Do you talk to people during campaigns and try to show them why they should vote for one of the parties or candidates?	33	172
Do you give money or buy tickets or anything to help the campaign for one of the parties or candidates?	26	139
Do you go to political meetings, rallies, dinners, or things like that?	23	119
Have you ever taken part in a party's nominations?	9	44
Do you do other work for a party or candidate?	8	42
Have you ever held an office or had a job in a political party?	5	25
Do you belong to any political club or organization?	4	22
Have you ever held a public office?	1	6

N = 525 registered voters.

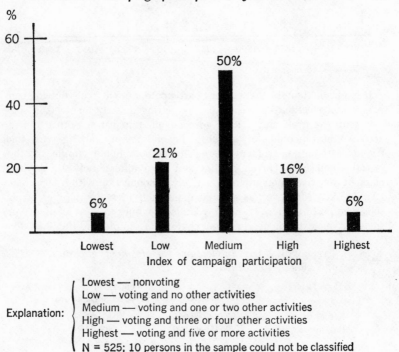

Figure 25.2. *Campaign participation, by number of activities*

Explanation:
{
Lowest — nonvoting
Low — voting and no other activities
Medium — voting and one or two other activities
High — voting and three or four other activities
Highest — voting and five or more activities
N = 525; 10 persons in the sample could not be classified
}

none of the things indicated in Table 25.3, and at the other extreme only three per cent claimed they had done all four.

As many studies of the national electorate have shown, the low rates of participation in political life by New Haven citizens are not unusual, for to stress a point that has been made before, in New Haven as in the United States generally one of the central facts of political life is that

TABLE 25.3. *Action in local affairs, by kinds of activities*

	Yes	
	%	N
When you and your friends get together, do you ever talk about New Haven politics and local affairs?	47	252
Have you ever contacted any local public officials or politicians to let them know what you would like them to do on something you were interested in?	27	141
In the past year or so have you had any contact with political or governmental officials in New Haven?	16	85
During the past year or so have you yourself done anything actively in connection with some local issue or local problem— political or nonpolitical?	13	66

N = 525.

politics—local, state, national, international—lies for most people at the outer periphery of attention, interest, concern, and activity. At the focus of most men's lives are primary activities involving food, sex, love, family, work, play, shelter, comfort, friendship, social esteem, and the like. Activities like these—not politics—are the primary concerns of most men and women. In response to the question, "What things are you most concerned with these days?" two out of every three registered voters in our sample cited personal matters, health, jobs, children, and the like; only about one out of five named local, state, national, or international affairs. It would clear the air of a good deal of cant if instead of assuming that politics is a normal and natural concern of human beings, one were to make the contrary assumption that whatever lip service citizens may pay to conventional attitudes, politics is a remote, alien, and unrewarding activity. Instead of seeking to explain why citizens are not interested, concerned, and active, the task is to explain why a few citizens *are*.

Whenever politics becomes attached to the primary activities, it may move from the periphery of attention, concern, and action to a point nearer the center. For most people in the United States (and probably everywhere else) this happens rarely, if at all. To be sure, if men are frustrated in their primary activities and if they find or think they find in political activity a means to satisfy their primary needs, then politics may become more salient. But in a political culture where individual achievement and nongovernmental techniques are assigned a high priority in problem-solving, men may be frustrated in their primary activities without ever turning to politics for solutions.

Even for someone to whom politics is important, it is easier to be merely interested than to be active. Considering the psychic economy of the individual, interest is cheap, whereas activity is relatively expensive. To be interested demands merely passive participation, requiring no more than scanning the political news in the newspaper or listening to news broadcasts. The merely interested citizen can go on reading the comics and watching his favorite Western on television; more than that, he may actually derive vicarious satisfaction from a spurious "participation" in politics that never requires him to turn from his passive engagement in the world described in newspaper, radio, and TV accounts to actual participation in the active world of politics. In this sense, to be merely interested in politics can be a kind of escape from politics. To be interested allows one to indulge in a great variety of emotional responses, from rage and hate to admiration and love; to derive a sense of superiority from the obvious inadequacies of men of action; to prescribe grandiose solutions to complex problems of public policy; to engage in fantasies about one's own achievements in a never-never-land of politics; to become an inside-dopester; and to follow each day's new events with the passionate curiosity of a housewife anxiously awaiting the next installment of her favorite soap opera; yet never to participate in politics in any way except by discussing political affairs with others and occasionally casting a vote.

To be interested in politics, then, need not compete with one's primary activities. By contrast, active political participation frequently removes one from the arena of primary activities. Since the primary activities are voracious in their demands for time, political activity must enter into competition with them. For most people it is evidently a weak competitor.

The sources of the myth about the primacy of politics in the lives of the citizens of a democratic order are ancient, manifold, and complex. The primacy of politics has roots in Greek thought and in the idealization of the city-state characteristic of the Greek philosophers. That initial bias has been reinforced by the human tendency to blur the boundaries between what is and what ought to be; by the inescapable fact that those who write about politics are deeply concerned with political affairs and sometimes find it difficult to believe that most other people are not; by the dogma that democracy would not work if citizens were not concerned with public affairs, from which, since "democracy works," it follows that citizens must be concerned; by the sharp contrast (noted by Tocqueville) between the low rate of uncoerced citizen participation in public affairs in authoritarian regimes and the *relatively* much higher rate in democratic ones; and by the assumption, based on uncritical acceptance of scanty and dubious evidence, that whatever the situation may be at the moment, at one time or in another place the life of the citizen has centered on politics.

This ancient myth about the concern of citizens with the life of the democratic polis is false in the case of New Haven. Whether or not the myth was reality in Athens will probably never be known.

26. Variations on a Theme

Given the fact that most citizens are not engaged very much in politics, several conclusions are evident. First, in so far as participation is a valid measure of resource use, we must conclude that comparatively few citizens use their political resources at a high rate. Second, in so far as the use of political resources is a necessary condition for political influence, only citizens who use their political resources at a high rate are likely to be highly influential. It follows that the number of highly influential citizens must be a relatively small segment of the population.

What kinds of factors are likely to induce people to use their resources at a relatively high rate? In Chapter 24, four hypotheses were advanced to help account for variations in the amount of political resources different individuals actually used. It was hypothesized that one group of citizens is likely to use more resources than another if (1) their political resources are greater in amount, (2) their expectations of success are higher, (3) the pay off they expect from using their resources for non-political purposes is lower, or (4) the value they attach to the outcome of political decisions is higher. On the assumption that the rate at which a registered voter participates in politics is a valid measure of the extent to which he uses his political resources, let us now examine these four hypotheses.

VARIATIONS IN THE SUPPLY OF RESOURCES

Political participation does tend to increase with the amount of resources at one's disposal. For example, participation in local political decisions is:

greater among citizens with high incomes than among citizens with low incomes;

greater among citizens with high social standing than among citizens with low social standing;

greater among citizens with considerable formal education than among citizens with little;

greater among citizens with professional, business, and white-collar occupations than among citizens with working-class occupation; and greater among citizens from better residential areas than among citizens from poorer areas.[1]

For want of a better term, I shall refer to citizens who are relatively well off with respect to income, social standing, education, occupation, or residence as the Better-Off. To summarize: participation in local political decisions is higher among the Better-Off than among the less well off.

For three reasons, however, the matter is much more complex than this simple statement suggests. First, all the relationships mentioned above represent *statistical tendencies*. For example, it is true that the more income one has the more *likely* one is to participate in local political activity. Indeed with some kinds of participation the relation with income is quite striking. (Figure 26.1) But it is also true that 42 per cent of our sample

FIGURE 26.1. *General participation in local political affairs* increases with income*

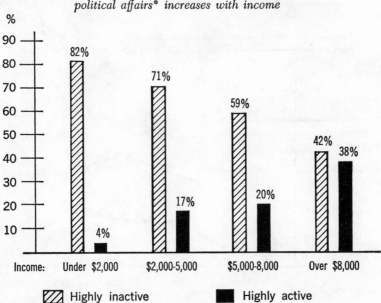

* Index of local action. Those with medium activity are not shown on the graph.

of registered voters who reported incomes over $8,000 were relatively inactive; on the other hand, 17 per cent of those with incomes from $2,000

1. Based on the index of local action in the sample of 525 registered voters. This index combines the two sets of activities shown in Tables 25.2 and 25.3. For details on construction of the index, see Appendix D.

to $5,000 and 2 per cent of those with incomes from $5,000 to $8,000
were highly active participants in local decisions.

Second, because the number of Better-Off citizens is inevitably rather
small, the *aggregate* activity of citizens with smaller resources is often
impressively large. In our sample of registered voters, for every citizen
who reported an income over $8,000, more than five reported incomes
less than that; in fact almost half the sample reported incomes less than
$5,000. Consequently even though citizens with incomes in the lower
brackets are much less likely to participate actively in local decisions
than citizens with larger incomes, there are so many more in the first
group that a smaller proportion of them can amount to an aggregate
greater than the group of participants with larger incomes. For example,
citizens with incomes less than $8,000 a year outnumbered those with
greater incomes at *every* level of political participation from the lowest
to the highest. In fact, as Figure 26.2 shows, citizens with incomes less

FIGURE 26.2. *Although general participation in local political affairs
varies with income, the Better-Off are a minority of all participants*

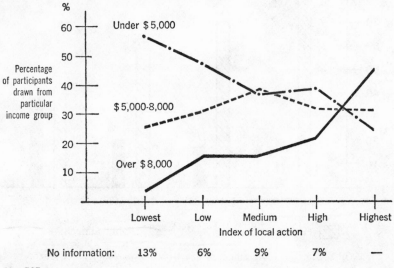

than $5,000 outnumbered citizens with incomes over $8,000 at every level
of activity except the highest; one-fourth of the people in the most active
category and nearly two-fifths in the second most active group have incomes under $5,000.

In the third place, the extent to which the Better-Off citizens participate in local decisions varies a good deal, depending on the nature of the participation. They participate much more heavily in noncampaign than in campaign activities. Even at the highest levels of campaign participation, citizens with incomes under $5,000 greatly outnumber citizens with incomes over $8,000; moreover the proportions drawn from the less well off are not much lower among the most active participants than among the less active participants. (Figure 26.3)

FIGURE 26.3. *Campaign participation varies only moderately with income, and the less well off are the largest category at every level of campaign participation*

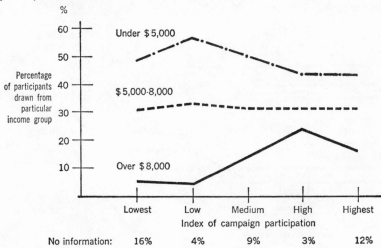

No information: 16%   4%   9%   3%   12%

N = 525

The greater readiness of the Better-Off to engage in *general* local action than campaign activities shows up in a variety of ways. Greater formal education, higher income, higher social position, better neighborhood, and a white-collar occupation are all associated less strongly with campaign participation than with general local action. If campaign activity is distinguished from exclusively noncampaign forms of political participation the differences are even more striking. Figure 26.4 shows that among the most active participants in noncampaign community activities the proportions of citizens who are Better-Off by four different criteria are all very much higher than among the less active. Figure 26.5, by contrast, shows that the participation of the Better-Off in campaign political activities is clearly much less pronounced.

Since the propensity among the Better-Off to engage more in noncampaign activities than in campaign activities evidently does not arise as a result of differences in access to resources among the Better-Off, other factors must be at work.

VARIATIONS IN POLITICAL CONFIDENCE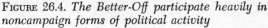

I have suggested that an individual who is relatively confident of success in attempting to influence decisions is much more likely to make the attempt than one who fears failure. Confidence might vary with the

FIGURE 26.4. *The Better-Off participate heavily in noncampaign forms of political activity*

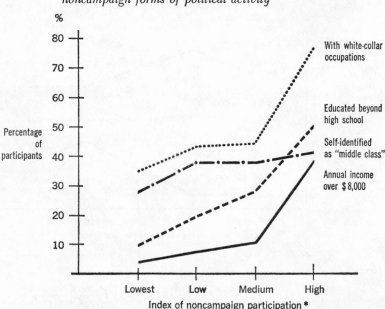

* For the construction of this index, see Appendix D.

specific political situation; if you happen to be a friend of the incumbent mayor and an enemy of his rival you might reasonably be more confident about succeeding now than if his rival wins the next election. However, confidence in capacity to influence government officials also seems to be a more general, pervasive, stable attitude in an individual. Some individuals bring into the political arena a durable optimism that survives occasional setbacks; others are incurably pessimistic. One of the striking characteristics of the activist in politics is his relatively high confidence that what he does *matters*; by contrast, the inactive citizen is more prone to doubt his effectiveness. A citizen who tends to feel that people like him have no say about what the local government does, or that the only way he can have a say is by voting, or that politics and government are too complicated for him to understand what is going on, or that local public officials don't care much what he thinks, is much less likely to participate in local political decisions than one who disagrees with all these propositions.[2] In short, the more one participates actively in local affairs the more

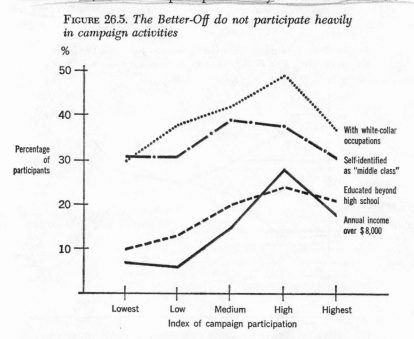

FIGURE 26.5. *The Better-Off do not participate heavily in campaign activities*

confident one is likely to be in one's capacity to be effective. (Figure 26.6)

Participation and political confidence evidently reinforce one another. A citizen with a high sense of political efficacy is more likely to participate in politics than a citizen pessimistic about his chances of influencing local officials. Participation in turn reinforces confidence. Evidently as a citizen becomes more familiar with the operation of the political system and develops more ties with leaders, subleaders, and activists, he tends to assume that he can get the attention of officials for his views and de-

2. The "sense of political efficacy" is a widely used and well-tested scale consisting of these four items. In Figure 26.6 registered voters who disagreed with three or four of the statements were regarded as having a "high sense of efficacy." Those who agreed with two or more of the statements were treated as having a "medium to low sense of efficacy."

mands. If he becomes a subleader, he is likely to have a very high sense of political efficacy. (Figure 26.7) Conversely, if one has little confidence in one's capacity to influence officials, one is less likely to participate and hence never acquires the skills, familiarity with the system, and associations that might build up confidence.

There is, however, a second and closely related factor associated with political confidence that might loosely be called the possession of "middle-class" attributes and resources: a college education, above-average income, a white-collar occupation, and the like. Level of education is par-

FIGURE 26.6. *The more one participates in local political affairs, the more likely one is to have a high sense of political efficacy*

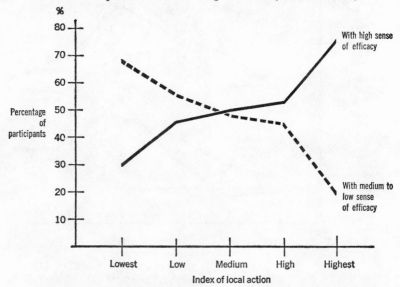

ticularly important. Among subleaders and registered voters alike political confidence is higher among citizens with a college education than among citizens with a high school education; the relation is much more apparent among registered voters than among subleaders. (Figure 26.8)

One might conjecture that the relationship between political confidence and "middle-class" attributes would disappear if one were to eliminate from consideration all those who are below a certain socioeconomic threshold and whose presence serves to pull down the averages for the working-class strata. However, this conjecture appears to be false. Table 26.1 includes only the registered voters in our sample who had at least a seventh grade education, over $2,000 income, and both parents born in the United States. Even among this group, twice as many persons with white-collar occupations of all sorts, from clerks to executives, were highly active as among persons with working-class occupations: one out of five registered voters with "middle-class" occupations was highly active compared with only one out of ten in working-class occupations.

FIGURE 26.7. *Subleaders have a very high sense of political efficacy*

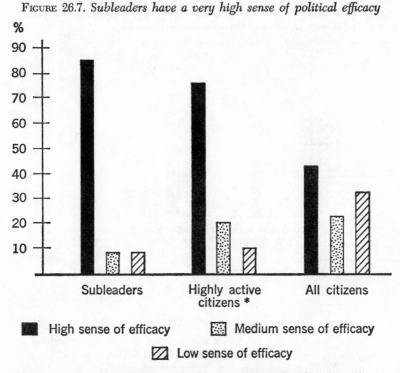

High sense of efficacy   **Medium sense of efficacy**

Low sense of efficacy

* Highest on index of local action. Those who did not answer are omitted from the graph.

Moreover, twice as many from the middling strata had a high sense of political confidence as from the working strata; conversely, twice as many persons in the working strata had a low sense of their political efficacy as in the middling strata. In fact, among the middling strata, one-third were highly confident and only one-sixth had little confidence in their political efficacy; among the working strata, it was precisely the other way around —one-sixth were highly confident and one-third had little sense of confidence. (Table 26.2)

The importance of confidence to political activity is indicated by the fact that the sharp differences between middling and working strata in

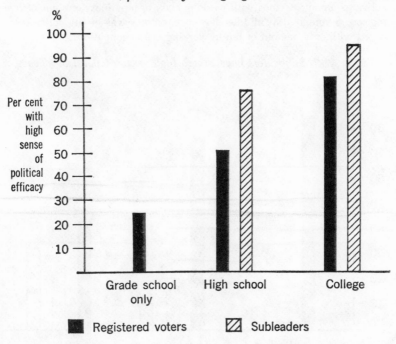

FIGURE 26.8. *A sense of political efficacy tends to increase with education, particularly among registered voters*

TABLE 26.1. *Registered voters with middle-class resources are more likely to be politically active than skilled and unskilled laborers, artisans, etc., even if groups below the "political threshold" are eliminated*

Index of political action	Middle-class occupations %	Working-class occupations %
High	21	11
Medium	22	21
Low	57	68
Total	100	100
N	*162*	*152*

Note: Table includes only respondents who reported seven or more grades of formal education, over $2,000 income, and both parents born in the United States.

TABLE 26.2. *Registered voters with middle-class resources are also more likely than workers to have a high sense of political efficacy*

Sense of political efficacy	Middle-class occupations %	Working-class occupations %
High	33	18
Medium	51	50
Low	16	32
Total	100	100
N	162	152

Note: See Note, Table 26.1.

the extent to which they participate in local affairs very nearly disappear if one considers their level of political confidence. Among persons from the middling strata who have a high level of political confidence, one-third are highly active participants in local affairs; the same proportion holds among the working strata. Conversely, among middling strata with a low degree of political confidence, slightly over two-thirds participate little or not at all in local affairs; the same thing is true among the working strata. (Table 26.3)

TABLE 26.3. *Registered voters with similar levels of confidence participate at about the same rate in local affairs whether they have white-collar or working-class resources*

Sense of political efficacy	Index of local action: High %	Medium %	Low %	Total %	N
HIGH					
Middle classes*	33	22	45	100	54
Working classes*	32	14	54	100	28
MEDIUM					
Middle classes	17	22	61	100	83
Working classes	5	19	76	100	75
LOW					
Middle classes	8	24	68	100	25
Working classes	6	29	65	100	49
Total					314

* Middle classes include executives, managers, professionals, administrative personnel, small businessmen, clerks, salesmen, technicians. Working classes include skilled manual employees, machine operators, semi-skilled and unskilled laborers.

Note: See Note, Table 26.1.

Because the Better-Off citizens with "middle-class" attributes and resources are also likely to participate more in political affairs, probably
an important circularity develops that increases the influence of the
Better-Off and decreases the influence of the working classes. In the way
suggested earlier each characteristic reinforces the other. This process of
reinforcement might be illustrated as follows:

Citizens with:

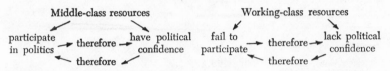

Although this can hardly be the whole explanation, it helps to account
for the fact that executives and professional people are more likely to
attempt to influence city officials than clerks, salesmen, and manual
laborers. (Table 26.4) The act of picking up a telephone and calling a

TABLE 26.4. *Professional men and executives are more likely to
attempt to influence city officials than are clerks, salesmen,
and manual laborers*

	Occupations			
	Professional and managerial %	Clerical and sales %	Manual laborers %	Not ascertained %
Attempt to influence politician or govern- mental official*	41	28	29	21
No attempt	59	72	71	79
Total	100	100	100	100
N	99	65	153	29

* "Have you ever contacted any local public official or politicians to let them know
what you would like them to do on something you were interested in?"

Note: See Note, Table 26.1.

public official in order to make a request has many familiar analogues in
the life of the business executive or professional man; it is hardly a
strange or formidable activity. To the clerk or artisan, however, it is more
unusual, though the easy availability of the alderman helps a great deal
to make it less difficult.

Why is campaign participation so much less popular among the Better-
Off citizens than other forms of participation? Evidently the circular

process by which participation and confidence reinforce one another is attenuated by the plain facts of party life. Once the ex-plebes had taken over control of the parties and used them as instruments to appeal to the immigrants and their children, it became difficult for the Better-Off to succeed in party affairs, nominations, and elections; they became estranged from the men who governed the parties and alien to their problems and tactics. Today, two generations later, it is by no means unrealistic for the Better-Off citizen to be somewhat pessimistic about his chances of success in *party* politics and at the same time relatively confident about his capacity for influencing city officials in various other ways.

VARIATIONS IN ALTERNATIVE OPPORTUNITIES

Citizens also vary in the rate at which they use their political resources because of differences in opportunities for achieving goals through means other than political action. In an affluent society dominated by goals that are typically sought through individual rather than collective action, citizens are confronted with a variety of opportunities for gaining their primary goals without ever resorting to political action at all. Essentially, this is why the level of citizen participation is so low.

Some citizens, however, have fewer alternatives to political action than others. Probably the most significant group in New Haven whose opportunities are sharply restricted by social and economic barriers are Negroes.

The Negroes are a relatively small though increasing minority in New Haven. In 1950 they were 6 per cent of the population. They comprised 9 per cent of our sample of registered voters. Although they are gradually dispersing, in 1950 they were concentrated in a few Negro ghettos; in fact, about 40 per cent of the Negro population was concentrated in only one of the city's thirty-three wards, the Nineteenth, where three out of four persons were Negroes.

Although discrimination is declining, in the private socioeconomic sphere of life New Haven Negroes still encounter far greater obstacles than the average white person. They find it difficult to move from Negro neighborhoods into white neighborhoods. Many private employers are reluctant to hire Negroes for white-collar jobs. In 1950, only four of the thirty-three wards had a smaller proportion of the labor force in white-collar jobs than the Nineteenth. Only three wards had a lower median income. These differences cannot be attributed solely to disparities in education, for in 1950 the median number of school years completed in the Nineteenth (8.8 years) was only slightly lower than for the whole city (9.1 years). Although nineteen wards were on the average better off in education, thirteen were worse off.

In contrast to the situation the Negro faces in the private socioeconomic sphere, in local politics and government the barriers are comparatively slight. There is no discrimination against Negroes who wish to vote; they have participated in elections for generations. Though they are a relatively small minority, both parties compete vigorously for their support. Partly because of their votes, Negroes are not discriminated against in city employment; they have only to meet the qualifications required of white applicants to become policemen, firemen, school teachers, clerks, stenographers. Negroes also share in city patronage, city contracts, and other favors. Because both parties nominate a Negro to run as alderman from the Nineteenth Ward, the Board of Aldermen always contains one Negro. Both parties nominate a Negro to one city-wide elective office. In 1954 Mayor Lee appointed a Negro as corporation counsel; in 1960 he appointed a Negro to the Board of Education.

In comparison with whites, therefore, Negroes find no greater obstacles to achieving their goals through political action but very much greater difficulties through activities in the private socioeconomic spheres. Consequently it is reasonable to expect that Negroes might employ their resources more in political action than the average white person does.

This hypothesis is strikingly confirmed by the evidence. For example, when we asked our sample of registered voters, "Assuming the pay is the same, would you prefer a job with the city government or with a private firm?" only 37 per cent of the white voters said they would prefer a city job, compared with 64 per cent of the Negroes. Thirty-eight per cent of the Negro voters said they would like to see a son enter politics, compared with 27 per cent among the whites.

What is even more impressive is the extent of Negro participation in politics. Although slightly less than one out of ten persons in our sample of registered voters was a Negro, nearly one out of four of the citizens who participated most in campaign and electoral activities was a Negro; in the next most active group one out of six was a Negro. With respect to local action generally, the percentages of Negroes in the two most active groups were 24 per cent and 16 per cent. Looking at the matter in another way, 44 per cent of the Negroes in our sample were among the two most active groups of participants in campaigns and elections compared with 20 per cent among whites (Figure 26.9); 38 per cent of the Negroes in our sample were among the two most active groups of participants in local affairs generally, compared with 17 per cent among the whites. (Figure 26.10)

The position of the Negro in New Haven helps us to explain why the Better-Off prefer to participate by means other than through political parties and campaigns. An important incentive for routine participation in party activities is the prospect of receiving favors from the city, par-

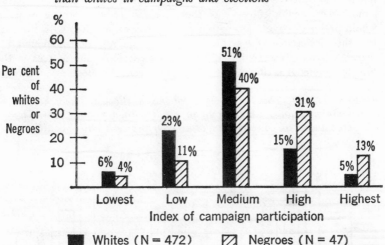

FIGURE 26.9. *New Haven Negroes participate more than whites in campaigns and elections*

ticularly jobs, minor contracts for snow removal, printing, and the like. The large contractor who constructs buildings, streets, highways and other expensive projects is likely to participate more through financial contributions than party activity. It follows that the parties must recruit their rank-and-file workers in great part from groups in the community to whom the prospect of a city job or small contract for themselves, their families, or their neighbors is attractive. To the Better-Off, who have

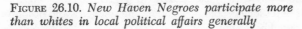

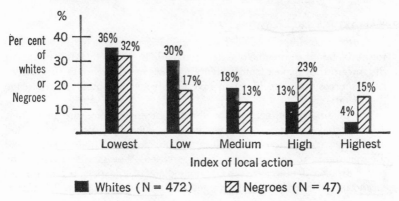

FIGURE 26.10. *New Haven Negroes participate more than whites in local political affairs generally*

many other and better opportunities, a job with the city is likely to be much less attractive than it is to the less well off. Now it happens that in almost every major category of the city's registered voters, a majority would prefer to have a job with a private firm rather than with the city. But this preference is less marked among the rest of the population than it is among the Better-Off, who have attractive alternatives in the private sphere. If a citizen has only a grade school education, an income

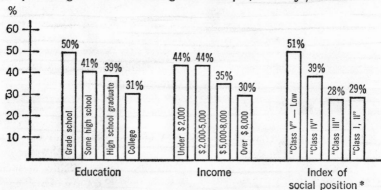

FIGURE 26.11. *The Better-Off a citizen is, the less likely he is to prefer a job with the city to a job with a private firm. The percentages in various categories who prefer a city job are:*

*A two-factor index based on residence and occupation. (See Appendix D).

under $5,000 a year, or a relatively low social position, he is just as likely to prefer a job with the city as with a private firm. But the higher a group is in its socioeconomic position, the smaller is the proportion which prefers city jobs. (Figure 26.11)

VARIATIONS IN REWARDS

As the preceding discussion suggests, citizens also vary in the value they attach to the outcome of a decision made by local officials. The bigger the reward they expect from a favorable decision, the more of their political resources they are likely to invest in trying to obtain the outcome they want.

The factors that affect one's evaluation of an outcome are numerous. As suggested earlier, citizens vary both in their objective situations and also, because of differences in information, predispositions, values, and identifications, in the subjective interpretations they give to events. The payoff from a decision may seem immediate to one person and remote to another; it may be specific or general, tangible or intangible. Almost always there is a set of citizens who feel that they benefit more from the existing situation, whatever it may be, than from any of the alternatives urged by those who favor a change. The results expected from a decision may vary from the concrete gain or loss of a job, a city contract, or a nomination to more abstract results like a better neighborhood, better schools, cleaner politics, or a sense of personal satisfaction in having performed one's duty as a citizen.[3]

Because of differences in objective situations, few decisions of government affect citizens generally and uniformly. Most decisions have strong and immediate consequences for only a relatively small part of the population and at best small or delayed consequences for the rest. Those to whom the consequences are small or delayed tend to be indifferent about the outcome and correspondingly uninterested in influencing it. By and large, only citizens who expect the decision to have important and immediate consequences for themselves, or for those with whom they feel strongly identified, try to influence the outcome. Even many of these people do little or nothing about a decision. As the character and consequences of decisions change, some of the actors change, and there is an ebb and flow in the numbers who participate. At any given moment, however, only the citizens who expect current decisions to have important and immediate consequences tend to be very active. And they are generally few in number.

However, a few citizens use their political resources steadily at such a high rate over such a broad range with such a comparatively high degree of skill that they might properly be called political professionals —even when they carefully cultivate the appearance of amateurism. To the professionals and the incipient professionals, the rewards from political activity are evidently very high indeed.

In a city like New Haven the number of highly rewarding positions, judged by the standards of the middling segments of the population, are few. The mayoralty is the key prize, and only one person in the city can be elected mayor. There are other prizes, but the number is not large. Hence at any given moment only a tiny number of people in the middling segments can have any hope of gaining rewards greater than those held out by careers in private occupations. For anyone who is

3. It is not unreasonable to suppose that a sense of civic duty might impel many citizens to action; the payoff would be their own sense of satisfaction in having performed their obligations as citizens. These considerations suggest that the most active participants in civic life might also have the strongest sense of civic duty. Unfortunately, the data from our study are inadequate for a good test of this hypothesis. While we cannot conclude that the hypothesis is false, it is clearly not confirmed by our data, and in fact such evidence as we have seems to run counter to it. However, given the nature of the evidence perhaps the best position one can take on the question is a combination of skepticism and open-mindedness.

not yet a member of one of the middling segments of the community, the chance of competing successfully for the chief offices is, as we have seen, dim. In sum, there are only a few large prizes; the only contestants with much chance of success are those from the middling layers who are prepared to invest their resources, including time, energy, and money, in the task of winning and holding the prize; and a full-time alternative career must be temporarily abandoned. Hence it is not too surprising that the number of professionals is small.

It is impossible to say with confidence why some citizens find participation in public life so highly rewarding that they are impelled along the path toward professionalism. Perhaps the most obvious requirement that one must have is an unusual toleration for creating and maintaining a great number and variety of personal relationships. This does not mean that the professional actually likes other people to any unusual degree or even that he has an unusual need to be liked by others. Indeed, a study by Rufus Browning indicates that among businessmen the "need for affiliation"—the desire to have the liking and approval of others— is lower among those who are active in politics than those who are inactive, and it is lower among leaders than among subleaders.[4] Browning's findings suggest the tantalizing hypothesis that the distinguishing characteristic of the professional is an inordinate capacity for multiplying human relationships without ever becoming deeply involved emotionally. Despite his appearance of friendliness and warmth, the professional may in fact carry a cool detachment that many citizens would find it impossibly wearisome to sustain.

Whether or not this hypothesis is true, the capacity of the professional to sustain a variety of human relations is revealed in his unusual propensity for joining organizations of all sorts. I have already alluded to this as a marked characteristic of subleaders. (Chapter 13) The same predisposition is evident in our sample of registered voters: the more a voter participates in local political life, the more likely he is to participate in other forms of community organization, and conversely. (Fig. 26.12) Now the propensity for joining organizations is partly a function of socioeconomic factors that are also associated with participation in political life; organizational memberships are higher among the Better-Off than among the worse off. However, one cannot explain the relation between political participation and other forms of participation merely by saying that *both* are functions of being better off, for the tendency of citizens who belong to numerous organizations to participate actively in political decisions holds up even when socioeconomic factors are held constant. For example, among citizens in our sample who were members

4. Rufus Browning, "Businessmen in Politics" (Doctoral dissertation, Yale University, 1960).

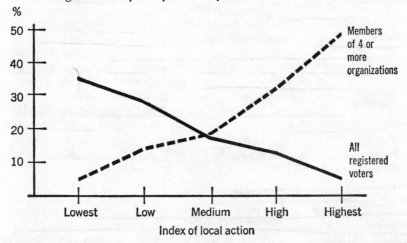

FIGURE 26.12. *The greater the participation in organizations, the greater the participation in politics*

Number of registered voters: 525

Number of registered voters who are members of four or more organizations: 89

of four or more organizations, the proportion of highly active citizens was just as great among those who had not completed high school as among those who had. (Table 26.5) Moreover, the relationship held for both partisan and nonpartisan forms of participation.

Joining organizations and participating in politics reinforce one another. If a person participates in local political decisions, he widens his range of relationships in the community; moreover, if he is serious about politics he may deliberately join organizations in order to establish more

TABLE 26.5. *Political participation among citizens who belong to four or more organizations does not rise with increasing education*

	Education	
	Less than 12th grade	12th grade or more
Participation	%	%
High	47	46
Medium	43	37
Low	7	15
None	—	2
No answer	3	—
Total	100	100
N	*30*	*54*

contacts. Numerous memberships in organizations in turn establish contact with people involved in various ways in local affairs and increase the probability that he too may become involved.

The professional politician has to tolerate a profusion of human contacts that many citizens would find abrasive and exhausting. He must interact with great numbers of people, cultivate friendships with as many as possible, and convey the impression that he enjoys meeting them all. To work with the zest and energy necessary to his success, probably he must actually enjoy this very proliferation of human contacts. If a citizen does not enjoy the process of cultivating friendly though not always very deep relationships with a great variety of people, he is not likely to find political life highly rewarding. For a person who does, politics is by no means the only possible outlet, but it is a natural and obvious one.

FLUCTUATIONS IN PARTICIPATION

The differences among citizens discussed here—in political resources, political confidence, alternative opportunities, and rewards—help to account not only for the persistent tendencies among various segments of the population to use their resources at different rates but also for the fluctuations in participation, and presumably in the use of political resources, that occur over time.

There are important differences among participants with respect both to the *frequency* with which they participate and the *range* of issue-areas in which they participate. Some citizens participate frequently; others occasionally. Some citizens participate only in one issue-area; some in several. By combining these two characteristics—frequency and range of participation—we arrive at a convenient classification of participants into four types. These are shown in Table 26.6.

TABLE 26.6. *Types of civic participation*

	Frequency	
Range	Low	High
One issue-area	a. Occasional, specialized participation	b. Frequent, specialized participation
Several issue-areas	c. Occasional, multiple participation	d. Frequent, multiple participation

Most citizens who participate at all are, as we have observed, occasional, specialized participants (*a* in Table 26.6) It may happen, however, that the consequences of policies under current discussion seem immediate and important to some of the occasional, specialized participants. Like the school teachers in 1945, or the citizens around Truman

Street in 1953, they enormously step up their activity and become frequent though still specialized participants (*b*). If the decisions are moderately favorable, many specialized participants revert to their earlier level of infrequent participation. If the decisions are unfavorable, some of them may continue for a time, until either a more favorable compromise is arranged or they become discouraged. Occasionally, however, a few citizens discover that they enjoy their new activities. They have made a place for it in their lives, acquired new associates, new opportunities for conviviality, perhaps an office with prestige or obligations. These few now continue as frequent, specialized participants, some of them as subleaders—PTA officers, members of League of Women Voters' committees, ward leaders, perhaps even members of the Board of Education. As a result of exposure to new situations, now and again one of the frequent, specialized participants finds himself pulled into another issue-area; for example, his prominence in education makes him an obvious candidate for the Citizens Action Commission. Or perhaps he is elected to the Board of Aldermen, where he engages frequently in a great variety of decisions. In Table 26.6, he has traveled the route *a–b–d*. It is also easy to see how he might move from *a* to *c* to *d*.

In addition to individual fluctuations there are changes in the level of political activity. Regularly recurring cycles of participation result from campaigns and elections. Political participation rises during a presidential campaign, reaches a peak on election day, and then drops rapidly into a long trough. Gubernatorial, congressional, and mayoralty elections create lower peaks followed by troughs. In New Haven, one of these elections occurs annually in November; hence there is an annual peak of activity on the Tuesday after the first Monday in November and an annual trough from election day to the start of the next campaign. Every four years a high peak is reached in presidential elections. Superimposed on these annual fluctuations are short-run cycles associated with meetings of the Board of Aldermen, Board of Finance, Board of Education, and the like. In addition, there are also erratic fluctuations associated with current decisions. Citizens to whom a decision is salient participate briefly and then for the most part return to their previous levels of activity.

Only a small group of citizens, the professionals, participate steadily throughout all the cyclical and erratic fluctuations. These are citizens to whom politics is a career, or at least an alternate career. They use their political resources at a high rate, acquire superior skills, and exert a very high degree of influence. These citizens, the professionals, are sources both of stability and instability in the political system.

Book VI

STABILITY AND CHANGE

27. Stability, Change, and the Professionals

New Haven, like most pluralistic democracies, has three characteristics of great importance to the operation of its political system: there are normally "slack" resources; a small core of professional politicians exert great influence over decisions; and the system has a built-in, self-operating limitation on the influence of all participants, including the professionals.

SLACK IN THE SYSTEM

Most of the time, as we have already seen, most citizens use their resources for purposes other than gaining influence over government decisions. There is a great gap between their actual influence and their potential influence. Their political resources are, so to speak, slack in the system. In some circumstances these resources might be converted from nonpolitical to political purposes; if so, the gap between the actual influence of the average citizen and his potential influence would narrow.

The existence of a great deal of political slack seems to be a characteristic of pluralistic political systems and the liberal societies in which these systems operate. In liberal societies, politics is a sideshow in the great circus of life. Even when citizens use their resources to gain influence, ordinarily they do not seek to influence officials or politicians but family members, friends, associates, employees, customers, business firms, and other persons engaged in nongovernmental activities. A complete study of the ways in which people use their resources to influence others would require a total examination of social life. Government, in the sense used here, is only a fragment of social life.

THE PROFESSIONALS

The political system of New Haven is characterized by the presence of two sharply contrasting groups of citizens. The great body of citizens use their political resources at a low level; a tiny body of professionals within the political stratum use their political resources at a high level. Most citizens acquire little skill in politics; professionals acquire a great deal. Most citizens exert little direct and immediate influence on the decisions of public officials; professionals exert much more. Most citizens have political resources they do not employ in order to gain influence over the decisions of public officials; consequently there is a great gap between their actual and potential influence. The professionals alone narrow the gap; they do so by using their political resources to the full, and by using them with a high degree of efficiency.

The existence of a small band of professionals within the political stratum is a characteristic of virtually all pluralistic systems and liberal societies. The professionals may enjoy much prestige or little; they may be rigidly honest or corrupt; they may come from aristocracies, the middle strata, or working classes. But in every liberal society they are easily distinguished by the rate and skill with which they use their resources and the resulting degree of direct influence they exert on government decisions.

Probably the most important resource of the professional is his available *labor time*. Other citizens usually have occupations that demand a large part of their labor time; they also feel a need for recreation. Measured by the alternatives he has to forego, the average citizen finds it too costly to sacrifice at most more than a few hours a week to political activities.

The professional, by contrast, organizes his life around his political activities. He usually has an occupation that leaves him freer than most citizens to engage in politics; if he does not, he is likely to change jobs until he finds one that fits easily into political routines. Celentano was an undertaker, Lee a public relations man for Yale, DiCenzo a lawyer, Golden an insurance broker—all occupations that permit innumerable opportunities for political work. As a public official, of course, the politician can work virtually full-time at the tasks of politics.

Most citizens treat politics as an avocation. To the professional, politics is a vocation, a calling. Just as the artist remains an artist even as he walks down a city street, and the scientist often consciously or unconsciously remains in his laboratory when he rides home in the evening, or the businessman on the golf course may be working out solutions to his business problems, so the successful politician is a full-time politician. The dedicated artist does not regard it as a sacrifice of precious time and leisure to paint, the dedicated scientist to work in his laboratory, nor the dedicated businessman to work at his business. On the contrary, each is likely to look for ways of avoiding all other heavy claims on his time. So, too, the dedicated politician does not consider it a sacrifice to work at politics. He is at it, awake and asleep, talking, negotiating, planning, considering strategies, building alliances, making friends, creating contacts—and increasing his influence.

It is hardly to be wondered at that the professional has much more influence on decisions than the average citizen. The professional not only has more resources at the outset than the average citizen, but he also tends to use his resources more efficiently. That is to say, he is more *skillful*.

SKILL

Skill in politics is the ability to gain more influence than others, using the same resources. Why some people are more skillful than others in politics is a matter of great speculation and little knowledge. Because skill in politics is hard to measure, I shall simply assume here that professionals are in fact more skillful. However, two hypotheses help to account for the superior skill of the politician.

First, the stronger one's motivation to learn, the more one is likely to learn. Just why the professional is motivated to succeed in politics is as obscure as the motives of the artist, the scientist, or the businessman. But the whole pattern of his calling hardly leaves it open to doubt that the professional *is* more strongly motivated to acquire political skills than is the average citizen.

Second, the more time one spends in learning, the more one is likely to learn. Here the professional has an obvious advantage, as we have just seen: he organizes his life, in effect, to give him time to learn the art of politics.

I have just said the *art* of politics. Although politicians make use of information about the world around them, and hence depend on "scientific" or empirical elements, the actual practice of politics by a skilled professional is scarcely equivalent to the activities of an experimental physicist or biologist in a laboratory.

Even the professional cannot escape a high degree of uncertainty in his calculations. If the professional had perfect knowledge of his own goals, the objective situation, and the consequences of alternative strategies, then his choice of strategy would be a relatively simple and indeed a "scientific" matter. But in fact his knowledge is highly imperfect. He cannot be sure at what point rival professionals will begin to mobilize new resources against his policies. When new opposition flares up, he cannot be sure how much further the battle may spread or what forces lie in reserve. He cannot even be certain what will happen to his own resources if he pursues his policies. He may lose some of his popularity; campaign contributions may fall off in the future; the opposition may come up with a legal block, an ethnic angle, a scandal.

Because of the uncertainty surrounding his decisions, the politician, like the military leader, rarely confronts a situation in which his choice of strategies follows clearly and logically from all the information at his disposal, even when he happens to be well-informed as to his own goals. Surrounded by uncertainty, the politician himself necessarily *imputes* a structure and meaning to the situation that goes beyond empirical evidence and scientific modes of analysis. What the politician imputes to the situation depends, in sum, not only on the information at his disposal but also on his own inner predispositions. His strategy therefore reflects his predispositions for caution or boldness, impulsiveness or calculation, negotiation or toughness, stubbornness or resilience, optimism or pessimism, cynicism or faith in others. The strategies of professionals may vary depending on the forces that generate needs for approval, popularity, domination, manipulation, deception, candor, and so on. The effect of inner dispositions on a professional's strategies is by no means clear or direct. But as one works back from a given situation with all its uncertainties to the professional's interpretation of the situation and his choice of strategies, usually some element in the interpretation or the choice is difficult to account for except as a product of his own special dispositions imposing themselves on his selection of strategies.

Differences in predispositions that result in differences in strategies often reveal themselves in dramatic differences in the style of a chief executive: the differences between a Roosevelt and Eisenhower, for example, or a Wilson and a Coolidge, or the early Truman doubtful of his inherent fitness for the presidency and the later, cocky, self-confident President. Differences also show up at the local level—for example, the contrast between the cautious demeanor of Mayor Celentano and the aggressive, programmatic behavior of Mayor Lee.

Just as individuals vary, so professionals vary in the extent to which they use all the resources at their disposal. Some professionals seem driven not only to use all the resources they have but to create new resources and thus to pyramid their influence. They are a kind of political entrepreneur. In an authoritarian milieu perhaps the political entrepreneur might even be driven to dictatorship. But in a pluralistic political system, powerful self-limiting tendencies help to maintain the stability of the system.

THE ART OF PYRAMIDING

We have seen that in the pluralistic political system of New Haven, the political order that existed before 1953—the pattern of petty sovereignties—was gradually transformed into an executive-centered order. How could this change take place? There were few formal changes in the structure of government and politics. The city charter not only remained unaltered, but as we have seen a proposed charter that in effect would have conferred full legality and legitimacy on the executive-centered order was turned down decisively in the same election in which the chief of the new order was re-elected by one of the greatest popular majorities on record.

The transformation of petty sovereignties into an executive-centered order was possible only because there were slack resources available to the mayor which, used skillfully and to the full, were sufficient to shift the initiative on most questions to the chief executive. Initially the new mayor had access to no greater resources than his predecessor, but with superb skill he exploited them to the limit. In this way, he managed to accumulate new resources; he rose to new heights of popularity, for example, and found it increasingly easy to tap the business community for campaign contributions. His new resources in turn made it easier for him to secure the compliance of officials in city agencies, enlarge his staff, appoint to office the kinds of people he wanted, obtain the cooperation of the Boards of Finance and Aldermen, and gain widespread support for his policies. Thus the resources available to the mayor grew by comparison with those available to other officials. He could now increase his influence over the various officials of local government by using these new resources fully and skillfully. An executive-centered order gradually emerged.

This transformation had two necessary conditions. First, when the new mayor came into office he had to have access either to resources not available to his predecessor or to slack resources his predecessor had not used. In this instance, the new mayor initially relied on a fuller and more efficient use of substantially the same resources available to his predecessor. By using slack resources with higher efficiency the new mayor moved his actual influence closer to his potential influence. Then because of his greater influence he was able to improve his access to resources. In this fashion he pyramided both his resources and his influence. He was, in short, a highly successful political entrepreneur.

There is, however, a second necessary condition for success. The policies of the political entrepreneur must not provoke so strong a countermobilization that he exhausts his resources with no substantial increase in his influence.

What then stops the political entrepreneur short of dictatorship? Why doesn't the political entrepreneur in a pluralistic system go on pyramiding his resources until he overturns the system itself? The answer lies in the very same conditions that are necessary to his success. If slack resources provide the political entrepreneur with his dazzling opportunity, they are also the source of his greatest danger. For nearly every citizen in the community has access to unused political resources; it is precisely because of this that even a minor blunder can be fatal to the political entrepreneur if it provokes a sizable minority in the community into using its political resources at a markedly higher rate in opposition to his policies, for then, as with the White Queen, it takes all the running he can do just to stay in the same place. Yet almost every policy involves losses for some citizens and gains for others. Whenever the prospect of loss becomes high enough, threatened citizens begin to take up some of the slack in order to remove the threat. The more a favorable decision increases in importance to the opposition, the more resources they can withdraw from other uses and pour into the political struggle; the more resources the opposition employs, the greater the cost to the political entrepreneur if he insists on his policy. At some point, the cost becomes so high that the policy is no longer worth it. This point is almost certain to be reached whenever the opposition includes a majority of the electorate, even if no election takes place. Normally, however, far before this extreme situation is approached the expected costs will already have become so excessive that an experienced politician will capitulate or, more likely, search for a compromise that gives him some of what he wants at lower cost.

Three aspects of Mayor Lee's situation made it possible for him to avoid costly opposition. These were: the wide degree of latent support for redevelopment that already existed in New Haven and needed only to be awakened; the evident need for a high degree of coordination among city agencies if redevelopment were to be carried out; and the Mayor's unusual skill at negotiating agreement and damping down potential disagreements before they flared into opposition. These aspects of Lee's situation are not prevalent in New Haven all the time, nor, certainly, do they necessarily exist in other cities. In the absence of any one of them, opposition might have developed, and the attempt to transform the independent sovereignties into an executive-centered order might have become altogether too costly.

Thus the distribution of resources and the ways in which they are or are not used in a pluralistic political system like New Haven's constitute an important source of both political change and political stability. If the distribution and use of resources gives aspiring leaders great opportunities for gaining influence, these very features also provide a built-in throttle that makes it difficult for any leader, no matter how skillful, to run away with the system.

These features are not, however, the only source of stability. Widespread consensus on the American creed of democracy and equality, referred to many times in the previous pages, is also a stabilizing factor. The analysis in the preceding pages surely points, however, to the conclusion that the effectiveness of the creed as a constraint on political leaders depends not only on the nature of the political consensus as it exists among ordinary citizens but also as it exists among members of the political stratum, particularly the professionals themselves. This is the subject of the next and final chapter.

Leaving to one side as a doubtful case the elected oligarchy that governed New Haven during its first century and a half, public officials in New Haven have been selected for the last century and a half through democratic institutions of a rather advanced sort. For more than a century, indeed, New Haven's political system has been characterized by well-nigh universal suffrage, a moderately high participation in elections, a highly competitive two-party system, opportunity to criticize the conduct and policies of officials, freedom to seek support for one's views, among officials and citizens, and surprisingly frequent alternations in office from one party to the other as electoral majorities have shifted. (Hereafter, when I speak of the political system of New Haven, I will assume what I have just enumerated to be the defining characteristics of that system: "stability" will mean the persistence of these characteristics.)

During this period New Haven has not, so far as I can discover, fallen at any time into the kind of semi-dictatorship occasionally found in other American communities. Violence is not and seems never to have been a weapon of importance to New Haven's rulers. Party bosses have existed and exist today; the parties tend to be highly disciplined, and nominations are centrally controlled. But despite occasional loose talk to the contrary, today the parties are too competitive and the community too fragmented for a party boss to be a community boss as well.

Like every other political system, of course, the political system of New Haven falls far short of the usual conceptions of an ideal democracy; by almost any standard, it is obviously full of defects. But to the extent that the term is ever fairly applied to existing realities, the political system of New Haven is an example of a democratic system, warts and all. For the past century it seems to have been a highly stable system.

Theorists have usually assumed that so much stability would be unlikely and even impossible without widespread agreement among citizens on the key ideas of democracy, including the basic rights, duties, and procedures that serve to distinguish democratic from nondemocratic systems. Tocqueville, you will recall, concluded that among the three causes that maintained democracy among the people of the United States—their physical, social, and economic conditions, their laws, and their customs—it was the customs that constituted "the peculiar cause which renders that people the only one of the American nations that is able to support a democratic government." By "customs," he explained, he meant "the whole moral and intellectual condition of a people." Considering his remarkable eye for relevant detail, Tocqueville was uncharacteristically vague as to the specific nature of these customs. But the general import of his argument is perfectly clear. "Republican notions insinuate themselves," as he says at one place, "into all the ideas, opinions, and habits of the Americans and are formally recognized by the laws; and before the laws could be altered, the whole community must be revolutionized." [1]

Before the days of the sample survey it was difficult to say with confidence how widely shared various ideas of democracy actually were in the United States, or even in New Haven. The data are still inadequate. However, some recent findings[2] cast doubt on the validity of the hypothesis that the stability of the American democratic system depends, as Tocqueville and others seem to argue, on an almost universal belief in the basic rules of the democratic game. These studies offer support for some alternative hypotheses. First, although Americans almost unanimously agree on a number of general propositions about democracy, they disagree about specific applications to crucial cases. Second, a majority of voters frequently hold views contrary to rules of the game actually followed in the political system. Third, a much higher degree of agreement on democratic norms exists among the political stratum than among voters in general. Fourth, even among the political stratum the amount of agreement is hardly high enough to account by itself for the stability of the system.

I propose, therefore, to examine some alternative explanations. Because my data on New Haven are not wholly adequate for the task at hand, the theory I shall sketch out might properly be regarded more as reflections on the process of creating consensus than as a testing of theory by a hard examination of the facts in New Haven. But New Haven will provide a convenient reference point.

SOME ALTERNATIVE EXPLANATIONS

There are at least five alternative ways (aside from denying the validity or generality of recent findings) to account for the stability of the political system in New Haven.

First, one may deny that New Haven is "democratic" and argue that

1. Tocqueville, *Democracy in America*, pp. 310, 334, 436.
2. Especially Samuel Stouffer, *Communism, Conformity and Civil Liberties* (New York, Doubleday, 1955) and James W. Prothro and Charles M. Grigg, "Fundamental Principles of Democracy: Bases of Agreement and Disagreement," *Journal of Politics*, 22 (1960), 276–94.

it is in fact run by a covert oligarchy of some sort. Thus the problem, it might be said, is illusory. Yet even in the absence of comparable studies our findings argue strongly that New Haven is not markedly *less* democratic than other supposedly democratic political systems. Some of these, we know, have proved to be unstable; hence the problem does not vanish after all.

Second, one might argue that things were different in the good old days. Yet it is hardly plausible to suppose that in 1910, when slightly less than half the population of New Haven consisted of first- and second-generation immigrants (many of them from countries with few democratic traditions), democratic beliefs were more widespread than they are now. In any case, the main characteristics of the political system— majority rule, the legitimacy of opposition, and so on—do not show any signs of disappearing.

Third, it might be said that the political system of New Haven is scarcely autonomous enough to furnish us with adequate explanations of its own stability, for stability may depend much less on the beliefs of citizens locally than on state and national institutions. There is much truth in this objection, but it does not altogether explain why some American towns, cities, and counties have at various times moved a good deal farther from democratic norms than New Haven has.

Fourth, one might argue that the system has not been entirely stable, that in fact most seemingly stable democratic systems are constantly in transition. Surely this is a valid point, but it is one that cuts both ways. In New Haven, as elsewhere, the rules of the game have altered in quite important, one is tempted to say fundamental, ways over the past century and a half. For example, organized, overt political competition, which was anathema to the patrician oligarchy, seems to have been fully legitimate since about 1840. Consider the electorate—the active voters. Partly as a result of the abolition of property qualifications in 1845, but probably more as a result of party organization and competition, the proportion of voting adults shot up and then stabilized at a moderate level. In most elections from 1800–33 the voters comprised less than a quarter of the adult males and sometimes less than 10 per cent; since 1834, however, they have made up from a half to three-quarters of the adult male (and since 1920, female) population. A final example: throughout the nineteenth century, an implicit norm excluded persons of foreign birth or non-Yankee origins from nomination or election to the mayoralty; since the mayoralty election of 1899, the norm has very nearly come to operate in reverse.

Because of, or in spite of, these changes, however, the essential characteristics of the political system as I described them have remained substantially intact for the past century. With appropriate techniques, probably one could detect and describe significant fluctuations in the "intensity," "degree," or "magnitude" of the various characteristics, but this line of inquiry would not help much in the present problem.

Fifth, one might argue that the stability of New Haven's political system does not depend on a widespread belief that certain democratic norms, rules, or procedures are highly desirable or intrinsically preferable to other rules; in some circumstances a democratic system could be highly stable if a substantial part of the electorate merely *accepted* them. A majority of voters who do not really believe in extending freedom of speech to individuals and groups beyond the pale of popular morality— and who would readily say so during an interview—might nonetheless acquiesce in such extensions on a variety of pragmatic grounds.

There is, I think, a good deal more truth in this view than many enthusiastic democrats care to admit. Let me suggest some circumstances in which this explanation might be valid.

Whenever the costs of disagreement are believed to be very high, there are innumerable conditions under which a collection of people might knowingly agree on a choice that no one preferred, simply because this was the only choice on which they could agree. Stable systems of international politics, such as the balance of power system in the nineteenth century, surely have been of this kind. Or suppose that 80 per cent of the voters are in favor of a more restricted suffrage than actually exists. Suppose that 40 per cent would like to restrict the suffrage to taxpayers, another 40 per cent would like to restrict it to college graduates, and only 20 per cent would like to retain the present suffrage. Suppose further that their other choices were as follows:

	40% prefer:	40% prefer:	20% prefer:
First choice:	Taxpayers	College graduates	Present requirements
Second choice:	Present requirements	Present requirements	College graduates
Third choice:	College graduates	Taxpayers	Taxpayers

One does not need to assume a great amount of rationality to conclude that they would retain the existing broad suffrage requirements, even though this would be the preferred choice of only a minority.

Moreover, this example hints at the fact that the stability of a political system, even a democratic one, is not merely a matter of the *numbers* of persons who adhere to it but also of the *amount of political resources* they use—or are expected to use—in acting on their beliefs. The amount of political resources an individual is likely to use is a function, among other things, of the amount of resources he has access to, the strength or intensity of his belief, and the relevance he sees in political action as a way of acting on his beliefs. Other things being equal, rules supported only by a wealthy, educated minority (money and knowledge

being important political resources) and opposed by the rest of the voters
are surely likely to endure longer than rules supported only by a poor,
uneducated minority and opposed by the rest of the voters. Likewise,
rules that are *strongly* believed in by a minority and weakly opposed by
the rest are more likely to endure than rules *weakly* believed in by a
majority and strongly opposed by a minority.

In addition to numbers and resources, however, skill is obviously a
critical factor. Rules supported by a politically skillful minority may
withstand the opposition of a less skilled majority, and in any case are
likely to endure longer than if they are supported only by an unskilled
minority.

Let us now imagine a society with a political system approximately like
that in New Haven. Suppose the rules, procedures, and essential characteristics of this system are strongly supported by a minority which, in
comparison with the rest of the population, possesses a high degree of
political skill. Suppose further that a majority of voters would prefer
rules different from those prevailing, though they might not all prefer
the same alternatives. Suppose finally that the majority of voters have
access to fewer resources of influence; that their preferences for other
rules are not salient or strong; that because of their relative indifference
they do not employ what potential influence they have; and that they
are not very skillful in using their political resources anyway. Such a
political system, it seems to me, might be highly stable.

On the other hand, if any of the characteristics of this hypothetical
minority were to shift to the majority, then the system would surely become less stable. Instability would increase, then, if the minority favoring the system no longer had superior resources, or if it became less
skillful, or if the question of rules became salient and urgent to a majority
of voters.

I should like to advance the hypothesis that the political system we
have just been supposing corresponds closely to the facts of New Haven,
and in all probability to the United States. If it errs, it is in supposing
that *even among the political stratum* the level of agreement on the rules
of the game is, at any given moment, high enough to explain the persistence of the rules.

CONSENSUS AS A PROCESS

Most of us, I suppose, are ready to recognize long-run changes in the
beliefs expressed by the more articulate segments of the political stratum
and the intelligentsia, and we can infer from various kinds of evidence—
all of it, alas, highly debatable—that changes of some sort take place
over long periods of time in the attitudes about democracy held in the
general population. We tend to assume, however, that except for these

long-run shifts beliefs about democracy are more or less static. I want
to propose an alternative explanation, namely that democratic beliefs,
like other political beliefs, are influenced by a recurring *process* of interchange among political professionals, the political stratum, and the great
bulk of the population. The process generates enough agreement on
rules and norms so as to permit the system to operate, but agreement
tends to be incomplete, and typically it decays. So the process is frequently repeated. "Consensus," then, is not at all a static and unchanging
attribute of citizens. It is a variable element in a complex and more or
less continuous process.

This process seems to me to have the following characteristics:

1. Over long periods of time the great bulk of the citizens possess a
fairly stable set of democratic beliefs at a high level of abstraction. Let
me call these beliefs the democratic creed. In Ann Arbor and Tallahassee,
Prothro and Grigg found that very nearly everyone they interviewed
agreed with five abstract democratic propositions.[3] We can, I think,
confidently conclude that most Americans believe in democracy as the
best form of government, in the desirability of rights and procedures in-
suring a goodly measure of majority rule and minority freedom, and
in a wide but not necessarily comprehensive electorate. At a somewhat
lower level of agreement, probably the great majority of citizens also
believe in the essential legitimacy of certain specific American political
institutions: the presidency, Congress, the Supreme Court, the states, the
local governments, etc.

2. Most citizens assume that the American political system is consistent
with the democratic creed. Indeed, the common view seems to be that
our system is not only democratic but is perhaps the most perfect expression of democracy that exists anywhere; if deficiencies exist, either they
can, and ultimately will, be remedied, or else they reflect the usual gap
between ideal and reality that men of common sense take for granted.
Moreover, because leading officials with key roles in the legitimate
political institutions automatically acquire authority for their views on
the proper functioning of the political institutions, as long as these various
officials seem to agree, the ordinary citizen is inclined to assume that
existing ways of carrying on the public business do not violate, at least
in an important way, the democratic creed to which he is committed.

3. Widespread adherence to the democratic creed is produced and

3. "Democracy is the best form of government." "Public officials should be chosen
by majority vote." "Every citizen should have an equal chance to influence government policy." "The minority should be free to criticize majority decisions." "People
in the minority should be free to try to win majority support for their opinions."
Prothro and Grigg, "Fundamental Principles of Democracy," 282, 284.

maintained by a variety of powerful social processes. Of these, probably formal schooling is the most important. The more formal education an American has, the more democratic formulas he knows, expresses, and presumably believes. But almost the entire adult population has been subjected to *some* degree of indoctrination through the schools. Beliefs acquired in school are reinforced in adult life through normal exposure to the democratic creed, particularly as the creed is articulated by leading political figures and transmitted through the mass media.

These social processes have an enormous impact on the citizen, partly because they begin early in life and partly because the very unanimity with which the creed is espoused makes rejection of it almost impossible. To reject the creed is infinitely more than a simple matter of disagreement. To reject the creed is to reject one's society and one's chances of full acceptance in it—in short, to be an outcast. (As a mental experiment, try to imagine the psychic and social burdens an American child in an American school would incur if he steadfastly denied to himself and others that democracy is the best form of government.)

To reject the democratic creed is in effect to refuse to be an American. As a nation we have taken great pains to insure that few citizens will ever want to do anything so rash, so preposterous—in fact, so wholly un-American. In New Haven, as in many other parts of the United States, vast social energies have been poured into the process of "Americanization," teaching citizens what is expected in the way of words, beliefs, and behavior if they are to earn acceptance as Americans, for it was obvious to the political stratum that unless the immigrants and their children quickly accepted American political norms, the flood of aliens, particularly from countries with few traditions of self-government, would disrupt the political system. In a characteristic response, the Board of Education of the city of New Haven created a supervisor for Americanization (a post, incidentally, that still exists). Something of the feeling of urgency and accomplishment that must have prevailed in many segments of the political stratum shines through these enthusiastic words in the annual report of the New Haven superintendent of schools in 1919:

> The public school is the greatest and most effective of all Americanization agencies. This is the one place where all children in a community or district, regardless of nationality, religion, politics, or social status, meet and work together in a cooperative and harmonious spirit. . . . The children work and play together, they catch the school spirit, they live the democratic life, American heroes become their own, American history wins their loyalty, the Stars and Stripes, always before their eyes in the school room, receives their daily salute. Not only are these immigrant children Americanized through

the public school, but they, in turn, Americanize their parents carrying into the home many lessons of democracy learned at school.[4]

For their part, the immigrants and their children were highly motivated to learn how to be Americans, for they were desperately, sometimes pathetically, eager to win acceptance as true Americans.

In one form or another the process of Americanization has absorbed enormous social energies all over the United States. As a factor in shaping American behavior and attitudes, the process of Americanization must surely have been as important as the frontier, or industrialization, or urbanization. That regional, ethnic, racial, religious, or economic differences might disrupt the American political system has been a recurring fear among the political stratum of the United States from the very beginning of the republic. Doubtless this anxiety was painfully stimulated by the Civil War. It was aroused again by the influx of immigrants. Throughout the country then the political stratum has seen to it that new citizens, young and old, have been properly trained in "American" principles and beliefs. Everywhere, too, the pupils have been highly motivated to talk, look and believe as Americans should. The result was as astonishing an act of voluntary political and cultural assimilation and speedy elimination of regional, ethnic, and cultural dissimilarities as history can provide. The extent to which Americans agree today on the key propositions about democracy is a measure of the almost unbelievable success of this deliberate attempt to create a seemingly uncoerced nation-wide consensus.

4. Despite wide agreement on a general democratic creed, however, citizens frequently disagree on specific applications. Many citizens oppose what some political philosophers would regard as necessary implications of the creed. Many citizens also disagree with the way the creed is actually applied—or perhaps it would be more accurate to say, with the existing rules of the game, the prevailing political norms. Again and again, for example, surveys indicate that a large number of Americans, sometimes even a majority, do not approve of the extension of important rights, liberties, and privileges to individuals and groups that do in fact enjoy them.

A citizen is able to adhere to these seemingly inconsistent beliefs for a great variety of reasons. For one thing, he himself need not see any inconsistency in his beliefs. The creed is so vague (and incomplete) that strict deductions are difficult or impossible even for sophisticated logicians. Moreover, propositions stated in universal terms are rarely assumed by men of common sense to imply universality in practice; to

4. "Report of the Superintendent of Schools," *Annual Report of the Board of Education of the New Haven City School District,* 1919.

the frequent dismay of logicians, a common tendency of mankind—and not least of Americans—is to qualify universals in application while leaving them intact in rhetoric. Then, too, the capacity for (or interest in) working out a set of consistent political attitudes is rather limited. As the authors of *The American Voter* have recently shown, most voters seem to operate at a low level of ideological sophistication; even among intelligent (though not necessarily highly educated) citizens, conceptions of politics are often of a simplicity that the political philosopher might find it hard to comprehend.[5] In addition, most citizens operate with a very small fund of political information; often they lack the elementary information required even to be aware of inconsistencies between their views and what is actually happening in the political system, particularly if the subject is (as most questions of rights and procedures are) arcane and complex. Again, questions that bother theorists are often not interesting or salient to most voters; their attention and energies are diverted elsewhere, usually to activities that lie entirely outside the political arena. As long as a citizen believes that democracy is the best political system, that the United States is a democracy, and that the people in office can be trusted, by and large, to apply the abstract creed to specific cases, issues of democratic theory and practice hotly discussed by political philosophers, or even by publicists and columnists, are likely never to penetrate through the manifold barriers to abstract political thinking that are erected by the essentially apolitical culture in which he lives. Finally, even if the issues do manage to get through, many citizens feel themselves incompetent to decide them; this, after all, is what Supreme Court judges, presidents, and members of Congress are supposed to do. Worse yet, many citizens feel that no one in public office will care much about their opinions anyway.

5. Members of the political stratum (who live in a much more politicized culture) are more familiar with the "democratic" norms, more consistent, more ideological, more detailed and explicit in their political attitudes, and more completely in agreement on the norms. They are more in agreement not only on what norms are implied by the abstract democratic creed but also in supporting the norms currently operating. This relatively higher degree of support for the prevailing norms in the existing political system is generated and maintained by a variety of processes. Because members of the political stratum have on the average considerably more formal education than the population as a whole, they have been more thoroughly exposed to the creed and its implications. Because they are more involved in, concerned with, and articulate about politics, they invest more time and effort in elaborating a consistent

5. A. Campbell, P. E. Converse, W. E. Miller, D. D. Stokes, *The American Voter* (New York, Wiley, 1960), Chs. 9 and 10.

ideology. Because they participate more extensively in politics, they more frequently express and defend their views, encounter criticism, and face the charge of inconsistency. They know more about politics, read more, experience more, see more.

Within the political stratum, the professionals tend to agree even more on what the norms should be, what they are, and the desirability of maintaining them substantially as they are. Agreement among the professionals is generated by all the factors that account for it among the rest of the political stratum and even among the apolitical strata. Mastery over the existing norms of the political system represents the particular stockpile of skills peculiar to the professional's vocation. Norms also tend to legitimate his power and position in the political system, furnish an agreed-on method of getting on with the immediate tasks at hand, carry the authority of tradition, and help to reduce the baffling uncertainty that surrounds the professional's every choice. Finally, the professional is likely to support the existing norms because his own endorsement of existing norms was initially a criterion in his own recruitment and advancement; complex processes of political selection and rejection tend to exclude the deviant who challenges the prevailing norms of the existing political system. Most of the professionals might properly be called democratic "legitimists."

6. The professionals, of course, have access to extensive political resources which they employ at a high rate with superior efficiency. Consequently, a challenge to the existing norms is bound to be costly to the challenger, for legitimist professionals can quickly shift their skills and resources into the urgent task of doing in the dissenter. As long as the professionals remain substantially legitimist in outlook, therefore, the critic is likely to make little headway. Indeed, the chances are that anyone who advocates extensive changes in the prevailing democratic norms is likely to be treated by the professionals, and even by a fair share of the political stratum, as an outsider, possibly even as a crackpot whose views need not be seriously debated. No worse fate can befall the dissenter, for unless he can gain the attention of the political stratum, it is difficult for him to gain space in the mass media; if he cannot win space in the mass media, it is difficult for him to win a large following; if he cannot win a large following, it is difficult for him to gain the attention of the political stratum.

7. Sometimes, of course, disagreements over the prevailing norms occur within the political stratum and among the professionals themselves. But these disagreements need not, and perhaps ordinarily do not, produce much effort to involve the general public in the dispute. The disagreements are not, to be sure, secret; the electorate is not *legally* barred from finding out about the conflict and becoming involved. It does

not need to be. Given the low salience of politics in the life of the average citizen, most conflicts over the prevailing norms might attract more attention if they were held behind locked doors. Unless a professional is willing to invest very great resources in whipping up public interest, he is not likely to get much effective support. In any case, public involvement may seem undesirable to the legitimist, for alterations in the prevailing norms are often subtle matters, better obtained by negotiation than by the crudities and oversimplifications of public debate.

8. Among the rules and procedures supported strongly by the legitimists in the political stratum, and particularly by the professionals, are some that prescribe ways of settling disagreements as to rules and procedures. These involve appeals to authorities who give decisions widely accepted as binding, authoritative, and legitimate—though not necessarily as "good" or "correct." Typically these include appeals to courts or quasi-judicial institutions that ostensibly arrive at their decisions by appeals to norms, codes, formulas, and beliefs that appear to transcend partisan and policy differences in the political stratum.

9. Ordinarily, then, it is not difficult for a stable system of rights and privileges to exist that, at least in important details, does not have widespread public support and occasionally even lacks majority approval. As long as the matter is not a salient public issue—and whether it is or not depends partly on how the political stratum handles it—the question is substantially determined within the political stratum itself. When disagreements arise, these are adjudicated by officials who share the beliefs of the political stratum rather than those of the populace; and even when these officials adopt positions that do not command the undivided support of the political stratum, members of the political stratum, and particularly the professionals, tend to accept a decision as binding until and unless it can be changed through the accepted procedures. This is the essence of their code of democratic legitimism.

10. Occasionally, however, a sizable segment of the political stratum develops doubts that it can ever achieve the changes it seeks through accepted procedures that are, in a sense, internal to the political stratum and the professionals. One or more of these dissenters may push his way into the professional group, or the dissenters may be numerous and vocal enough to acquire a spokesman or two among the professionals. The strategy of the dissenters may now begin to shift. Instead of adjudicating the matter according to the accepted procedures, the dissenters attempt to arouse public support for their proposals, hoping that when a sufficient number of voters are won over to their cause, other professionals—legitimist or not—will have to come around.

The professionals, as I have said, live in a world of uncertainty. They search for omens and portents. If the auguries indicate that the appeal to the populace has failed, then the legitimists may confidently close ranks against the dissenter. But if the auguries are uncertain or unfavorable, then the legitimists, too, are forced to make a counter-appeal to the populace. Since public opinion is often as difficult to interpret as the flights of birds or the entrails of a sheep, political professionals may and frequently do misread the auspices. In October 1954, the Survey Research Center discovered that only 12 per cent of their sample said they would be more likely to vote for a candidate who had the support of Senator McCarthy; 37 per cent said they would be less likely, and 43 per cent said it would make no difference.[6] In retrospect, these proportions do not look wildly off, but in 1954 belief in McCarthy's mass following was widespread throughout the whole political stratum and not least among the professionals. The legitimists could probably have ignored the late Senator with impunity—as they later did—but he followed a classic strategy—(required, I am suggesting, by the tendency of the legitimists to monopolize the internal devices for adjudicating disputes over norms) —by taking the issue out of the hands of the professionals, where the rules of the game were bound to run against him, and appealing instead to the populace.

If the dissenters succeed in forcing the issue out beyond the political stratum, and dissenters and legitimists begin making appeals to the populace, then the nature of the debate begins to change. Technical questions, subtle distinctions, fine matters of degree are shed. The appeal is now shaped to the simple democratic creed which nearly every citizen believes in. Because the creed does not constitute a tightly logical system, it is possible for the legitimists to demonstrate that existing norms are necessary consequences of the creed, and for the dissenters to show that existing norms run counter to the creed. Because the creed is deeply laden with tradition and sentiment, emotion rises and reasoned discussion declines.

11. Ordinary citizens who normally remain outside these debates now find their attention—and their votes—solicited by both sides. They become aware that the very officials who ordinarily decide these matters, to whom the citizen himself turns for his cues as to what is legitimate and consistent with the creed, are locked in deadly, heated battle. These citizens must now find ways of applying the creed to the issue. One way is to withdraw even more deeply into the political shadows; a citizen can simply refuse to choose. Many do. In March 1937, at the height of the debate over President Roosevelt's proposal to enlarge the Supreme Court, 50 per cent of the people interviewed in a Gallup poll had listened

6. Angus Campbell and Homer C. Cooper, *Group Differences in Attitudes and Votes, A Study of the 1954 Congressional Election* (Ann Arbor, Mich., University of Michigan Survey Research Center, 1954), p. 145.

to neither of the President's two recent radio speeches defending his plan. A month later, one out of seven persons who were asked whether Congress should pass the President's bill expressed no opinion.[7] In New Haven, after several years of public discussion and debate over charter reform, when a sample of registered voters was asked in 1959 whether they personally would do anything if a revision of the charter was proposed that would make the mayor stronger, over 40 per cent of those who disapproved of such an idea said they would do nothing to oppose it, and nearly three-quarters of those who approved said they would do nothing to support it. (These seemed to be tolerably honest responses; in the preceding election, after wide discussion among the political stratum and hot debate among the professionals over a new charter, less than half the voters who went to the polls even bothered to vote on the charter.) Thus when dissenters and legitimists appeal to the populace to settle questions they ordinarily decide among themselves, they cannot be at all sure that they will actually produce much of a response no matter how much they try to stir up the public.

However, citizens who *do* make up their minds must find some ways for arriving at a choice. For many citizens the decision is eased by their existing loyalties to parties or political leaders. In April 1937, 68 per cent of the Democrats in a Gallup poll said that Congress should pass Roosevelt's court plan; 93 per cent of the Republicans said Congress should not. Those who had no strong party identifications were, as one might expect, split—42 per cent in favor and 58 per cent against.[8] In 1954, attitudes toward McCarthy were closely related to party identifications. Among strong Democrats, those who said that McCarthy's support would make them *less* likely to vote for a candidate were six times as great as those who said his support would make them *more* likely; strong Republicans, by contrast, split about evenly. Among Catholics who were strong Democrats, the ratio was two to one against McCarthy; among Catholics who were strong Republicans it was nearly two to one in his favor.[9]

If the parties give no clear guidance, citizens may look to particular leaders or institutions. They may turn to spokesmen in their churches, for example, or trade unions, or regions. They often turn, of course, to attitudes prevalent in their own circle of intimates, friends, associates, acquaintances. If their search yields no consistent cues, they may give

7. Hadley Cantril, ed., *Public Opinion, 1935–1946* (Princeton, Princeton University Press, 1951), p. 150.

8. Ibid.

9. Campbell and Cooper, *Group Differences in Attitudes,* Tables VI–VIII (p. 92) and B-81 (p. 149). See also Nelson W. Polsby, "Towards an Explanation of McCarthyism," *Political Studies, 8,* No. 3 (1960), 250–71.

up. In the struggle over charter reform in New Haven in 1958, when Democratic leaders were split from the top down, judging from a sample of registered voters interviewed shortly after the election the proportion of people who went to the polls and voted on the general election but did not vote either for or against the charter was higher among Democrats than among either Republicans or independents.

12. An appeal to the populace may terminate in several ways. The appeal may simply fail to create a stir. Interest in political matters wanes rather quickly; since complex issues of democratic norms nearly always lack a direct relation to the on-going life of an individual, they have even less capacity for holding attention than many other issues. However passionately the dissenters feel about their case, life does move on, old questions become tiresome, and the newspapers begin to shove the conflict to the inside pages. Perhaps the legitimists, buoyed by their reading of the electorate, defeat the dissenters in a clear-cut trial of strength and, having done so, close ranks and go on to the next business. Perhaps the dissenters win, or a compromise is worked out; if so the dissenters, like as not, turn into the next generation of legitimists.

THE ROLE OF DEMOCRATIC BELIEFS

The specific beliefs of the average citizen thus have a rather limited though important function. Ordinarily, conflicts over democratic norms are resolved among the professionals, with perhaps some involvement by parts of the political stratum but little or no involvement by most citizens. Thus the fact that a large number of citizens do not believe in the political norms actually applied, particularly extending political liberties to unpopular individuals and groups, has slight effect on the outcome.

The beliefs of the ordinary citizen become relevant only when professionals engage in an intensive appeal to the populace. Even then, the actual outcome of the appeal does not necessarily reflect majority attitudes at all accurately. These are not always known; they are guessed at in a variety of inaccurate ways, and they have to be filtered through the tighter mesh of the political stratum and the professionals before they can become public policy.

Nonetheless, wide consensus on the democratic creed does have two important kinds of consequences. On the one hand, this very consensus makes occasional appeal all but inevitable, for the creed itself gives legitimacy to an appeal to the populace. On the other hand, widespread adherence to the creed limits the character and the course of an appeal. It insures that no appeal is likely to succeed unless it is framed in terms consistent with the creed—which is perhaps not so small a constraint. Some solutions pretty evidently are *not* consistent. Because an appeal must take place in the face of criticism from legitimists and extensive appraisal by members of the political stratum, blatant inconsistencies are likely to be exposed. Moreover, because the appeal is legitimized by the creed, it provides an orderly way to conduct a dispute that exceeds the capacities of the professionals to resolve among themselves.

No one, I imagine, has ever supposed that the existence of the creed entails no risks. People can be deceived by appeals intended to destroy democracy in the name of democracy. Dissenters who believe in the democratic creed may unwittingly advocate or legitimists may insist on preserving rules of the game destined to have unforeseen and unintended consequences disastrous to the stability and perhaps the survival of the democracy.

Nonetheless, we can be reasonably sure of this: even if universal belief in a democratic creed does not guarantee the stability of a democratic system, a substantial decline in the popular consensus would greatly increase the chance of serious instability. How the professionals act, what they advocate, what they are likely to believe, are all constrained by the wide adherence to the creed that exists throughout the community. If a substantial segment of the electorate begins to doubt the creed, professionals will quickly come forth to fan that doubt. The nature and course of an appeal to the populace will change. What today is a question of applying the fundamental norms of democracy will become tomorrow an inquiry into the validity of these norms. If a substantial number of citizens begin to deny not merely to *some* minorities but to minorities *as such* the rights and powers prescribed in the creed, an appeal to the populace is likely to end sooner or later in a call to arms.

Thus consensus on political beliefs and practices has much in common with other aspects of a democratic system. Here, too, leaders lead—and often are led. Citizens are very far indeed from exerting equal influence over the content, application, and development of the political consensus. Yet widely held beliefs by Americans in a creed of democracy and political equality serve as a critical limit on the ways in which leaders can shape the consensus.

Neither the prevailing consensus, the creed, nor even the political system itself are immutable products of democratic ideas, beliefs, and institutions inherited from the past. For better or worse, they are always open, in some measure, to alteration through those complex processes of symbiosis and change that constitute the relations of leaders and citizens in a pluralistic democracy.

Appendixes

A. COMPARISON OF NEW HAVEN
WITH OTHER URBAN AREAS, 1950[1]

	Urban areas[2]	New Haven
Total population	69,249,148	164,443
Population increase, 1940–50	19.5%	2.4%
14-17-year-olds in school	86.9%	86.7%
18-19-year-olds in school	36.6%	52.5%
20-24-year-olds in school	15.9%	32.2%
Median years of schooling for adults 25 years old or over	10.2	9.1
Number of males per 100 females	94.6	98.9
Population over 65 years old	8.2%	9.3%
Married males over 14 years old	68.6%	60.0%
Married females over 14 years old	63.8%	60.1%
Median family income	$3,249	$3,301
Families with income of $5,000 or more	24.7%	19.9%
Foreign-born white population	8.8%	7.7%
Nonwhite population	10.0%	6.0%
Owner-occupied dwellings	50.6%	31.7%
Owner-occupied dwellings, 1940	37.5%	26.2%
Median value of owner-occupied dwelling units	$8,380	$12,187
Median monthly contract rent	$37.54	$29.32
Dwellings with more than one person per room	13.3%	11.0%
Dwellings not dilapidated, with private toilet, bath, and hot water	77.8%	81.1%
Most numerous occupational group for males and percentage of males in this occupation	Operatives, 21.7%	Operatives, 23.8%
Most numerous occupational group for females and percentage of females in this occupation	Clerical, 29.9%	Clerical, 26.8%

1. Population data from U.S. Bureau of the Census, *U.S. Census of Population: 1950*, Vol. II, *Characteristics of the Population* (Washington, D.C., U.S. Govt. Printing Office, 1952), Part I, U.S. Summary, Chs. B and C, and Part 7, Connecticut, Chs. B and C. Housing data from U.S. Bureau of the Census, *U.S. Census of Housing: 1950*, Vol. I, *General Characteristics*, Ch. 1, U.S. Summary (Washington, D.C., U.S. Govt. Printing Office, 1953), and Ch. 7, Connecticut (Washington, D.C., U.S. Govt. Printing Office, 1952).

2. According to U.S. Census criteria, there were 157 urban areas in the U.S. in 1950. The total population of these areas was 46% of the total population of the U.S.

B. METHODS AND DATA

I. The Definition and Measurement of Influence

During three and a half centuries from Thomas Hobbes to Max Weber little was done to make widely used notions of power or influence more precise. In the last quarter century, and particularly in the last decade, the problem of providing operational meaning and measurements for the concepts of power and influence has received a good deal of attention. Nonetheless, no entirely satisfactory solutions to the numerous problems involved have yet been set forth, and this book necessarily reflects the fact that concepts and methods in the analysis of influence are undergoing rapid changes.

One who wishes to consider more rigorous formulations of the concept of influence used in this volume and problems of measuring differences in the influence of different individuals or actors should consult my article, "The Concept of Power," *Behavioral Science*, 2 (1957), pp. 201–15 and the works cited there at pp. 214–15. I later expanded some of the ideas set out in that article and applied them to local politics in an article, "The Analysis of Influence in Local Communities," in a monograph edited by Charles R. Adrian, *Social Science and Community Action* (East Lansing, Mich., Michigan State University, 1960), pp. 25–42. I cite my own papers on this topic simply because they happen to be the most relevant to this volume. However, the modest progress recently made on the analysis of influence is a product of an interchange among many scholars; the number of articles and books that any serious student of influence must now consult is too large to cite in this Appendix. Moreover the number rapidly increases. Indeed, what promises to be a highly important addition to the analysis of influence came to my attention too late to be incorporated into this study; this is a forthcoming work by Professor John C. Harsanyi of the Australian National University entitled "Two Papers on Social Power" of which the first, "Measurement of Social Power, Opportunity Costs, and The Theory of Two-Person Bargaining Games" (mimeo., Jan. 1961), explicitly brings out what is sometimes only implicit in the present volume, the importance of opportunity costs as dimensions of power and influence.

II. Operational Measures of Influence

One of the most serious problems in the study of influence arises from the fact that, no matter how precisely one defines influence and no matter how elegant the measures and methods one proposes, the data within reach even of the most assiduous researcher require the use of operational measures that are at best somewhat unsatisfactory.

One way to compensate for the unsatisfactory character of all existing operational measures of influence is to be eclectic. In this study, an eclectic approach was adopted deliberately, not only to avoid putting all our eggs in one methodological basket but also in order to take advantage of the existence of a very wide assortment of data. Six methods of assessing relative influence or changes in influence were used in this study. These were:

1. To study changes in the socioeconomic characteristics of incumbents in city offices in order to determine whether any rather large historical changes may have occurred in the sources of leadership. Except for Chapter 6, Book I relies mainly on this method.

2. To isolate a particular socioeconomic category and then determine the nature and extent of participation in local affairs by persons in this category. This method was applied to the Social and Economic Notables in Chapter 6.

3. To examine a set of "decisions" in different "issue-areas" in order to determine what kinds of persons were the most influential according to one operational measure of relative influence, and to determine patterns of influence. Books II and III (except for Chapter 13) rely mainly on this method.

4. To survey random samples of participants in different issue-areas in order to determine their characteristics. This method was used in Chapter 13 to locate the socioeconomic sources of the subleaders in different issue-areas.

5. To survey random samples of registered voters in order to determine the characteristics of those who participate in varying degrees and in varying ways in local affairs. This method was used in Books IV and V.

6. To study changes in patterns of voting among different strata in the community.

It may be helpful to clarify some methodological questions with respect to each of these methods.

III. HISTORICAL CHANGES IN INCUMBENTS IN CITY OFFICES

Fortunately, the amount of data available on the social origins and characteristics of incumbents in certain city offices in New Haven over the last century and three-quarters is very great. Anyone interested in the history of New Haven necessarily incurs a large debt to Professor Rollin Osterweis; in addition to his own distinguished history of New Haven—*Three Centuries of New Haven, 1638–1938* (New Haven, Yale University Press, 1953)—which was a constant reference for descriptions of social, political, and economic developments, Professor Osterweis generously provided a wealth of information in a series of lengthy discussions about the social history of New Haven.

The occupational data used in tables and charts in Book I came from a variety of sources, chiefly annual City Directories and material in the Arnold Dana Collection of the New Haven Colony Historical Society. Except for the last few decades, biographical information on business and political leaders was obtained chiefly from the following sources:

> *Encyclopedia of Connecticut Biography*, 5 vols. (New York, American Historical Society, 1917)
> *Dictionary of American Biography*, 22 vols. (New York, Scribner's, 1946)
> Edward E. Atwater, *History of the City of New Haven* (New York, W. W. Munsell, 1887)
> N. G. Osborn, ed., *Men of Mark in Connecticut*, 5 vols. (Hartford, William R. Goodspeed, 1906–10)

M. H. Mitchell, ed., *History of New Haven County*, 3 vols. (Chicago and
  Boston, Pioneer Historical Publishing Co., 1930)
Carleton Beals, *Our Yankee Heritage, The Making of Greater New
  Haven*, 2nd ed. (New Haven, Bradley and Scoville, 1957)

In addition to the Osterweis volume mentioned above, descriptions of
social, political, and economic developments are to be found in:

Charles H. Levermore, *The Republic of New Haven, A History of
  Municipal Evolution* (Baltimore, Johns Hopkins University, 1886)
Richard J. Purcell, *Connecticut in Transition, 1775–1818* (Washington,
  American Historical Association, 1918)
Jarvis M. Morse, *A Neglected Period of Connecticut's History, 1818–1850*
  (New Haven, Yale University Press, 1933)

Sources of voting data are described below in section VIII.

IV. The Social and Economic Notables

The criteria of selection are fully indicated in Chapter 6 and therefore need
not be repeated here. A list of the 50 property owners with the largest assessed valuations was obtained from official records for the years 1948–57.
Lists of Social Notables were obtained from the society page of the New
Haven *Register*, which printed in full the guests invited to attend the Assemblies. Lists of Economic Notables, other than large property owners, were
obtained from City Directories, company reports, *Poor's Register of Directors
and Executives, United States and Canada* (New York, Standard and Poor's
Corp., 1961) and *The Directors Register of Connecticut, 1958* (Hartford,
Directory Publishing Co., 1958)

V. Decisions in Different Issue-Areas

This method is intended to penetrate the veil of official position and overt
participation in order to determine, as far as possible, who *really* influences
decisions.

A. The Distribution of Influence

The method of analyzing decisions in different issue-areas in order to determine the distribution of influence among various overt and covert participants rests upon the assumption that the following operations furnish a
method, crude but useful, for estimating the relative influence of different
actors:

a. Restrict attention to "comparable" respondents who directly participate in a "single" scope.
b. Examine decisions where the number of direct participants is more
   or less the same during the period under investigation.
c. Assume that the following collective actions are responses of roughly
   the same strength or extent:
   When a proposal initiated by one or more of the participants is adopted
   despite the opposition of other participants.

When a proposal initiated by one or more of the participants is rejected.

When a proposal initiated by one or more of the participants is adopted without opposition.

d. Determine the number of successful initiations or vetoes by each participant and the number of failures.

e. Consider one participant as more influential than another if the relative frequency of his successes out of all successes is higher, or the ratio of his successes to his total attempts is higher.

Three issue-areas were chosen because they promised to cut across a wide variety of interests and participants. These were redevelopment, public education, and nominations in the two major parties. Events leading up to a proposal for a new city charter and its rejection by voters in November 1958 were also examined in detail. In each of these issue-areas, all the decisions that the participants regarded as the most important since about 1950 were selected for detailed study. These decisions were:

Decisions on redevelopment, 1950–59:

1. Creating the Redevelopment Agency.
2. Building and extending the Oak Street Connector.
3. Redeveloping the Oak Street area.
4. Creating the Citizens Action Commission.
5. Redeveloping the Church Street area.
6. Redeveloping the Wooster Square area.
7. The Long Wharf project.
8. Negotiations between Savitt, a jeweler, and the city over the proper price for his property.

Decisions on public schools, 1950–59:

1. Selling the high schools to Yale and building two new ones.
2. Accepting or rejecting a proposal to change procedures on promotions.
3. Major appointments, particularly an assistant superintendent for secondary education.
4. An eye-testing program.
5. A proposed ratio plan on salaries.
6. Budgets.
7. A proposal to deal with delinquency.
8. Proposals to increase appropriations for school libraries.

Decisions on nominations, 1941–57:

In order to cover a larger number of elections than would have been possible if the decisions on nominations had been confined to the period 1950–59, it was decided to extend the examination of nominations back to 1941. During this period there were 9 elections and 18 nominations by the two major parties for candidates for mayor. The events preceding each of these were reconstructed, though the more remote the time, in general the scantier the information. Information for the more recent period was also collected on nominations for the Board of Aldermen and the Board of Finance, but this information was general rather than specific to particular nominations.

Decisions relating to the proposal for a new charter and its defeat, 1958:

1. The initial proposal.
2. The selection of a charter commission.
3. The work of the charter commission.
4. The reception of the proposal by the Board of Aldermen.
5. Activities of special groups: the parties, the League of Women Voters, the New Haven Taxpayer's Research Council.
6. The response of the voters at the referendum in November.

These decisions were reconstructed by means of interviews with participants, the presence of an observer, records, documents, and newspapers.

Interviews lasting up to six hours were conducted in 1957 and 1958 with 46 persons who had participated actively in one or more of the key decisions. The persons interviewed had the following occupations and responsibilities:

Major occupations

	Total	President, chief executive, partner, or head of organization
Business		
Banks and investment houses	4	4
Public utilities	4	2
Manufacturing firms	3	2
Retail firms	2	2
Other	1	—
Total	14	10
Education		
Administration	5	5
Teaching	2	—
Other	1	—
Total	8	5
Public Office		
Executive	7	7
Judicial	1	—
Total	8	7
Insurance	1	1
Law	4	3
Labor Organizations	2	2
Other	9	—
Total	46	28

Major area of policy responsibility

Total

Redevelopment
  CAC members   12
  Redevelopment Agency   4
  General   4
    Total   20

Education
  School Board members and
    top school executives   7
  CACE and general   7
    Total   14

Politics (Parties)
  Top party leaders   8
  Other   4
    Total   12

          Grand Total   46

Some of these people were reinterviewed several times. Many of the interviews were recorded; the others were reconstructed from extensive notes. With one exception, all of the interviews were conducted by the author, usually with the assistance of Nelson Polsby.

Everyone interviewed was promised anonymity and full preservation of the secrecy of the actual interview document. (The interviews are still stored in a locked file.) Respondents were assured that any information directly attributed or traceable to them would not be published without their explicit consent. Participants who cooperated extensively and were the source of much detailed information were also promised the opportunity to see any section of the manuscript involving them. In actual fact, a large number of the persons interviewed were given an opportunity to review parts or all of the manuscript before publication. Various draft chapters in mimeographed form were sent to 24 persons with a covering letter asking for corrections, criticisms, and comments. This resulted in a number of corrections of fact, some differences in interpretation, and a very small number of deletions; the deletions, though interesting as "inside dope," were in no case vital evidence.

The impression of the interviewers, fortified by cross-checking among the interviews and other sources of information, was that most of the persons interviewed were remarkably candid, though they were not always accurate in their memories of events. Only two people with whom interviews were sought refused to be interviewed. Both were strategically placed in the local scene, and both gave reasons of health as an excuse. It is doubtful, however, whether they would have added anything significant to the sum total of information contained in the other interviews.

A remarkable opportunity to check the validity of many of the interviews and to gain a rich supply of additional background information was provided by an internship held by Raymond Wolfinger in the office of the Development Administrator and in the office of the Mayor. Among other events, Wolfinger was in a position to observe from the beginning the course of the struggle over the charter proposal. A detailed reconstruction of several key decisions that Wolfinger was uniquely situated to study will be found in his forthcoming volume, *The Politics of Progress.*

The detailed record of decisions, reconstructed from interviews—frequently with the aid of Wolfinger's observations—provided the most complete and objective history attainable as to what really happened in the course of each decision: what the participants saw as the alternatives, who proposed the alternatives, how the participants responded, which alternatives were approved, modified, or rejected. Thus from the record it was usually possible to determine for each decision which participants had initiated alternatives that were finally adopted, had vetoed alternatives initiated by others, or had proposed alternatives that were turned down. These actions were then tabulated as individual "successes" or "defeats." The participants with the greatest proportion of successes out of the total number of successes were then considered to be the most influential. This is the method used in Tables 10.1, 10.2, 10.3, 14.1, 14.2, and 14.3. The rankings resulting from this somewhat crude measure confirmed our qualitative judgments based on interviews, records, and observations. Thus it was not necessary to face the troublesome question of the relative weight one should assign to the results of this method as compared to qualitative judgments.

B. The Patterns of Influence

The influence rankings arrived at by the study of decisions in the three different issue-areas also provided a method for determining patterns of influence in Book III. It was a simple matter to see from the rankings of influentials in each issue-area where individuals in one issue-area ranked in the others (see Chapter 14).

However, patterns of influence are much too complex to be described by simple numerical measures; the loss of information would be enormous. Consequently, our analysis of patterns in Book III was supplemented with a great amount of qualitative information. In addition to the record of the decisions listed above, other important sources of qualitative information were:

1. Studies of the proposal for a new city charter

Wolfinger's contribution has already been mentioned. A survey of registered voters was conducted just after the referendum; this is discussed below (Survey No. 1). In addition, students in a graduate seminar interviewed participants, studied documents and other data, and wrote research papers on various phases of the charter story. These included:

> "The operation of the Charter Revision Commission," by Richard Merritt
> "A statistical analysis of demographic and historical factors in the patterns of ward voting on the charter," by Leroy N. Rieselbach

"The activities of the most interested and active unofficial organizations, including the League of Women Voters and the New Haven Taxpayer's Research Council," by William Foltz

"The role of the Board of Aldermen," by Bruce Russett

2. A case study, the metal houses

The evidence on patterns of influence during William Celentano's mayoralty, which ended four years before active research on this study began, was naturally more fugitive. Fortunately, as a Yale senior in 1954, William K. Muir, Jr., had written a senior essay of over 100 pages, under the supervision of Professor Herbert Kaufman, entitled "Avalanche: A Study of a Pressure Group in New Haven." The essay was a detailed and careful reconstruction of the events surrounding the proposal to erect the metal houses described in Chapter 16. Muir's study was later published in shorter form under the title *Defending "The Hill" Against Metal Houses*, ICP Case Series, No. 26 (University, Ala., University of Alabama Press, 1955). The description in Chapter 16 is drawn from both the published and unpublished versions, supplemented by some additional material.

VI. SURVEYS OF SUBLEADERS IN THREE ISSUE-AREAS

In 1958, a questionnaire of about 70 items was mailed to all persons who were members of the Citizens Action Commission, members of the various CAC committees, or officials in the Redevelopment Agency—a total of 435 persons; to all persons who held any offices in either of the two parties, were delegates to party conventions, or held local elective office—a total of 497 persons; and to all persons on the Board of Education, all officials in the public school system with the rank of principal or higher, and all PTA officials—a total of 131 persons. The returns from the mailed questionnaire were so limited, however, that random samples from each of these three groups were drawn, interviewers were hired, and the persons in the sample were interviewed. This resulted in 286 completed interviews, distributed as follows:

	Political parties	Redevelopment	Education	Total
Number in all	497	435	131	1063
Number in original sample	150	130	50	330
Number of interviews completed	130	112	44	286

Data from this survey were used to determine the characteristics of subleaders described in Chapter 13.

VII. SURVEYS OF REGISTERED VOTERS

A. Survey No. 1

In November and December 1958, after the charter was defeated in a referendum vote, a survey of 197 persons in a random sample of registered voters was carried out under the direct supervision of William Flanigan, then a graduate student in the Department of Political Science at Yale, now Assistant Professor of Political Science at the University of Minnesota. The official registration lists for the November 1958 election were used as the population. A sample of 220 names was selected as follows: from the list for each ward, names were drawn at regular intervals after a random start. The number of respondents drawn from each ward was determined by the percentage of the total vote in the election accounted for by the ward. Nonvoters in the sample were replaced by names from the same ward, drawn at random. Interviewers made three attempts in all to complete the interview.

The rate of refusal was high, around 33%, partly no doubt because the interviewers were untrained.

B. Survey No. 2

In the summer of 1959 a second, much more extensive and much more carefully planned and executed survey of registered voters was conducted, again under Flanigan's direct supervision. The sample was drawn as before from the registration lists used in the 1958 election as revised down to June 1959. The number of respondents drawn from each ward was in the same proportion to the total sample as the registered voters in the ward bore to the total number of registered voters in the city. Although in this survey persons who had registered but had not voted in recent elections were interviewed, the sample, drawn as it was from registered voters, greatly underrepresented the number of nonvoters in the adult population. This was a deliberate choice, since the purpose of the survey was to study the active electorate, not the nonvoters.

In the first drawing of the sample, some of the names drawn from the registration lists were of persons who were no longer living or had moved out of New Haven. These names were eliminated and new names were then drawn from the same ward as replacements; thus wards in which such persons had lived continue to be represented proportionally in the final sample. Persons who moved to another address within their ward were kept in the sample; for those who had left the ward and continued to live in New Haven no problem arose, since they were registered in their new ward rather than the old. Hence the population from which the final sample was drawn comprised all registered voters living in New Haven at the time of the survey in the same ward in which they were shown on the most recent registration lists.

All of the interviewers were given a period of training before they began; 525 persons were interviewed in a random sample of 818. Although the number of uncompleted interviews was high, partly because many people were on vacation and difficult to reach, those not interviewed do not appear to have differed in significant respects from the ones actually interviewed. For example, in the total sample of 818, 49% were males and 51% were females; of the 525 interviewed 49.4% were males and 50.6% were females; among those not interviewed, 48% were men and 52% were women. Judging from the neighborhoods in which they lived, the socioeconomic characteristics of the persons not interviewed were about the same as those interviewed:

Neighborhood ranking	Interviewed	Not interviewed
	%	%
I	5	5
II	11	12
III	15	16
IV	14	13
V	30	30
VI	23	22
No answer	2	—
Total	100	100

The most common reason for failing to get an interview was illness or infirmity, which made up 19% of all refusals. Other important reasons for failure to complete interviews were: 16% of those not interviewed said they were "too busy," 10% refused because of lack of interest, 14% were never located, and 15% were out of town for the summer on business trips, vacations, or military service. Five per cent of the failures occurred because of language difficulties.

VIII. Changes in Voting Patterns

1. Voting data

For the period before 1900, election returns were drawn from many different sources since no single collection exists, official or unofficial. The best sources for the early period are newspapers and occasional lists of voting returns found in histories such as Atwater's and Levermore's, cited above. The Arnold Dana Collection was also used. Returns are missing for some mayoralty elections before 1877. Since 1900 newspapers and official records provide a complete series. From these it was possible to compile the number of votes cast in each ward for every candidate for president, governor, and mayor from 1901–59. Votes for Republican and Democratic candidates were then converted into percentages of the total two-party vote. These percentages were then correlated with various indices of the socioeconomic characteristics of the wards, as explained below.

2. Data on socioeconomic characteristics of the wards

The U.S. Census of Population reported its data for New Haven by wards until 1950. In the census of 1940, the census tracts were identical with the wards. However, in 1950 the Census reported its data according to census tracts that were not identical with the wards; thanks to a grant to the author from the American Philosophical Society to cover the costs, the Census Bureau retabulated certain New Haven data along ward lines. The ward boundaries were changed in 1920, when 15 wards were divided into 33; the new wards were, for the most part, carved out of the old. Thus by grouping the present wards it is possible, without much error, to trace changes in the character of the population of a region of the city from 1900 to 1950.

Only a few relevant characteristics have been continuously reported over the 50-year period. The most important are the number of foreign-born, which except for 1930 are also reported by country of birth: whites and Negroes or colored; males of voting age, and, since 1930, females of voting age. These and additional data from the 1940 and 1950 censuses were converted into indices, usually percentages of a total; interpolations for years between census years were made on the assumption that all changes from one census to the next were linear over the ten-year period.

3. Correlations between voting returns and census data

Some of the charts in Chapter 4 are based on the correlation between percentages of the two-party vote cast for the candidate of one of the two parties in each ward and a socioeconomic index based on the census data (e.g., the percentage of foreign-born population in each ward). The measure used is the Pearson linear correlation coefficient. If two variables are perfectly correlated, the coefficient takes a value of 1 or −1, depending on whether the correlation is positive or negative; if two variables are not correlated at all, the coefficient is 0. Correlations need to be interpreted with caution; in the case of census data on foreign-born and country of birth, the usual hazards are increased because the percentage of persons in a ward who were born in, say, Italy, may not be a good index of the percentage of persons of Italian origins in that ward. However, the tendency of persons of similar ethnic stock to cluster together is well-known; in New Haven this tendency has been very strong. Hence to use the census data on foreign-born and country of birth as indices seems fully justified.

C. INDICES OF SOCIAL POSITION

THE RESIDENTIAL SCALE

All references to social rankings of New Haven neighborhoods are based on a classification of neighborhoods developed by Yale sociologists and recently described as follows:

> The residential scale was based upon ecological research carried on by Maurice R. Davie and his associates in the New Haven community over a 25-year span. In the early 1930s, Davie mapped the city of New Haven ecologically, and ranked residential areas on a six-position scale that ranged from the finest homes to the poorest tenements. Jerome K. Myers brought Davie's data up to date as of 1950, within the city of New Haven, and mapped the suburban towns in the same way that Davie had mapped New Haven in earlier years.[1]

The criteria used in mapping the neighborhoods in the 1950s were: predominant land-use (whether one-family, two-family, multiple-family dwellings, or mixed); percentage of dwelling units owner-occupied; value of one-family houses; average monthly rent; percentage of population Italian; religious affiliation; occupational characteristics; and level of education. The criteria used by James Davie in the study referred to in Chapter 11 were slightly different.

THE INDEX OF SOCIAL POSITION

The index of social position was developed by A. B. Hollingshead and is described in detail in Hollingshead and Redlich, *Social Class and Mental Illness*. Unless otherwise indicated, the index is based on three factors: residential area, an occupational scale, and education. Where one of the factors was missing, a two-factor index was used instead; according to Hollingshead and Redlich, the two-factor index is almost as good a predictor as the three-factor index (e.g., the multiple correlation of residence and occupation with class position as assigned by judges is 0.926, as compared with 0.942 for all three factors).[2]

1. A. B. Hollingshead and F. C. Redlich, *Social Class and Mental Illness: A Community Study* (New York, Wiley, 1958), p. 390.
2. Ibid., p. 394.

D. INDICES OF POLITICAL PARTICIPATION

Registered voters in Survey No. 2 (see above) were classified according to levels of participation in political affairs by means of three different indices.

THE INDEX OF CAMPAIGN PARTICIPATION

This index was constructed from the list of activities in Table 25.2, p. 278. Registered voters were located on the five points of the scale according to the following criteria:

		%	N
Lowest	nonvoter (had not voted for president in 1956, mayor in 1957, and governor in 1958)	5.6	29
Low	voted in one of these elections but engaged in no other activities on the list	20.6	108
Medium	voted in one election and engaged in one or two other activities on the list	48.0	253
High	voted in one election and engaged in three or four other activities on the list	15.6	82
Highest	voted in one election and engaged in five or more other activities on the list	6.1	32
	No answer, etc.	4.0	21
	Total	99.9	525

THE INDEX OF NONCAMPAIGN PARTICIPATION IN LOCAL AFFAIRS

This index is a simple cumulative score of responses on four items. If a respondent reported talking about politics with friends, he received one point. He also received one point for each of the following: getting in touch with local officials or politicians on an issue, taking an active part in a local issue or problem, and reporting any contact with political or governmental officials in the past year or so. The distribution along the five points of the scale was:

		%	N
Lowest	engaged in none of these activities	39	207
Low	engaged in one	32	168
Medium	engaged in two	17	89
High	engaged in three	9	46
Highest	engaged in all four	3	15
	Total	100	525

THE INDEX OF LOCAL ACTION

This index was constructed from the two indices just described. Weights were assigned to respondents in the following way:

			Index of noncampaign participation				
		Weight	*Lowest* 0	*Low* 1	*Medium* 2	*High* 3	*Highest* 4
	No answer	0	0	°	2	°	°
Index of	Lowest	0	0	1	2	°	°
campaign	Low	0	0	1	2	3	°
participa-	Medium	0	0	1	2	3	4
tion	High, highest	1	1	2	3	4	5

° No cases in sample

The index of local action was then defined as follows:

		%	N
Lowest	no points according to table above	36	188
Low	one point	28	148
Medium	two points	17	89
High	three points	13	68
Highest	four or five points	6	29
	Unclassified, etc.	—	3
	Total	100	525

List of Tables and Figures

FIGURES

Index

Italicized numbers refer to tables and figures.